CORRECTIONAL INSTITUTIONS

VERNON FOX
Florida State University

PRENTICE-HALL, INC., *Englewood Cliffs, New Jersey 07632*

Library of Congress Cataloging in Publication Data

Fox, Vernon Brittain, (date)
    Correctional institutions.
    Bibliography: p. 303
    Includes index.
      1. Correctional institutions—United States.
I. Title.
HV9304.F69 1983   365'.973   82-24061
ISBN 0-13-178228-2

Editorial/production supervision and interior design by Margaret Rizzi
Cover design by 20/20 Services, Inc.
Manufacturing buyer: Ed O'Dougherty

© 1983 by Prentice-Hall, Inc., Englewood Cliffs, New Jersey 07632

All rights reserved. No part of this book may be
reproduced, in any form or by any means,
without permission in writing from the publisher.

Printed in the United States of America

10 9 8 7 6 5 4 3 2

ISBN   0-13-178228-2

Prentice-Hall International, Inc., *London*
Prentice-Hall of Australia Pty. Limited, *Sydney*
Editora Prentice-Hall do Brasil, Ltda., *Rio de Janeiro*
Prentice-Hall Canada Inc., *Toronto*
Prentice-Hall of India Private Limited, *New Delhi*
Prentice-Hall of Japan, Inc., *Tokyo*
Prentice-Hall of Southeast Asia Pte. Ltd., *Singapore*
Whitehall Books Limited, *Wellington, New Zealand*

Dedicated to Louie L. Wainwright

Secretary of the Florida Department of Corrections,
whom I have watched develop into an effective
and progressive correctional administrator.

CONTENTS

II   THE PHYSICAL PLANT

2
Organization of Correctional Institutions,   *19*

III   THE PROGRAM AND THE RESIDENTS

3
Custodial Control,   *41*

4
Classification and Treatment,   *59*

8

Effects of Imprisonment,   *130*

9

Contacts with the Outside,   *140*

10

Staff Society,   *154*

IV SPECIAL INSTITUTIONS

V ADMINISTRATION AND MANAGEMENT OF INSTITUTIONS

16
Fiscal Management,   *264*

17
Personnel Management,   *281*

FOREWORD

Dr. Vernon Fox, through this work, has presented a comprehensive and knowledgeable overview of the field of corrections. The text demonstrates the complexity of the correctional system as it developed and currently exists. This extensive knowledge of the historical development of the field of corrections allows the reader to gain an understanding of sociological, religious, cultural, and political factors which have shaped the present system. Without an appreciation of this historical evolvement, the philosophically contradictory components within correctional systems are difficult to comprehend.

The book is enhanced by the author's blending of his experiences as a practitioner with his academic maturity. Rarely has a text elaborated on the human elements involved in corrections. All too frequently the orientation to corrections addresses the system in which the incarcerated offender must live and neglects to address the system in which the correctional employee must survive. Dr. Fox has poignantly discussed the social, psychological, and physical isolation experienced by staff. The public's lack of knowledge and, more importantly, its failure to appreciate the unrelenting pressure which correctional personnel experience, deny deserved recognition to those who carry out unpopular missions without adequate pay or status.

Those of us who are responsible for the operation and management of correctional systems have gained most of our expertise through experience and without benefit of comprehensive literature to aid in gaining a broad perspective of the field, understanding its historical development, or appreciating its subtle intricacies. It is all too easy to become involved in the daily decisions of operation and the frustrations inherent in the management of a correctional system. Each of us needs to pause occasionally and view our profession in its totality. This book presents an opportunity to do so.

The subject matter presented is not only of value to practitioners but is appropriate for study by a wide variety of audiences. Students pursuing careers in corrections can gain a realistic perspective of the complexity of the field. Legislators, whose decisions determine the scope and depth of correctional missions, can glean from these pages significant insight regarding their role in the field of corrections. Special interest groups, both liberal and conservative, can assess their positions more objectively by examining all aspects of corrections as set forth in this text. Finally, the public in general would benefit from Dr. Fox's presentation since it is the public who, in the final analysis, dictates the parameters of the correctional system.

Special interest groups, while perhaps motivated by genuine concern, champion extreme and narrowly defined causes. Pressure is then applied to both legislators and correctional executives to respond to philosophically diverse viewpoints—a process which perpetuates rather than resolves the illogical contradictions found in correctional missions. Without a full understanding of the correctional system by special interest groups and the general public, legislators and correctional executives will, out of necessity, continue to temper their decisions as a result of pressures applied from subjectively skewed viewpoints.

The most significant contribution that can be realized from this book is for it to reach all of its potential audiences. If accomplished, the field of corrections can come even closer to attaining recognition as a bonafide profession.

Dr. Fox is to be commended for his efforts to elevate corrections to a bonafide professional status through his work in general, and this book specifically.

Gordon H. Faulkner
Commissioner
Indiana Department of Correction

PREFACE

The correctional institution or prison is the core of the criminal justice system. Within the American system of correctional institutions and prisons, facilities range from the maximum security prison to the medium security prison to the minimum security institution and, finally, to the community-based facility. Additional institutions serve juveniles, women, and mentally disordered offenders. Correctional institutions, particularly those designated maximum security, represent the last resort for the placement of offenders in the criminal justice system.

The purpose of this book is to present a much needed comprehensive view of all correctional institutions, including their historical development, physical plants, and programs and the residents that they serve; their administration and management; and their future.

Institutions date back to ancient times, the first public institution being the temple, which served in part as a sanctuary for offenders fleeing from justice. The first courts appeared four to five thousand years later, around 2000 B.C., to issue sanctions against those guilty of slavery, to administer public works, and to order banishment and death. Places of detention emerged in Jerusalem by the seventh century B.C. After the rise of Christianity, monasteries provided for the long-term detention of offenders. Then, when the monasteries were closed, in the sixteenth century A.D., major offenders were often transported to distant lands. Prisons began to be constructed in the late eighteenth century.

Assessing the need for prisons, determining their location, planning their architecture, and constructing them is an important part of the correctional process that has received too little attention in the past. Most of the literature regarding correctional institutions has focused on the programs in the institution and the residents of the prison community. Staff society, although an important part of correctional institutions, has been neglected. And there is a need to investigate institutions for the "criminally insane" or the mentally disordered, including the dangerous sex offender.

The administration and management of correctional institutions requires additional attention today given the recent increase in court intervention in prison procedure that now affects the decisions and procedures of administrators. In the 1950s, the courts considered prison administration to be beyond judicial review. In the 1960s, increasingly in the 1970s, and continuing in the 1980s, the courts have intervened more and more in prison administration. In fact, the correctional programs of thirty-nine states were operating under court order in 1981. The increase in union activity and the development of collective bargaining agreements have further limited the autonomy of the administrator. In the 1960s, a strong prison administrator could personally dominate an institution. By the 1970s and the 1980s, the administrator had to be guided by statutes, court orders, collective bargaining agreements, and regulations by governmental commissions concerned with discrimination. Moreover, within the current economy, fiscal management has become more sophisticated. No longer can professionals call for needed programs yet adopt the attitude, "I do not know where the money is coming from and I don't care; that's not my responsibility." This lack of fiscal responsibility needs to be corrected. Similarly, personnel management, an important factor in the effectiveness of any program, requires greater administrative attention.

The future of prisons is a matter of debate. Some scholars want to build more prisons, lock up more people, and "throw the key away," to make streets safe. Others believe that imprisonment has been ineffective and that prisons should be abolished. More moderate writers have indicated that there is an overuse of prisons in America, that prisons are needed for violent offenders, but that some nondangerous property offenders could be handled better in other ways. The future of imprisonment depends on political concerns, on economic factors as seen by the taxpayers, and on resolving the social problems caused by the imprisonment of breadwinners in the family, and, particularly, mothers whose children are their sole responsibility. All these concerns must be dealt with in the future.

Appreciation goes to Mrs. Carolyne Richardson and Ms. Edwina Ivory for their excellent typing of the manuscript and to Mrs. Mary Harris for coordinating the process. Without their assistance, this project could not have been completed.

Vernon Fox
Florida State University

1

THE RISE
OF INSTITUTIONS

A social institution is a system of interrelated folkways and laws organized to
perform a given function of society.[1] Social institutions, such as education, religion, health care, and the economic system, for example, exemplify humanity's
attempt to meet the needs of society in an organized manner.[2] Each system, in
turn, is housed in physical plants or buildings, for example, schools and universities, churches and temples, hospitals, and banks. In the case of the criminal
justice system, that institution is housed in a variety of physical plants and buildings ranging from the police station through the courts to the correctional institution. Correctional institutions are the residential facilities in which custody
and treatment of offenders occur to protect society and rehabilitate the
offender.

[1]David Dressler, *Sociology: The Study of Human Interaction* (New York: Alfred A. Knopf,
Inc., 1969), p. 607.
[2]T. Lynn Smith, ed., *Social Problems* (New York: Thomas Y. Crowell Company, 1955), p.
215.

1

THE FIRST INSTITUTIONS

Temples

Temples were the first physical buildings designed to house the functions of a social institution, as the development of agriculture led to emergence of cities and permanent buildings. Of these cities, Jericho was probably the first to have been considered sufficiently important to require the protection of walls from the nomadic plunderers who inhabited the region at that time. It was apparently built between 8000 and 7500 B.C. just north of the Dead Sea in what is now called the West Bank, and it is still there today under the modern name of Aribā. Contemporary with Jericho was Qual'al Jarmy, a settlement about 170 miles north of present-day Baghdad, which remains to this day as Jarmo. The first evidence of temples above ground were excavated there in 1959. The site contains twenty to twenty-five foundations of homes built of packed clay as well as two oval-shaped foundations that were interpreted as being the first temples, dated at about 6750 B.C.[3] At Abu Shahrein, now called Eridu, about 175 miles southeast of Baghdad, near Ur, the remains of a single-room shrine or temple tower, a building about 40 feet by 80 feet, were found standing on a terrace, probably to prevent flooding, dating back to about 4000 B.C.

Early temples served all the needs of people outside the home in ancient times, including socializing, fortune-telling, and the purchase of small items. Commerce first started in the temples, and then quickly moved to the marketplaces near the temples for more room. The temple was the social center of the community, as was the church in colonial America. Primitive religion began about 60,000 B.C., according to excavations in the rugged Zagros Mountains in what is now Northern Iraq, and primitive organized religion began about 23,000 B.C., with the shaman (or other religious leader) making the clergy the first profession. Many rites were instituted in the temple, including the 12 loaves of "shewbread" on the Sabbath as a remnant of older nomadic times and prostitution as a "rite of fertility."[4] The "rite of fertility" was important in agrarian societies and was in the context of the theological concept of "sympathetic magic," in which fertility in the temple enhanced fertility throughout the land. "Sacred prostitution" or "shrine prostitution" was performed by the priestesses, while women not identified with religion provided "lay prostitution." Religion at that time was *practical*. The ancients had a "sky god," who was male, and an "earth god," who was female, because she was fertile and produced. While banking did not begin until the thirteenth century, A.D., rudimentary beginnings of banking appeared in the temples about the seventh century B.C. Ancient man had used hundreds of objects as "money," including slaves, salt, stones, and the jawbones of pigs, until coinage began in the late eighth century B.C. After that, the rudimentary beginnings of banking appeared in the temples where travellers could exchange their money for "coin of the realm" in strange lands. These practices were gradually taken from the temples and found their places in general society.[4]

The Egyptians built pyramids, rather than temples, between 2700 B.C.

---

[3]"Temples," *Encyclopaedia Britannica, Macropaedia,* Vol. 11 (Chicago: Encyclopaedia Britannica, Inc., 1974), pp. 967 ff.

[4]Harry Benjamin and R. E. L. Masters; *Prostitution and Morality,* New York: The Julian Press, 1964, pp. 35–36. Elmer W. K. Mould; *Essentials of Bible History,* New York: Thomas Nelson

and 2300 B.C.[5] The largest and oldest in that of Khufu, called the Great Pyramid, and has been referred to as the greatest single building ever erected by man. Structures of this general type have been built in other parts of the world, including the Sudan, Ethiopia, West Asia, Greece, Italy, Thailand, Mexico, and some islands in the Pacific Ocean. Similar in construction were the approximately twenty-five *ziggurats* that were built in Mesopotamia, beginning with the *ziggurat* at Ur, built around 1800 B.C., which stands about 70 feet tall on a base of 30,000 square feet.[6] It is referred to in Genesis 18:12 as "Jacob's ladder." In Babylon in 656 B.C., King Nebuchadnezzar II built the largest *ziggurat* in the world, rising to a height of 650 feet and referred to as the "Tower of Babel."

The first Jewish temple was built by King Solomon, who died in 934 B.C. after a reign of forty-nine years. It was destroyed by the Babylonians under Nebuchadnezzar in 586 B.C. when the conquered Jews were taken into slavery. In 538 B.C., Cyrus, the Persian king, authorized the Jews to build a new temple on the site of the original temple. In the fifty years during which the Jews had had no temple, they developed the synagogue. Because animal sacrifices could only be made in a temple, communal prayer was the practice in the synagogue. Israel had fallen to the Assyrians in 722 B.C., and ten of the twelve tribes were lost. The second temple was destroyed by the Romans in 70 A.D.; its western wall remained intact, however, and it became the focus of pilgrimages for two millenia: the Wailing Wall. After exiling many and forbidding Jews to inhabit Jerusalem, Rome further cut off Jews from Judea by renaming it Syria Palaestrina, which became Palestine soon after the 70–72 A.D. conquests.

Hospitals

As society grew in population and complexity, the social institutions that had been served by the ancient temple gave way to separate functions and gradually disappeared from the temples. Hospitals emerged to take over health care in Ceylon (now Sri Lanka) in 437 B.C. and made their way to India soon afterward.[7] By the first century A.D., hospitals could be found in Rome. These institutions were merely places of refuge for the hopeless, the homeless, and the sick, however; physicians did not work in or around hospitals. It was not until surgery was moved from the barber shop to medical practice under the leadership of John Hunter (1728–1793) in the eighteenth century that hospitals became places of healing.

Universities

In higher education, the earliest universities were in India in the sixth century A.D. as the University of Nālāndā and the University of Valadhi.[8] They became firmly established in Europe between the eleventh and sixteenth cen-

and Sons, 1939, pp. 173–179. Also, personal conversation with Rabbi Richard L. Rubenstein, Ph.D., Distinguished Professor of Religion, Florida State University, October 20, 1982.

[5]"Pyramid," *Encyclopaedia Britannica*, Vol. 18, p. 894.

[6]Melville Bell Grosvenor, editor-in-chief, *The Story of Man—Everyday Life in Bible Times* (Washington, D.C.: National Geographic Society, 1967), pp. 59–61.

[7]"Hospitals," *Encyclopaedia Britannica, Macropaedia*, Vol. 8, p. 1114.

[8]"Education in Classical Cultures," *Enclycopaedia Britannica, Macropaedia*, Vol. 6, p. 319.

turies. Other social institutions, such as welfare, were continued in the religious context, particularly by monasteries and abbeys of the Middle Ages.

Criminal Justice

In primitive times, conflicts between persons were handled in the consensus model rather than by the adversary prosecution and defense model of modern civilized countries. For example, in Alaska, primitive Eskimo and Athabascan Indians always plead guilty in white man's courts, whether innocent or not, because it was deemed the first step in resolution of conflict and gaining consensus. Many judges have had to call a recess and convince the accused to plead not guilty when it became apparent that the interface of primitive custom and "white man's law" was creating confusion. In primitive society, the elders and the religious leaders enter a case only when the accused and the victim or his or her family are unable to resolve it. It was somewhat similar to the practice in ancient society where deviant persons were considered to be under control of evil gods and the religious leaders had to "cast out the demons."[9] The Old Testament mentions the process of exorcism in Deuteronomy 18:9–12 and the New Testament notes it in James, Luke, Matthew, Acts, the Corinthians, and elsewhere. Jesus said, "I cast out devils," in Luke 13:32.

Temples were associated with the oldest type of mitigation, the right of sanctuary.[10] Certain places were set aside to which the accused might flee and escape punishment. Mosaic law designated certain cities and places where an unwitting manslayer would be safe for a time from the vengeance of his victim's kin: he could stay in that city until he stood before the congregation and until death of the priest, at which time he could return to his own city.[11]

BEGINNING OF CONFINEMENT

Sanctions in the ancient world consisted primarily of slavery or indentureship to the victim or his family, employment in public works projects, mutilation or amputation, banishment, or death. One of the basic tenets of the Code of Justinian (529 A.D.), which synthetized all the ancient codes, was that long-term confinement would not be used as a punishment for crime. There were no trials or sentences. The first court probably appeared around 2000 B.C., depicted on the shield of Achilles in Homer's *Iliad* for the purpose of mitigating blood feuds. The beginnings of the ancient codes were about at this time.

Many people date the Code of Hammurabi between 2200 and 2000 B.C., but this was simply the beginnings of formulations that became the Code of Hammurabi about 1750 B.C. The code of King Hammurabi (1792–1750 B.C.) was prepared from many earlier attempts and was based firmly in the *lex talionis*

---

[9]W. A. Schenck, *A History of Psychiatry* (Philadelphia: J. B. Lippincott Company, 1952), p. 11. Also, see Carl Richardson, *Exorcism: New Testament Style* (Old Tappan, N.J.: Fleming H. Revell Company, 1974), pp. 128.

[10]Numbers 35:6 and Joshua 20:2–6.

[11]Joshua 20:6.

or the "eye for an eye" doctrine. Again, long-term confinement was not a part of punishment for what is now called crime.

The first "police" were messengers who carried letters from the priests and elders commanding or permitting them to enforce certain orders about 2100 B.C.[12] They were also mentioned in the New Testament when Christ was arrested in the garden by those who came from the chief priests and elders of the people (Matthew 26:47) and when Paul bore letters from the high priests and elders granting him the right to arrest, bind, and commit to prison both men and women (Acts 22:4). Detention in some way was possible under this system, even without a facility built specifically for confinement of people. Prison is mentioned nine times in the Old Testament[13] and eight times in the New Testament.[14] The first incident, in Genesis, involved the imprisonment of Joseph in Egypt, which, historically, is estimated to have been around 1700 B.C.

The problem appears to be one of semantics and translation without any clear concept of what prison was. The Bible evolved not as a single book but as a contribution of many writers and many stories.[15] The first five books, or the Pentateuch, came to be regarded in the sixth century B.C. as the supreme law of the Hebrews. By the second century A.D., twenty-four books had been accepted as having been inspired by God. Translated first from Hebrew into Greek, the Bible came eventually to be translated into many languages. The first Bible in English was the 1382 translation by John Wycliffe. William Tyndale's New Testament appeared in 1526, and he and his Testament were both put to the torch. The King James version, used most predominantly in the English-speaking world, was issued in 1611. The Revised Version of the King James, with more than 35,000 changes, was published in 1885. The basic King James version, released in 1611, came more than a century and a half before the emergence of the modern concept of "prison."

It is obvious that places for the detainment of people existed during this ancient time. Without documentary or archeological evidence, however, it is apparent that facilities built for other purposes were used for this detention. This was not unusual. In the castles built in the Middle Ages, the towers and the bases of the towers used as dungeons were not built for this purpose, but they were used to keep prisoners nonetheless. Even the Tower of London, not built as a detainment center, was used as a prison on occasion. In the American involvement in Vietnam from 1964 to the early 1970s, similar substitutions were made. There were no prisons as commonly known, but there were errant military personnel who had been court-martialed for offenses. They were imprisoned in

---

[12]A. C. Germann, Frank D. Day, and Robert R. J. Gallati, *Introduction to Law Enforcement* (Springfield, Ill.: Charles C. Thomas, Publisher, 1962), p. 37.

[13]Genesis 39:20–23; Genesis 42:16, 19; Judges 16:21, 25; 2nd Chronicles 18:26; Psalms 142:7; Isaiah 53:8; Isaiah 60:1; and Jeremiah 38:6. In the last reference, Jeremiah was dropped into a dungeon filled with mire. In addition, Numbers 12:34 refers to a "ward."

[14]Matthew 5:25, 25:36; Luke 22:33; Acts 16:24; 2nd Corinthians 11:23; 1st Peter 3:19; and Revelations 20:7. In addition, Acts 4:3 refers to a "hold" and to stocks for the feet.

[15]Gilbert M. Grosvenor ed., "From Oft-Told Epic to Printed Page: How the Bible Comes to Us," in *Everyday Life in Bible Times* (Washington, D.C.: National Geographic Society, 1967), p. 445.

"kennel runs" originally built for dogs and in *conex boxes*.[16] The process resembles that of sending an unruly child to his or her room as punishment, although the room had not been designed for that purpose.

The first documented existence of detention facilities built specifically for the purpose of confining prisoners can be traced to the seventh century B.C. when the Greeks constructed large rooms and underground chambers to hold prisoners awaiting trial.[17] In the sixth century B.C., Jerusalem had three such institutions: the Beth-ha-keli, or house of detention; The Beth-ha-asourin, a facility to hold people in chains; and the Beth-ha-mahpecheth, a facility to hold people whose hands and feet were chained.[18] In the fifth century B.C., Plato wrote in his *De Legibus* that there should be three prisons: one in the city for persons awaiting trial or sentence; one for the reform of disorderly persons, vagrants, and misdemeanants; and a third far from the city for the punishment of felons. Rome had an underground prison in the first century B.C., a reconstruction of the Tullianum, now called the Mamertine Prison. It consisted of an upper rectangular room to hold persons not condemned to death and a lower dungeon into which condemned persons were thrown, generally to be starved or strangled to death.

MONASTERIES

Long-term confinement was used first by the Roman Catholic Church after the fourth century A.D. in the form of imprisonment in the gatehouse of the abbey or monastery. Monasteries began when the Christians were persecuted by the Roman Emperor Decius and many Christians fled into the desert in Egypt. Monasteries became important as institutions throughout the Middle Ages because, in addition to their religious functions, they served as centers for rudimentary welfare services, maintained early hospitals, and confined offenders in their gatehouses.

Paul of Thebes (not to be confused with the Apostle Paul) is considered by St. Jerome to have been the first hermit to have adopted a life of prayer and meditation and excessive austerity about 250 A.D. Later, Anthony of Egypt, a hermit-disciple of Paul of Thebes, gathered other solitaries around him in loosely constructed communities, meeting for instruction and reception of the Eucharist. Pachomius gave organization to the cenobitic life and wrote the rules for the first monastery at Tabennisi about 318 A.D. Subsequently, leadership for the monasteries and monastic life was provided by the monastery at Basil in the East and at Nursia in the West. Founded by St. Benedict, Nursia's influence is

[16]Conex boxes were steel containers about 4 feet by 4 feet by 4 feet in which supplies were shipped to military units. They could be laid on their sides, the double lids being used as doors and slits cut in the sides for ventilation, and were used to house one prisoner each. Entire prisons, though small, were made up of conex boxes.

[17]Leslie Fairweather, "The Evolution of the Prison," in Giuseppe di Gennaro, project director, et al., *Prison Architecture: An International Survey of Representative Closed Institutions and Analysis of Current Trends in Prison Design* (London: The Architectural Press Ltd., for the United Nations Social Defense Research Institute, 1975), p. 13.

[18]Ibid., p. 13.

still in the spirit of religious orders in the West. Monasteries were established throughout Europe and served many social purposes in addition to or as a part of the religious life of the residents.

——The Council of Nicaea in 325 A.D. was called to determine the relationship of Jesus to God. The issue was hotly debated, but the vote was that Jesus was divine and could be called "the Son of God." Those who opposed this view were prosecuted by the new church, which was no longer a sect of Judaism, but a separate religion of Christianity. Heresy, blasphemy, and similar offenses against the church were met with burnings-at-the-stake, confinement in the gatehouses of the abbeys or monasteries, and other sanctions. The fifth ecumenical council came close to becoming a trial of the pope.

By the fourth century A.D., Christian church members had established hospitals for lepers, cripples, the blind, and the ailing poor. An important hospital was founded at Lyons, France, in 542 A.D., and hospitals were developed throughout the Arab countries in Spain, North Africa, and western Asia. Religious communities continued to play a central role. The first solely nursing order was organized in about 1155 A.D. by the St. Augustine nuns.

The monastery or abbey became the source of sustenance for many vagabonds and travelers throughout the Middle Ages and, therefore, central to the social services of that time. Christian cathedrals became central to the life of ecclesiastical leaders in the eighth and early ninth centuries. Replacing the monastery in some places, the cathedral represented a trend toward a stricter form of life.

The monasteries grew throughout the Middle Ages reaching a number approximating sixteen hundred from Iceland to the Danube by the sixteenth century.[19] While the monasteries did perform welfare functions for the important poor, some became dens of iniquity, inadvertently encouraging able-bodied beggars to lead a life of idleness.[20] Seeing all this and having to pay for it by tithing to the church, the taxpaying citizenry grew increasingly resentful. In England, Henry VIII closed all the poorer monasteries in 1536[21] and the rest in 1539.[22] About 608 monasteries had been closed in England during this short span.

THE PRIVATE PRISON

The breakdown of the feudal system caused the economy to shift from a primarily agricultural one to a commercial shipping and trading one, accompanied by the growth of intellectual pursuits known as the Renaissance following Thomas Aquinas's *Summa Theologica*, often referred to as the sum total of human knowl-

[19]Melville Bell Grosvenor, ed., *Middle Ages* (Washington, D.C.: National Geographic Book Service, The Story of Man Library, 1977), p. 79.

[20]C. J. Ribton-Turner, *A History of Vagrants and Vagrancy and Beggars and Begging* (Montclair, N.J.: Patterson Smith, 1972), p. 83. Published originally in London by Chapman & Hall Ltd. in 1887.

[21]27 Hen. VIII., e. 28, 1536.

[22]31 Hen. VIII., 13, 1539.

edge in the thirteenth century. Entrepreneurs in business and scholars had changed society. Other movements in the social structure followed, including a more equitable balance between church and state. In the twelfth century, the criminal tribes of India moved into Europe, making their living by kidnapping for ransom or slave sales and murder. The people thought they were from Egypt, so they called them "gypsies." The Mafia in Sicily is reported to have begun in 1298 to fight French domination of that island and is thought to have continued for other reasons. The legendary Robin Hood was supposed to have roamed Sherwood Forest with his band of outlaws during the last half of the twelfth century. In general, the social structure of the Middle Ages had been disrupted and a new order was coming.

Custody of violators of the social order during ancient and medieval times was primarily private, a vestigial remnant of the blood feud among primitive man. In fact, the duel as a solution to private disputes continued into early America. Private prisons were built in the twelfth century and after. Any person with sufficient power and influence could build his own private prison and incarcerate those who interfered with his political ambitions or his personal inclinations.[23] Some of the outstanding places of private confinement during the twelfth century were the Tower of London, the Castle of Spielberg, the Conciergerie and the Bastille in Paris, the *pozzi* or wells of the ducal palace in Venice, and the Seven Towers of Constantinople.[24] Thieves were incarcerated in Baulk House on High Street in Winchester as early as 1103.[25] The first prisoner to die in the Tower of London was Rannulf Flambard in 1128, and a special facility was built by Brian Fitzcourt in 1128, called Cloere Brien, to accommodate the famous William Martel.[26] The Florentine prison, Delle Stinche, erected as early as 1300, had a system of classification, a board of inspectors, recreational and work programs, segregation, and both definite and indefinite sentences.[27] The last private prison appears to have been built in 1785 by Sir Thomas Beever at Wymondham in Norfolk, England.

The first public building for the criminal justice system was the jail, authorized by Henry II at the Assize of Clarendon in 1166, along with the formulation of the jury system and the delineation of the functions of the sheriff. At approximately the same time, harsh punishments and ingenious torture devices were introduced throughout Europe. Transportation of serious offenders to distant lands began in England and elsewhere after 1600, with England's first law for deportation passed in 1597, elaborated in 1617, and finalized in 1717, all to the American colonies.[28] France and Russia instituted this practice in

[23]Fairweather, "The Evolution of the Prison," in Gennaro et al., *Prison Architecture*, pp. 13–14.

[24]Ibid., p. 13.

[25]N. Vidmar and P. Ellsworth, "Public Opinion and Death Penalty," *Stanford Law Review*, Vol. 26 (1974), pp. 1245–70.

[26]P. N. Walker, *Punishment: An Illustrated History* (Newton Abbot, Devon, England: David & Charles Publishers, Ltd., 1972), p. 35.

[27]Harry Elmer Barnes and Negley K. Teeters, *New Horizons in Criminology*, 3rd ed. (Englewood Cliffs, N.J.: Prentice-Hall, Inc., 1959), p. 329.

Tower of London.

Photo taken by Professor Franklin G. Ashburn in 1979. Courtesy of Dr. Ashburn.

the middle of the nineteenth century.[28] The practice of transportation delayed for a while the construction of prisons for serious offenders.

Felons ceased to be deported from England to America in 1776 as a result of the outbreak of the American Revolution, and this created temporary havoc in England.[29] Criminals crowded the jails and something had to be done. Some were sent to Africa, where they died of tropical diseases. Then, many were placed in old boats or "hulks" anchored in the rivers and harbors. Some were transport ships converted into nautical prisons. Despite the development of transportation to Australia, halfway around the world, they remained part of the British penal system until 1858. It was during this period that "convict ships"[30] made their appearance. They were equipped with chains, torture devices, and other implements of punishment and death, among them the "iron maiden," an iron container shaped like a casket, attached to the mainmast, and equipped with hinges and 8-inch spikes that would kill a man placed there when the enclosure was shut.

[28]Harry Elmer Barnes, *The Story of Punishment: A Record of Man's Inhumanity to Man*, rev. ed. (Montclair, N.J.: Patterson Smith, 1972), pp. 68–71. Published originally by The Stratford Company, New York, in 1930.

[29]Barnes and Teeters, *New Horizons in Criminology*, pp. 296–98.

[30]This writer has been aboard two of these ships as a child in the late 1920s, when they were on tour like the *U.S.S. Constitution* ("Old Ironsides") in Boston harbor, but the public was not aware of their history, so the old convict ships disappeared.

ASYLUMS, ALMSHOUSES, WORKHOUSES, AND BRIDEWELLS

The closing of the monasteries from 1536 to 1539 left a void in welfare and social services in England. The first welfare laws, passed in 1557, were designed to have the government provide for the poor, the destitute, and abandoned needy children. Vagrancy and unemployment during the Tudor period, roughly the fourteenth and fifteenth centuries, had caused economic and social problems that needed public attention. The Royal Palace of Bridewell had been constructed by Henry VIII in 1522 at St. Bridget's Well, but Bishop Ridley convinced him to open it as a public institution for the poor, homeless children, debtors, minor offenders, and other public charges. These bridewells were built elsewhere in England and on the European continent, beginning in The Netherlands and Belgium, in the next several decades. The accelerated rate of construction of these institutions continued into the eighteenth and nineteenth centuries. Serious welfare problems resulted in the passage of the famous Elizabethan Poor Law of 1601 that consolidated the previous welfare laws and coordinated all the social services, including those for minor offenders and delinquent youths as well as the poor and homeless.

Institutionalization had become the solution to most economic problems by the eighteenth century. The poor, the criminal, the insane, the delinquent, and the retarded were all housed together as public charges. Custodial care in institutions was seen as a way of training social deviants to work. The insane were considered to be better off in a custodial hospital than in a filthy cellar, prisoners were better off in a crowded cell than on the gallows or whipping post, the poor were happier eating the miserable fare of the almhouses than starving on the streets,[31] and, certainly, destitute children were better off in orphanages than on the streets having to steal their living like Charles Dickens's Oliver Twist.

Separate treatment for the mentally ill began to emerge in the early eighteenth century. The old methods were restraint, confinement, purging, bleeding, and blistering. The first treatment of the insane began in the United States in 1732 at the Philadelphia Alms House, which had been established by the Quakers in 1713. Philippe Pinel (1745–1826) was chief physician in two mental hospitals in Paris, the Bicêtre and the Salpetrière. It was at the Bicêtre in 1797 that Pinel removed the shackles and chains from the patients, some of whom had been held for thirty to forty years, and more humane treatment of the mentally ill was introduced in Europe. Further improvement of the treatment of the mentally ill came in the United States as a result of a crusade undertaken by Dorothea Lynde Dix (1802–1887). She began her campaign for mental health care in 1841 when she taught Sunday School in the East Cambridge, Massachusetts, jail and saw the mentally ill housed with other prisoners and reported this to the legislature in 1843. Her subsequent efforts resulted in the construction of fifteen hospitals for the mentally ill and improved treatment methods.

[31]David J. Rothman, *The Discovery of the Asylum* (Boston: Little, Brown and Company, 1971), p. 294.

As asylums and almshouses were developing in Europe, they were also developing in the United States. In Charleston, South Carolina, in 1734, the vestry of St. Philip's Church took care of the needy. Later, a congregate institution for the sick, poor, and minor offenders was established. In New York City in 1735, a combined House of Correction, Work House, and Poor House was established to house dependents and misdemeanants under the same roof. During the colonial period in the eighteenth century, procedures reflected the idea that poverty and crime did not indicate a basic defect in the community organization but, rather, a defect in the individuals involved from being lazy to disobedience to God.

Not long after the American Revolution, however, the situation changed. During the Jacksonian period, particularly in the 1820s and 1830s, a new concept of the cause of deviance, poverty, and crime began to emerge, ascribing it to the faulty organization of the community.[32] This is when the asylum was built to fulfill a dual purpose that would rehabilitate inmates and set an example of right action for the larger society.

In 1824, the New York State legislature appointed the secretary of state, John Yates, to investigate the poor and administration of relief throughout the state.[33] The Yates report found that (1) about one-ninth of the cost of welfare was spent in moving people back to their legal residences, (2) the education and morals of children of paupers were almost completely neglected, (3) provisions for employment of the poor were virtually nonexistent, (4) the administration of welfare was expensive and uneconomical, (5) idiots and lunatics did not receive sufficient attention, and (6) the system encouraged henchmen and fraud. The proposals were as follows: (1) a primary system should be undertaken for the care of people by establishing institutions or almshouses; (2) these almshouses should be houses of employment with agriculture being primary, though there was question as to whether this solution could be implemented in an urbanized society; (3) these houses should be connected with a penitentiary to provide suitable employment for those who will not work; (4) free education for the children should be provided; and (5) the county should be the governmental unit to erect these almshouses because the town is too small. The Yates report was accepted and implemented in New York State.

Subsequently, these almshouses begin to split off into more specialized institutions, including those for dependent children, handicapped children, juvenile delinquents, the mentally ill, and adult delinquents or minor offenders. More institutions were constructed in the nineteenth century than ever before in history. Institutions for handicapped children appeared. The first voluntary asylum for the deaf and dumb and for idiots and the feebleminded was constructed in Maine in the mid-1820s. The first institution for blind children was constructed in Ohio in 1837.

While the first treatment of the mentally ill in the United States was at the Philadelphia Alms House in 1732, the first separate hospital for the mentally ill opened in the colony of Virginia in 1773. Kentucky opened the second hospital in 1824, and South Carolina opened a hospital in 1830. The first state hospi-

[32]Ibid., p. xix.
[33]Ibid., p. 157.

tal for the mentally ill in the North was opened by Maine in 1833. There were several private voluntary hospitals in the North.

The first institution for children was the St. Vincent de Paul permanent asylum for wandering children opened in Paris in 1848. The first institution for "juvenile delinquents" was established by the Roman Catholic Church in 1650, when Filippo Franci began a work house for recalcitrant and vagrant boys in Florence, Italy. The success of this venture prompted Pope Clement XI to build the Hospital of St. Michael in Rome in 1704. This was the first cellular institution and was destined to influence prison architecture for the next two hundred years.

In the United States, the early institutions for children were voluntary, particularly from religious orders. The first was established in New Orleans in 1727 by the Ursuline order to care for children in need. The first home for Jewish children was in Charleston, South Carolina, in 1787. The first governmental unit for dependent children was also in Charleston, South Carolina, in 1790. The first home for children in the North was the St. Joseph's Home in Philadelphia in 1798.

The first home for juvenile delinquents was voluntary, the House of Refuge in New York City in 1825, established one year after a similar house of refuge had been established in Danzig, Germany, in 1824. The first state school for delinquents was the Lyman School for Boys in Massachusetts in 1847, another was opened in Maine in 1848, and a third began operation in New York in 1849. After that, state training schools for juveniles were established in every state. In the meantime, private training schools were also being established.

Until late in the 1880s, dependent people, including the sick, the elderly, the blind and the deaf, the physically handicapped, the mentally ill, the poor, and orphaned children, who had no family or others to care for them, were herded together in almshouses or poor farms that provided primarily custodial care.[34] Sanitary facilities, heat in the winter, and even bedding were minimal in these institutions.

With the development of prisons and penitentiaries in the late eighteenth and early nineteenth centuries, serious offenders who had previously been transported to distant lands were housed in them and the lesser felons and misdemeanants were sent to the almshouses, from which they might be transferred to the prisons and penitentiaries. Thus began the administrative separation of the criminal from the poor cared for by governmental and public agencies. The first state hospital for the criminally insane was opened at Ionia, Michigan, in 1867. Throughout the nineteenth century, welfare and correctional functions were administered by the same agency and were seen as similar functions. For example, the Conference of Board and Public Charities was organized in 1874. The name was changed in 1879 to National Conference of Charities and Corrections. In 1947, it became the National Conference of Social Work, and in 1956 it became the National Conference of Social Welfare. Juvenile institutions have been administered by welfare departments in many states.

---

[34]Charles Zastrow, "Prologue for Social Workers," in Dae H. Chang and Warren B. Armstrong, eds., *The Prison: Voices from Inside* (Cambridge, Mass.: Schenkman Publishing Company, 1972), p. 9.

They are still so administered in Georgia, Michigan, Pennsylvania, and Virginia. Many states had the same departments administering welfare and correctional functions. As late as the mid-twentieth century, several states still performed in that manner, namely, Kentucky, Minnesota, and Wisconsin. Wyoming still has a State Board of Charities and Reform that handles these functions. South Dakota has a State Board of Charities and Corrections. By the twentieth century, however, with impetus from the enormous welfare program developed during the Great Depression of the 1930s and the attention to crime brought by the gangland activities in Chicago and New York in the 1920s, culminating in St. Valentine's Day Massacre in 1929, these functions of welfare and corrections tended to be separated. Even so, they had a common origin.

Prisons, penitentiaries, and correctional institutions were eventually seen as the substitute for banishment and for capital punishment. England had no "prisons" in the modern sense because there was no sanitation and no discipline inside; they were simply holding areas. The infamous Newgate prison, built in London in 1769, was demolished in 1902. The Penitentiary Law of 1775 was passed by the British Parliament under the sponsorship of John Howard and Sir William Eden. John Howard and William Blackstone sponsored an act known as the Blackstone Act of 1778, which established penitentiary houses, confirmed the principle of separate confinement and labor, stressed a need for more religious instruction, fixed minimum sizes for cells, and provided for regular inspection of prisons by justices. Even so, the first prison in England was built at Millbank in 1821, fully forty-three years after the act. It must be noted that a previous General Prisons Act of 1782 emphasized the need for separation of offenders and segregation of men from women.

PRISONS AND CORRECTIONAL INSTITUTIONS

The modern prison is generally considered to have begun with the penitentiary movement in 1790 when the Quakers reformed the old Walnut Street Jail in Philadelphia, although there had been some prior movements in Europe, England, and elsewhere in America. The first solid evidence of a building approaching the modern prison was at Milan in 1628 and the "New Prison" or Carceri Nuove on the Via Giulia in Rome.[35] The first prison opened in America was at Simsbury, Connecticut, about 50 miles North of New Haven, in 1773 when administration buildings were built near the shaft of an old abandoned copper mine.[36] The first prisoner to be sent to this institution, called Newgate of Connecticut, was John Hinson who was sent there on December 2, 1773 and escaped eighteen days later when a "strong-handed Phyllis," who worked on a neighboring farm, pulled him up with a waterbucket at the end of a rope. From

[35]Giuseppe di Gennaro and Sergio Lenci, "Architecture and Prisons," in Gennaro et al., *Prison Architecture*, p. 8.

[36]Orlando F. Lewis, *The Development of the American Prison and Customs, 1776–1845* (Montclair, N.J.: Patterson Smith, 1967), p. 65. Published originally in New York by Prison Association of New York in 1922.

that first prison in America emanated tales of cruelty, riots, insurrections, vice, and crime among the prisoners, where the debauched and the decent, the young and the old, were forced into intimate physical association and unnatural sex.[37] It was reported that the system was well suited to turn men into devils, but it could never turn devils into men. A Newgate prison was constructed in New York City in 1796 about a block from the Hudson River in the area now known as Greenwich Village.

The emergence of the prison coincided with the Industrial Revolution. "Crime" was considered to be personal injuries between people, there was no criminal law, and the amount of damage and the sanctions were decided by the court almost as civil suits are today. Beccaria's famous *Essays on Crime and Punishment*, written in 1764, began a movement that culminated in the development of criminal law and procedure in England and America between the time of the American Revolution and the War of 1812. In England, the primary contributions were made by Jeremy Bentham, William Blackstone, and Samuel Romilly, while Edward Livington performed the same service in America. Prisons became the implementation of public concern for crime.

In 1815, New York established a prison at Auburn that imposed a silent system, individual confinement at night, convicts' working during the day, and harsh discipline. For the next two or three decades, there was intense debate between advocates of the Pennsylvania system and the less expensive Auburn system. It was soon apparent that prisons were costly, and efforts were made to ameliorate that cost. Some states, such as Kentucky, leased the prison to the highest bidder.[38] The prison, then, became a profit-making enterprise rather than a tax burden on the citizens. The direction of the state prisons became quite varied with some, for example, those in Alabama, Tennessee, and Kansas, going into mining; some, such as those in Texas and Mississippi, going into agriculture; and many Northern prisons going into industrial production of various types.

In the 1820s, the penitentiary and the reformatory coincided, and New York, Philadelphia, and Boston led the way in new prison construction and the movement to erect structures for juvenile offenders.[39] Overcrowding had become a problem by the middle of the nineteenth century, as had unemployment of inmates.

The use of contracts provided for almost everything from housekeeping functions to industry in the early American prisons. Even feeding of prisoners was by contract at Auburn, Sing Sing, Boston, and elsewhere.[40]

In 1870, the first meeting of the organization now known as the American Correctional Association was held in Cincinnati to discuss the directions that American prisons should take and to attempt to coordinate professional effort in the field of corrections. Then known as the National Congress on Penitentiary

---

[37]Ibid., p. 67.

[38]Ibid., Chap. 20, "Kentucky," pp. 253–59.

[39]Rothman, *The Discovery of the Asylum*, p. 257.

[40]Gustave de Beaumont and Alexis de Tocqueville, *On the Penitentiary System in the United States and Its Application in France* (Carbondale and Edwardsville: Southern Illinois University Press, Arcturus Books Edition, 1979), p. 69. Published originally in France in 1833.

and Reformatory Discipline, thirty-seven principles were worked out as guide-lines for the operation of prisons. There were considerable emphases upon (1) education, (2) consideration of the Irish system of incarceration by stages going from maximum custody to release for work in the community during the day, as well as (3) discussion of the indeterminate sentence preparatory to pa-role. Classification was considered to be paramount to separate people with various problems and concentrate programs on the basis of their needs. As a direct result of this conference, the first reformatory, built at Elmira, New York, subscribed to education, the indeterminate sentence, and the concept of parole. Zebulon R. Brockway, formerly superintendent of the Detroit House of Correc-tion and an instrumental figure in Michigan's having the first indeterminate sentence law in 1867, was made superintendent at Elmira. In that position, he became the first paroling authority to decide which inmates should be released under parole supervision prior to expiration of the sentences. Dissatisfaction with his choices soon led to the appointment of a separate and independent parole commissioner, but better classification, educational programs, and parole had received considerable impetus from the 1870 meeting in Cincinnati.

Minimum custody institutions began to be developed with the Borstals in England in 1908. Along with variations in custody, classification became more important. Classification began at rudimentary level in England with the emergence of the Borstals and in Belgium with the use of minimum custody institutions as well. Classification procedures were adopted in New Jersey in 1927. The U.S. Bureau of Prisons began using classification procedures in the early 1930s. Illinois developed classification procedures at the Diagnostic at Joliet in 1931. The first discussion of classification procedures in the Annual Congress of Correction sponsored by the American Correctional Association, then called the American Prison Association, was in 1936, with Dr. F. Lovell Bixby of New Jersey taking leadership. Other states began introducing classifica-tion procedures soon afterward, such as Michigan in 1937. Although, for a long time, Florida had a classification system based on whether or not a person could do a good day's work on the roads, conventional classification procedures were introduced in 1957. By the 1970s, all states had classification procedures of some type. It must be added, however, that all prisons had some type of informal classification since the beginning of institutionalization, though mostly by judg-ment of the administrators rather than by conventional procedures.

Prisons developed in different ways in different parts of the country. Historically, the older prisons in the Northeast and Kentucky followed the con-ventional plans of the Pennsylvania system, Auburn system, or leasing to the highest bidder. The majority of prisons in the North, Midwest, and California were built at a time when the large industrial prison was in vogue. Many of the prisons in the Northwest and mountain states were developed from territorial jails, such as Arizona, Walla Walla in Washington, Calgary in Canada, Deer Lodge in Montana, and others. Texas, Oklahoma, Arkansas, Louisiana, and Mississippi developed large agricultural operations to provide what some Texas officials refer to as "work therapy." Other states in this group boast about how much money they turn back to the legislature, sometimes over the amount appropriated to them in the first place. Prisons in the Deep South developed in a still different manner. Plantations provided private control over slaves, leaving prisons at the state level to handle people primarily from the cities. Mississippi built a prison at Jackson in 1808, known as "The Walls," which was a small operation. The first significant penitentiary in Mississippi was at Parchman in 1900. Georgia built a prison in 1823, but closed it in about eight years because it was not profitable; Georgia opened another prison in 1841, and Alabama opened its first in that same year. The Civil War left the formerly affluent South impoverished. There was not enough tax money to support good schools, much less to support prisons, so the South turned to the practice of leasing prisoners to the highest bidder. This altered the prison system from a tax burden to a profit-making venture. Abuses within the lease system and the invention of the automobile led to road gangs to construct and maintain roads. Some of these early abuses are well documented in J. C. Powell's *The American Siberia*, published originally in 1891.[41] Florida's first prison at Raiford was constructed in 1913 to house infirm men, who could not work on the roads, and women. The Southern prisons were considered a disgrace to penology until World War II.

Efforts after World War II resulted in vast improvements in Southern prisons to the point of achieving positions of leadership. This is evidenced by the series of presidents of the American Correctional Association who have been elected from the South, such as Ellis MacDougall of South Carolina (1968–1969), Dr. George Beto of Texas (1969–1970), Louie L. Wainwright of Florida (1970–1971), Oliver J. Keller of Florida (1975–1976), William D. Leeke of South Carolina (1976–1978), and Amos Reed of North Carolina (1980–1982).

THE TOTAL INSTITUTION
AND ITS POPULATION

In *Asylums,* Goffman pointed out that the social conditions in all total institutions are essentially similar, be they mental hospitals, monasteries and convents, jails, orphanages, military establishments, slave quarters, or *seraglios* (harems).[42] They develop special subcultures with an articulate set of values and informal rules and roles. The underlife of institutions is a way of surviving as easily as possible.

It should be noted that the term "asylum" is an old word meaning a place of refuge. Ancient peoples provided refuges in the temples, where offenders could be safe as long as they stayed there. The houses of refuge were institutions for the poor and the mentally ill. The modern meaning of "asylum" has a political connotation, that of permitting a defector from the Soviet Union political asylum in the West, for example, or enabling Eldridge Cleaver to leave the United States and find asylum in Algeria.

All institutions have residents with similar problems. The institutions, also, have some similar problems. They have to have a building site, where it is built, an architect to design the structure to house the program, a budget, an administrator, a staff, and a program designed to work with the residents of the

[41]J. C. Powell, *The American Siberia* (Montclair, N.J.: Patterson Smith, 1969). Published originally in Chicago by Chapman in 1891.
[42]Erving Goffman, *Asylums: Essays on the Social Situations of Mental Patients and Other Inmates* (Chicago: Aldine Publishing Company, 1961).

Table 1-1 Inmates of Institutions in America, 1970*

INSTITUTION	NUMBER	AS A % OF ALL INMATES
Homes and institutions for the aged and dependent	927,514	43.6%
Mental hospitals	433,890	20.4
Correctional institutions (adults)	328,020	15.4
Mentally handicapped	201,992	9.5
TB and chronic diseases hospitals	84,032	4.0
Training schools for juvenile delinquents (public and private)	76,729	3.6
Dependent and neglected children and unwed mothers	51,803	2.4
Physically handicapped	22,739	1.1

*U.S. Bureau of the Census, *Census of Population: 1970.* Vol. 2, *Persons in Institutions and Other Group Quarters.* Reprinted in *Statistical Abstract of the United States, 1978,* 99th ed. (Washington, D.C.: U.S. Bureau of the Census, 1979), p. 52.

institution. They have similar sets of operating procedures to provide requisites for survival in terms of shelter, clothing, food service, medical services, and all the basic necessities of life.

According to the 1970 census of the United States, the institutionalized population in America is divided above in Table 1-1. Of the 19.0 percent of the total institutionalized population in the United States in juvenile and adult correctional institutions, some 15.4 percent are in adult prisons and correctional institutions.

CONCLUSIONS

It took a long time for correctional institutions to emerge from other institutions and replace the practice of banishment and capital punishment. Temples were the first public institutions to house offenders. Places of dentention were situated in ancient Greece, Jerusalem, and Rome. The Code of Justinian, which held that places of confinement were not to be used as a result of a crime, influenced the thinking in Europe for a thousand years. Even so, the Roman Catholic Church was the first to condone the use of incarceration for crimes of a minor nature, using excommunication and turning offenders over to secular courts for severe punishments in other cases. By the twelfth century and into the eighteenth century, influential men could build private prisons to hold political opponents and people who were personally obnoxious to them. Criminal justice was really a private matter until the emergence of the national state was combined with the emergence of the criminal law in the last part of the eighteenth century and the early nineteenth century. Almshouses, workhouses, and asylums began to be developed by counties and local units of government in the seventeenth century and supplemented the jails that developed in the twelfth century. The use of prisons, penitentiaries, and correctional institutions began to be used after the codification of criminal law and court procedure in England and the United States, generally between the American Revolution and the War of 1812. More institutions were built during the nineteenth century than at any time ever before and continued into the twentieth century. Prisons and correctional institutions today, then, are the product of long-term metamorphosis, evolution, and development.

Prisons have not eliminated criminals, but have defined, refined, and perpetuated crime itself.[43] Prisons cannot be separated from the societies they serve. The modern prison in America is a concentrated expression of discipline that has spread throughout schools, armies, factories, and hospitals since the seventeenth century. Regularized routines and rigidly organized labor are a part of modern society in which prisons epitomize the ways in which people are controlled and repressed.

CHAPTER QUESTIONS

1-1.   What function or functions did the temple serve for the criminal justice system during ancient times?

1-2.   What role did the monastery play in the criminal justice system during the Middle Ages?

1-3.   What did the Council of Nicaea in 325 A.D. contribute to criminal justice?

1-4.   Why has slavery been associated with criminal justice since ancient times?

1-5.   What was the contribution of the Code of Justinian (about 456 A.D.) to the criminal justice system?

1-6.   What was the contribution of the Roman Catholic Church to the criminal justice process?

1-7.   What was the role of the private prison?

1-8.   Why were asylums, almshouses, workhouses, and bridewells built to serve the criminal justice system?

1-9.   How and why did prisons begin?

1-10. What proportion of all institutionalized persons in the United States are considered to be in the criminal justice system?

---

[43]Michel Foucault, *Discipline and Punish: The Birth of the Prison* (New York: Pantheon Books, Inc., 1977), p. 33.

2

ORGANIZATION OF CORRECTIONAL INSTITUTIONS

Modern correctional institutions have a long history of development of the delivery of services related to social institutions. The delivery of these services has been housed necessarily in physical plants or buildings. Originally, of course, all these services were provided by the tribe or kinship group. With the beginning of contained agriculture, in about 8000 B.C., land became important for permanent housing as tribes abandoned the nomadic life. Many of the social services provided by the tribe began to be taken over by newly constructed temples, the first about 6750 B.C. near the modern Jarmo in Iraq. The first temple with a purely religious focus appears to have been at Qulbān Layyah in lower Mesopotamia about 4000 B.C.[1]

While some services began to split off from the temples, many of the welfare and criminal justice functions were taken over by the monasteries beginning in the fourth century A.D. Jails were authorized by Henry II in 1166 A.D. When the monasteries were closed in England in the sixteenth century A.D., the government took over, with welfare being coordinated under the Elizabethan

[1]Note on *Lands of the Bible Today with Descriptive Notes* (Washington, D.C.: National Geographic Society, 1967). Map associated with Melville Bell Grosvenor, editor-in-chief, *The Story of Man—Everyday Life in Bible Time* (Washington, D.C.: National Geographic Society, 1967).

Poor Law of 1601 and other functions handled by asylums, workhouses, and houses of correction; major offenders were transported across the seas.

In America, no such transportation was possible, and this resulted in the construction of the first prisons. Prisons and penitentiaries that developed in America attracted world attention in the early 1800s.[2] The other components of the adult correctional system, such as the reformatory and various degrees of security from maximum to minimum and community security, were offshoots of this system. Juvenile institutions developed from the asylums. Special units and separate institutions for the criminally insane developed along with the criminal justice system.[3] From all this emerged the criminal justice system and its correctional institutions.

Organization refers to the relationship of the component parts of the whole of any system, the purpose being to arrange these parts into a coherent unit in which each part has a special function in achieving the final objective or objectives of the system. The objective of the criminal justice system is to protect society and to reform the individual offender sufficiently so that he or she can adjust to the free community. The criminal justice system, itself, is a component of larger society. It has close relationships with the welfare system, the mental health system, the educational system, and all other systems. Crime, itself, is not a unitary phenomenon. If a series of maps of a city were to show the places where crimes are committed, where offenders live, the incidence of welfare recipients, the incidence of health problems from dental caries through venereal disease to tuberculosis, the incidence of truancy from school, the incidence of unemployment, and many other indices of social breakdown, the configurations on each map would be similar. Crime is an index, but only one index, of social breakdown. Consequently, the criminal justice system must relate to all other systems in society for the common welfare.

Within the criminal justice system, correctional institutions form but one of several components. They serve as the hard-core entity in the system, holding the most serious problems that cannot be handled by the other components. In the total adult system, 63 percent are on probation, 16 percent are in prison or in other correctional institutions, 12 percent are on parole, and the rest are in jail. It can be seen that correctional institutions are a relatively small part of the total criminal justice system, but a most important part because they are "at the end of the line."

Organization within the institutions is most important in contributing to the success of the total criminal justice system. The primary components of the institutional organization can be classified as (1) custody, (2) "treatment," and (3) housekeeping. They are supposed to be coordinated by administration. Custody includes all personnel and equipment needed to maintain peace and order inside the institution and to prevent escapes, which generally takes 65 to 70 percent of the budget in a maximum security institution and less than 20 percent

---

[2]See Gustave de Beaumont and Alexis de Tocqueville, *On the Penitentiary System in the United States and Its Application in France* (Carbondale and Edwardsville: Southern Illinois University Press, 1971). Published originally in 1833.

[3]Seymour L. Halleck, *Psychiatry and the Dilemmas of Crime: A Study of Causes, Punishment and Treatment* (New York: Harper & Row, Publishers, 1967), p. x.

in a community-based facility. Treatment refers to the classification process, psychiatry and psychology, social work and counseling, education, recreation, religion, and any other program that serves the individual inmate. Housekeeping refers to the services anyone would need in his or her own house: food services, plumbing, electricity, radio, television, water, heat, laundry, sanitation, and general maintenance.

ASSESSMENT OF NEED

Assessment of need for correctional institutions, as for any other public expenditure, is required for planning, for the political leaders who appropriate funds, and for the public. Many of the larger states and the Federal Prison System (known as the U.S. Bureau of Prisons between 1930 and 1981), maintain a section on research and planning in the corrections system. Information is gathered regarding the potential needs of the agency, computerized projections of future needs, and other pertinent information for decision making and planning. In 1946, Congress established an Advance Planning Unit within the Bureau of Prisons for these purposes and to gather and maintain architectural designs and plans for future use.[4] Between 1968 and 1982, the Law Enforcement Assistance Administration (LEAA) provided federal assistance to the states, but this function was taken over by the National Institute of Corrections in 1980 and the National Institute of Justice in 1981, as LEAA was being phased out. The National Jail Center in Boulder, Colorado, opened in 1978, serves jails and local detention facilities. The National Academy of Corrections opened there in 1982. All these services are provided for the improvement and planning for the criminal justice system, including correctional institutions.

Prisons or other correctional institutions now appear in civilized societies around the world. Assessment of the need for further institutions requires an accounting of where the strains and problem areas are in society and in the present institutions and prediction of the type and size of the population expected to arrive at the prisons in the future.

Projections of future prison populations are present in most states. Projections generally are from five to ten years in the future, although the District of Columbia has projected only three years and Florida has projected twenty-five years. There are a variety of ways in which to produce these projections. The simplest way, of course, is to review the increase in the past ten years and project an equivalent increase for the next five to ten years, attempting to take into account other factors that might disturb the even continuation of the trend. This linear regression curve is probably the most frequently used method of predicting prison populations. More refined prediction includes an assessment of the population, particularly the high-risk category of males between 17 and 29 years of age. Unemployment rates also affect prediction of prison populations, since prison populations are more a reflection of unemployment than of crime rates. The extent of urbanization and increase of the problems of the inner cities in a

---

[4]See *Handbook of Correctional Institution Design and Construction* (Washington, D.C.: United States Bureau of Prisons, 1949).

geographical area also influence the prediction of prison populations. The extent of the use of probation and parole and other means of removing or diverting offenders from the institution must be considered.

There are several ways in which to predict prison populations and assess future needs. By January 1978, thirty-three states and the U.S. Bureau of Prisons had population projections for their prisons. Linear regression methods have been used frequently. The SIMMODG method, developed in early 1976, uses a simulation of the criminal justice system from arrest through trial and sentence. The SPACE model was developed by the Council of State Governments in Lexington, Kentucky, in early 1977, using proportion of arrests placed on probation and has a time lag built into it. The Congressional Budget Office (CBO) developed a method in 1977 using (1) young adult population, which was placed at ages 20 to 30; (2) historical inmate population; and (3) unemployment rates.[5] Other factors have been noted, such as predicted parole rates, rates of probation and parole violations, and the extent of use of probation and parole.

Unemployment and "population at risk" are the primary factors in predicting prison population increases. Wisconsin employed multiple regression to predict population increases, using age, economic factors such as unemployment, and arrest and conviction data. Texas uses new inmates per year, parolees per year, and discharges per year. New Mexico uses intake statistics over the past decade, state population change, and critical age groups in the work force. Arizona uses number of admissions, typical length of sentences, and pattern of parole decisions. South Carolina uses number of parolees, economic variables, and population at risk.

Prison populations had been reduced significantly in the United States in the early 1970s, resulting in empty cell blocks in some states, such as Michigan and California. By the late 1970s, however, prison populations reached a record high, the apparent result of economic conditions and high unemployment. Louisiana and Maryland both considered the purchase of old World War II ships to house prisoners on the Mississippi River and in the Chesapeake Bay, respectively. Florida erected tents and had its famous "Tent City" at the Reception and Medical Center at Lake Butler. Projections of prison populations *can* be made at least as accurately as the weather can be predicted, which realistically reflects a rather high degree of accuracy, at least considerably better than chance.

In planning for new institutions, their sizes become important in terms of the numbers of new prisoners anticipated and the cost factor. Institutions have been constructed in many sizes ranging from small jails to prisons of 5,000 capacity. If the institution is too small, the cost of its administration will be disproportionately high. At the other extreme, a massive penal institution has a lower per capita cost, but the resulting mass treatment inundates efforts to rehabilitate, educate, and provide other constructive programs. In the 1950s, general thinking was that adult correctional institutions should not exceed populations of 1,200. In the 1960s and 1970s, general opinion held that these institu-

---

[5]Congressional Budget Office, *Federal Prison Construction: Alternative Approaches* (Washington, D.C.: Government Printing Office, January 1977), p. 35. Also, see William H. Robinson, *Prison Population and Costs—Illustrative Projections to 1980* (Washington, D.C.: Congressional Research Service, April 24, 1974), pp. 19–20.

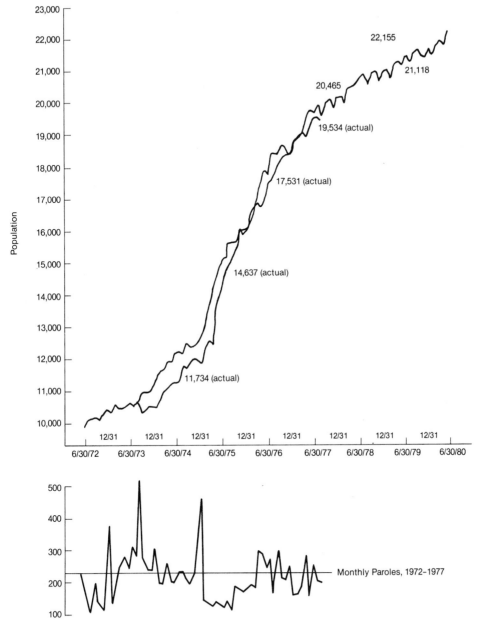

Inmate Population Projections: Short- and Long-Range Estimates, 1977 to 1980 and 1977 to 2000, (Tallahassee, Fl.: Department of Offender Rehabilitation, Bureau of Planning, Research and Statistics, July 27, 1977), p. 4.

Figure 2-1   Inmate population projections, June 30, 1977 through June 30, 1980.

tions should not exceed populations of 600. Women's institutions are small, anyway, because of the disproportionately small number of female inmates. Juvenile institutions should not exceed 150 in population, according to general concensus in this field. The largest juvenile institution in the United States had been at Gatesville, Texas, with a population of 1,500, but that institution was closed in 1978. An example of the computerized projections of prison needs in Florida appears in Figure 2-1.

In summary, the accurate assessment of the need for institutions is a most important phase of planning institutions. Failure to take advantage of the best available knowledge and experience provided by architects and engineers, sociologists and statisticians, economists and political scientists, and competent correctional practitioners and administrators has in the past resulted in expensive and tragic consequences in terms of cost and inability to implement constructive programs.

FINDING THE SITE

Two apparently paradoxical factors take primary consideration in finding a site for the institution. First, the facility should be located far enough from urban centers so that security is not threatened. Cities had grown up around the old Eastern state penitentiary in Philadelphia that was closed in 1970 and the old Ohio state penitentiary in Columbus that was replaced by the Ohio correctional facility at Lucasville in 1972. The same thing occurred at the Illinois Youth Center at St. Charles, opened in 1901, where public transportation today runs on all its four sides. Second, the institution should be sufficiently close to urban centers so that easy access to markets for supplies and public utilities can be maintained and families can visit their loved ones in prison. The Stateville–Joliet complex, for example, has the largest prison population in Illinois and is located 30 miles southwest of Chicago, from which the majority of its inmates come.

From a transportation viewpoint, a good location for a correctional institution is where main east-west and north-south highways and railroads cross. There are also advantages to being near a good airport.

If common water, sewage, gas, and electric utilities are available, considerable money can be saved. Most maximum custody institutions, however, have their own power supplies as backup to accommodate the institution in case of power failure, particularly in the case of electric power of the public utilities. All correctional institutions need two independent sources of electric supply to eliminate security hazards. The most economical arrangement is an institutional connection to two high-power transmission lines from different sources or a standby gasoline or diesel generating facility.

Probably the most difficult part of finding the site for a prison or correctional institution is in getting the consent of the people in the neighborhood of the proposed site. To accomplish this, the best approach generally is to identify the leadership in the neighborhood, including the local political leaders, and approach them diplomatically to explore their attitudes toward such an institution being in their locality. The strongest argument for a location is the fact that the facility would provide a payroll and economic stimulus for the area. The most difficult objection to overcome is that many persons who own homes in the area fear that property values will go down if a prison is located there. Further, many residents dislike the idea of their city being known as the site of the state prison. For example, the huge State Prison of Southern Michigan at Jackson is frequently referred to around the country as the "Jackson State Prison" or simply as "Jackson." Many would prefer to have the state university located in their cities.

A well-advertised public hearing should be held to give everybody an opportunity to voice his or her support or objections and to permit the citizens to vote for or against using the proposed site for a prison or correctional institution. If this is not done, trouble will start as the construction starts! This writer was present at an institution during a visit from the state director of corrections who was, in turn, visited by a committee of citizens in the area where a minimum security correctional institution was located. The citizens told him that they wanted the institution vacated and eliminated from their community. The director of corrections asked them how much time he had to find new space in the state and to relocate the prisoners. The citizens' committee gave him six months! Other developments in the area in the few months following dissipated the resolve of the citizenry and the institution continues to function today. The attitudes of the citizenry and political leadership is a primary reason that many major institutions are located in the rural areas—in the "boondocks"—far from urban centers.

Over and above the expense and inconvenience of being far from the markets, away from the availability of public utilities, and the inaccessibility by poor families for visiting their loved ones in prison, is what such isolation does to the program. Psychiatrists, psychologists, physicians, dentists, social workers, and teachers frequently want to be in or near urban cultural centers with their universities and libraries. They do not want to live and work in isolated rural areas. Consequently, it is difficult to maintain a positive and constructive rehabilitation program there, and the prison or correctional institution simply becomes a place for warehousing and deep-freezing the humanity it incarcerates.

In summary, facilities should be located in reasonable proximity to urban areas because most of the residents who come from urban areas will be close to their families and the supply of goods and services to the institution will be close and less costly. Government and, particularly, state land is preferred because of costs. Local zoning considerations must be taken into consideration. The relationship of the proposed facility to the adjacent property use and the local planning commission's view on how the facility will fit in with local comprehensive plans is important. Physical features of the site, such as soil conservation, composition, and susceptibility to flooding are important features. Community opinion and opposition must be dealt with and accommodated. It is important to (1) establish strong and continuous contact with various key people in the community while alternative sites are being considered, (2) demonstrate how the site fits in with the comprehensive plan and criteria for site selection, (3) recommend one of the sites to the governor, who will make the recommendation to the legislature, and (4) have community leaders favorable to the site support it in various meetings and forums.

New Facility at Oak Park Heights, Minnesota, dedicated March 4, 1982. Earth to the top of the walls on three sides (with 1.3 million cubic yards of earth moved) giving low visibility to the facility, maximum security, and energy conservation.

Courtesy of the Minnesota Department of Corrections.

ARCHITECTURE

After the need has been assessed, the size and security classification of the proposed institution has been determined, and the site has been found, attention can be focused on the design and construction of the institution. Design refers to the type of program the institution should have. Academic education, vocational training, an industrial operation, a farm, work and study release, specialized drug or alcohol programs, programs for mentally disordered or mentally defective offenders, group counseling, psychodrama and other role-playing programs, and many other types of programs in combination of programs may be selected.

The design of the program is more important than any proposed buildings planned. After the program has been designed and probably a couple of building suggestion sketched out, the project is turned over to an architect. Architects do not want sketched plans. Rather, architects want to know for what kind of program and for what type of offender the institution is being designed. The architect will then plan a building or a complex in which to house the program. The architect may suggest two or three preliminary sketches for the correctional administrator to approve or discuss possible changes. After some consultation, the architect will complete a final plan for the institution.

Standards of construction of institutions have been developed in several ways down through the years. The American Correctional Association recommends 60 square feet per single cell if the inmate spends no more than ten hours a day there, but recommends 80 square feet if more than ten hours are spent in the cell per day.[6] Lighting should be at least 20 footcandles, and circulation of at least 10 cubic feet of fresh or purified air should enter per minute. If a dormitory houses no more than fifty inmates each, they should have a minimum floor area of 60 square feet per inmate and the air circulation and footcandles should be the same as those in a cell block. Many other standards are also suggested. The Federal Prison System has designed new construction standards at 70 to 80 square feet per cell, but in several systems, overcrowding has forced double-celling. It also requires acoustics that ensure noise levels that do not interfere with normal human activities.[7] The National Clearinghouse for Criminal Justice Planning and Architecture indicates that this means normal conversation levels at decibel levels of 66 or less, but shouting would be required to be heard at 85 dB.[8] To sleep, the noise level would have to be less than 45 dB. Excessive noise levels in correctional institutions, as well as elsewhere, is a contributing factor to the people exposed, inmates and staff alike. Many institutions have reduced noise levels by installing individual radio headsets in each cell that are connected to a central receiver, moving televisions to special rooms with architecture that avoids acoustically "hard" surfaces and noisy locking mechanisms, and using plastic or other nonmetallic meal service equipment.

In the well-known Alabama case, Federal Judge Frank Johnson ordered that a minimum of 60 square feet of cell space be provided for each inmate.[9] On appeal to the Fifth District Court in New Orleans, some of the case was overturned, but the minimum cell space was upheld.

The hourly change of air in living quarters is dependent upon the number of people, their eating habits and diet, and personal hygiene, among other factors. A federal district court in Pennsylvania in 1979 held that the special housing unit for disciplinary cases at the federal penitentiary at Lewisburg did not meet constitutional standards[10] because (1) its ventilation system failed provide a minimum of nine air changes per hour, (2) it failed to provide inmates with two hours of exercise per week and two showers per week, and (3) it failed to provide proper and timely hearings to the inmates placed there. The problem in environmental health control involves air changes per hour and square feet

---

[6]*Manual of Correctional Standards for Adult Correctional Institutions* (Rockville, Md.: American Correctional Association Commission for Accreditation for Corrections, August 1967), pp. 27–28.

[7]Ibid., pp. 27–28.

[8]*Noise in Jails* (Champaign-Urbana, Ill.: National Clearinghouse for Criminal Justice Planning and Architecture, 1979), p. 2.

[9]*Pugh* v. *Locke*, 406 F. Supp. 318 (1975), and *Newman* v. *Alabama*, 559 F. 2nd 283 1977 (C.A. New Orleans, 1977).

[10]*Jordan* v. *Arnold*, Civ. No. 75-1334 (M.D. Penn. April 30, 1979).

Southern Ohio Correctional Facility at Lucasville, opened 1972.
Courtesy of the Ohio Department of Rehabilitation and Corrections.

per inmate. In addition, planning and implementation of environmental health services in penal and correctional institutions necessitates teamwork across disciplines that include legal, economic, and health components.[11]

Space has been found to be very important in prison architecture. There is a direct relationship between the availability of "personal space" and the dehumanizing aspects of prisonization. This relationship is reflected in the higher number of misconduct reports in crowded prisons and the lower number in less crowded prisons.[12]

Some have suggested underground construction of prisons and correctional institutions, but the majority of progressive correctional administrators do not favor of it, primarily because inmates in many prisons today may go for years without seeing a tree or a landscape. Underground institutions would eliminate

[11]Bailus Walker, Jr., and Theodore Gordon, "The Role of the Environmental Health Specialist in Penal Correctional Systems," *Journal of Environmental Health*, Vol. 38, no. 6 (May–June 1976), pp. 387–89.

[12]Peter L. Nacci, Hugh E. Teitelbaum, and Jerry Prather, "Population Density and Inmate Misconduct Rates in the Federal Prison System," *Federal Probation*, Vol. 41, no. 2 (June 1977), pp. 26–31.

Administration Building, Texas Department of Corrections, Huntsville.
Courtesy of the Texas Department of Corrections.

natural light that is considered to be "essential" by the Commission on Accreditation for Corrections.[13]

It has been pointed out that many buildings have been constructed underground recently, including homes, schools (in Fort Worth, Texas, and Reston, Virginia), libraries, and other buildings, for the purpose of conserving energy:[14] underground construction costs about 11 percent more than does building above ground, but the cost is made up within six years in maintenance and operating costs, after which time, the savings continue indefinitely.[15] The only underground correctional institution is the Ramsey County detention center in St. Paul, Minnesota, which was built into a bluff in the east bank of the Mississippi River.[16] But this is a short-term facility, not a long-term maximum custody institution.

After a final plan has been completed by the architect, the project is turned over to a general contractor or other person within the system of criminal justice to supervise inmate labor to construct the buildings. Texas, for example, has been very successful in having construction work done by inmates, including the buildings housing the Institute of Contemporary Corrections and Behavioral

[13]*Manual of Standards for Adult Correctional Institutions*, p. 27.

[14]Michael Barker, *Building Underground for People: Eleven Selected Projects in the United States* (Washington, D.C.: American Institute of Architects, 1978), 30 pp.

[15]Andrea O. Dean, "Underground Architecture," *AIA Journal*, Vol. 67, no. 4 (April 1978), p. 37.

[16]"Ramsey County Detention Center, St. Paul, Minnesota," in "Correctional Facilities: Building Types Study 518," *Architectural Record*, June 1978, pp. 128–29.

Sciences at the Sam Houston State University at Huntsville, which was established by the Texas legislature in 1965 to serve the criminal justice system in that state. On the other hand, when Michigan wanted to build a new chapel within the State Prison of Southern Michigan, the contract had to be let to a private contractor and the inmates stood around watching the project as "sidewalk superintendents."

In states with strong labor unions, the project must be let out to private contractors, generally on bids. A minimum of three bids is required. While the department of corrections is not required to choose the lowest bid, the reasons for passing by the lowest bid and selecting another must be clearly delineated.

TABLES OF ORGANIZATION

The organization of a prison varies with its type and its level of security. Custody is always a primary concern, but its implementation varies from maximum security to community-based security. The public, fearing crime, demands it. Further, many correctional administrators who have an average tenure in the United States of less than six years because they frequently find themselves in a "Catch-22" between treatment-oriented people and more conservative individuals in both the public and the political leadership. To protect their positions, they frequently have to focus on "the mandate of the court" as their primary concern. In the supermaximum custody, legendary U.S. penitentiary at Alcatraz, people were kept in their cells for twenty-two hours per day, were not permitted newspapers or radios, and were completely cut off from the outside. In the general maximum security prison, such as the California state prison at San Quentin and the U.S. penitentiary at Atlanta, contact with the outside, including radio, television, and newspapers and other journals, is permitted, although security is tight and counts are made every two hours. In the medium custody institutions, like the federal correctional institution at Danbury, Connecticut, and the Michigan Reformatory at Ionia, the perimeter is strong, but the security inside is more relaxed. In minimum security institutions, there may or may not be fences, there are no weapons in evidence, and the counts may be at meal time and bed check. In a community custody facility where the residents can work and study in the town and participate in community programs, security is not in evidence, although the residents must be in the center and in bed by specified times and abide by the rules designed to facilitate successful participation in the community, such as no drugs or alcoholic beverages and a definite check-out and check-in procedure. There is some security in probation and parole, also, since the rules must be followed and the probation and parole status can be revoked in case of violation. Custody is dependent upon how much external control a resident needs.

Examples of organizations frequently found in prisons and correctional institutions appear in Figures 2-2, 2-3, and 2-4.

Custody is the primary concern in maximum and medium security institutions, whereas treatment and other concerns are emphasized in minimum security and community-based facilities. Over one-third of the prisoners in the United States are doing their time in maximum security facilities and approx-

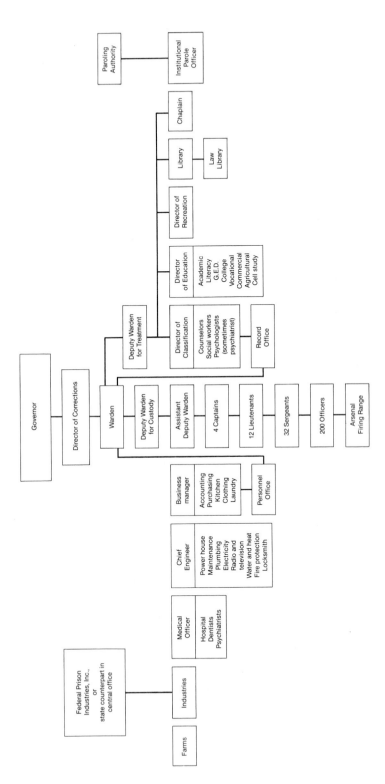

Examples of prisons this size would be the U.S. penitentiaries at Atlanta and Leavenworth, the Ossining correctional facility (Sing Sing) and the Auburn correctional facility in New York, and many other institutions in the United States. There are many variations from this table of organization, but this represents a typical system. Some prisons have an additional associate superintendent or deputy wardens for administration whose duties include the supervision of business, maintenance, and other functions at the left of the chart. The chief administrative officer may be called a warden or a superintendent.

Figure 2-2 Table of organization for an average prison of 2,000 residents or prisoners.

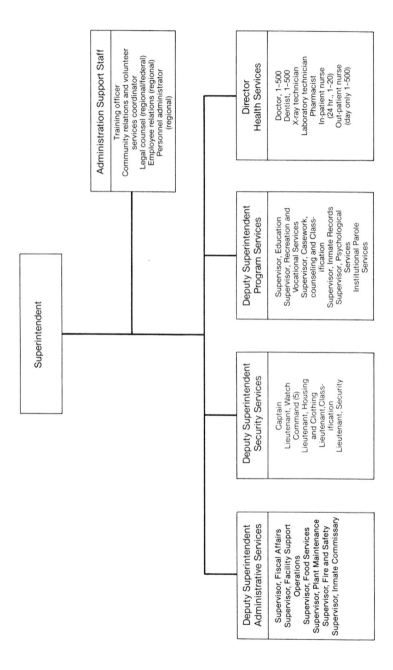

Facility Administrative Structure (Albany: New York State Department of Correctional Services, 2 n.d., received 1979), p. 7. Reprinted by permission.

Figure 2-3 Table of organization with deputy superintendents.

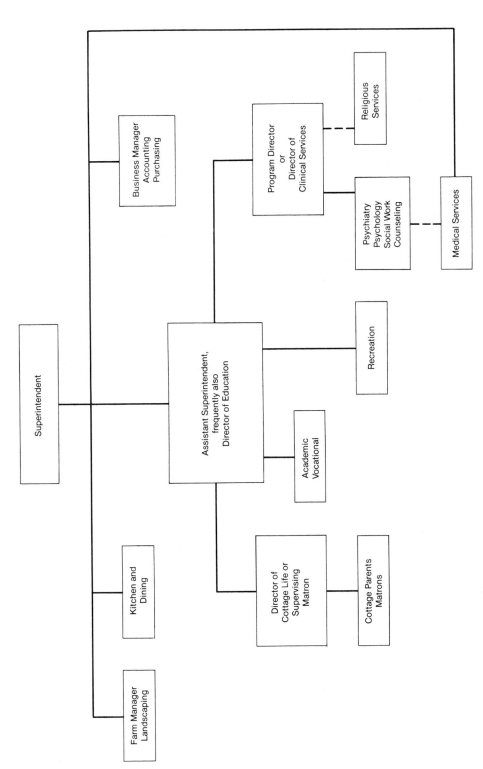

Figure 2-4 Table of organization for a "typical" juvenile training school.

imately one-third are doing their time in medium custody institutions. Therefore, custody is the primary concern in most correctional institutions in America. It has been traditional in American prisons that the warden, sometimes a political appointee, "runs the outside," including meeting legislative committees and doing the public relations while the deputy warden for custody "runs the inside." The latter is responsible for the security and order in the institution, disciplinary procedures, preventing escapes, and keeping down disturbances.

The "treatment" personnel include a classification department that prepares admission summaries on all new residents, participates in their job and program assignments, and prepares preparole progress reports when they become eligible for a parole hearing.

The record office, not unlike the registrar in a university, keeps the records. Consequently, it must be close to classification because they prepare many of the prison records. Since those and other records are filed there, the record office must be close to the warden's office as well. They maintain the court records and any records the warden might need to answer inquiring reporters' questions about specific inmates.

The education department generally has academic and vocational divisions, but may sometimes also have commercial and agricultural schools. The academic division focuses on teaching illiterates to read and write and helping non-high school graduates pass the G.E.D. (General Education Development) test and gain a high school equivalency diploma. They may also have extension courses from nearby universities and cell study, which is made up of correspondence courses that can be taken by inmates in their cells at night.

The recreation department is important because it attempts to provide constructive use of leisure time that might transfer outside. The library varies widely from institution to institution, ranging from a vault-type establishment from which residents may order books to be delivered to their cells to an open-stack arrangement where residents can browse and check out books. Since residents of prisons are generally nonreaders, it takes a personable librarian and a good selection of books to attract the residents to a library.

The law library is frequently attached to the general library. The law library has recently been declared in several states an essential element of the prison. California has listed the required books to be in these law libraries. In all states, law books must be available to all residents.

The chaplaincy is a difficult post to fill in the prison for a variety of reasons, including the reticence of many inmates to participate in religious activities and the wide diversity of religious beliefs among those who do participate. This writer has heard inmates say, "If there *is* a God, He sure as hell wasn't on *my* side!" The best chaplain appears to be one who does not "push" his own creed but can use counseling and general ethics effectively.

Other departments within the prison are for maintenance and daily operation of the small city that is the prison. The business manager is concerned with accounting, purchasing, kitchen, clothing, laundry, and other functions that involve rapid turnover of funds. The personnel office is often part of his function, but it may also be close to the warden because of interest and, in some situations, handling political patronage from outside politicians. The chief engineer is responsible for the power house, maintenance, and the smooth functioning of the plumbing system, the electrical system, radio and television, the water system, sewage system, heating, and other phases of the general maintenance and operation of the institution.

The medical officer is in charge of the hospital. Dentists generally serve under the medical officer. In some systems, the psychiatrists and psychologists are in the medical department, as in U.S. Public Health Service, which provides psychiatric and psychologist services to the U.S. Bureau of Prisons, while others house them administratively in the classification department. Many prisons have contracts with nearby university hospitals for specialized services such as cosmetic surgery.

The farms vary in size from prison to prison. Some prisons have eliminated the farms as being unproductive, while others, such as those in Texas, Mississippi, Arkansas, and Louisiana, maintain large farms. Industries present special problems in prison organization because of objections by the National Association of Manufacturers and various state counterparts against producing prison-made goods for sale on open markets; in addition, many object to prisons producing goods for other state agencies, such as state hospitals, state highway departments, and other subdivisions, such as county jails and schools. Legislation against prison industries has been passed in most states and in the U.S. Congress as a result of these lobbies in the name of protection of "free enterprise." Sufficient difficulty has arisen that most industries do not report to the institution warden but to the central office. In the case of the U.S. Bureau of Prisons, they report to a corporation formed by the government, the Federal Prison Industries, Inc. In many prisons, there is no common administrator to supervise the services of the business manager, chief engineer, medical officer, industries, or farms. Rather, they tend to work informally in cooperation with the deputy warden of custody and the warden. Other prisons, such as the Attica correctional facility in New York, have an associate superintendent for administration to provide this supervision and coordination.

The institutional parole officer (IPO) is not really part of the institution, but of the parole system. He or she maintains an office in the institution but is paid by the parole board or parole field services. The parole officer's function is to coordinate the program of the prison with the parole program. Within the institution, the officer interviews residents about to be released to assist with possible problems. A primary function is to operate the prerelease preparation program, which is a series of lectures, films, and other types of instruction to prepare residents about to be released for successful adaption to free society after a period of time in the closed prison. The IPO's association with others within the institution is informal, but his or her successful functioning depends upon getting along well with other prison personnel.

Tables of organization vary with the size and needs of the institution. The charts presented earlier are simply examples. In smaller institutions, there would be fewer top administrators. Because institutions may range from less than fifty in a community-based facility to over four thousand and as high as over five thousand, these tables of organization *must* vary with the size and needs of the institution.

HOUSEKEEPING

Housekeeping refers to the services anyone would expect in his or her own home—food, plumbing, electricity, radio, television, water, heat, laundry, and sanitation. Control of living conditions in the institution is very important for morale and health. Further, these services are perpetual; around the clock, 365 days a year, without vacation. Any interruption constitutes an emergency.

Food Services

Food services are the most important segment of this operating area. The residents work in the kitchen and dining hall to prepare the food and serve it and to clean the kitchen and dining hall afterward three times a day under the supervision of the chief steward. All inmates who handle food must pass a rigid medical examination. In some states, the menus are made up by a dietician in the central office and are sent to each institution with permission to modify according to the unusual availability of certain foods, such as tomatoes in season, if cleared by the central office. This has resulted from several court cases in which diets have been challenged. The Black Muslims won a court case in 1962 that resulted in modifying the diet at the District of Columbia Youth Center at Lorton, Virginia.[17] The U.S. Bureau of Prisons was also required to provide kosher food to Orthodox Jewish inmates[18] in a suit that had been brought by an Orthodox Jewish rabbi who had been convicted and sentenced in the Eastern District of New York for conspiracy to violate the Federal Firearms Act (18 U.S.C. 371). The Bureau of Prisons appealed to the Second District Court of Appeals, but lost. The U.S. Bureau of Prisons now has a kosher line in all institutions.

Prison diets are not exotic. In fact they are quite plain. Some of this has to do with public opinion and frequent remarks that many prisoners eat better in the institution than they did at home! This may well be true, but it is also true that many are on a schedule that they did not observe at home. Their daily lives have been changed and are under control. It is interesting to note that many prison farms raise prize cattle, exhibit their prize bulls in county and state fairs, and produce other outstanding crops and animals. In these cases, the fruits and vegetables raised on the prison farm can be consumed at the prison. The prize bulls and other animals, however, must be sold and cheaper commercial grades of meat purchased for consumption at the prison.

For a prison housing two thousand residents, as portrayed in Figure 2-2, a typical breakfast might be oatmeal, stewed apples, toast with jelly, and coffee.

- Rolled oats: 100 lb rolled oats ⎫
               28 gal milk   ⎬   cooked together
               8 lb salt   ⎭
- Milk: 140 gal
- Sugar: 50 lb

[17]*Fulwood v. Clemmer*, 205 F. Supp 370 (District of Columbia, 1962).
[18]*Meir Kahane v. Norman Carlson*, 527 F. 2nd 492 (1975).

- Stewed apples: 130 lb dried apples, 50 lb sugar
- Apple jelly: 24 gal
- Coffee: 38 lb
- Bread: 380 lb
- Margarine: 60 lb

A typical noon lunch featuring potted noodles with diced beef might be as follows:

- Potted noodles with diced beef: 150 lb noodles
  400 lb diced beef
  100 lb onions
  10 lb salt
  2 lb black pepper
  1½ lb celery salt
  1 lb marjoram
  ½ lb salad oil
- Mixed fruit: 53 lb dried apples
  60 lb raisins
  38 lb dried peaches
  45 lb sugar
- Coconut bars: 150 bars
- Bread: 380 lb
- Radishes: 240 lb
- Iced tea: 35 lb black tea, 13 lb sugar, 1,050 lb of ice

Evening dinner or supper with hamburger steak in brown sauce may take the following ingredients:

- Hamburger steak in brown sauce: 950 lb beef or 1½ head of cattle
  40 doz eggs
  50 lb bread crumbs
  3 lb black pepper
  8 lb salt
  1 lb whole dried peppers
  75 lb onions
  2 lbs garlic
  8 gal milk
  1 lb marjoram
- Brown sauce: 250 lb soup bones for stock
  50 lb flour
  50 lb drippings
  8 lb salt
  1½ lb black pepper
- Boiled potatoes: 11 bu potatoes
  8 lb salt

- Buttered green beans: 100 #10 cans green beans
                            13 lb margarine
                             4 lb salt
                             1 lb black pepper
                           210 lb green onions
- Pickled cucumbers and onions: 900 lb cucumbers
                                   160 lb onions
                                    18 gal vinegar
                                     4 gal vegetable oil
                                     6 lb salt
                                     1 lb black pepper
- Rice pudding with raisins: 100 lb rice
                                30 doz eggs
                                90 lb sugar
                                 2 qts vanilla extract
                                 1 lb salt
                                12 lb margarine
                                 1 qt food coloring
                                90 gal milk
                                 1 lb cinnamon
- Bread: 39 lb
- Tea: 22 lb black tea
         38 lb sugar
- Margarine: 60 lb

This is a typical prison meal for inmates. In addition, there are special diet lines for special cases, such as diabetics and others who require them for medical reasons. Special meals are made for persons in the hospital and for persons in disciplinary status, solitary confinement, and administrative segregation. It must be noted that expenses are watched at all times. In fact, due to high prices, many prisons mix the coffee with roasted grains, such as barley. During times of shortage, as in wartime, many prisons use roasted grains exclusively for coffee and, therefore, do not have to ration it.

Laundry

The laundry is run by inmates under the supervision of a civilian. Because of the heat, the laundry is generally not considered to be a good place to work, so assignment to the laundry is sometimes used as a disciplinary measure. In a large prison, each cell block or housing unit may have its "laundry day" in which an inmate *corps de honeur* delivers the dirty clothes from the inmates to the laundry and brings back the clean ones. Each resident generally has three sets of prison clothes: one in the laundry, one being worn, and one in reserve.

Maintenance

Skilled maintenance jobs, such as plumbing, electrical services, and other functions, are done by inmates skilled in these trades under the supervision of the chief engineer and assistants. Crews work in various parts of the prison and may be called at any time of the night or day in case of emergency. The power house is the main source of energy, including the alternate power system in case the public utility supply breaks down. In an industrial prison, heating in the winter generally is a by-product of industry.

Sanitation

Keeping the corridors, auditorium, and the entire physical plant clean is done by inmates working in crews. There are enough inmates in most prisons so that all institutions should be spotless.

CONCLUSIONS

Architecture has the capacity to contribute to correctional programs at four significant levels. First is the provision of adequate space in which program activities can be conducted. The sensory deprivation that results from sterile, routinized, and mechanical environments must be avoided. Second, architecture has the potential for positive or negative impact on activity patterns that permit or do not permit flexibility. An extreme example is the attempt at the old Eastern state penitentiary in Philadelphia to play softball within a "V" between the radial cell blocks that crowded first and third base so that each was only about 10 feet from the pitcher's mound. Architecture must recognize and accommodate to change. Third, architecture has an impact on organizing relationships between people, where the very location of the facility permits or limits visits by the family, specialized services, and community reintegration. Internally, architecture determines the internal spatial organization of human interaction, just as the presence or absence of a civic center expands or limits sporting and other entertainment events in a city. Identification of residential clusters or modules may provide a reference place that contributes to the identity of the individual living there. Fourth, architecture has an impact on the communications patterns of the correctional environment in which hostile physical environments may carry threatening connotations to the activities attempted in that setting and impede rehabilitative methods. In summary, architecture must provide adequate space for the program, permit flexibility in design to accommodate new programs, provide settings that permit outside contacts and inside positive identification, and provide a nonthreatening environment that permits positive communication of socially approved values and attitudes.

In conclusion, the organization of the prison and its services are a microcosm of any large city. It has its law enforcement component in custody, education, religious services, recreation, library, and its counselors, social workers, and psychologists. It has its medical services, including dentists and psychiatrists. Industries, farm produce, and other supplies and distributions of goods and services are made through the business manager. The prison, then, is a complete city with all its services operating behind the walls.

In assessing the need for institutions, it is important to determine the type of persons anticipated to be in the institution, whether they are young first-offenders, older hardened offenders, young hard-core delinquent and young adult offenders, older low-risk embezzlers and moonshiners, or any other group. It should be determined whether the planned institution is to house juveniles or adults, males or females, and what type of security is to be provided. Maximum custody prisons are usually constructed first and modified institutions generally follow. Medium custody, reformatory-type institutions generally serve young first-offenders or older low-risk offenders. Minimum custody serves similar groups with lower security risks. Community custody institutions, such as halfway houses and community correctional centers, serve offenders who can work or study in the community and participate in community programs, but need their evenings and weekends controlled. The type of institution to be constructed must be well planned if the construction and programming of the institution is to be effective and efficient.

CHAPTER QUESTIONS

2-1. When discussing social institutions and the need for various services in society, why is the physical plant or building important?

2-2. What factors are generally considered during the assessment of the need for a prison or a correctional institution?

2-3. What was the method developed in 1977 by the Congressional Budget Office to predict growth in prison population?

2-4. What factors should be considered in finding a site for a prison or correctional institution?

2-5. How can the consent of the people be obtained for the construction for a prison or correctional institution in or near their community?

2-6. Why is architecture important in the prison or correctional institution?

2-7. Why is a definite table of organization needed for each institution?

2-8. To what does "housekeeping" refer in an institution?

2-9. Why are food services most important in the housekeeping function?

2-10. Why is the physical plant and the services it houses so important in a prison or correctional institution?

3

CUSTODIAL
CONTROL

Custodial control has been regarded by many as the primary mission of the maximum security prison. With varying degrees of intensity, control is the central function of all correctional institutions and programs. Three elements appear in all positions in the criminal justice system from police to institutions to parole: (1) investigations, (2) counseling, and (3) enforcement. The custodial function in the prison and in the correctional institution also includes these three elements. Enforcement refers to the control necessary to maintain the safety and security of the institution and to prevent escapes. Investigation in the institution refers to the identification of disciplinary problems and potential areas of trouble and disruption. Counseling is an ongoing function of custody because of the closer proximity of correctional officers to the residents or inmates while in the cell block, on-the-job counseling while supervising work assignments, recreational programs, and other activities.

Correctional officers provide probably more counseling than do any other personnel in the prison, including psychiatrists, psychologists, and social workers, because of the former's numbers and their accessibility to residents or inmates. Whether this counseling is good, bad, or indifferent gives way to the fact that the correctional officer is available, whereas the "professionals" tend to be in offices more distant from where the inmates live and work. Appointments

41

have to be made with the professional, whereas the correctional officer is immediately available.

It becomes apparent that custody, through its mission to control the institution, and correctional officers, through their accessibility to residents or inmates and their numbers, are central to the operation of all maximum and medium custody institutions; their visibility is diminished and their functions are somewhat lessened in the more open minimum custody institutions and community-based facilities.

Court decisions on litigation brought by inmates against correctional systems, frequently against treatment by custodial officers, have changed in recent years. In the 1950s and before, courts maintained a "hands-off" policy that considered prison administration and operation essentially beyond judicial review.[1] At that time, approximately 500 cases per year were brought to litigation by inmates. In the 1960s, the courts grew more interested in prison administration and operation, and a "hands-on" policy developed.[2] About 1,600 cases of litigation were coming into the courts at that time. In the early and middle 1970s, there was the beginning of concern about the safety and security of the institutions and a "restrained-hands" policy appeared to be emerging.[3] By 1976, there were 19,000 cases of litigation brought by inmates against correctional systems. By 1979, over 21,000 cases were brought to court. Chief U.S. district court Judge James Burns of Portland, Oregon, told the Annual Congress of the American Correctional Association in Miami Beach on August 20, 1981 that some judges were then calling for a policy of "hands on, hands in, and hands all over."[4] At that time, eight entire prison systems had come under court order, and eighteen other states had one or more prisons that were under court order or had been declared unconstitutional.

While this litigation brought by inmates covers all phases of prison operation from food to religion, most of it involves the custodial operation, particularly with the "cruel and unusual punishment" prohibited by the Eighth Amendment and "due process" as set forth in the Fifth Amendment in the federal system and as the Fourteenth Amendment makes it applicable to the states. Also, violation of civil rights is frequently charged under Title 42 of the United States Code (U.S.C.), Section 1983, which is the Civil Rights Act of 1871. These legal constraints bear on the custodial operation in all jurisdictions in the United States.

FUNCTIONS OF CUSTODY

The functions of custody include the incapacitation of the offender to protect society and treatment of the offender through rewards and punishments to modify behavior. The major mandate of the court is to hold dangerous or

---

[1]John W. Palmer, *Constitutional Rights of Prisoners,* 2nd ed. (Cincinnati: W. H. Anderson Publishing Company, 1977), p. 174. Referred as an example to *Garcia* v. *Steele,* 193 F. 2d 276 (8th Cir., 1951).

[2]Ibid., p. 174. Referred as an example to *Cooper* v. *Pate,* 378 U.S. 546 (1964).

[3]William G. Archambeault and Betty J. Archambeault, *Correctional Supervisory Management* (Englewood Cliffs, N.J.: Prentice-Hall, Inc., 1982), pp. 195–215.

[4]Reported *Corrections Digest,* Vol. 12, no. 19 (September 11, 1981), p. 4.

disruptive offenders in confinement for the protection of society. On the other hand, the treatment phase of custody is to modify behavior by providing disciplinary action or punishment for unconforming behavior, on the one hand, and providing rewards by reduction of custody and additional privileges, on the other. The long-term purpose of custody is to provide external control for persons who do not have internalized controls sufficiently strong to get along in society. Enlightened custody reduces those controls when possible to provide only that amount of external control that is immediately necessary.

The more immediate purposes of custody are (1) to prevent escape, (2) to maintain peace and order within the institution, and (3) to perform these two functions with the least possible hindrance to the primary treatment objectives of the program, thereby promoting efficient functioning of the overall institutional program. It should be noted here that in the mid-1970s there has been a movement away from the treatment or rehabilitation ideal. One such contention has been that "rehabilitation" has not worked.[5] Another major factor has been a series of court cases concerning the right to refuse treatment. The U.S. Parole Commission has gone to a system of "salient factors" to decide for or against parole in most cases, in which social factors outside the prison, not institutional records, are taken into consideration. Many states have followed suit by developing "objective parole criteria" that permit them to defend parole action. Any deviations have to be explained in writing. This has resulted in more difficult custodial control in many institutions, since "good behavior" in the institutions no longer affects parole chances unless it is obvious and extreme. This has also caused some correctional administrators to think that flat sentencing regardless of institutional record and abolition of parole is, itself, a viable course of action.[6]

This conflicting situation has brought several correctional administrators, including Norman A. Carlson, director of the former U.S. Bureau of Prisons, now the Federal Prison System, and former Commissioner Ben Ward of the New York State Department of Correctional Services to conclude that treatment programs should be made available in prisons but that the residents or inmates should not be forced to participate in them; moreover, parole should not be used to reward such participation or to punish lack of participation. This "justice model" would leave the custodial function only as holding securely or incapacitating the offender, without real concern for the treatment objectives. A survey of the top prison officials in all fifty states in 1975 indicated that 73 percent favored continuing the rehabilitation objective, 15 percent wanted more information, and 12 percent wanted to institute the "justice model" and forget rehabilitation.[7] It is apparent that the majority of correctional administrators in the United States favor continuing efforts at treatment and rehabilitation and will retain that as a part of the custodial function. In fact, many prison systems have already selected from the

[5]Douglas Lipton, Robert Martinson, and Judith Wilks, *The Effectiveness of Correctional Treatment* (New York: Praeger Publishers, Inc., 1975).

[6]David Fogel, ". . . *We Are the Living Proof. . . " : The Justice Model of Corrections* (Cincinnati: W. H. Anderson Publishing Company, 1975).

[7]Michael S. Serrill "Is Rehabilitation Dead?" *Corrections Magazine*, Vol. 1, no. 5 (May–June 1975), pp. 3–12.

correctional officer ranks competent persons as correctional counselors and have provided them with special training and extra pay for the service. A few administrators will continue to view their correctional officers as "guards" and function under the "justice model."

Techniques by which custody achieves its purposes are (1) segregation or separation of inmates, (2) controlled movement of inmates, and (3) counseling inmates. In the more secure prisons, each resident or inmate is in an individual cell, although overcrowding has required doubling cell occupancy in some cases. Some medium custody institutions have two inmates per cell, while other medium and minimum custody institutions may use dormitories. Each type of housing has its own custodial advantages and disadvantages.

CONTROL OF THE YARD AND THE INSTITUTION

Control of the yard and the institution as a whole depends on the development of systematic distribution of custodial personnel and assignments into various parts of the institution and assuring that shifts of custodial personnel meet each other around the clock all days of the year. These assignments may be made by the lieutenants or the captain. There is generally a rotation of shifts so that one correctional officer or sergeant will not have to be on the same shift all the time.

Segregation is used to maintain discipline and to isolate problem residents or inmates. Persons who violate institutional rules may be disciplined by solitary confinement or other procedures. Segregation for disciplinary purposes is one technique by which custody achieves its purposes. Administrative segregation is provided for many troublemakers and agitators, assaultive and quarrelsome people who cannot get along with others, as well as some uncontrollable homosexuals and for the protection of young and weak residents from attack.

The controlled movement of inmates within a prison is an important feature in custody. Moving inmates from cell blocks to central dining halls and back must be organized. Moving inmates from cell blocks to work assignments in an orderly manner requires coordination in housing. For example, if the kitchen crew reports at 5:00 A.M. or 5:30 A.M. for the purpose of preparing breakfast for the institution, they should all be moved from one cell block to the kitchen so that supervision can be done by a single officer, if necessary. Similar arrangements should be made for other assignments within the institution. At the other extreme, many minimum security institutions exercise little or no such control, permitting inmates to go from their domicile to the work assignment and to the dining hall at specific times with little or no supervision. These varying degrees of institutional security and custodial control are designed for the gradual reduction of custodial security from maximum to community custody as the resident no longer needs the more secure external controls.

General custodial control of the institution is coordinated from a control room that becomes the "nerve center," usually in the charge of a lieutenant. From this control room are coordinated the functions of the outside towers and wall towers and supervision of various work assignments, schools, cell blocks or dormitories, kitchens and dining halls, chapels and auditoriums, recreational

Prison yard on a weekend, State Prison of Southern Michigan at Jackson.
Courtesy of the Michigan Department of Corrections.

areas, industries, and the yard. Depending on the size of the prison, the lieutenant reports directly to a captain, who generally has an office separate from the control room. The captain, in turn, reports directly to the deputy warden or associate warden or to the deputy warden in charge of custody, depending upon administrative structure. In most prisons, the deputy warden is in charge of custody and reports to the warden; the warden is more frequently concerned with the broader aspects of the institution and its relationship to the legislature, political leaders, and the public through the news media.

The differentials in custodial personnel coverage in an institution is known as *custodial zoning*. For example, correctional officers assigned to industries, schools, and other programs that operate from 8:00 A.M. to 4:00 P.M., five days a week, do not provide coverage for these facilities nights and weekends. Further, the shifts for general security vary in size depending on the activities anticipated. The night shift or "morning watch" most frequently works from 10:00 P.M. to 6:00 A.M. or from midnight until 8:00 A.M. and is generally the smallest shift because most of the residents are supposed to be sleeping and no institutional activities are supposed to be in progress. On the other hand, the afternoon shift, frequently from 2:00 P.M. to 10:00 P.M. or from 4:00 P.M. to midnight generally has most of the activity, particularly recreational or leisure-time activity; this is the time, experience indicates, during which most escapes and disturbances occur. This shift is generally the largest. The remaining shift is a morning-daytime shift that has most to do with the supervision of industries, schools, and other programmed activities in the institution and is generally between the other two shifts in size.

Direct telephone lines run from the outside or wall towers to the control room. They are without dials so that communication can be only between the tower and the control room. Similarly, direct telephone lines run from the cell blocks or the dormitories to the control room, but these generally have dials leading to an internal telephone system only, so that the hospital, some work assignments, and some other specific points can be contacted—but no outside calls can be made. There are several systems by which the control room can be notified of emergencies in cell blocks and other areas, one system being simply that the telephone has been knocked off its cradle and sets up an alarm in the control room, while other systems frequently require three-digit dialing for the same purpose.

A system of passes and details (group passes) is used to control movement within the institution. When an individual prisoner is to go from a work assignment to a counselor, the hospital, or any other destination for which he has no assignment, the correctional officer must write a pass that includes the time of departure, the inmate's destination, and the officer's signature. All these passes are returned to the control room at the end of each shift for future reference in case they are needed.

Control of gates is necessary for security. In maximum security institutions, there is generally a main gate, a freight gate for trucks, and sometimes a railroad spur. Adequate supervision is always provided when these gates are open. While in the older prisons these gates are opened and closed manually by key, some of the newer institutions have remote-control locking systems. At the main gate and the freight gate, for example, an officer may be in a secure enclosure containing a television monitor some distance from the gate. Signals from the officer at the gate tell the officer in the subcontrol room with the remote-control capability when to open and close the gates electronically. Within the prison in some newer institutions, the cell blocks themselves can be similarly controlled by an officer in a remote and secure subcontrol room with a bank of television monitoring screens carrying messages from cameras focused on each gate. Opening and closing of these gates can be done remotely.

Searches of cell blocks and dormitories, generally referred to as "shakedowns," are routine in security-oriented institutions. In maximum security institutions, shakedowns are frequent. Contraband or articles that are not permitted in the prison vary widely depending upon the type of security and the practices of the institutions. Unfortunately, much of the contraband, particularly drugs and alcohol, is brought into the institution by untrustworthy officers and other prison personnel. Some of it is brought in by inmates who have outside assignments and return to the prison each evening, and some is brought in by visitors. Most maximum security prisons do not permit money inside the walls, but some medium, minimum, and community security institutions permit varying amounts of money. Some other items that have been listed as contraband are matches, razor blades, broken spoons, metal objects, rocks, earth or sand (which may have come from a tunnel being dug somewhere or be used as a weight in a sock to make a blackjack), alcoholic beverages, narcotics, jail plants (marijuana), keys and key-making materials, cutting tools, gambling equipment, spices (particularly mace and nutmeg), buzzers, knives, and tools for breaks.

Alcohol is a primary problem in prison. "Spud juice" is made from a potato base and is found frequently in the North and Midwest. "Raisin jack" or "pruno" has a raisin or prune base and is found frequently in the West. "Cane buck" has sugar cane as a base and is found frequently in the South. A greater problem is the smuggling of bonded liquor into the prison.

By the mid-1970s, the drug problem in prisons and correctional institutions appeared to exceed the alcohol problem. Despite valiant attempts at control by the custodial force, many medium security and some maximum security prisons have been known to have "pot parties." Officers could smell the odor of marijuana but have remained helpless to find or stop it. Hard drugs are even more difficult to control as they emit no odor. Many of the fights in maximum and medium security institutions are drug related. Recently, phencyclidine (PCP) or "Angel Dust" has been a problem.

There are other types of contraband that are not dangerous or undesirable, but are against the rules of the institution. These types of contraband rules have been upheld in the courts. For example, confiscation of religious books have been held not to be a denial of religious freedom when twenty-two of these religious books were confiscated from an inmate's cell when the institution had a four-book limitation.[8] Searches are the basic approach to the control of contraband. Strip searches are the most thorough search in prison. It involves stripping the prisoner nude, examining the inmate's hair, ears, and all body openings, including the anus, which can be distended with a tool designed for the purpose. In one case, a roll of bills amounting to $600 was found in that orifice.

The Fourth Amendment rights of prisoners are commonly construed to apply to search and seizure practices by officers in correctional institutions. Careful formulation of institutional rules may effectively circumscribe the searching guard's discretion in initiating and executing the search.[9]

Fourth Amendment protection against unreasonable searches and seizures was found to survive to some extent during incarceration in *Bonner* v. *Coughlin.*[10] The decision in this case held that entry into a controlled environment entails a dramatic loss of privacy but that the surrender of privacy is not total and that some residuum meriting the protection of the Fourth Amendment survives the transfer into custody. What privacy remains and the conditions under which a correctional officer must get a search warrant to search an inmate's cell remains for the court to decide. These searches are the routine in most jurisdictions at present, but they could be challenged. This is true also of personal and body searches. General searches can still be authorized at any time without specific cause, since prisonwide searches for contraband may still be

[8]*Taylor* v. *Cupp*, 564 P. 2d 746 (Oregon App., 1977).

[9]Gianelli and Gilligan, "Prison Searches and Seizures 'Locking' the Fourth Amendment Out of Correction Facilities," *Virginia Law Review*, Vol. 62 (1976), pp. 1045–98.

[10]*Bonner* v. *Coughlin*, 517 F. 2d. 1311, (7th Cir. Ill., 1975).

instituted by prison officials as reasonable unless there is abuse or wanton conduct during the search.[11]

Through the many court actions from litigation brought by inmates, some upholding the right to search for the protection of the institution and others suggesting that the Fourth Amendment protections against "unreasonable searches" hold and that no warrants can be issued without probable cause, some prison systems have become concerned about what the future directions in search procedure might be. The U.S. Bureau of Prisons has developed rules covering various levels of searches.[12] The least intrusive search is the "par search," in which an inspection may be made of a fully clothed resident by hand or by a metal detector. Next most intrusive is the "visual search," which includes visual inspection of body surfaces and cavities. The "cavity" or strip search refers to internal inspection of all body cavities; recent rulings state that it can be done only by a medical staff member upon approval by the warden and that a written explanation must be filed. An X-ray search for contraband may be made.

Tool and key control are important in a maximum security prison because stolen tools and keys can be used in escape attempts and in making weapons. The basic factor in tool control is a rigid check system with receipts for the tools available in the shop and the classification system for different storages of tools. Class A tools, for example, are those that can cut steel, for example, welding torches, the parts of which must be stored in the arsenal overnight and checked out by the maintenance supervisor or the vocational school instructor each morning for the day's work. Class B tools may be stored in the machine shop but under close scrutiny. Class C tools, such as screwdrivers and pliers, need observation but do not require unusual surveillance. While Class A tools are frequently stored in the arsenal at night, other tools must be accounted for in the tool crib.

Key control is of primary importance, of course, and the key rings are stored in the control room arranged according to the tour of duty of each correctional officer. An officer may have twenty-five keys on a ring or he may have only one or two, depending upon his duties. These key rings must be checked out and precise records kept. If an officer takes a key ring home, he must be called and made to bring it back immediately. Keys inadvertently left on a table for only a moment have been pressed into a bar of soap for models. Inmates have even been known to observe keys and be able to manufacture replicas from visual recall. When a key is lost, there is no recourse but to change the locks and issue new keys to the affected areas. While it may seem paradoxical to maintain close control of tools and keys and then permit people to work in the kitchen and butcher shops with knives and cleavers, the inmates who work in the kitchen with knives and cleavers must be selected carefully and the correctional officer in the kitchen and butcher shop has to supervise them closely. Because operating a kitchen or butcher shop with civilian help would be prohibitively expensive, the use of residents becomes an economic necessity.

The arsenal is essential to the custodial operation because it maintains

[11]*Aaman* v. *Helgemoe*, 20 Cr. L 2351 (D.N.H., 1976).

[12]"BOP Proposes Rules for Inmate Searches," *Criminal Justice Newsletter*, Vol. 11, no. 8 (April 4, 1980), p. 5.

and services the firearms to be used in the guard towers and in outside patrols, particularly in the case of escapes and sometimes in the supervision of outside work details. These firearms are classified in various ways from the high-powered rifle to the pistol. There are also machine guns, carbines, shotguns or riot guns, and gas guns. The high-powered rifle is usually used from a tower to stop an escape. The machine gun is thought of as a "scare" weapon and is generally used to cover an area without intending to kill anybody. The shotgun or riot gun is generally filled with buckshot for short-range operation and has a sleeve on the barrel so that it can be used as a hand weapon after it has been fired and the barrel, itself, is hot. The gas gun is designed to propel a projectile filled with tear gas, CN, or other type of gas for controlling disturbances. The pistol, generally .38 or .45 caliber, is most frequently issued in time of escape and patrols are sent out. The officer in charge of the arsenal is generally also in charge of the firing range. Many prisons have inside firing ranges and outside firing ranges, and all custodial personnel are required to qualify periodically. Generally, the slugs are retrieved from the bank behind the targets in an outside range or from the floor after they have been dropped by the wall on an inside range and the ammunition is remade by restoring the slugs into the shells with new powder, which is far more economical than attempting to purchase new ammunition on a continuing basis. Also in the arsenal are the leg irons, hand-cuffs, belly belts, and other restraining equipment for controlling inmates. Leg irons are bands that go around the ankles and are connected by short strands of chain that reduce stride and eliminate a footrace between resident and the officer in charge. Belly belts are belts with handcuffs that hold the person's wrists to a belt to reduce the chance of assault. There are other types of restraint equipment, such as a long chain that goes through the handcuffs of a line of residents to be transferred to another facility or institution.

The locksmith generally works in the arsenal. He may be a correctional officer in the custodial department or a civilian working for the chief engineer in maintenance. In any case, he works closely with both custody and maintenance. His function is to inspect all locks for wear and damage and to replace or maintain them. When a key is lost, the locks in the area must be replaced and new keys issued. Locks are, of course, very important in a prison or correctional institution.

Correctional officers have a right to use force in dangerous situations. In one case, an inmate filed an action under Title 42 U.S.C., Sec. 1983 (a civil rights litigation). Some pens had been confiscated from his cell, the inmate was ordered to return to his cell, but he refused to do so. After threatening force, the officers put him in the cell and he sustained several bruises, swellings, and minor ailments in the scuffle. The court held that the officers were justified in taking swift and forceful action.[13]

Force is differentiated as deadly and nondeadly. Each can be used only in certain circumstances. The use of deadly force is permissible to prevent the commission of a felony.[14] Nondeadly force, such as physical force or chemical

[13]*Suits* v. *Lynch,* 437 F. Supp. 38 (D. Kans., 1977).

[14]*Beard* v. *Stephens,* 372 F. 2nd 685 (5th Cir., New Orleans, 1967). In re: *Riddle,* 57 Cal. 2d 843, 372 P. 2d 304 (1962).

agents, can be used for self-defense, to prevent riot or escape,[15] and to prevent the commission of a misdemeanor.[16]

Sykes has noted that guards' authority erodes through the close working relationship they have with inmates on a long-term, day-to-day basis.[17] Guards frequently fail to report infractions of the regulations, transmit forbidden information to inmates, neglect elementary security requirements, and join inmates in outspoken criticism of higher officials. Corruption through friendships occurs as a product of the confinement and close proximity that guards and inmates share on a daily basis. Corruption through reciprocity is an indirect consequence of the guards' need to control the inmates efficiently, and effectiveness depends upon how well the guards get along with the inmates. Corruption by default occurs when guards permit inmates to assist in some tasks or even take over some responsibilities.

Correctional officers and personnel are always outnumbered by the residents. Consequently, real control of the institution is accomplished best in at least a partially cooperative manner. This is why correctional officers have to be selected carefully with concern toward empathic skills or ability to get along well with people while maintaining their positions as authority figures. Discretion by correctional officers in the prison is similar to discretion by the police in the community. Order is accomplished best with a minimum of confrontation and conflict, but with the ability to use coercion and force when it is needed. There is an informal type of social control exerted by the inmate population in most prisons, with the long-term older residents providing a stabilizing influence. Sensitive correctional officers can use this informal social control to advantage, while less sensitive officers may fail to use it constructively.

COUNTS

The count is the procedure by which residents are accounted for in a prison or correctional institution. In a maximum custody institution, counts are generally made every two hours. There are in counts, out counts, flesh counts (or "meat counts"), and details. The in count occurs when a resident is supposed to be in the cell and the officer walks along the tiers and counts to make sure that all inmates are in their cells. The guard reports to the control room by the direct-line telephone when somebody is not in his or her cell as he or she should have been. In the out count, the officer also walks the tiers, generally during the daytime when the residents are on assignments and reports to the control room persons who are in their cells who should have been on assignment or otherwise out of their cells. The flesh count or "meat count" is a major count, made generally at about 4:00 P.M. and during the night, in which residents have to be identified in a lineup or at the front of their cells or during the night when the

---

[15]*National Advisory Commission on Criminal Justice Standards and Goals, Corrections*, 2.4 (Washington, D.C.: Task Force on Corrections, 1973).

[16]*State* v. *Jones*, 211 SC 300, 44 S.E. 2d 841 (1947).

[17]Gresham Sykes, "The Corruption of Authority and Rehabilitation," *Social Forces*, Vol. 34, no. 3, March, 1956, pp. 257–262 (1956).

officer has to see flesh to know that there is a person in the cell. The details are lists of residents who are authorized to be elsewhere for a variety of purposes, including seeing the parole board, visiting attorneys, in the hospital, out on court order for a new trial, furlough, or any other authorized function.

Counts are reported from cell blocks, work assignments, school, and other areas of endeavor in the prison or correctional institution. Most experienced correctional officers report that they are always counting, whatever their assignment may be. As indicated previously, maximum security institutions generally have counts every two hours. Medium custody institutions may have counts every four hours. Minimum custody institutions would have counts at meal time and bed check. Community custody institutions would have counts at breakfast, the evening meal, and bed check.

RULES AND REGULATIONS

Rules and regulations in prisons and correctional institutions vary widely in numbers, depending upon local custodial attitudes and needs, but sanctions covering the most serious offenses are generally similar. Under the wardenship of Joseph Ragen at Stateville in Illinois in the 1950s, the inmate rule book included almost two hundred rules and regulations! In addition, Stateville had a massive list of rules and regulations covering personnel on eighty-three assignments.[18] There were seventy-six rules at the Iowa State Penitentiary at Fort Madison in the 1960s.[19]

Most prisons have a more simplified set of rules and regulations, numbering probably twenty-five to thirty. These rules generally prohibit the same type of behavior that would be prohibited by law in the civilian community outside the prison, for example, assaults, fighting, gambling, homosexuality, theft, and other activities that violate the criminal law anywhere. In addition, there are rules that would be found in any military organization, such as sanctions against disrespect and insolence to correctional officers and other civilian personnel. A few rules are inserted in some prisons to reduce irritation and quarreling between inmates, such as no bartering between inmates, that might lead to developing obligations and ultimately to conflict. Probably the most serious infractions are gambling, sex, and fighting, with fighting being frequently the result of the other two.

Objectional behavior by men in prisons is so diverse that no single set of rules could possibly encompass it all without being too long and complex for practical application or so arbitrary as to arouse resentment.[20] The dispositions of rule infractions include segregation or solitary confinement, restriction of

[18]*Rules and Regulation for the Government of Officers and Employees* (Stateville: Illinois State Penitentiary, printed by the Vocational School, Stateville, n.d.), p. 132.

[19]Norman Johnson, Leonard Savitz, and Marvin E. Wolfgang, eds., "Rules for Inmates," in *The Sociology of Punishment & Corrections*, 2nd ed. (New York: John Wiley & Sons, Inc., 1970), pp. 387–92.

[20]Daniel Glaser, *The Effectiveness of a Prison and Parole System* (Indianapolis: The Bobbs-Merrill Co., Inc., 1964), p. 507.

privileges and loss of good time, warnings and suspended sentences, and other miscellaneous actions, such as extra work. Some offenses, such as sex infractions, racial provocation, attempted escape, and assaulting an officer, are dealt with by segregation in about 90 percent of the cases.[21] Segregation is used in 89 percent of the cases of group disturbances, 59 percent of the cases of insolence and refusal to work or obey direct orders, and 52 percent of the cases involving destruction of property. Other violations, such as those related to contraband and gambling, lead to segregation in less than one-third of the incidents.

DISCIPLINARY PROCEDURES

Disciplinary procedures have moved in recent years from a universal central summary court in the institution to some decentralization. The majority of prisons still use the centralized summary court for all infractions, but some use the decentralized system for the more minor offenses, reserving the summary court for the major infractions that threaten the security of the institution. The centralized summary court is generally made up of high-ranking custodial personnel headed by a deputy warden or a captain, with a lieutenant and one or two sergeants, and some recently have included a counselor or someone from the classification department. Several recent court decisions in the early 1970s have determined that due process is required in institutional disciplinary hearings just as it is in criminal court outside.[22]

In *Wolff* v. *McDonnell,* due process was established in federal prisons, including (1) advance written notice of the charges, (2) written statement of the decision as to evidence and reasons, (3) permitting inmates to call witnesses and present documentary evidence "when permitting him to do so would not be unduly hazardous to institutional safety or correctional goals," and (4) use of counsel or counsel substitute for illiterate accused persons or those who otherwise cannot understand the proceedings. Similar procedures have been mandated by court orders in several states.

This movement may have contributed to the decentralization of handling lesser offenses. In team treatment and functional unit management, which is discussed more fully in Chapter 4, a team of three or four personnel is assigned to each resident or inmate or the unit personnel in the cell block or dormitory, and responsibility for disciplinary action is taken below the level of the summary court. Punishments may be reduction of privileges, extra work, or other punishment that does not require confinement in punitive status.

Dispositions as a result of summary court action in serious infractions are frequently punitive segregation in a type of solitary confinement. The sentences range from ten days to thirty days in punitive segregation, but they have been longer in the past. The court and administrative concerns tend to hold that no stay in punitive segregation should be longer than thirty days. This writer knows of two cases in which residents were held in punitive segregation for twelve years as a result of very serious offenses, including the killing of a deputy

[21]Ibid., p. 177.
[22]See *Wolff* v. *McDonnell,* 418 U.S. 539 (1974).

Prisoner being escorted to disciplinary segregation.

Courtesy of the Washington State Department of Corrections.

warden, and has heard of a case in punitive segregation for as long as twenty-three years (unverified). Probably the longest time anyone has spent in solitary confinement was Jesse Pomeroy, who had been convicted in Massachusetts at age 14 of a series of atrocious sexual murders and was sentenced by the court to solitary confinement for life. He served approximately thirty-eight years in solitary and was transferred to the farm at Bridgewater where he died a few years later.[23]

There is general consensus among administrators and the courts that these long times in punitive segregation in the institution should not occur and that serious infractions should be handled by trial in an outside criminal court. Lesser institutional infractions may be punished by keep lock or top lock, which is locking a person in his or her own cell, therefore denying privileges; reprimand; withdrawal of privileges; and similar action. Other disciplinary dispositions include institutional transfer, segregation, suspension of visiting privileges, solitary confinement, restriction of privileges, extra work, administrative segregation of repeat offenders, loss of furlough and other community privileges, and reduction of good time.

[23]A. Warren Stearns, "The Life and Crimes of Jesse Harding Pomeroy," *Journal of the Maine Medical Association*, Vol. 39, no. 4 (April 1948), pp. 49 ff.

A study of 1,331 inmates (64 percent white and 36 percent black) and 30 correctional officers (67 percent white and 33 percent black) at the Federal Correctional Institution at Tallahassee indicated that there were no differences between the frequency of disciplinary reports or severity of disciplinary procedures or sanctions on a racial basis.[24] There was, however, a difference in the kinds of offenses the officers wrote up on the charging tickets. White officers tended to write more contraband charges, whereas black officers wrote more charges relating to drugs, alcohol, and trouble on the job. A survey of confinement practices in the fifty states in 1979 indicated that the wide variations in administrative segregation and punitive segregation are being narrowed.[25] This is undoubtedly the result of the widespread inmate litigation.

PROPERTY CONTROL

Property control is an important custodial function in a prison or a correctional institution. Personnel in many prisons and correctional institutions "appropriate" more state property than do the inmates, including gasoline, foodstuffs, machinery, and other type of property. When inmates steal, it is primarily to obtain food, materials for escape, or items for making a weapon. When employees steal it is generally to obtain things to take home. Clothing, radio equipment, office supplies, and other inventories tend to "shrink." Even some superintendents and wardens have taken hams and other items from the institutional supplies to send to their relatives for Christmas. Some top and middle management personnel have filled 55-gallon drums of gasoline from the institutional garage in preparation for hunting and other trips. When inmates become aware of this practice—and they do—any rehabilitation programs become negated, as they view that type of stealing as equivalent to or worse than the crime for which they are serving time.

A rigid system of property inventory and control is important in the prison. While the business office has responsibility for this in terms of records, the custodial force has primary responsibility for implementing the control through more immediate surveillance. Unfortunately, it is sometimes the correctional officers who are involved. Many wardens have said that, if they could gain full control over the personnel, they would have fewer problems with the inmates!

Manifests are important in property control by recording the property that goes through all gates. These manifests are forms on which are listed property that goes through any gate, inside or outside, together with the dates and times and are signed by the employee carrying the property. This property may be anything from wire for the radio or electrical system to heavy equipment brought through the salley port or truck gate. The manifests are kept generally in the control room or other custodial storage place for future reference as

[24]Jeffery L. Boyd, "*Race of Inmate Proceedings at a Federal Correctional Institution,*" *FCI Research Reports,* Vol. 8, no. 1 (1976), pp. 1–35.

[25]"Lock Them Up, and Throw Away the Key," *Corrections Compendium,* Vol. 3 (August 1979), pp. 1–4.

needed. If an inordinate amount of property is carried out by one or two employees, manifests can be used as part of any informal or formal inquiry.

ESCAPES

Escapes vary widely from institution to institution and among the various types of programs. The majority of escapes are not escapes, but walkaways. There are very few escapes from inside the walls—and these make news. In 1973, there were 8,083 escapes for a rate of 39.6 per 1,000 prisoners.[26] From juvenile institutions, the runaway rate can be generally estimated at one-half the population, but it involves probably one-fifth of the juveniles, since many who run away do it several times annually.

All major prisons have an escape plan. These escape plans involve stationary and mobile patrols. The prison or correctional institution determines the areas of high risk in terms of walking away from the institution, such as railroad lines, highways, significant crossroads, and similar lines of easy movement in the areas around the institution. The mobile patrols are officers in automobiles patrolling the roads where custodial personnel suspects that the resident may have gone, generally toward his hometown or where his wife or girlfriend is living, particularly if there had been a disturbing letter or visit recently. In some rural areas, particularly in the South, several days may be spent on such a manhunt and may include the use of dogs. In most prisons, however, the manhunt after an escape is relatively short, since, if the escapee has not been caught within twelve to twenty-four hours, the chances are that he has been able to get a ride out of the vicinity. Then, a copy of his fingerprints will be sent to the FBI in Washington, D.C., with a notification of the escape and that, if he is picked up anywhere, the prison or correctional institution would like to be notified. As a consequence of this procedure, the number of successful escapes is very small.

Escapees tend to be the younger inmates of a correctional institution.[27] Some studies have indicated that escapees tend to be serving sentences for robbery or property offenses, rather than for personal crimes,[28] while others found that escapees were committed more frequently for personal crimes.[29] Escapees also have a history of prior arrests, prior commitments, and prior escapes. Es-

[26]*Prisoners in State and Federal Institutions on Dec. 31, 1971, 1972, and 1973,* Bulletin No. SD-NPS-PSF-4 (Washington, D.C.: National Prisoner Statistics, May 1975).

[27]Norman Holt, *Escape from Custody,* Research Report No. 52 (Sacramento: California Department of Corrections, 1974); W. S. Loving, F. E. Stockwell, and D. A. Dobbins, "Factors Associated with Escape Behavior of Prison Inmates," *Federal Probation,* Vol. 49 (September 1959), pp. 49–51; David I. Morgan, "Individual and Situational Factors Related to Prison Escapes," *American Journal of Corrections,* Vol. 29 (March–April 1967), pp. 30–32.

[28]Faye Farrington, *The Massachusettes Furlough Program: A Comprehensive Assessment* (Boston: Massachusetts Department of Corrections, 1976); D. A. Dobbins, F. E. Stockwell, and W. S. Loving, "Individual and Social Correlates of Prison Escape," *Journal of Consulting Psychology,* Vol. 14 (1960), p. 95.

[29]*Report of Escapes During the Fiscal Years Ended June 30, 1974–1978* (Richmond: Virginia Department of Corrections, 1978).

capees are more often single than married. Escapes tend to occur more frequently during the warmer spring and summer months. Norman Holt has said that "once a classification staff knows an inmate's race, escape history, type of offense, age and criminal background, they probably know about all that is worth knowing in term of escape potential."[30] Whites are overrepresented in most escape populations; blacks escape at a significantly lower rate.[31]

There are some psychometric measures that can predict escape. Beall and Panton in 1956 found a constellation of forty-two personality variables in the MMPI (Minnesota Multiphasic Personality Inventory) that showed predictive ability in identifying potential escapes, which Panton referred to as the *Ec scale*.[32] This has subsequently been challenged as an oversimplification.[33]

Litigation brought by escapees to avoid the charge of escape has indicated that some escapes may be justifiable, while others are not. An escape from prison may sometimes be justified on the grounds of protecting oneself from threats of sexual attack from fellow inmates.[34] To avoid mass escapes of inmates shouting "rape!," certain criteria must be followed. The situation has to be immediate and without time to report to authorities, and no force or violence can be used during the escape, according to *Johnson* v. *State* in Delaware, where three prison escapees were denied the defense of justification because of the failure to give sufficient proof that such intolerable conditions existed.[35]

MISCELLANEOUS FUNCTIONS OF CUSTODY

There are many miscellaneous functions of custody and they frequently vary from prison to prison. In some prisons, approval of visiting and correspondence has been traditionally under custody, whereas in other prisons, these functions are handled by the classification department. In any case, immediate supervision of visiting is a custodial function.

Transferring prisoners from one place to another is the responsibility of custody. When prisoners are taken home for funerals or sick visits, taken to court for new trials, or transferred from one institution to another, it becomes a custodial function that must be well planned.

Supervision of barbers within the institution is a frequent custodial func-

[30]Holt, *Escape from Custody*, p. 4.

[31]Paul R. Maurer and James C. Payne, *A Statistical Study: An Offender Profile—Escape* (Tallahassee: Florida Division of Planning and Evaluation, 1975); W. Stone, "Factors Related to Escape Prediction" (Ann Arbor, Mich.: University Microfilms, unpublished dissertation on Texas data, 1975, by the Texas Department of Corrections, Huntsville).

[32]Herbert S. Beall and James H. Panton, "Use of M.M.P.I. as an Index to Escapism," *Journal of Clinical Psychology*, Vol. 12 (1956), pp. 392–94; James H. Panton, "Predicting Prison Adjustment with the M.M.P.I.," *Journal of Clinical Psychology*, Vol. 14 (1958), pp. 308–12.

[33]David M. Pierce, "The Escapism Scale of the M.M.P.I. as a Predictive Index," *Correctional Psychologist*, Vol. 4 (1971), pp. 230–32.

[34]*People* v. *Lovercamp*, 118 California Reporter 110, 1974.

[35]*Johnson* v. *State*, 379 A. 2d 1129 (n/d Dela., 1977).

tion, the reason being that the barber is in a position to establish himself in a lucrative economic position. It must be noted here that all barbering is done by residents. The cost of an outside professional barber would be prohibitive. While every inmate is entitled to one haircut a month, in many prisons, inmates must give the barber a pack of cigarettes to get a "decent" haircut. Therefore, the barber can accumulate cigarettes, which have traditionally been the medium of exchange in prisons, and be near the top of the economic hierarchy among the prison population. Further, barber supplies, such as bay rum or other liquids containing alcohol or certain drugs, have to be controlled. The barbershop can be a meetingplace for any inmates that the administration wants to keep separated and can be a place of communication for a variety of purposes. Consequently, part of the custodial function is to control the barbering operation in the prison or correctional institution.

Residents sometimes want to wear long hair or beards and mustaches. While some courts have differed as to length of hair, the general approach is that hair can be worn below the ears but above the neck if it is "neat and well groomed." Some institutions permit short and well-groomed beards and mustaches, while others forbid facial hair. The courts have indicated that enforced shearing of hair does not violate civil rights when it is for sanitary purposes.[36]

The inmate commissary or inmate store is a place where residents can purchase personal goods, such as cigarettes, candy bars, and other supplies from their own funds. In some prisons, inmates can carry a small amount of money, but in most prisons, there is a scrip check system where all the money is kept in the office and transactions are made on paper and are accounted for in the office. Many inmates going to the commissary may subsequently be hijacked in the yard and lose their goods. Custody has the responsibility of protecting weak inmates from the strong.

Fire protection is considered to be a responsibility of custody, although like the locksmith, it may be also a matter to concern of the chief engineer responsible for maintenance. Custody's concern is that fires are frequently used as expressions of hostility or as attempts at diversion to cover other activities, such as an attempted escape. Consequently, custody is always concerned with fire protection.

In fact, custody is concerned with everything in the prison. The safety and security of the institution may be threatened in the hospital, in the recreation yard, in the cell blocks, in the schools, or in any other place within the institution. Consequently, custody always keeps a watchful and alert eye on all procedures within the institution.

CONCLUSIONS

Because custody is involved in all activities within the prison or correctional institution, custodial personnel are constantly in confrontation and conflict in the course of their work. While inmate litigation has to be brought against the administration, it is frequently based on challenging the work of a correc-

---

[36]*Williams* v. *Hoyt,* 556 F. 2d 1336 (5th Cir., 1977).

tional officer and/or other line personnel. In some cases, officers and employees involved in these actions can move for an award of attorney's fees under the Civil Rights Attorney's Fees Award Act of 1976.[37] Further, when the inmate or resident brings civil rights action under Title 42 U.S.C., Sec. 1983 that is deemed "frivolous," the prisoner, himself, must pay the costs[38] and even an indigent person has no right to "prostitute" the process by bringing frivolous and warrantless litigation.

Brodsky has suggested a "Bill of Rights" for correctional officers.[39] The proposed rights for correctional officers include (1) participation of all levels in boards, committees, and decision-making structure; (2) clearly defined roles and loyalties; (3) education and training relevant to job activities and career development; (4) differential assignments related to skills and abilities; (5) informed behavioral science consultation on managing people; and (6) the development of professionalism.

In conclusion, custody is responsible for the safety and security of the institution. As such, it maintains control in all possible ways to prevent escapes and to secure the peace and order of the community. It does this through many procedures beginning with secure perimeter control and the guard towers and weaponry to orderly movement of inmates and protecting them from each other. Custody is the controlling system within the prison or correctional institution.

CHAPTER QUESTIONS

3-1.   What elements appear in all positions in the criminal justice system, from police to institutions to parole, but become more intense in custody than do most other components of the criminal justice system?

3-2.   What are the immediate functions of custody?

3-3.   What is involved in the control of the yard in an institution?

3-4.   Describe count procedures.

3-5.   What are the functions of rules and regulations?

3-6.   Describe the disciplinary procedures usually found in prisons and correctional institutions.

3-7.   Why is property control an important custodial function in a prison or correctional institution and how is it accomplished?

3-8.   Describe escape procedure.

3-9.   Why is the supervision of barbers within an institution a function of custody?

3-10.   Why is fire protection a function of custody?

---

[37]*Rinehard* v. *Morland,* U.S. District Court (M.D. Fla., 1979).

[38]*Moss* v. *Ward,* 434 F. Supp. 69 (S.D. N.Y., 1977).

[39]Stanley L. Brodsky, "A Bill of Rights for the Correctional Officer," *Federal Probation,* Vol. xxxviii (June 1974), pp. 38–40.

4
CLASSIFICATION AND TREATMENT

Classification and treatment are services provided by the staff of a correctional institution to bring to the residents such helpful and corrective services as education, counseling, medical and dental care, religious services, recreation, and whatever other services might be provided by the institution or contracted for from outside. Social services in society as a whole are divided into (1) employment, (2) mental health, (3) physical health, (4) housing, (5) education, (6) income maintenance, and (7) justice.[1] Classification is intended to assist in the optimum distribution of these services to the residents of the institution.

Farms and industries have been viewed by some correctional administrators as "treatment" through on-the-job training in some areas and the development of better work habits. With its large farm operation, the Texas Department of Corrections personnel frequently refer to their forced agricultural labor as "work therapy."

Realistically, treatment in prisons refers to those services conducive to the socialization process that would ordinarily be found in any community, such as schools, churches, recreational programs, medical and dental services, and

---

[1]"Program for NCSW Forum Begins to Take Shape," *NASW News,* March 1978, p. 16.

some mental health, intensive counseling, and group therapy. Some prisons have chapters of Alcoholics Anonymous and Addicts Anonymous, and others have community-oriented civic clubs or groups, such as the Jaycees in men's institutions and the Junior League in women's institutions. In-depth diagnosis, psychotherapy, casework, and counseling are very rare in American prisons, since legislatures and political leaders simply will not fund them, placing other public services in higher priority.

CLASSIFICATION

Classification is the administrative organization that attempts to allocate available treatment resources to achieve optimum results. This is done by making a brief study of all new residents and then separating them according to several characteristics, such as sex, age, and criminal history, as well as basic problem category. Because of the large volume of persons coming into the prison and being processed there, the relatively small staff in classification has no choice but to make that initial study brief. Nevertheless, the initial classification is based on that study.

Classification is at two levels, jurisdiction-wide and institutional. Jurisdiction-wide classification refers to state-wide assignment of residents to various institutions, while institutional classification refers to assignment of residents within the institution. Based primarily on sex, age, and criminal history, as well as on other problem areas, the individual offender may be sent to a specific institution. Within the institution, the inmate may be classified for security on the basis of whether or not he or she might be an escape risk or dangerous. The resident would also be assigned to a program, such as school or a specific type of job. In addition, the prisoner may participate in group sessions or in other special programs. During the period of institutionalization, the resident may be classified and reclassified several times while changing programs to meet his or her changing needs. Toward the expiration of an inmate's minimum sentence, a preparole progress report will be written to advise the parole board or the parole hearing examiner as to the prisoner's progress or lack thereof in the institution, together with a recommendation for or against parole with the reasons provided. As noted earlier, some parole boards base their decisions on factors outside the institution, ignoring institutional records for all practical purposes unless an extreme case justifies considering such records. This is the practice of the U.S. Parole Commission and several state parole authorities. By 1978, four states had abolished parole and went to flat sentencing—Maine in 1976, California and Indiana in 1977, and Illinois in 1978. Five more states had adopted this approach by the end of 1979.

Formal classification as constituted in the modern prison is a twentieth-century development, but there has always been classification of some sort on an informal basis. In Spain, institutions began separating women from men in 1519. This was also accomplished by the Quakers who began the penitentiary movement by remodeling tbe old Walnut Street Jail in 1790 and who separated women from men and prohibited whisky and beer in the institutions. Children began to be separated from adults in Milan in 1695 and in Rome in 1704 when Pope Clement XI constructed the Hospice di San Michele for youthful offenders. From an historical perspective, separation by sex came first, then separation by age, followed by separation by problems.

By 1908, the beginnings for formal classification appeared with the development of minimum security institutions in England and Belgium. New Jersey is credited with having the first formal classification system for juveniles at Vineland Training School in 1911 when Goddard brought intelligence testing from France to that school by translating into English the Binet-Simon intelligence tests. New Jersey is also credited with establishing the first classification system in the adult prisons in 1927. Illinois established the Diagnostic Depot at Joliet in 1931. During the 1930s, many states established classification programs on a formal basis. By the 1960s, all states had some form of formal classification. The historical development of classification in the various states appears to have followed the same general pattern. It began with what might be called (1) preprofessional classification and progressed through (2) traditional classification, (3) integrated classification in which the process began to develop real effectiveness, (4) professional classification, (5) team treatment, and (6) functional unit management. Preprofessional classification refers to classification by the staff without the assistance of professional personnel. The second development was the addition of a psychologist, sociologist, or social worker to prepare admission summaries or social history for the new residents arriving at the prison, but the same staff, frequently twelve to fifteen in number, met weekly or twice weekly for a half a day to classify the new residents who had come in within the past month. This traditional approach was the most popular from the 1930s through the 1960s and it still prevails in many institutions. The third approach, the integrated classification committee, represented the first time that a classification committee's "recommendation" actually became an order. For the first time, a copy of the proceedings of the classification meeting went forward to the headquarters of the department of corrections for filing in the resident's file in the central office. Any variation between that record and the actual assignment of the resident in the institution could result in disciplinary action from the central office. This was an effort to achieve coordination. The fourth development was the professional committee in which the large twelve- to fifteen-person committee was reduced to the resident's counselor, the director of classification, and a high-ranking custodial officer. This three-member committee was much more efficient than the former large committee. The fifth development was the team treatment concept developed at the federal correctional institution at Ashland, Kentucky, and at the 3320th Retraining Group at the Amarillo Air Force Base in Texas (now at the Lowry Air Force Base in Denver) in 1959. Rather than having a central committee meeting formally, each resident was assigned a team, usually a counselor, a correctional officer, and another staff member. The other staff member would probably be from the education department if the resident were young and participating in the educational program, but he or she could be any staff member. The team, then, made the classification decisions, handled counseling for the resident, and dealt with minor behavioral problems.

The sixth and most recent development in classification procedures has been the functional unit management system. Each domiciliary unit, whether a cell block or a dormitory, is to be autonomous. As a refinement of the treatment team concept, it is designed to decentralize treatment services. It has a unit manager, one or two caseworkers, two counselors from among the correctional officers, an administrative assistant, and a secretary. There would be fewer personnel in smaller units, of course, and there may be more personnel in the larger units. In any case, all problems and classification procedures would be handled within the unit. This brings the services and the classification procedure closer to the residents. The functional unit management concept was introduced into the U.S. Bureau of Prisons and several states in 1973 and 1974 and has been regarded as an improvement over the older centralized system because it takes less time for communication between the residents and the staff and many problems can be handled immediately.

As part of the diagnostic process in classification, intelligence and personality tests are routinely administered to the new residents and are kept in the record. The most frequent intelligence tests used are revisions of the Army Alpha for literates and the Army Beta for illiterates. The most frequently used personality test is the Minnesota Multiphasic Personality Inventory (MMPI). While testing has been challenged by several minority groups, particularly by blacks and Hispanics in the United States and by native Americans in Canada, these tests appear to have emerged as most useful, particularly when clinical judgment in their use is applied to account for cultural differences.

A study of 262 male offenders of widely different ages, based on the Minnesota Multiphasic Personality Inventory, showed significant differences between younger and older offenders.[2] The greater the age difference between groups, the larger the personality differences on the MMPI scales. The older groups showed increases on the neurotic scales and decreases on the psychotic scales. There was an abrupt decrease in the older group in impulsivity and acting-out tendencies. This confirms the view that offenders over 60 years of age are in greater need of noncriminal, more traditional, treatment programs than are other offenders.

As a resident approaches his or her minimum sentence expiration, the classification department collects reports from persons in the prison who have had contact with the inmate, such as the cell block officer, work assignment supervisor, and others, to prepare a preparole progress report. This is generally begun about ninety days prior to the expiration and is sent to the parole board sixty days before expiration, and the parole board considers parole thirty days before expiration to give the resident and his or her family time to prepare for release. The final section of the report is a recommendation for or against parole supported by reasons. In some jurisdictions where objective parole criteria are used without much concern for the institutional record, the forms are scored by classification committee personnel or by the parole hearing examiner. Whatever system is followed, the classification department makes and keeps the record.

[2]Charles F. McCreary and Ivan N. Mensch, "Personality Differences Associated with Age in Law Offenders," *Journal of Gerontology,* Vol. 32, no. 2 (1977), pp. 164–67.

RECORDS AND THE PRIVACY LAWS

The problem of privacy is an old one in English-speaking countries. In 1938, Professor Winfield in Great Britain proposed that a new tort for offensive invasion of privacy be established.[3] On November 4, 1950, the Council of Europe held a convention for the protection of human rights and fundamental freedoms and issued the European Convention on Human Rights, which held that everyone has a right to respect for his or her private and family life.[4] Judge Thomas Cooley wrote in 1888 in America that everyone has the right to be left alone. Warren and Brandeis wrote in 1890 on the issue as to whether, according to the Constitution, an individual has a right to privacy in the United States.[5] Many court cases on this issue ensued. In *Griswold* v. *Connecticut* in 1965, Justice Douglas wrote that the right of privacy emanates from the First, Fourth, Fifth, Ninth, and Fourteenth Amendments and that certain zones of privacy were created by logical necessity.[6] This decision became a basic one in privacy litigation and legislative action.

The Freedom of Information Act passed in 1967 gives the general public and mass media a particular statutory right of access to the increasing store of information held by the federal government.[7] The Fair Credit Reporting Act of 1970 addressed confidentiality, accuracy, relevance, and the use of personal information, allowing individuals to challenge the contents of the files, and aimed at prohibiting a consumer reporting agency from issuing records of arrest or conviction. The Family Educational Rights and Privacy Act, known as the Buckley Amendment and passed in 1974, allows parents and students access to records held by educational institutions and simultaneously prohibits educational institutions from revealing to others any of these records, even to the point of prohibition against posting grades. The Privacy Act of 1974 was directed at personal record systems maintained by federal executive agencies, limiting dissemination of information and allowing individuals access to knowledge of such records through public notice and permitting challenging the information contained in the record systems. Further, state and local governments were affected. Restrictions were placed on the use of social security numbers as a common identifier.

The SEARCH Group, Inc., has developed guidelines for keeping records on individuals within the privacy laws. Their recommendations are as follows:[8]

[3]Francis G. Jacobs, *The European Convention of Human Rights* (Oxford: Clarendon Press, 1975), Chap. 1. p. 1

[4]Thomas M. Cooley, *A Treatise on the Law of Torts,* 2nd ed. (Chicago: Callaghan and Co., 1888), p. 29.

[5]Samuel D. Warren and Louis D. Brandeis, "The Right to Privacy," *Harvard Law Review* (1890), p. 193.

[6]*Griswold* v. *Connecticut,* 381 U.S. 113, 85 S. Ct. 1678 (1965).

[7]For example, see Title 13 U.S.C., Sec. 8, and Title 38 U.S.C., Sec. 3301.

[8]George B. Trubow, "Informational Privacy and the Policy Foundations for Criminal Justice Information Management," in *Advisory Bulletin: Perspectives on the Evolution of Criminal Justice Informational Privacy Issues* (Sacramento, Calif.: SEARCH Group, Inc., October 1976), pp. 38–39.

3 X

1. Keep no secret personal information or double records system. This is characteristic of the "police state."

2. Gather only what is needed for lawful and authorized purposes. There can be debate as to what is actually *needed* in any given case.

3. Keep information accurate, complete, and relevant. One phase of criminal justice management not yet perfected is disposition reporting. Relevance and timeliness also pose questions.

4. Give the subject file access. Except for intelligence or investigative files that might be kept confidential for a reasonable length of time, no files can be kept confidential from the individual concerned. The individual has a right to review the file and challenge the information.

5. Use data only for the purposes gathered. Particularly troublesome in criminal justice are (a) access by law enforcement to nonlaw enforcement records and (b) access by nonlaw enforcement to law enforcement records.

It is apparent that litigation will continue regarding the use of the records in prisons and correctional institutions. Many correctional administrators are not sure now what information can be gathered and kept for purposes of classification and treatment.

EDUCATION

Education in prisons and correctional institutions is really only about a century old. The first teacher was hired in the penitentiary at Cherry Hill in Philadelphia in 1844. Since the chaplains came into the prisons in 1790 when the Quakers developed the penitentiary movement based on religion and penitence, the chaplain sometimes also provided education. The first formalized movement toward education in prisons was in 1876 at the Elmira Reformatory in New York, a concept developed in the discussions of the first Congress of Correction held in Cincinnati in 1870, now the American Correctional Association (then the National Congress on Penitentiary Reform Discipline). Earlier, New York State had permitted elementary education to be taught to "meritorious convicts" during the winter months by other prisoners. Even the experiment at Elmira Reformatory did not improve education in prisons very much, although it was a symbol of leadership in this field and "blazed the trail" for other institutions to establish educational programs. The first broad survey of education in prisons was made in 1927 and 1928 by Austin H. MacCormick, who found that there were no schools in thirteen of the sixty prisons he visited and that not one had a program of vocational education; he concluded that he had not found a single educational program approaching adequacy.[9]

As with so many other programs in the correctional field, education had joined the "history of good intentions" that was never adequately financed.

[9]Austin H. MacCormick, *The Education of Adult Prisoners* (New York: The Osborne Association, 1931), p. 5.

Bricklayer school at the Federal Correctional Institution at Tallahassee, Florida.
Courtesy of the Federal Prison System.

Better funding began to be available after World War II, and correctional education improved in the 1960s with federal funding and increased interest at the state level. The Correctional Educational Association developed in 1945 from a relatively new Committee on Prison Education of the American Prison Association (now the American Correctional Association), and the *Journal of Correctional Education* was initiated in 1949.

The improved educational programs in recent years in prisons and educational institutions have taken several forms, depending upon local conditions, available funding, and the philosophy of the administration. Academic programs are now central to education in prison, with vocational training also being highly regarded. Agricultural schools exist in some prisons, with a few holding classes in the winter months and "on-the-job training" during the growing season. Some prisons also have commercial schools for the residents who learn typing and other similar skills.

The academic schools focus on two primary objectives, the development of literacy skills and the earning of the high school equivalency diploma through the G.E.D. (General Educational Development) test. As a secondary focus, the introduction of college-level courses has been a more recent development. The U.S. Office of Education indicates that 12.3 grades have been completed by the average citizen in the United States. The average resident of a prison or correctional institution, however, is conceded to be about three grades retarded, probably dropping out at the beginning of the ninth grade. Publishers of academic achievement tests, such as the Iowa Placement Test and California Achievement Test, and others place the standard retention level at 10.5 and 11.0 grades, while an LEAA (Law Enforcement Assistance Administration) study in 1973 indicated that the average retention in a sample of prisoners was 4.9 grades.[10]

Functional illiteracy refers to persons who read below the fifth-grade level. Since the average retention level was 4.9 grades according to the LEAA study, the problem of illiteracy in prison populations becomes apparent. Consequently, much of the effort of the academic school is toward teaching illiterate residents basic reading, writing, and arithmetic. The other primary thrust is assisting residents to pass the G.E.D. and earn the high school equivalency diploma from the state department of education. This is important because many jobs in the American labor market require a high school diploma for entry. In fact, many people who have earned the high school equivalency test have gone on to college and some even into academic careers.

College courses at the freshman level have been introduced in many prisons through extension from nearby universities. In a few instances, residents of the prison have been able to earn the bachelor's degree inside the walls; for example, William Heirens earned his bachelor's degree from Lewis University while inside the walls of the Illinois state penitentiary at Stateville in the early 1970s. Study release has been used in many jurisdictions to permit residents to go from the prison to nearby schools and universities to study.

Vocational education has also become standard in prisons and correctional institutions. Learning a trade has been a highly accepted objective in correctional programs. In addition to state funding of vocational training, the U.S. Department of Labor has contributed significantly to this endeavor. In 1965, the Manpower Development and Training Act (MDTA) funded special programs in vocational training in many prisons and correctional institutions through the Department of Labor. This act was replaced in 1973 by the Comprehensive Employment Training Act (CETA), which has continued this effort.

There have been other special approaches to education in prison. Night school has sometimes been used for residents in prisons who have jobs during the day but would also like to study. Cell study is the equivalent of correspondence courses in the prison and is carried on in the academic school in many prisons and correctional institutions.

The primary problem in education is that new residents are entering the system continually. The courts cannot be told that the semester starts in September! Further, a variety of levels of experience, intelligence, and education exists among the prisoner population. Therefore, it is difficult to handle large classes in a lecture course, although it is done in many places. The most effective type of education is individual tutoring or monitoring so that an individual can study his or her own subjects at his or her own pace. Computer-assisted instruction (CAI) has been used effectively in prisons and correctional institutions. For example, some jails and short-term institutions have indicated that the residents' stay is too short for an educational program but that CAI can be used in some way for any length of stay from a day to a year or more.

[10]Ken Carpenter, LEAA representative at the Southern Conference on Corrections, Tallahassee, Florida, February 1974.

Welding training at the State Prison of Southern Michigan, Jackson.

Courtesy of the Michigan Department of Corrections.

Studies of the intelligence of offenders and residents of institutions and correctional institutions indicate the equivalency with the general public. Offenders are representative in terms of intelligence and native ability of the population from which they have been drawn. On the other hand, the average achievement is three or more years behind the general public. In prison education, then, it must be remembered that educators are working with a group with the same intelligence they expect to encounter on the outside but that the institutional population, juvenile or adult, as a group is composed almost entirely of serious underachievers. This requires special treatment. For example, many persons do not want their colleagues to know that they cannot read or write, so some prisons help tutor illiterates in the vocational school, in the bakery, or elsewhere where they can be taught to read instructions and compute measurements and do not have to be seen returning to their cell block with *Run, Jane, Run* under their arms.

For purposes of funding and improving the level of instruction, some prisons and correctional institutions have taken action to become officially separate school districts. This makes them eligible for state and federal funds for educational purposes. When this is done, the institutional school can be funded and accredited and enjoy the same benefits as any school district in the state.

RELIGION

Religion has been a central component of the correctional process since the Quakers introduced the penitentiary concept in 1790 at the old Walnut Street Jail in Philadelphia. The chaplain was central to the "treatment" programs in the prisons throughout the nineteenth century and took the lead in bringing humane treatment into the prison. In fact, the development of the early American prison system was characterized by serious debate between religious factions. The Quakers, organized as the Philadelphia Society for Alleviating the Miseries of the Public Prisons, backed the Pennsylvania system of humane treatment, solitary confinement, work in the cells, and meditation for the purpose of penitence. On the other hand, Reverend Louis Dwight of the Boston Prison Disciplinary Society supported the Auburn system, and Elam Lynds, warden of the early Auburn and Sing Sing prisons, believed in harsh punishment, whipping, silence to avoid moral contamination, and congregate labor. Quakers contended that the Auburn system was not only cruel but a repudiation of the tenets of the New Testament. Reverend Dwight contended that the Pennsylvania system was expensive to construct and operate, that labor with power machinery in workshops would be more productive than handcrafts in the individual cells, and that the tendency to separate people from others in solitary confinement tended to induce insanity or mental deterioration. The high cost of maintaining prisons concerned taxpayers, and any feasible work plan that would help prison inmates to defray the cost was viewed with more favor. Consequently, the Auburn system of harsh discipline and congregate labor became the basic model for American prisons.

The chaplain has always been in the prisons, but his acceptance has not always been complete. Many correctional officers see him as a "do-gooder" who is inclined to side with the inmates. In many prisons, he is "tolerated" by the administration and custody, but it is difficult to challenge religion and the philosophy for which it stands. Even so, there has been discussion in the military and among correctional officers following the elimination of prayer in the public schools that maintaining a chaplain with public funds might be challenged under the freedom of religion clause in the First Amendment, but voluntary participation in religious services appears to have silenced that issue.

Most residents or inmates in prisons or correctional institutions do not attend chapel services. In addition, they are divided among Protestants, Roman Catholics, and other denominations. For these reasons, a rather small chapel can serve a rather large prison or correctional institution. The chaplain is seen by many inmates as a person who is selling intangibles without much security.

To serve the needs of residents in a prison or correctional institution, the chaplain has to be selected carefully. If funds were available, most correctional administrators would like to have a full-time white Protestant chaplain, a black Protestant chaplain, a Roman Catholic priest, and, depending upon the composition of the population in the institution, a Spanish-speaking chaplain, probably from the Roman Catholic faith. In addition, several part-time chaplains would be desirable on some type of contract, including a Jewish rabbi, probably Reformed rather than Orthodox or Conservative; a Black Muslim chaplain, depending upon the composition of the institutional population; and other part-time chaplains as needed. While this is a larger group of chaplains than most

Religious services at the Huntsville Unit, Texas.
Courtesy of the Texas Department of Corrections.

institutions can afford, modifications downward can be made by appointing a chief chaplain and other chaplains as can be funded on a part-time basis. Outside clergy can be permitted inside the prison or correctional institution to serve their particular membership.

Repeating for emphasis, the chaplain must be selected with care. The best chaplain is one who can work with people and who is not confined to the creed in which he may have been educated. He has to serve everybody in the population. On the other hand, everybody in the population has different emotional needs and requires different approaches to religion. Consequently, the creeds and the symbolism must give way to the basic ethical systems that appear in all major religions and the understanding interpersonal empathy that exists when a chaplain is helping a person in trouble.

The problems of the chaplain in correctional institutions appear to be generated from the fact that most of the prison populations have had little contact with churches and religion on the outside. Volunteers from religious groups from the outside can be of assistance. Inmate congregations can be developed within the prison.[11] Counseling on an individual basis appears to

[11]D. C. Pace, *Christian's Guide to Effective Jail and Prison Counseling* (Old Tappan, N.J.: Fleming H. Revell Company, 1976), 318 pp.

Muslim religious services, Auburn Correctional Facility.
Courtesy of the New York State Department of Correctional Services.

remain the best contribution of the chaplain. Some writers contend that the chaplain should concern himself with his co-religionists outside the prison to arouse their sympathies for those within the prison.[12]

The safety, security, and tranquility of the institution also has to be taken into consideration when selecting any personnel—including the chaplain.

COUNSELING

Counseling and psychotherapy are virtually nonexistent on a professional basis in prisons. When one psychologist or psychiatrist is available for a prison of two thousand residents, there is no way to get realistic counseling to the population. A good mental health or child guidance clinic permits no more than twelve to fifteen cases per worker, as compared with prisons that are fortunate if they have one professional worker or counselor for five hundred residents.

Recognizing this problem, many states and the U.S. Bureau of Prisons in the early 1970s began selecting from among the correctional officers those persons who could work well with inmates. Historically, correctional officers had always provided informal counseling on job assignments, in cell blocks, and in other areas where inmates and correctional officers come together. Conse-

[12]J. W. Oliver, "To Whom Should the Prison Chaplain Minister?" *Federal Probation*, Vol. 36, no. 1 (March 1972), pp. 19–22.

quently, most of the counseling in American prisons has been done by correctional officers—good, bad, or indifferent—because of their accessibility. They are present when the resident has a problem. To get to a counselor, the resident would have to write a note to his or her counselor and wait to be called, probably several days or a week later. Recognizing that correctional officers are available and have in fact provided most of the counseling in prisons, the selection of competent people from the correctional officer force for special training and assignment as counselors, together with a pay raise, has appeared to be the best approach in view of the lack of funding for professional counselors.

Counseling has been defined as a "planned interaction between the correctional worker and the clients or group of clients—probationers, prisoners, or parolees—with the aim of changing the pattern of the recipient's conformity to social expectation."[13] While this does not clearly separate counseling activities from psychotherapy, psychotherapy is generally aimed at resolving internal personal problems that might be related to delinquent and criminal behavior. Counseling does not make the assumptions that the individual is "sick," so it is not in this context considered to be in the "medical model."

Counseling is a relationship between the counselor and the client, the goal of which is to understand the client's problems and help him or her solve them by mutual consent, rather than by giving advice or admonition.[14] Casework includes professional services in (1) obtaining case histories and description, (2) solving immediate problems involving family and personal relationships, (3) exploring long-range problems of social adjustment, (4) providing supportive guidance for inmates about to be released, and (5) providing supportive guidance and professional assistance to probationers and parolees.

There is no common and all-encompassing definition of casework accepted by everybody, no single "right way," and different approaches may be used by counselors or caseworkers with different academic backgrounds. Many psychiatrists, psychologists, social workers, and other counselors have adopted varying approaches depending upon their orientations and personalities, although a common understanding of the development of behavior and personality is necessary. On the other hand, the requirement of specific academic degrees in the social and behavioral sciences does not assure competence in changing the behavior of others. In fact, some of the employees of a prison or a correctional institution most effective in changing inmates' behavior for the better are correctional officers, shop teachers, recreation directors, or others whose duties are not directed specifically to the casework effort. Unfortunately, individuals who may have a negative effect on inmates also hold these positions. This is why selection of caseworkers and counselors followed with close professional supervision is vital to the casework effort in prisons.

Preparation for correctional casework involves three kinds of learning: (1) information and concepts, (2) skills, and (3) professional role and self-devel-

[13]Lawrence A. Bennett, Thomas S. Rosenbaum, and Wayne R. McCullough, *Counseling in Correctional Environments* (New York: Human Sciences Press, 1978), p. 10.

[14]American Correctional Association, "Counseling, Case Work and Clinical Services," in *Manual of Correctional Standards,* 3rd ed. (Washington, D.C.: ACA, 1969), p. 422.

opment.[15] Professional development is undoubtedly the most important, although it has to be based on information and skills. Without professional development, the "caseworker" simply becomes a mechanic who records facts and processes people through a program. Effective casework requires professional orientation and empathic skills.

Communication between counselor and inmate is dependent upon many factors, including common culture, common communication levels, and generally common frames of reference. When the social distance is too great, there is little or no real two-way communication. Consequently, two-way communication between staff and inmates is frequently better in the reputably poorer institutions where inmates and staff come from essentially similar cultural backgrounds than in some of the reputably better institutions where staff is carefully and professionally selected and the social distance between staff and inmates may be too great for meaningful two-way communication. Even so, the rehabilitative effects of the reputably better prisons appear to show positive results in terms of lesser recidivism rates. Better communication in the better prisons can be achieved by learning more about the cultural backgrounds of the inmate population and the prison subculture itself. There are several approaches to learning about culture.[16]

Treatment people, including psychiatrists, psychologists, social workers, counselors, and others, are often faced with confidential material that comes from clients. How to handle it responsibly has been a problem for the "helping" professions. Some responsible psychiatrists have learned of crimes committed in the past and have considered that their privileged relationship with their clients makes such reporting unethical. Most professionals in this situation have considered three issues to be the only ones in which breaking confidentiality in the therapeutic or casework situation is permissible: (1) when the welfare of the client is threatened, (2) when the situation is potentially dangerous, and (3) when duty to the institution or employer becomes overwhelming. Errors in judgment in these situations have produced tragic results in the past. In most cases, the relationship of trust between the therapist and the client may be irreparably broken to the extent that the client will never again trust a professional. In some other cases, people have been killed when the therapist has made the wrong judgment in maintaining confidentiality. The California Supreme Court has held that a doctor or psychotherapist treating a mentally ill person has a duty to use reasonable care to give threatened persons such warnings as are essential to avert foreseeable danger arising from the patient's condition or treatment. In the case noted, the court held that the parents of a murdered girl could recover damages on the basis that the patient announced his intentions to the psychotherapist and the psychotherapist did not warn the girl or her parents.[17]

[15]Hayes A. Hatcher, *Correctional Casework and Counseling* (Englewood Cliffs, N.J.: Prentice-Hall, Inc., 1978), p. 9.

[16]For example, see James P. Spradley, *The Ethnographic Interview* (New York: Holt, Rinehart and Winston, 1979).

[17]18 California Reporter 129, 529 P. 2nd.

In summary, counseling is central to the treatment program in prisons and correctional institutions. Unfortunately, caseworkers in prisons are generally spread so thinly that they could do adequate counseling with only a small percentage of their case loads. Legislatures and other political leaders simply do not place a high enough priority on prison casework to fund it.

GROUP METHODS

Group therapy, group counseling, guided group interaction (GGI), psychodrama, and other group methods were introduced in the correctional field after World War II. The earliest significant uses of these methods were made at the Army facility at Ft. Knox, Kentucky, during the last phases of World War II. Subsequently, group methods were used by Dr. Lloyd McCorkle (who was at Ft. Knox) and Dr. F. Lovell Bixby in New Jersey in the late 1940s. Albert Elias also operated a group program at Highfields for youthful offenders in New Jersey during that time.

California developed a program of group counseling in the late 1940s and 1950s. Under the leadership of Dr. Norman Fenton, training programs were established with volunteer personnel from within San Quentin who would lead groups in the evening. Correctional officers, record clerks, and anybody who was interested could participate—after having undertaken several weeks of training on their own time. Once the groups were started, the assessment was that they helped everybody, especially the group leaders. Wives of correctional officers who participated in the programs stated that their husbands were better fathers and more understanding of human behavior as a result of their experience in group counseling.

In recent years, several types of group methods have been developed, one of which is reality therapy. Introduced in 1965 by Dr. William Glasser,[18] reality therapy does not look at causes, but starts with behavior in the present. It seems to work well with offenders. There are thirteen steps to reality therapy:

1. Be warm, friendly, subjective.
2. Reveal yourself (self-disclosure).
3. Be personal (I, me).
4. Concentrate on the present.
5. Concentrate on behavior.
6. Ask "what" not "why."
7. Have client evaluate his or her own behavior.
8. Work out a plan.
9. Negotiate a contract.
10. Accept no excuses.
11. Work in groups as soon as possible.

[18]William Glasser, *Reality Therapy* (New York: Harper & Row, Publishers, 1965).

12.   Praise, approve, reward, touch.
13.   Never give up, maintain the relationship.

Reality therapy has been helpful in the correctional field probably because its principles are easy to understand; hence correctional officers can accept and use it effectively.

There are several advantages to group methods. First, more persons can be reached than in individual counseling. Most important in the correctional field is the dilution of the image of threatening authority. The peer group does most of the acting and discussing. The leader says as little as possible, only asking questions or making suggestions to make sure that the session remains objective and purposeful. When problems are handled by one's peers, they are acceptable more easily than when they are dictated or coerced by an authoritarian leadership. The presence of authority is diluted in group methods. Too frequently, a one-to-one relationship between a staff member and a resident of the prison becomes threatening to the counselee.

Group methods appear to be a more important element in correctional treatment. They are economical in that they allow one leader to handle more than one client at a time. Further, their effectiveness appears to be at least as good as that achieved in the one-to-one counseling process.

MEDICAL AND DENTAL CARE

Medical and dental care are most important in prisons and in correctional institutions because inmates tend to have been neglected and are deficient in these areas. Just as prisoners tend to be dropouts from school, they also tend to be dropouts from medical and dental care. An initial examination of all incoming residents is an important step in evaluating their medical conditions. In the group of people generally admitted to prisons, there is a high incidence of all sorts of diseases, including venereal disease, tuberculosis, and epilepsy, as well as poor dental health.

Estimates vary, but it is believed that between 2 and 5 percent of the persons accused of committing crimes are mentally disordered or psychotic. Estimates are that 2 or 3 percent of them are found insane in the courts and are disposed of by a civil commitment to a hospital setting. The remainder, however, is processed by courts as being criminal and those individuals are sent to prisons. The prisons, in turn, have to establish centers within their facilities to treat these psychotic offenders. Some prisons have set aside a certain cell block for the treatment of mentally disordered residents or inmates; others have built separate units designed for their treatment.

Cosmetic and plastic surgery is more important in prisons and juvenile institutions than anywhere else. There are crossed eyes that need to be straightened. There are prominent facial scars, including knife and gunshot wounds that need to be removed. There are disfigurements that are the result of fights, accidents, and tattoos that need to be corrected. Beyond the regular dental attention needed by any population, dental surgery of cosmetic variety is also important in a prison population.

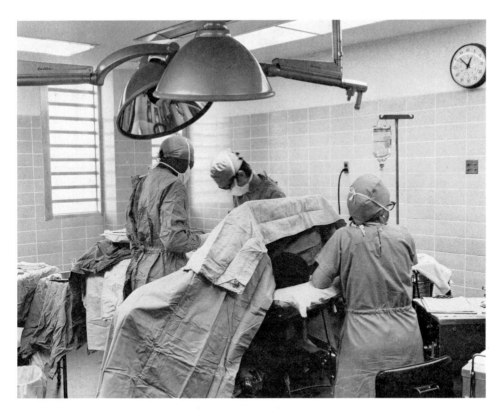

Surgery at the Reception and Medical Center, Lake Butler, Florida.
Courtesy of the Florida Department of Corrections.

Psychopharmacology has been used in some prisons to control violent behavior. Anectine has been used to reduce violence. Prolixin is a "supertranquilizer." Psychopharmacology, however, has also encountered legal difficulties as being a violation of the First and Fourth Amendments.

Inmates have a constitutional right to psychiatric care under the Eighth and Fourteenth Amendments. An inmate sued that he was denied parole because of psychological evaluation indicating that he would not complete a parole period successfully. The decision in *Estelle* v. *Gamble*[19] held that deliberate indifference to serious medical needs of prisoners constituted cruel and unusual punishment and that there was no difference between the right to care for physical ills and the right to care for mental or emotional ills; the court held that treatment would be given, although it would be limited to that which could be provided on reasonable and time and cost basis and that the treatment must be a medical necessity, not merely desirable.[20]

[19]*Estelle* v. *Gamble*, 97 S. Ct. 285 (1976).
[20]*Bowring* v. *Godwin*, 551 F. 2d 44 (4th Cir., 1977).

Hobbycraft store to sell items made by residents in their spare time.
Courtesy of the New Hampshire State Prison

The American Medical Association has a correctional project, headquartered in Chicago, which is concerned with the physical and mental health of inmates in jails, prisons, and juvenile facilities.[21]

LEISURE-TIME ACTIVITIES

Leisure-time activities are potentially one of the most important phases of a prison program, but, unfortunately, they have received little attention in prisons as being central to the treatment process. Yet it has been during leisure time that people became involved in conflict with the law outside. People tend not to get into trouble while they are working, sleeping, or eating; they get into trouble during their leisure time. Consequently, an effective leisure-time activity program in prisons and correctional institutions should be designed to transfer to activities after release.

Many such activities do transfer, such as chess, hobbycrafts, or other activities that might be pursued upon release. Some prisons have tennis courts, but they have been the subject of derision by those who see them as "country club activities"—nobody would dare put a golf course or putting green in their

[21]*The Correctional Stethoscope*, published bimonthly by the American Medical Association, Vol. 1, no. 10 (June 1978), pp. 1–2.

correctional facility! Even so, there are many hobbies, games, and other activities that can transfer outside the institution in a constructive way.

Most recreational pursuits in the prisons are generally comprised of individual or programmed athletics, either varsity or intramural. Most major prisons and correctional institutions have athletic teams in football, basketball, and baseball that play outside teams, many of which are local teams from the industrial leagues and universities or semiprofessional teams. The most popular individual sport in prison is boxing. Many of the leading contenders in boxing, as well as a champion or two, have been in prisons or training schools and learned to fight there. Boxing is an individual sport, rather than a team sport, and thus it appeals to people who do not relate well to others.

Libraries are important in prison for a variety of reasons, even though the percentage of residents who check out books and read is quite low. Most residents in prisons and correctional institutions are nonreaders, either by lack of ability to read or by choice. It takes a competent librarian who can "sell" reading to make a library function in a prison or correctional institution.

A law library is important in the prison, also, as a manner of access to the courts and as a leisure-time activity. Many correctional administrators who see the rise of litigation brought by residents of institutions against prison administrations conclude that much of this activity is really related to leisure time. This view was supported by Judge Henley in an Iowa case in 1978, in which he said that inmates may use this suit or threat of a suit to obtain more favorable treatment or a desirable work assignment and that these inmates have "essentially nothing to lose, including time, by prosecuting such actions and they may gain something even if it is nothing but the satisfaction of harassing, inconveniencing, and annoying those who have them in charge."[22] While this is not condoned by correctional administrators personnel or the judiciary—or many other people, for that matter—it does become a use of leisure time. It may induce somebody to make a serious study of the law after release.

Playing-cards are considered to be contraband in most prisons because gambling games such as poker, which are popular among the inmates, result in generating obligations to the winners on the part of the losers that the latter could not possibly pay. This leads to fights, sometimes serious assaults resulting in homicide, and a wide variety of attempts to satisfy the obligations or evade the consequences. Further, these games do not provide for constructive transfer to positive recreational pursuits outside.

A few prisons, such as the U.S. penitentiary at Leavenworth, have introduced bridge.[23] The context in which bridge is played does not promote the heavy gambling stakes found in poker and similar games. Outside guests, including women, are invited into the prison to play with the inmates, and the playing cards are generally brought in by the outside bridge club sponsoring the project. In this situation, there is no problem with contraband, the inmates groom themselves as well as possible for the visiting players, and there is no rudeness. Inmates have reported that the bridge project has improved their attitudes as

---

[22]*Wycoff* v. *Brewer*, 572 F. 2d 1260 (Iowa, 1978).

[23]Henry Francis, "Bridge Behind Bars Prepares Convicts for Life Outside," *The Contract Bridge Bulletin*, Vol. 46, no. 3 (March 1980), pp. 54–57.

well as their lives. Of considerable importance is the fact that the transfer of bridge as a recreational pursuit outside tends to bring them into contact with the middle-class segment of our society.

In conclusion, the basic objective of a recreational program in prisons or correctional institutions is to assist each resident, if possible, to find a recreational pursuit that will occupy some of his or her leisure time outside. Sometimes it is learning to play a musical instrument or other skills or becoming competent in chess or some other socially approved game. Other transferable recreational activities include painting and writing.

PRISON AS A THERAPEUTIC COMMUNITY

Some correctional institutions have been converted to therapeutic communities, but these are generally small institutions housing first-offenders or juveniles, such as the Minnesota State Training School at Red Wing. These institutions promote good relationships between officers and inmates and emphasize peer pressure and control among the inmates themselves. Group counseling is generally a basic ingredient in the program.

CONCLUSIONS

Classification and treatment are approaches by which constructive programs in the prison can be delivered to the residents or inmates who need them. Classification is an administrative device by which the residents are separated according to sex, age, criminal history, and other factors. Then, education, religion, counseling, group therapy, and other desired programs can be delivered to relatively homogeneous groups of residents. Classification, then, becomes the optimum delivery of treatment resources available to the residents of the institution.

An analysis of ten thousand state prison inmates nationwide indicated that 41 percent participated in some type of treatment programs while incarcerated.[24] About 31 percent of this group needed job training, 68 percent needed further education, 23 percent needed drug rehabilitation, and 22 percent needed alcohol rehabilitation. Younger inmates received more education and job training, whereas older inmates needed alcohol rehabilitation. Blacks received more drug treatment, whereas whites received more alcohol treatment.

In summary, classification and treatment in prisons and correctional institutions are designed to assist individual offenders to readjust to the free community after release. Incorporated in the institution are the services that become a microcosm of the larger society, including education, religion, health care, recreation, and all the social institutions considered to be normal in the larger society. Mobilization of these services to assist the individual offender becomes the central thrust of this service.

[24]John R. Petersilia, "Which Inmates Participate in Prison Treatment Programs?" in *Selected Rand Abstracts*, Vol. 17, no. 1 (January–March 1979), p. 18.

CHAPTER QUESTIONS

4-1. What is classification?

4-2. What are the general patterns seen in the development of classification and in classification systems throughout the country?

4-3. What appear to be the best recommendations regarding guidelines for keeping records on individuals within the privacy laws?

4-4. What are the primary objectives of education in prisons and correctional institutions?

4-5. What is the function of religion in a prison or a correctional institution?

4-6. What is the function of a counselor in a prison or a correctional institution?

4-7. What are the advantages of group methods in prisons and correctional institutions?

4-8. Why is cosmetic and plastic surgery more important in prisons and juvenile institutions than anywhere else in society?

4-9. Why is recreation and participation in constructive leisure-time activities important in prisons and correctional institutions?

4-10. Can a prison or correctional institution be made into a therapeutic community?

5

EMPLOYMENT OF RESIDENTS— PATTERNS OF PRISONER EMPLOYMENT

There is an old adage that prison labor is the essence of prison discipline.[1] After the opening of Bridewell in 1557 as a workhouse and other workhouses or "bridewells" throughout England, The Netherlands, and other parts of Europe, work became basic in these institutional programs for minor offenders. In other places of detention, however, such as Newgate in London, opened in 1769, there was no work and no discipline. Work has been central to the discipline in prisons down through the history of prisons. The modern correctional administrator considers idleness of prisoners a primary problem.

The public believes that prisoners should work. Work release outside the prison is accepted when jobs are plentiful, but during periods of unemployment, the public resists prisoners' taking jobs from law-abiding citizens. Work with the prison should be productive, but not in competition with "free enterprise" outside. The reasons frequently given for working prisoners are (1) to administer punishment, (2) to achieve discipline in prison, (3) to relieve the monotony of the prison term, (4) to reduce operating costs through production of goods that may be sold or used within the prison's limits, (5) to assist inmates to aid in the support of their families, (6) to give the prisoner a small sum of money so that he

[1]Scott Christianson, "Corrections Law Developments—Prison Labor and Unionization— Legal Developments," *Criminal Law Bulletin*, Vol. 14, no. 3 (May–June 1978), p. 243.

or she may purchase notions, candy, cigarettes, and other items from the prison commissary, (7) to teach prisoners trades, and (8) to maintain control.[2]

Slavery had been used as a disposition of the court from ancient man to the sixteenth century. Working prisoners were confined to rowing the galleys, working the quarries, and assisting on some public works projects. Labor was introduced in correctional institutions with the development of workhouses, or "bridewells," beginning in 1557. The early institutions were not well maintained, were unsanitary, and lacked discipline. An early type of vocational training was established during the 1830s by Colonel Manuel Montesinos in Valencia, Spain, who took over an old Augustinian convent and supervised fifteen hundred prisoners by developing about forty trades that made the prison self-supporting. At the same time, George Obermaier, who became superintendent of the Kaiserslautern Work Prison in Bavaria, developed trade training and productive work at a time when exploitation of prisons was the prevailing practice.

In England, however, overcrowding of jails, houses of correction, and the later penitentiaries forced the development of unproductive machines, such as the treadwheel in 1818 and the crank about 1846, both providing useless work because there was not enough productive employment available. The first formalized program of inmate labor, a contract and piece-price system, was instituted in the years 1790 to 1800 at the old Walnut Street Jail where the penitentiary movement was begun by the Quakers. The contractor furnished the raw material and received the finished product, paying the prison a certain amount for each completed unit accepted by him. Since the prison hired its own supervisors and custodial force, exploitation of the inmates was at a minimum. Full development of the contract system was accomplished between 1825 and 1840 in various prisons. The contract system, of which the piece-price system was a variation, involved letting out prisoner labor to an outside contractor who furnished the machinery and raw materials and provided the supervision. Prison management had nothing to do with the operation, its responsibility only being that of custody.

The contract system received impetus following 1825 with the rise of the merchant-capitalist in America. The entrepreneur was willing to furnish the raw material and take the finished product at an agreed-upon rate. The prisons in New York and other states adopted this new method of working prisoners enthusiastically. By 1828, the Auburn and Sing Sing prisons were self-supporting. The same developments were occurring in other states. Kentucky, for example, opened the prison at Frankfort in 1800 and contracted with private individuals until 1844 when the profits were so high that the prison was subsequently contracted to a corporation rather than to an individual.[3] In most contract systems, the prison became self-supporting or made a profit for the state. With the organization of the American Federation of Labor in 1900, a concerted political campaign evolved to abolish the contract system.

[2]Harry Elmer Barnes and Negley K. Teeters, *New Horizons in Criminology*, 3rd ed. (Englewood Cliffs, N.J.: Prentice-Hall, Inc., 1959), pp. 523–24.

[3]Orlando F. Lewis, "Kentucky," in *The Development of American Prisons and Prison Customs, 1776–1845* (Montclair, N.J.: Patterson Smith, 1967), pp. 253–59. Published originally in 1922 by the Prison Association of New York.

The lease system developed primarily in the South after the Civil War, as a result of the impact of the Civil War on that economy. The antebellum South was a prosperous "agricultural kingdom."[4] Mississippi had been the most prosperous state in the country with Alabama second, while the North was struggling with a beginning industry subsidized by federal funds. The Civil War resulted in the full development of industry in the North and the destruction of the economy of the South. When the Union forces left the South in 1877, many formerly profitable plantations had been taken out of production, now owned by Northerners who bought them at panic prices from Southerners attempting to replace worthless Confederate money with whatever U.S. currency they could obtain.

The South did not have enough tax funds to support schools for their children, much less prisons for offenders. Consequently, Southern states leased their convicted offenders to the highest bidder, generally to individuals or companies from the North. A good documentary of this era was written by a captain of the Florida "convict camp" at Lake City about his career from 1874 to 1890.[5] Some states went so far as to eliminate the state prison system and turn the prisoners over to the counties, thereby avoiding the cost of prisons at the state level. Leasing was gradually abolished between World War I and 1936, at least partially as a result of the invention of the automobile and the need for building and maintaining roads. The leasing system, then, really moved from leasing to the highest bidder to the "chain gang" or "road gang" throughout the South.

In the public works and ways system, which succeeded the lease system, prisoners were used in the construction and repair of roads, public streets, highways and in other public projects. Many states still use prisoners to maintain their capitol and other state office buildings. Many states still use their inmates to construct recreational areas, such as Michigan's Iron Mountain Ski Jump and California's conservation camps. Some states, such as Texas, use inmates to construct new prisons, new prison cell blocks, and the building to house the criminal justice program at Sam Houston State University at Huntsville. Opposition from labor unions has eliminated the construction of buildings in states with strong unions.

The state-use system of prison labor is currently the most widely used in American prisons. In this system, prison-made goods and agricultural products are provided to the prison system and other governmental agencies and local units of government by some type of contract between the prison system and the other units of government. While this appears to be the best compromise between productive employment of prisoners and the marketing of their product, even this approach has encountered opposition and restrictive legislation from associations of manufacturers, retail merchant groups, some unions, and other groups and individuals who regard *any* marketing of prison-made goods or produce as a threat to free enterprise.

[4]William Warren Rogers, *Ante-bellum Thomas County—1825–1861* (Tallahassee: Florida State University Press, 1963), pp. 118–20.

[5]J. C. Powell, *The American Siberia* (Montclair, N.J.: Patterson Smith, 1970). Published originally in Chicago in 1891 by H. J. Smith & Co.

MAINTENANCE
OF THE INSTITUTION

In most prisons and correctional institutions, the majority of residents or inmates are employed in the maintenance of the institution and its services. The largest number are generally employed by the food services, including the kitchen, bakery, butcher shop, and dining hall. In addition, special food services have to be provided to the hospital, disciplinary units, and mental ward, and special food lines have been legislated for Black Muslims, Jews (Kosher lines) and other religious groups, and diabetics and others with medically prescribed special diets. In addition, the officers' dining room and the special containers to be delivered to officers in the guard towers assigned there for eight hours each shift must be served. In some prisons, the officers get a special menu, but they receive the same menu as the residents do in the more progressive prisons, including facilities maintained by the Federal Prison System. The officers' dining quarters may be separated from the inmate dining hall, or it may be in a separate section within the same dining hall. Most of the work done by the residents is in the preparation of food and in cleaning the utensils, kitchen, dining hall, and other physical space after meals.

Physical maintenance of the institution probably employs the next largest number of residents. Most of the skilled tradespeople who happen to be in the prison population, such as electricians, plumbers, carpenters, welders, radio and television technicians, painters, and other skilled persons, are generally assigned to maintenance. A civilian supervisor heads each specialty and reports to the chief engineer.

There are many other jobs in the prison that serve to maintain the institution, such as the laundry, which is used as a disciplinary assignment in many prisons. The majority of unskilled residents are classified in the "labor pool," which means that they are eligible for menial work and can be assigned anywhere that does not require social skills, commensurate with their custodial classification.

FARMS

Agriculture employs many residents in most prisons. In some systems, such as those in Texas, Arkansas, Louisiana, and Mississippi, the primary prison employment is on their large farms. The large farm production in these states has prompted some of the administrators to point out that they are self-supporting and sometimes return to the legislature more than their original appropriation each year.

At the other extreme, many smaller institutions have abolished their farms because they were not profitable, because of their smaller size or the fact that they were trying to work the farms with a population mostly from the cities who were not accustomed to farm work, or both. A cost-benefit analysis of several farms has indicated that they were an economic liability. Many institu-

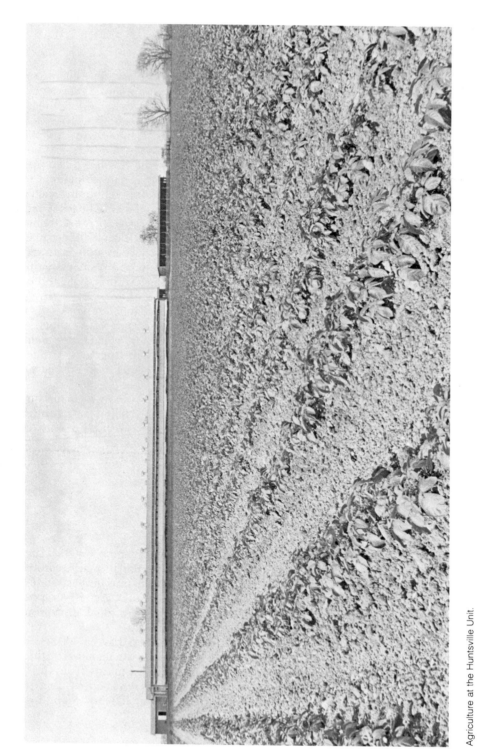

Agriculture at the Huntsville Unit.

Courtesy of the Texas Department of Corrections.

Dairy operation at the Huntsville Unit.
Courtesy of the Texas Department of Corrections.

tions, including those maintained by the Federal Prison System, have declared their farmlands to be surplus and have divested themselves from it to focus on other phases of their program, such as industries, education, and vocational training.

PRISON INDUSTRIES

Industrial prisons began to develop rapidly with the industrialization of society in the Northeast and Midwest, largely between Boston and Washington, D.C., west to St. Louis, and in California. New York had developed industrialized prisons beginning earlier at Auburn and Sing Sing, and industrialization was part of the programs in prisons built later. Major industrialized prisons were developed as the Ohio penitentiary at Columbus opened in 1834 with subsequent additions; the California state prison at San Quentin opened in 1852 and Folsom opened in 1880; the Illinois state penitentiary at Stateville opened in 1925, although construction was begun in 1919; and the largest of them all, the state prison of southern Michigan at Jackson, opened in 1926. Industry had become the central focus for most of the new prisons in these areas. It thrived during the last half of the nineteenth century and the first quarter of the twentieth century.

Prison industry has been organized in several ways. The patterns have been (1) piece-price, (2) contract, (3) lease, (4) public-account or state-account, (5) state use, and (6) public works and ways. *Piece-price* was common up until the middle of the nineteenth century in which the outside entrepreneur furnished the raw materials, the inmates did the work, and the entrepreneur bought the finished product at an agreed-upon price. *Contract* was the system that was common through the first two thirds of the nineteenth century in which the outside entrepreneur contracted for the prison labor and did his work inside the prison in prison shops. It was in this arrangement when a riot occurred at Sing Sing on November 27, 1855, when the contractor placed an inmate who had refused to work into solitary confinement for discipline. The other workers picked up their hammers and tools, refused to work, and became hostile until the disciplined inmate had been released. Fortunately, nobody had been hurt. *Lease* became popular in the South after the Civil War. While the South had been one of the richest areas of the country prior to the Civil War, the devastation of the war and confederate money becoming worthless resulted in impoverishment to the extent that the states could not maintain goods for their children, much less prisons for offenders. Leasing had been in existence before the Civil War, but it had not been as popular as it was in the South after the Civil War. States simply leased their inmates to the highest bidder, many of whom were Northern companies or entrepreneurs who used the inmates to produce products like turpentine to be sold to the Navy, lumber, and other types of work. *Public-account* or *State-account* was a system in which prison-made goods were sold on the open market. Despite many restrictions, including congressional and state legislation against prison-made goods, some states have always produced something that could be sold on the open market, such as binder twine in Minnesota. Recent industrial experiments in Minnesota, Kansas, and Arizona, called "Free Venture" have revived to some extent this practice. *State Use* refers to a system in which prison-made goods can be sold only to other state institutions and agencies or to governmental subdivisions. For example, prison-made goods could be sold to mental hospitals, state offices, other departments of state government, county jails, and schools. Agricultural products have been sold to local jails and school lunch programs. *Public Works and Ways* refers to using inmates for the maintenance of roads, parks, and recreational facilities. California has, for example, a forestry conservation program. Some other states have used inmates to build and maintain public recreational facilities. This approach simply focuses the effort of inmate work toward public installations, roads, and service.

Resistance to prison industry began to develop during the first quarter of the twentieth century and has grown stronger since. The Hawes–Cooper Act of 1929, which went into effect in January 1934, divested state prison products of their interstate character. The Ashherst–Summers Act passed in 1935 prohibited transportation companies from accepting prison-made goods. The Walsh–Healy Act of October 1940 excluded almost all prison-made products from interstate commerce. By 1940, every state had passed some sort of similar limitation on prison-made products. Some labor organizations have made themselves felt in legislation against prison labor, particularly in preventing use of skilled labor on

Auto tag shop at the Powhatan Correctional Center in Virginia.
Courtesy of the Virginia Department of Corrections.

public highways or other public projects—if they come from the prison. National industrial associations and their state counterparts have lobbied successfully for limitation of prison-made goods. Arguments that prisons could make license tags, street signs, and other stamped-metal products carried no weight in the legislative bodies in the face of lobbyists for the industrial organizations who maintained that prison products became government interference with free enterprise. The highest productivity in peacetime in the prison industry was in 1923 when almost $74 million worth of materials was made in the prisons. This amount has declined dramatically since. The only period since that prison-made products have been welcomed was during World War II, when the director of the U.S. Bureau of Prisons, James V. Bennett, and the Prison Industry Section of the War Production Board requested that prison industries be put to work manufacturing war goods. Between 1941 and 1945, inclusive, American prisons produced about $138 million in manufactured goods and about $75 million in farm products, considerably less per year than the 1923 output. After World War II, prison industries declined further. Idleness in prison has since become a major problem.

Correctional administrators are convinced that full employment of the residents is essential, whether by industry, farming, or education. There is general agreement, though not unanimous, that prison farming is a "make-work" effort because using residents from urban centers who have never worked or who do not plan to work on farms is hardly productive and only a few of the largest prison farms break even financially. It becomes a political matter as to how this employment must be financed and how much it costs the public in tax funds to cut off prison production and substitute other programs.[6]

During argument and debate, some representatives of private industry have suggested a willingness to establish and support vocational training programs in the prisons, themselves, using some of their surplus equipment; nevertheless, although some correctional administrators have been willing to accept the offer, no such program has ever been implemented. Prison industries administrators, on the other hand, have indicated that their primary goals are to provide useful and meaningful work, to provide training and practice, to instill self-discipline, to inculcate work habits, and generally to prepare a person for release back to the community as a self-respecting wage-earning citizen.[7] With a peak prison industries production in 1923 at slightly under $74 million, many correctional industries administrators find it difficult to understand how prisons could compete with the total GNP (gross national product) of the United States. In addition, many restrictions of prison products have placed other governmental units in jeopardy. For example, several states had customarily sold agricultural products and other goods to county jails, county schools, and other local governmental agencies, which had to cut back or find other resources when the restrictive legislation passed into law.

The Federal Prison Industries, Inc. (UNICOR), appears to have achieved the best organization in the field of prison industries. Of about 30,000 inmates in the U.S. Bureau of Prisons system in 1977, an average of 5,995 worked for Federal Prison Industries, Inc.[8]

A study supported by the U.S. Department of Labor has indicated that, as constituted currently, prison industries do not achieve either the goal of rehabilitation or that of providing valuable work for inmates and prisons. The goals of prison industries should be revised and developed as industries rather than as correctional programs. Real work experiences, full workdays, job compensation, minimum wages, and merit pay increases would provide a closer relationship to private industry.[9]

INMATE PAY AND INCOME

Inmate pay and income derives from several sources. About three-fourths of the states pay something to all residents on assignment. Residents working on industrial programs generally earn more than do the others. In addition, monetary awards for good behavior or positive contributions to the programs are available. For example, for many years, the Federal Prison System had a meritorious

---

[6]Ernest E. Means, *Prison Industries and Rehabilitative Programs* (Tallahassee: Florida Division of Corrections and Florida State University Institute of Governmental Research, March 1964).

[7]*The Correctional Industries Association Newsletter,* Vol. 1, no. 2 (October 1968), p. 4.

[8]Carolyn Johnson and Marjorie Kravitz, *Prison Industries: A Selected Bibliography* (Rockville, Md.: National Criminal Justice Reference Service, LEAA, May 1978), p. vi.

[9]V. A. McArthur and M. R. Montilla, *"Role of Prison Industries Now and in the Future—A Planning Study* (Washington, D.C.: Georgetown University Institute of Criminal Law and Procedure, 1975), p. 68.

Tailor shop at the Coxsakie Correctional Facility.
Courtesy of the New York State Department of Correctional Services.

service award, which it has now adjusted to an incentive pay program. Several states also have some type of monetary reward for outstanding performance. Many residents receive money from their families outside the institution.

Three-fourths of the states pay something to all residents or inmates on assignment. They may start at a nickel or dime a day and gradually work up, usually in four stages, to fifty cents to a dollar a day, which with an average of twenty-three working days per month, would range from $1.15 to probably about $17.00 per month. The Federal Prison System is one of the better paying systems. For ordinary work, the range is $7.50 per month to a high of $20.00 per month, with an average of $15.00 per month. In addition, an average resident's incentive pay would be probably $9.70 per month, based on contribution to industries, recommendations by work assignment supervisors, and reports and recommendations by the treatment team or unit management reports. These awards are made on the basis of recommendations by work supervisors and the treatment team. Some residents, of course, would get more; others may get nothing. The average pay for the resident of the Federal Prison System, then, is about \$24.70 per month. As indicated previously, state systems pay considerably less for ordinary assignments. In the higher range of state systems are prisons in Oregon, California, Minnesota, and South Dakota. States that have traditionally paid nothing to inmates have been Arizona, Arkansas, Colorado, Florida, Georgia, Idaho, Louisiana, Maine, Mississippi, Montana, Nevada, New Mexico, North Carolina, and Texas. Jurisdictions that pay little or nothing are in accordance with *Ruffin* v. *Commonwealth*, 21 grat. 760 (Virginia, 1871), which held that prisoners were "slaves of the state," and the Thirteenth Amendment, which prohibits involuntary servitude "except as a punishment for crime."

Prison industries pay more to residents than do ordinary maintenance assignments. Industries generally have a dual system of piecework and hourly rates and award pay differentials according to skill levels. Generally, the high might be about \$135.00 per month, the low being dependent upon time invested and productivity that would be difficult to state conclusively, with an average of \$75.00 per month. In addition, the incentive pay averaging \$9.70 per month could be awarded. It should be noted here that some jobs in industry can provide time for the resident worker to his or her credit in the social security system. As also indicated previously, other income may come from the resident's family outside. Income may also be earned in the hobbycraft program or arts and crafts program, which may be recreational. It consists of making wallets and leather goods, smoking stands, cedar chests, lamps, and other items that could be sold to visitors in the prison's hobbycraft shop. Earnings from this source, of course, depend upon productivity by the resident and sales in the shop.

There have been some recent suggestions that the entire system be changed. The proposal has been made that residents or inmates of prisons and correctional institutions be paid the legal minimum wage and then be charged board, room, and other maintenance. The argument is that they *are* citizens of the United States and should be covered by all its laws.

Another source of income for many inmates derives from the Veterans Administration as a result of disabilities sustained from their service in the U.S. military.

After adjusting for race and sex, the potential productivity of inmates in American prisons and jails is estimated at over \$2.5 billion annually.[10] The actual productivity in educational, training, industrial, and maintenance activities is estimated at \$1 billion or less, which indicates that there is considerable loss or wasted potential inmate productivity that exceeds \$1 billion each year.

CRITERIA FOR ASSIGNMENT

Prisons and correctional institutions need to be maintained constantly. The rehabilitative or treatment objective, including education and other helping services, must also be maintained. All the various offices in the prison need clerical assistance that legislatures do not support with funds, and the prison's staff has to select from the prison population the residents who can do the job. Inmate

[10]N. M. Singer, "Value of Inmate Manpower," *Journal of Research in Crime and Delinquency,* Vol. 13, no. 1 (January 1976), pp. 3–12.

clerks work in most of the offices, including those of the director of education, the classification department and its various professional staff, the hospital, the chaplain, various custodial divisions, and even the deputy warden. Trusted residents are used as "runners" assigned to cell blocks and elsewhere to carry messages for officers and other authorized personnel from one office to the other. These people have to be selected for their trustworthiness and dependability even ahead of their clerical skills. Residents in these positions generally consider them to be a "good go" (meaning a pleasant, comfortable, and rewarding existence as compared with an unpleasant and punitive existence) and seldom flagrantly violate that trust.

Occasionally, of course, they may use their positions to their own advantage vis-à-vis the rest of the population. For example, jobs and cell assignments are coordinated in large maximum custody institutions. If workers in the kitchen have to move from the cell block to their work assignment to prepare breakfast at 5:00 A.M., they must go as a group accompanied by an officer. Consequently, the people who work in one assignment in a maximum custody institution generally are housed in the same cell block or living quarters. Inmate clerks frequently handle the clerical routines in changing cell blocks and jobs. In many prisons, the officials do not have time to supervise this closely, and the inmate clerk may charge a carton of cigarettes to another inmate who is assigned to a desirable job or the card will be "lost" in the file. Of course, if the civilian supervisor presses it, the card can be "found" quickly. Consequently, many of these deals are by default because the staff does not have time to keep up with them all. If the practice becomes flagrant, however, the inmate clerk will be replaced.

One such case involved an inmate working in the records office who was serving thirty years. He removed materials from his file that reduced his sentence by twenty years and had himself transferred to another institution and released.[11] This case is extreme, but it demonstrates the need for supervision. When these data are placed in computers, the danger will be even greater because immediate supervision will be much more difficult.

A real problem in prison maintenance and programming is that of determining who should go to school and who should be sacrificed in this regard to maintain the institution. These selections are made daily in the assignment process. The U.S. Bureau of Prisons (now the Federal Prison System) implemented a system of classification in 1969 that formalized the selection process that has been traditional for these different assignments. On the basis of experience in placing offenders in the treatment categories of (1) intensive, (2) selective, or (3) minimal as to the likelihood of change according to staff judgment, a RAPS system was developed that could be translated into categories I, II, or III, depending upon whether there should be a great, medium, or no expenditure of resources above the essential level of service.

The "R" (rehabilitation potential) is based on the staff's professional opinion regarding the prospect of change. The "A" refers to age as under 30, 30 to 45, or over 45. The "P" is the number of prior sentences ranging from none to one or two or more. The "S" refers to the nature of the sentence in terms of

---

[11]Robert M. Carter, Richard A. McGee, and E. Kim Nelson, *Corrections in America* (Philadelphia: J. B. Lippincott Company, 1975), p. 150.

special classification (Federal Juvenile Delinquency Act, Youthful Offender Act, or Narcotic Addict Rehabilitation Act) or length of sentence. These codes are fed into the computer as the digit 1, 2, or 3, with 1 being the most hopeful and 3 being least hopeful. Translated into assignments, inmates in category I are most hopeful and get first chance at all educational and other treatment programs. Those in category II get the available spaces left in the treatment programs and are assigned to the better work assignments. Those in category III are not provided educational or other positive opportunities but are assigned to the menial jobs necessary to maintain and operate the institution.

FREE ENTERPRISE IN PRISON INDUSTRIES

Minnesota and Kansas have invited private industry to establish industries in which inmates can work for free-world wages, pay social security, and enjoy the same status as workers in outside industry.[12] Arizona has subsequently joined the movement. Minnesota has always had some type of industry competing with private ventures, particularly in binder twine. In 1973, the Minnesota legislature passed a law allowing private entrepreneurs to set up shop inside the state's penal facilities. Since 1975, the project, Free Venture, has been active in Minnesota, funded by the former LEAA and operated by the American Institute of Criminal Justice in Philadelphia, which has provided some funds to seven states. The goals of Free Venture projects are to make prison industries self-sufficient, to have them employ more workers, and to pay them wages well above the normal institutional scales and provide a real-world job situation.[13]

Throughout the first half of the eighteenth century until the Civil War, it was not uncommon for states to lease their prisons to the highest bidder for industrial purposes. In fact the practice continued in the South until the twentieth century. With the rise of industrial prisons, however, federal and state legislation began to be enacted to restrict prison-made goods, and prison industries were reduced dramatically. The present move in a few states appears to be a modest attempt at bringing industries back to prisons at a level considered to be "normal" in the free world.

CONCLUSIONS

It has been suggested that prisoners be recognized as public employees and that prisoner labor unions may be a possible means of securing improved employment conditions on a par with those of public employees.[14] On the other

---

[12]Michael Fedo, "Free Enterprise Goes to Prison—In Kansas and Minnesota, Private Firms Hire Inmates at Free-World Wages—and Teach Them Valuable Skills," *Corrections Magazine*, Vol. 7, no. 2 (April 1981), pp. 5–15.

[13]Ibid., p. 11.

[14]S. M. Singleton, "Unionizing America's Prisons—Arbitration and State Use," *Indiana Law Journal*, Vol. 48, no. 3 (Spring 1976), pp. 493–502.

hand, a Pennsylvania court has held that inmates in penal institutions are not within the protection and benefits of Pennsylvania's Public Employee Relations Act in regard to the work they perform.[15] Previously, the U.S. Supreme Court held that an inmate's constitutional rights are not violated when denied the protection of labor laws and that prison administrations can refuse to permit the existence of prisoners' unions if they become a threat to the security of the institution.[16]

In every appropriate way, including employment-related injury and disability, minimum wages, job seniority and security, pensions, and unions, prisoners should be accorded the same rights as other workers and be integrated into the general work force.[17] The state-use system of prison labor should be eliminated so that prisoners can learn skills and work in jobs that they can perform on release. Arbitrary disqualification of prisoners from certain employment should be eliminated, and legislation should authorize prisoners' unions.[18]

A move to eliminate the jobs on which ex-felons cannot work has to be incorporated into the rehabilitative process. Florida began taking the lead in 1971 to reduce the number of jobs denied ex-felons by state law. By the mid-1970s, there were at least 315 civilian occupations in some states from which ex-felons were barred.[19]

There is a close relationship between youth crime and the unemployment of youth.[20] For many, crime is a primary or secondary form of employment. A major public policy in criminal justice should be, therefore, to develop employment opportunities that are responsive to human needs. While the theories of crime have varied from time to time, the need for employment and its resources have consistently been reported by the offenders themselves.

Constructive work is basic to prison discipline. Keeping a person active in a positive and productive way tends to preclude some of the deterioration that results from idleness or nonproductive "make-work" assignments. The maintenance and service functions of the institution provide the work for the majority of inmates. Agriculture provides the primary work for institutions with large farms, such as those in Texas, Arkansas, Mississippi, and Louisiana. In many other states, agriculture provides work for a number of persons. Prison industries are used to make goods that are useful to the prison system and other state

---

[15]*Salah* v. *Commonwealth*, 24 Cr. L. 2249 (Penn. Commonwealth Ct, November 31, 1978).

[16]*Jones* v. *North Carolina Prisoners' Union, Inc.*, 433 U.S. 19 (1977).

[17]L. D. Clark and G. M. Parker, "Labor Law Problems of the Prisoner," *Rutgers Law Review*, Vol. 28, no. 4 (Spring 1975), pp. 840–60.

[18]T. E. Holliday, "Granting Workmen's Compensation Benefits to Prison Inmates," *Southern California Law Review*, Vol. 36, no. 4 (September 1973), pp. 1223–62. A similar view is presented by the National Council on Crime and Delinquency, *Policies and Background Information* (Hackensack, N.J.: National Council on Crime and Delinquency, 1972), 32 pp.

[19]James W. Hunt, James E. Bowers, and Neal Miller, *Laws, Licenses and the Offender's Right to Work* (Washington, D.C.: American Bar Association, National Clearinghouse on Offender Employment Restrictions, 1974), Appendix, pp. A-2 to A-12.

[20]Leon Leiberg, director of the Employment and Crime Project; *"Crime and Employment Issues"—A Collection of Policy Relevant Monographs* (Washington, D.C.: Institute for Advanced Studies in Justice, American University Law School, 1978), pp. 14–18.

and local governmental agencies, such as hospitals, jails, schools, and other facilities as permitted by federal and state law. The use of industries has declined since the peak in 1923, after which federal and state restrictions on prison-made goods were enacted as a consequence of objections from private inudstry and businesses.

The problem in American prisons today is that of finding enough meaningful work to go around. Even where the residents can work, the prison is fortunate if it can function five or six hours a day because of interruptions by counts, frequently a major count at 4:00 P.M. Prisons and correctional institutions, then, face a problem of idleness and are attempting to meet it by educational programs, using the residents for maintenance of the institution, on farms, and in industry.

CHAPTER QUESTIONS

5-1.   What are the reasons given most frequently for making prisoners work?

5-2.   What systems have been used for marketing prison-made goods and products?

5-3.   Where is the largest number of inmates employed in the maintenance of the institutions and its services?

5-4.   What is the debate regarding the operation of farms in connection with prison and correctional institutions?

5-5.   Why have prison industries had difficulty in being accepted historically?

5-6.   Why do correctional administrators desire industry in their prisons?

5-7.   From what sources do inmates receive funds?

5-8.   What is the potential productivity of inmates in American prisons and jails?

5-9.   Is there an advantage in having inmates do much of the clerical work in a prison?

5-10. What are the criteria for assignment to jobs in prisons?

6

MAXIMUM SECURITY SOCIETY

The maximum security institution has been compared with a totalitarian state in miniature,[1] and social formation and interaction within institutions differ considerably from that in free society.[2] In fact, some prisons consider themselves to be in competition as to which is the toughest or the worst.[3] The prison is a closed social system that lends itself to clique formation, the prison code as a defense against prevailing authority, and institutionalization.[4] It is characterized by constant supervision by visible and hostile authority, complete lack of privacy, assaults by inmates, deprivation of normal amenities, regimentation, and general degradation of the individual. Similar conditions exist in some medium security institutions, particularly those for younger offenders, generally 15 or 16 years of age to the mid-20s, called "reformatories." There is supervision, of course, in minimum security institutions, but it is not rigid, and weapons are not visible.

[1] Henry Burns, "A Miniature Totalitarian State: A Maximum Security Prison," *The Canadian Journal of Corrections*, Vol. 2, no. 2 (July 1969), pp. 153–64.

[2] Irving Goffman, *Asylums* (Chicago: Aldine Publishing Company, 1962), p. 1.

[3] Joseph Ragen and Charles Finston, *Inside the World's Toughest Prison* (Springfield, Ill.: Charles C. Thomas Publisher, 1962).

[4] Donald Clemmer, *The Prison Community* (Boston: Christopher Press, 1940); reissued in New York by Holt, Rinehart and Winston in 1958.

Other than a count at breakfast, the evening meal, and bed check, there is little supervision in community custody facilities, and the only custodial concern arises when someone on work or study release returns to the facility intoxicated or not at all. The people in less than maximum security are selected as the least security risks. This chapter concentrates on the maximum custody institution, although it can relate to other institutions in decreasing intensity from medium to minimum and to community-based facilities.

AUTHORITARIAN SOCIETY

The maximum security prison is generally run according to an authoritarian system. Probably one of the best known extremes in American prisons was that at the federal penitentiary at Alcatraz. From its opening in 1933 to its closing in 1963, the inmates were not permitted to have newspapers, radios, or television. The strict and rigid inside control was disturbed only once, by the riot on May 2–4, 1946, which drew national publicity. And some suggested later that an overreaction was planned to display the authoritarian stance of Alcatraz. With the arrival of General "Vinegar" Joe Stilwell began rumors of a large-scale revolt. Then Coast Guard boats and planes circled the island and the Marines landed, and the riot was quelled after two guards and three inmates died. In actuality, six inmates armed with a rifle and a pistol taken from the gun gallery had caused all the commotion. That was the extent of inmate resistance.

There have been many other lesser known depictions of authoritarian prison societies, such as that shown in the movie released in the 1960s, *Cool Hand Luke*, starring Paul Newman, that described rather accurately the Florida road camp system in the 1950s and earlier. After a riot at the Arizona state prison at Florence in the late 1950s, Warden Frank Eyman, formerly sheriff of Pima County (Tucson), went into the yard with his own firearms and assisted in quelling the riot, then locked the ring leaders in solitary confinement, and had the doors welded shut. The Illinois state penitentiary under Warden Joseph Ragen, formerly a sheriff in southern Illinois, also exemplified the authoritarian prison. The personal domination of the institution by Warden Ragen between 1931 and 1963, when he became director of the system, was characterized by an authoritarian regime.[5]

Most correctional administrators point out that a maximum security prison must be operated on an authoritarian basis. Most prison violence consists of inmates assaulting other inmates.[6] Violent men and women from violent subcultures live in prisons. As violence behind the walls becomes acceptable behavior, prison becomes a "subculture of violence" that has to be controlled. The only way in which it can be controlled is by developing an authoritarian society managed by an authoritative administration. That does not mean that the

[5]See James B. Jacobs, *Stateville: The Penitentiary in Mass Society* (Chicago: University of Chicago Press, 1977), which traces Ragen's domination at the Illinois State penitentiary.
[6]Albert K. Cohen, "Prison Violence: The Sociological Perspective," in Albert K. Cohen, George F. Cole, and Robert G. Bailey, eds., *Prison Violence* (Lexington, Mass.: Lexington Books, 1976), p. 9.

administration has to meet violence with violence; rather the prison must have sufficient controls so that violence is contained.

Prison inmates have several salient concerns: privacy, safety, structure, support, emotional feedback, activity, and freedom and autonomy.[7] On the basis of nine hundred interviews with inmates and correctional officers in five New York prisons, Hans Toch has documented the devastating impact of the prison environment on those who must live within its walls. Inmates differ widely in their concern for physical safety, with many who become obsessive in their fear seeing survival as "fight" or "flight." If "fight" is chosen, then violence is directed toward real or imagined foes. If "flight" is chosen, the inmate is branded as a coward or a "punk" and becomes a target for further exploitation. Most aggressors come from urban environments, have been involved in violent crimes, and tend to be members of a minority. Courage is evidenced by an inmate's willingness to fight.

An inmate market system similar to that in any outside community is necessary both psychologically and economically for most prisoners to facilitate reintegration into the free community after release.[8] At present, the source of economic exchange in prison is a barter system that involves food, cigarettes, cash, privileges, and "personal services" (homosexual partnerships). The economy inside the prison will continue for as long as the residents have the psychological and financial demand and access to goods and jobs that are desired.[9] The working capital is represented by cigarettes, "green" (money), script (legitimate exchange within the prison), and transfers between men's accounts. Residents in the prison estimate that it costs $40 to $50 per month to live comfortably inside.

An interesting and popular descriptive account of prison life in Green Haven, New York, was presented in *The New Yorker* in three issues in 1977.[10] Descriptions of poor food and gang rapes with other homosexual behavior appeared in the first issue. The ability to buy groceries and clothing and other services, the lack of which constitutes deprivation, which most were not willing to tolerate on the streets, was discussed in the second installment. The third installment discussed the routines of prison life and relations with the police and parole board and indicated that people who have not experienced prison life would not believe it and could not appreciate it.

The "prison syndrome" or enforced acquiescence, passivity, anxiety, and hopelessness would also appear generally to exert negative self-concept. A study of autonomic or involuntary reactions was conducted on 236 inmates at the federal correctional institution at Tallahassee, of whom 118 were controls, to

[7]Hans Toch, *Living in Prison: The Ecology of Survival* (New York: The Free Press, 1977), p. 144.

[8]H. Strange and J. McCrory, "Bulls and Bears in the Cell Block," *Society,* Vol. 11, no. 5 (July–August 1974), pp. 51–59.

[9]Sandra E. Gleason, "Hustling: The 'Inside' Economy of a Prison," *Federal Probation,* Vol. 42, no. 2 (June 1978), pp. 32–40.

[10]Susan Sheehan, "Annals of Crime: A Prison and a Prisoner. I. Maximum Security," *The New Yorker,* October 24, 1977, pp. 48–142; "Annals of Crime: A Prison and a Prisoner." II. "Same as on the Street," *The New Yorker,* October 31, 1977, pp. 46–99. "Annals of Crime: A Prison and a Prisoner. III. You Wouldn't Understand," *The New Yorker,* November 7, 1977, pp. 124–303.

measure the effects of stress on the basis of systolic blood pressure, diastolic blood pressure, galvanic skin response, and finger pulse volume.[11] Results showed that autonomic response was greatest to a stimulus that affected the inmates' sense of adequacy and personal identity and was least vis-à-vis negative self-concept.

The mortification process, or reduced feelings and appetites as in death, occurs in prisons and other institutions, first, with the barriers between the inmate and the outside world.[12] Admission programming is the second phase of mortification, in which self-identification is curtailed by stripping; being sprayed with deodorants, taking showers, standing naked, and being strip searched; posing for mug shots; being issued prison clothing; and losing one's name. The third phase of mortification involves humiliating postures and verbal responses, such as submitting to regular searches and shakedowns, clothing of substandard quality and design, and other reminders of subservient status. Fourth, the invasion of self-territory in which the inmate cannot claim his or her personal space, not even the cell, and continuous searches and regimentation is degrading, with humiliating postures and invasions of privacy characterized by open supervision of toilet and other personal activities. The fifth phase of mortification is the disruption of the usual relationship between the actor and his or her actions, such as the development of the inmate code, prison customs and folkways, and the "pains of imprisonment" outlined by Gresham M. Sykes, discussed later in this chapter.

LACK OF PRIVACY

One of the most dehumanizing aspects of maximum security prisons is the complete lack of privacy. In a well-controlled maximum security prison, a resident can never escape supervision. The toilets are in one large space where full visibility is available to the officers. The closest one can come to privacy is in disciplinary segregation, where the inmate is also subject to check whenever the supervising officer decides to see what is going on the cell.

A rather uncomfortable problem occurred regarding privacy when the State of New York was prevented from obtaining race and sex information on application and other personnel forms. Male officers were assigned to the women's prison at New Bedford. When they began supervising showers and other personal activities in accordance with their assigned duties, the inmates rebelled. The problem had to be worked out informally.

In any case, there is no privacy in prison. In the free community, many people have said, "I'm 'peopled out' and want to be alone for a while." This is not possible in prison.

---

[11]Jorge L. Gonzalez, Marva P. Dawkins, and Jack E. Hokanson, "Autonomic Reactions to Stress: The Effects of Several Therapy Analogues on Prisoners," *Criminal Justice and Behavior*, Vol. 6, no. 2 (June 1979), pp. 107–17.

[12]Goffman, *Asylums*, pp. 1–40.

Lonely inmate at the State Prison of Southern Michigan.
Courtesy of the Michigan Department of Corrections.

DEPRIVATION

Probably the best discussion of deprivation in prison is Gresham M. Sykes chapter, "The Pains of Imprisonment," in his *The Society of Captives*.[13] He discusses (1) the deprivation of liberty, (2) the deprivation of goods and services, (3) the deprivation of heterosexual relationships, (4) the deprivation of self-concept and autonomy, and (5) the deprivation of security. The prisoner is not free to go downtown for dinner, take in a ball game, or take a two-week vacation. The inmate cannot have a prime steak, join a civic club, get a "styled" haircut, have specialized medical attention, or enjoy other high-quality goods and services. Sexual activity of any sort is forbidden. Only a few institutions in the United States are co-correctional, that is, housing men and women in the same institu-

[13]Gresham M. Sykes, "The Pains of Imprisonment," in *The Society of Captives, a Study of a Maximum Security Prison* (Princeton, N.J.: Princeton University Press, 1958), pp. 63–83.

tion, the first being a facility in Framingham, Massachusetts, that opened in 1972; although most prisons prior to 1870 housed men and women in the same institution, sexual activity was discouraged. Institutions in many other countries, however, do permit sexual activity, particularly those in Scandinavia. At Ringe, in Denmark, for example, the sixty men and thirty women about ages 18 to 22 housed there can spend the night in each other's cells. Elsewhere prisoners cannot decide when they will go to bed or rise in the morning, cannot decide their menus or time of eating, and generally lack autonomy over their schedules. Security is lacking, too, because prison is a subculture of violence and one's safety there is always in jeopardy.

In a homogeneous young male population in the federal correctional institution at El Reno, Nevada, violent behavior was close to becoming the norm in the survival-of-the-fittest socialization that existed there.[14] When a group of older inmates from the federal correctional institution at Texarkana was brought to El Reno and a group of younger inmates was transferred to Texarkana from El Reno, the violence level at El Reno dropped, but the violence level at Texarkana rose initially, followed by a general leveling off. Institutional age heterogeneity tends to provide more informal inmate social control than does a homogeneous younger population.

BY THE NUMBERS

Everything in a maximum security prison is regimented—by the numbers. This regimentation is necessary for control. Groups of residents are marched to and from cell blocks on their work assignments, the dining hall, and other areas. A rigid pass system controls movement inside the walls. Mass treatment is needed for the efficient operation of the maximum security prison.

The activity schedule is primarily a custodial responsibility, but it involves all departments, offices, and activities in the prison. It is the time schedule for rising in the morning, having breakfast, reporting to assignments, taking the noon meal, reporting back to the assignment in the afternoon (the major count being taken around 4:00 P.M.), eating the evening meal, going to the yard for recreational pursuits depending upon the season, returning to the cell in the evening, and administering "lights out" in the cells. Yard privileges for recreation depend upon the time of year: light into the evening during the summers permits outdoor activity, but the early sunsets in the winters preclude yard privileges during that season. Visibility is important in a maximum custody prison. Also, "lights out" refers only to lighting in the cells. The lights never go out in prison.

The activity schedule is a sensitive issue. All departments, offices, and activities have to be coordinated. In one federal correctional institution holding six hundred men in 1970, it was necessary to serve the evening meal a half-hour

---

[14]Jerome Mabli, Charles S. D. Holley, Judy Patrick, and Justine Walls, "Age and Prison Violence: Increasing Age Heterogeneity as a Violence-Reducing Strategy in Prisons," *Criminal Justice and Behavior*, Vol. 6, no. 2 (June 1979), pp. 175–86.

earlier. It took three days to work out the activity schedule and get all departments, offices, and activities in agreement and cooperating.

Regimentation is needed to control a group of people who have not known discipline, whose behavior is unpredictable, and whose backgrounds lack much in the way of orderly living.

The autobiographies of nineteen inmates in a Midwestern prison consistently included two themes: (1) a poor home environment when young, one lacking in affection or discipline and characterized by conflict between parents or a broken home and parental drinking or other personal problems, and (2) subpar school performance, behavioral problems, difficulty in relating with peers, and dropping out of school.[15] Because of the time spent in institutions, learning to adjust in normal society is difficult. The regimentation of the prison is inadequate as a means of preparing anybody for a responsible role in the larger society after release from prison. It seems to be paradoxical to remove someone from the community because he or she has been in "bad company" and put that person in a prison!

THE INMATE CODE

The inmate code in the maximum security prison is made up of the customs and folkways by which the residents protect themselves from the repressive measures of the administration: the inmates have nothing to do with the administration or correctional officers, and they do not "squeal" or "snitch" on fellow inmates.

This inmate code, which is fundamental to prisoner organization, manifests itself in a type of informal control, in which inmates do not interfere with inmate interests, do serve the least possible time by not being subject to disciplinary action, and enjoy the greatest possible number of pleasures and privileges. Other maxims are "Never rat on a con," "Don't be nosey," "Don't have a loose lip," "Keep off a man's back," and "Don't put a guy on the spot," all of which adds up to being loyal to the inmate group.[16] Other tenets are "Don't lose your head," "Play it cool," "Do your own time," "Don't bring heat," "Don't exploit inmates," "Don't break your word," "Don't steal from cons," "Don't sell favors," "Don't be a racketeer," "Don't welsh on debts," "Be right," "Don't weaken," "Don't whine," "Don't cop out," "Be tough," "Be a man," "Don't be a sucker," "Skim it off the top," "Never talk to a screw" (guard, hack), "Have a connection," and "Be sharp."[17]

Inmates learn the code by word of mouth. It is basic to the prison subculture. Prisoners are guided by it in the prison and after they are released. This part of the prison culture becomes a permanent part of the personality of long-term institutionalized prisoners. The code is frequently violated by weaker prisoners and by those who are trying to manipulate a good recommendation for

---

[15]Dae H. Chang and Warren B. Armstrong, eds., *The Prison: Voices from Inside* (Cambridge, Mass.: Schenkman Publishing Company, 1972), 331 pp.

[16]Edwin H. Sutherland and Donald R. Cressey, *Criminology*, 9th ed. (Philadelphia: J. B. Lippincott Company, 1974), p. 532.

[17]Ibid., p. 532.

early parole. These "infractions" are dealt with harshly when other inmates discover them. In fact, this was basic to the thirty-three killings in the riot at the New Mexico prison at Santa Fe, February 15–16, 1980, when inmates broke into the cell block where "informants" and other inmates needing protection were being held. The thirty-three dead men had been informants. Some were so burned and mangled that they could not be identified.

Repeating, there is an informal type of social control maintained by the inmates, particularly the long-termers. The inmate code is basic to this control. When this informal social control breaks down, riots and disturbances ensue.

INMATE-STAFF RELATIONS

One study of prison experiences as seen from the polarized positions of an habitual criminal and a prisoner counselor provides some insights as to the relationship between treatment personnel and inmates in the prison.[18] The opposing yet independent perspectives and relationship between inmates and prison officials can be interpreted as a strong caste system. Rehabilitation in a maximum custody prison may be nearly impossible, because the caste system impedes communication and attempts at rehabilitative efforts. Prison life is frequently a manipulative game played by both inmates and staff.

A study of 194 inmates in the Glen Mills School for Boys in Pennsylvania attempted to study staff-inmate relationships in conflicts.[19] Inmates who had favorable relationships with the staff tended to promote conventional behavior; inmates with closer ties with other inmates tended to perpetuate delinquent and deviant behavior. The social backgrounds of the inmates determined to some extent the strength of ties to other inmates.

Staff and residents of correctional institutions in Kentucky showed significant differences in their perceptions of the institutional environment.[20] Residents of maximum security institutions have less favorable perceptions of the institution and resist attempts at "treatment." The relationship between staff and inmates was better in the less secure institutions. The staff also scored very low on scales that measured involvement and support of the institution and acceptance of the residents. When poor communication and mutual disrespect exist between residents and staff, effective treatment is difficult to achieve.

Discipline must be viewed as an extension of the treatment program in which custody-treatment conflicts can be resolved. This can occur only when the role conflicts between the custodial and treatment staff are resolved so that they can function harmoniously. This can occur when group interaction programs are used with prison discipline as part of the treatment process. Prison discipline

---

[18]A. J. Manocchio and J. Dunn, *Time Game—Two Views of a Prison* (New York: Dell Publishing Company, 1970), 267 pp.

[19]B. Schwartz, "Peer vs. Authority Effects in a Correctional Community," *Criminology*, Vol. 11, no. 2 (August 1973), pp. 233–57.

[20]C. D. Scully and M. R. Young, *Resident and Staff Perceptions of the Prison Environment—Psycho-Social Evaluation* (Frankfort: Kentucky Department of Corrections, 1973), 28 pp.

is the focal point around which the various groups in the prison revolve and interact.[21]

Many inmates and staff can function harmoniously and spontaneously on a private, one-to-one basis, but they become conflicted when role expectations of their respective group positions are involved.[22] When an inmate and an officer know each other and become friends, they function as individual partners in the relationship. On the other hand, the impersonal relationship between staff and inmates reverts to role expectation and lack of communication.

Mortality from all causes is lower among prison inmates than it is for a male population of similar age outside, frequently because many terminally ill inmates are released on "medical parole" to be taken care of at home. The probability that they would die from natural causes is about three-fifths of what it would be on the outside and about one-twentieth of what it would be from accidental causes.[23] General pressures and negative influence from excessive staff control reduces bodily and mental processes.

Training correctional officers to function in a helping relationship with inmates can improve the rehabilitative efforts of an institution, as demonstrated by one training program implemented in South Carolina.[24] Criteria of the program included three therapeutic conditions: (1) genuineness, referring to an honest openness to the helping relationship; (2) nonpossessive warmth as a precondition for helping people; and (3) accurate empathy, involving sensitivity as to what a person being helped is feeling and the ability to communicate this understanding. After the counseling program, the correctional officers significantly increased their ability to provide effective counseling and support for the institutional program.

Yochelson and Samenow at St. Elizabeth's Hospital in Washington, D.C., have identified what they call the "criminal personality," one whom nobody can trust and who fails to respond to the orthodox approaches of treatment. They have identified fifty-two errors in thinking that permeate these individuals' behaviors.[25] The basic pattern is lying constantly. Criminals are victimizers rather than victims of society. They possess extreme fearfulness, which results in striking-back responses. Extreme and persistent anger is sometimes expressed outwardly, but it always boils from within. Sometimes this is accompanied by feelings of worthlessness and a belief that life is hopeless, which accounts for some death row inmates who want to die. Superoptimism, on the other hand, con-

---

[21]D. McLaren, "Cons, Hacks, and Educated Screws—The Prison Politics of Discipline and Rehabilitation," *Canadian Journal of Criminology and Corrections*, Vol. 15, no. 1 (January 1973), pp. 25–38.

[22]Stanton Wheeler, "Role Conflict in Correctional Communities," in Donald R. Cressey, ed., *The Prison: Studies in Institutional Organization and Change* (New York: Holt, Rinehart and Winston, 1961), pp. 229–59.

[23]Sawyer Sylvester, John P. Reede, and David O. Nelson, *Prison Homicide*, (New York: Spectrum Publications, 1977), 126 pp.

[24]William D. Leeke and Hubert M. Clements, *Correctional Officer as a Counselor—A Promising Development in Manpower Utilization* (Columbia: South Carolina Department of Corrections, n.d., ca. 1973), 11 pp.

[25]Samuel Yochelson and Stanton E. Samenow, *The Criminal Personality*, Vol. 1 (New York: Jason Aronson, 1976), pp. 251–406.

vinces them that they can commit a crime and not be caught. This "criminal personality" is difficult to communicate and associate with in a *positive manner.*

A California study has shown that black inmates tend to have liberal political attitudes, whereas white inmates tend to have conservative political attitudes.[26] White guards have even more conservative political attitudes. These differences between the conservative attitudes of white prison guards and inmates, on the one hand, and liberal attitudes of black inmates, on the other, create social tension and conflict in prisons and·correctional institutions, which intensifies the already wide social distance between white guards and black inmates to a greater extent than the social distance between white guards and white inmates. White guards become socially isolated, black inmates become socially isolated and dichotomized from all the guards, and white inmates tend to be isolated from both groups, somewhere in between the more extreme groups. Racial differences seem to be more important than status.

Some career criminal subgroups, such as the younger hard-core inmates, present major disciplinary problems in prison.[27] Career criminals generally wait longer to become involved in treatment programs, even though they participate in these programs at a rate similar to that of all other prisoners. Less than a quarter of all prisoners needing special treatment, such as rehabilitation from drugs or alcohol problems, actually receive such treatment.

The U.S. Supreme Court has held that correctional authorities can prevent prisoners' unions from meeting and organizing inmates.[28] It upheld a North Carolina prison regulation that forbade solicitation for membership, holding of union meetings, or delivery of bulk mail within the walls.[29] Normal First Amendment rights of free association may be withdrawn or limited in prison for good cause. Maintaining order is good cause.

In summary, inmate-staff relations take on a variety of aspects. The role conflicts find their way into disciplinary problems, legal action, and violence. In the helping professions, in which corrections must take the treatment and rehabilitative approaches, conflict has to be reduced. Cooperation between custody and the rest of the staff can be achieved by better communication and participation in all activities.

DANGER

Living in almost constant fear of assault is emotionally exhausting for many residents of maximum security prisons. Many weaker inmates are subjected to homosexual attacks and gang rapes. Others are subjected to highjacking on the

---

[26]Lonnie H. Athens, "Differences in the Liberal-Conservative Political Attitudes of Prison Guards and Felons," *International Journal of Group Tensions,* Vol. 5, no. 3 (September 1975), pp. 143–55.

[27]P. K. Honig, "The Prison Experience of Career Criminals: Current Practice and Future Considerations," *Selected Rand Abstracts,* Vol. 16, no. 3 (January–February 1978), p. 45.

[28]"Prisoners' Unions Barred by Court," *LEAA Newsletter,* Vol. 6, no. 12 (August 1977), p. 13; "Supreme Court Strikes Down Inmate Unions," *Corrections Magazine,* Vol. 3, no. 4 (December 1977), p. 58.

[29]*Jones* v. *North Carolina Prisoners Labor Union, Inc.,* No. 75-1874 (1977).

yard after store day. Minor arguments and personal differences can result in stabbings.

In a study of prison homicides in 1973, the victimization rate for inmates nationally was 7.44 per 10,000 inmates. The rate for the U.S. Bureau of Prisons institutions was 5.43 deaths per 10,000 inmates. The victimization rate of staff was 2.62 per 10,000 staff members.[30]

The maximum custody prison forces physical contact between antagonists because these prisons permit no option of withdrawing or leaving. The fight-flight premise is a frequent response to aggression.[31] Either the victim turns away and leaves the scene, in which case he becomes vulnerable to further aggression, or he fights. When other men sense fear, they tend to exploit it by further aggression. Frequently, also, fear is camouflaged by an angry and explosive reaction, which precipitates a fight even when the victim would prefer flight. Table 6-1 shows some *reported* violence figures for 1974 and 1975.

The victimization rate in prison is difficult to establish because many victims are afraid to report aggressors to the authorities.[32] The victims are disproportionately white, young, and smaller than the aggressors, while the aggressors tend to be black and older and have a record of more serious assaultive felonies.[33] Of course, both aggressors and victims come from all races, all ages, and all backgrounds.

A state-raised youth who has grown up in juvenile and early-adult institutions holds violence as the proper mode of settling an argument.[34] Second, memberships in cliques developed in institutions also command loyalties and define values that differ from those held in the free community. Third, the homosexual culture defines an exploitative and violent caste system in which sexual conduct is based on physical ability to exercise force and the deprivation of masculinity that derives from subjugation. Fourth, it is a fantasy from the "streets" that institutionalization is the "real world," and they see "the streets" from the perspective of the institution. Success comes with willingness to fight.

At the Massachusetts correctional institution at Walpole, which houses approximately six hundred men, in the two-year period from January 1972 to January 1974, there were three mass escapes attempted and over two hundred felonies committed. Of these felonies, there were eleven murders and five other violent deaths, twenty-nine attempted murders, thirty-five violent assaults on inmates and correctional officers other than simply fighting, three explosions caused by inmate activity that resulted in two inmate deaths, and three cases of inmates taking correctional officers hostage.[35] During this same period, there were four major and four minor disturbances at a cost of over $2 million.

[30]Sawyer F. Sylvester, John H. Reed, and David O. Nelson, *Prison Homicide* (New York: Spectrum Publications, 1977), p. 5.

[31]Toch, *Living in Prison*, pp. 157–78.

[32]Ibid., p. 144.

[33]A. J. Davis, "Sexual Assaults in the Philadelphia Prison System and Sheriff's Vans," *Trans-Action*, Vol. 6 (1968), pp. 8–12.

[34]John Irwin, *The Felon* (Englewood Cliffs, N.J.: Prentice-Hall, Inc., 1970), pp. 26–29.

[35]William A. Miller, "Crime in Our Prisons," *FBI Law Enforcement Bulletin*, Vol. 46, no. 10 (October 1977), p. 6.

Table 6-1 Violence Statistics for 1974 and 1975

STATE	INMATES KILLED BY INMATES		INMATE SUICIDES		INMATES KILLED IN DISTURBANCES OR RIOTS		STAFF KILLED BY INMATES		STAFF KILLED IN DISTURBANCES OR RIOTS	
	1974	1975	1974	1975	1974	1975	1974	1975	1974	1975
Alabama										
Alaska	0	0	0	0	0	0	0	0	0	0
Arizona	0	2	0	2	0	0	0	1[a]	0	0
Arkansas	0	1	0	0	0	0	0	0	0	0
California	23	17	14	9	0	0	0	0	0	0
Colorado	3	3	0	3	0	0	0	0	0	0
Connecticut	0	0	4[b]	0	0	0	0	0	0	0
Delaware	0	0	0	0	0	0	0	0	0	0
District of Columbia	4	4	0	0	1	0	0	0	0	0
Florida	2	8	0	3	0	0	0	0	0	0
Georgia	11	6	4	2	0	0	0	0	0	0
Hawaii										
Idaho										
Illinois	0	1	5	2	0	1[c]	0	0	0	0
Indiana	1	1	1	0	0	0	0	0	0	0
Iowa	1	2	2	4	0	0	0	0	0	0
Kansas	4	3	0	1	0	0	0	0	0	0
Kentucky	1	2	7	3	0	0	0	0	0	0
Louisiana	10	11	2[d]	0	0	2	0	0	0	0
Maine	0	1	0	2	0	0	0	0	0	0
Maryland	0	3	3	2	0	0	0	0	0	0
Massachusetts	0	0	1	0	0	0	0	0	0	0
Michigan	0	2	0	1	0	0	0	0	0	0
Minnesota	1	3	6	1	0	0	0	0	0	0
Mississippi										
Missouri	6	4	1	1	0	0	0	1	0	0
Montana	1	0	1	0	0	0	0	0	0	0
Nebraska	1	0	2	1	0	0	0	0	0	0
Nevada	1	0	0	0	0	0	0	0	0	0
New Hampshire	1	0	0	0	0	0	0	0	0	0
New Jersey	0	0	1	1	0	1	0	0	0	0
New Mexico	0	1	1	1	0	0	0	0	0	0
New York	2	2	5	4	0	0	0	0	0	0
North Carolina										
North Dakota	0	0	0	0	0	0	0	0	0	0
Ohio	2	2	0	2	0	0	0	0	0	0
Oklahoma	3	1	3	0	0	0	0	0	0	0
Oregon	0	0	0	0	0	0	0	0	0	0
Pennsylvania	4	1	2	3	0	0	0	0	0	0
Rhode Island	0	1	1	2	0	0	0	0	0	0
South Carolina	0	5	1	1	0	0	0	0	0	0

Table 6-1 *(Continued)*

STATE	INMATES KILLED BY INMATES		INMATE SUICIDES		INMATES KILLED IN DISTURBANCES OR RIOTS		STAFF KILLED BY INMATES		STAFF KILLED IN DISTURBANCES OR RIOTS	
	1974	1975	1974	1975	1974	1975	1974	1975	1974	1975
South Dakota										
Tennessee	3	2	2	3	0	1	0	0	0	0
Texas	1	1	7	10	1	0	0	0	2	0
Utah	2	0	3	1	0	0	0	0	0	0
Vermont	0	0	0	0	0	0	0	0	0	0
Virginia	4	0	1	1	4e	0	0	2	0	2
Washington	5	3	3	7	0	0	5	7	NA	NA
West Virginia	0	0	0	1	0	0	0	0	0	0
Wisconsin	1	0	0	1	0	0	0	0	0	0
Wyoming	0	0	1	0	0	0	0	1	0	0
Federal Bureau of Prisons	16	18	5	4	0	0	1	2	0	0

aThis occurred in a juvenile institution.
bOccurred in correctional centers.
cInmate also reflected in "Inmates Killed by Inmates."
dOne occurred while on escape.
eIncludes escape attempts.
SOURCE: *Corrections Compendium,* Vol. II, no. 8 (February 1977), published by CONtact, Lincoln, Nebraska.

Violence is caused by (1) violence-prone inmates; (2) the lower-class value system that emphasizes "masculinity," "toughness," and violence; (3) the use of violence as a means of control within the prison; (4) the anonymity of large prisons; and (5) the utility of violence in furthering inmate objectives, such as better living conditions.[36] Needless to say, constant fear of danger is emotionally draining. It has resulted in unwilling but complete submission to homosexual advances, emotional disturbances, and suicides.

ASSAULTS AND MURDERS

Assaults in prison are frequently generated by homosexual activities and its ramifications, debts from gambling, perceived personal insults against the individual or his family, and "snitching," "ratting," or otherwise informing the administration or custodial force of illicit inmate activities.

Homicides in prison appear to be grossly underreported. There were 116 homicides reported officially from the federal penitentiary at Lewisburg for

[36]John Conrad, "Violence in Prison," *The Annals of the American Academy of Political and Social Science,* Vol. 364 (1980), pp. 113–19.

the fifteen months prior to May 1977, which resulted in a change of administration in that institution. An inmate told a judge, however, 25 homicides a year is "not bad" in a prison of 1,600 population and when a "hit can be bought for two cartons of cigarettes, when the individual, himself, does not want to do it." Warden Ken McKeller of the maximum security unit of the South Carolina state prison at Columbia has told of an incident that occurred at his institution in December 1976, when he was in the yard and observed an inmate with a knife chasing another inmate. Since an officer was not immediately available, Warden McKeller took up the chase, but as they went around the corner of a building, he could not see them. When he rounded the corner, one inmate was lying on the ground, having been stabbed by a knife, and subsequently died. Several hundred residents or inmates were in the area but they "Didn't see nothin'." The offender was subsequently convicted. Realistically, few inmate homicides can be proved in a criminal court because of lack of witnesses. Some 107 homicides were reported in 1977, but most correctional administrators agree that these may be the only cases that could be proved and that the real homicide rate is much higher.

In one survey of homicides in prison in 1973, 170 prisons were contacted, and 126 responses indicated that 54 institutions had 128 murders that year. There were 78 inmates killed by other inmates, of whom 49 were killed by an individual assailant, 29 were killed by multiple assailants, and the assailants of 35 inmates were unidentified.[37] Ten inmates killed staff members, 1 staff member shot another officer, and 3 staff members had killed inmates. Size, security status, and, to a lesser extent, density of the institutional population are related to these homicides. One conclusion was that the homicide rate is only about one-twentieth that of assaults, the rate of murders being about that expected of a similar number of men of that age group in the general population.[38] About twice the number of suicides occurs in prison as would be expected from a population of similar size outside.

As indicated previously, homicide in a sample of prisons studies (1974) was found to occur at a rate of 7.44 per 10,000 inmates in state correctional institutions and 5.43 per 10,000 in federal institutions.[39] This compared with a Uniform Crime Report homicide rate in 1974, or 0.97 per 10,000 citizens in the general public. There were five correctional staff killed in 1977 and eleven in 1978 whose families received compensation under the Public Safety Officers' Benefit Act administered by LEAA.[40]

The 128 reported homicides committed in 1973 in state and federal prisons indicates that staff was victimized much less than the inmates.[41] Institutional staff committed four homicides in that year, three justifiable in escape attempts and one excusable in an accident. Of the 124 homicides committed by

[37]Sylvester et al., *Prison Homicide*, p. 29.

[38]Ibid., p. 73.

[39]Samuel Sylvester, *Homicides in Prisons*, Grant 74-NI-99-0022 (Washington, D.C.: National Institute of Law Enforcement and Criminal Justice, 1976), p. 7.

[40]*Corrections Compendium*, Vol. 3, no. 14 (September 1979), p. 9.

[41]Wendy P. Wolfson, *The Patterns of Prison Homicide* (Ann Arbor, Mich.: University Microfilms, 1978), 78 pp.

inmates, there were 113 inmate victims and 11 staff victims. Eight (7 percent) of the inmate homicides were the result of homosexual jealousy, 29 were related to personal disputes, and 21 were related to violations of the inmate code, such as informing on another inmate.

On August 9, 1978, Gary Bowdach, a convicted murderer, testified before the U.S. Senate Permanent Subcommittee on Investigations that there were many killings at the federal penitentiary at Atlanta and described the killing methods as "degutted," "decapitated," "hatcheted," burning by throwing cleaning fluid that was then ignited in a cell, and simple stabbing.[42] Further, he pointed out that "everybody has a weapon except the guards."

In a psychiatric study of thirty-six aggressors, of thirty historical or background factors noted, the most frequent behaviors in the nine most violent men were as follows:[43]

1. Repeated violent behavior with little provocation.
2. Usually violent without an accomplice.
3. Frequent behavior requiring forcible restraint.
4. Frequent fighting with a weapon.
5. Carrying a weapon for prolonged periods "for protection."
6. History of repeated violence between parents.
7. Serious self-perpetrated accidents.
8. Self-mutilation.
9. Bisexual behavior.
10. Hypersensitivity to humiliating names.
11. Hypersexual behavior.
12. History of cruelty to domestic animals.
13. Conspicuous lack of repression of childhood sexuality.
14. Relative absence of fantasy formation.

These factors should be helpful in evaluating the violent predisposition in prison inmates.

One set of "official statistics" set the number of homicides for 1973 at 107. A survey by *Corrections Compendium* for 1974 revealed 114 homicides reported in forty-four states. As can be seen, the true number of inmate homicides is difficult to ascertain. One state with a large prison system lost 13 in one year, but not one was reported in the news media or in official statistics. On the basis of informal conversations with prison administrators, this writer suspects that the "official" statistics on a national basis could be doubled to approach a more accurate figure. It is noted that the better systems, like those at the U.S. Bureau

---

[42]"Confessed Killer Gives Congress Details on Inmate Murders at Federal Prison at Atlanta," *Corrections Digest,* Vol. 9, no. 16 (August 11, 1978), pp. 7–8.

[43]August F. Kinzel, Lewis Merklin, and Warren B. Miller, "Violence in Prison," in *A Handbook of Correctional Psychiatry,* Vol. 1 (Washington, D.C.: U.S. Bureau of Prisons, 1968), pp. 19–20.

of Prisons and in California, report a significantly higher rate of inmate homicides than do other jurisdictions.

SEXUAL ATTACKS

Sexual attacks by aggressors against their targets appear to be a frequent type of assault in the maximum security prison. The young, weak first-timer is generally the target. In many cases, he has already been "made" in the county jail, being forced, as in the case of some heterosexual rapes in the outside community, either to submit or to be beaten and possibly killed. When word gets around in the prison that he has already been "made" in the jail, he quickly becomes a target for homosexual aggressors.

Even if a young, weak, first-timer has not been "made" in the jail and has been protected, he still becomes a target for homosexual aggressors. Sometimes, these young people may decide that being a partner to one person in exchange for protection is better than being a general target for everybody. Unfortunately, even when such a partnership is made and the young man becomes the older man's "kid," sometimes the older man may farm out his "kid" in payment of debts, obligations, and favors. Sometimes, this situation winds up in assaults when the "kid" does not want to be farmed out.[44] (In *Cowart* v. *United States*, the inmate, Cowart, was "farmed out" by his "daddy," hit the aggressor in the mouth whereupon Cowart was stabbed, which resulted in the loss of oxygen to his brain. The family sought damages for his resulting retardation.)

Gang rapes also occur when a group of homosexual aggressors attacks a single, young, weak, resident. It is a frequent occurrence in the weight-lifting room or other small area in which officers are occasionally not present, particularly when a shift happens to be short.

A study of 152 incidents of homosexual aggression in the New York State prisons showed that about half (75) featured physical violence.[45] About 50 percent of this violence came from aggressors attempting to rape others, and 50 percent came from men who were reacting to aggression. Most men interviewed considered fighting as the best way to make the aggressors leave them alone. Exploitative violence on the part of the aggressors can be traced to cultural patterns learned on the streets where strong-arming, "mugging," and other types of assault for gain or satisfaction are part of the subculture of violence.

Victims have unanimously held that the only defense against rape in prison is to respond violently.[46] Alternative traditional responses have been largely ineffective.

---

[44]*Cowart* v. *United States*, Civil Action No. C75-1568-A (D.C. Northern District of Georgia, Atlanta, March 1977).

[45]Daniel Lockwood, *Maintaining Manhood: Prison Violence Precipitated by Aggressive Sexual Approaches*, State University College at Utica/Rome, New York, prepared for the Academy of Criminal Justice Sciences, March 1978, p. 39. From Daniel Lockwood, "Sexual Aggression Among Male Prisoners," unpublished Ph.D. dissertation, State University of New York at Albany, 1977.

[46]Daniel Lockwood, *Prison Sexual Violence* (New York: Elsevier-North Holland, 1980).

SELF-INJURIOUS BEHAVIOR
AND SUICIDE

Suicide and self-mutilation, sometimes in the form of attempted suicide, occur in prison populations about twice as frequently as they do in the general population of the United States. Many of these incidents are the result of gang rapes or otherwise forceful assaults by homosexual aggressors, which leads to a self-concept of worthlessness and lack of manhood.

When inmates are so demoralized that they are unable to rebel, sometimes self-mutilation occurs. For example, four inmates broke their own legs to escape quarry work at the Dallas prison camp on March 25, 1940. At the Buford Prison in Georgia, thirty inmates slashed their heel tendons on December 26, 1951, to thwart their captors attempting to make them work the quarry there. At the Louisiana state prison, seventeen inmates slashed their arms on January 29, 1954. This type of self-mutilation occurs generally when conditions would ordinarily precipitate a riot, but where the inmates are too demoralized to fight back.

In May and June 1978, three men in Colorado committed suicide and twenty other attempts at suicide were recorded.[47] All events had taken place in Cell House 3, the disciplinary unit, where men spent twenty-two hours a day in 7 foot by 10 foot cells. Inmates interviewed said that the unit was all they saw and that they "couldn't take it no more."[48]

The literature on suicides is divided among suicides, suicide gestures, (unsuccessful suicide attempts) and suicide threats.[49] The Minnesota Multiphasic Personality Inventory was used in a study of 40 inmates making consecutive suicide gestures as compared with 323 airmen of the nonpsychiatric population. There were 258 adult males of the general nonpsychiatric population, and 538 psychiatric patients seen at the Chanute Air Force Base psychiatric clinic. The study revealed that the MMPI can be of value when used as a screening device in predicting the potential of suicide gestures of an individual.

EXECUTIONS IN THE INSTITUTION

Death row prisoners are impotent where custody is the vehicle by which men are kept alive and safe for eventual execution.[50] Psychological survival involves avoiding the slightest deviation where safety is a matter of nonaction. The death sentence dramatically affects the social environment of death row in which the

---

[47]"Colorado Suicides: Getting Their Lollipops," *Investigative Newsletter on Institutions/Alternatives*, Vol. 1, no. 7 (July 1978), pp. 11–12.

[48]Ibid., p. 12.

[49]*Cloyd v. Martin;* Jack R. Alvord, and Gary C. Horner, "The Prediction of Suicide Gestures," *Corrective Psychiatry and Journal of Social Therapy*, Vol. 34, no. 3 (Fall 1968), pp. 153–65.

[50]Robert Johnson, "Warehousing for Death," *Investigative Newsletter on Institutions/Alternatives*, Vol. 2, no. 6 (June 1979), pp. 1–10.

keepers and the kept become polarized in an atmosphere of tension and fear and where the sentence, itself, becomes a source of stress and suffering for the condemned. Medical and emotional needs take a back seat to the impersonal requirements of custody. Death row prisoners see that the ritual of execution and the rubric of legal punishment does nothing to alter its cruelty.[51]

The institution is generally tense for several days after an execution. This writer visited several prisons in the 1950s and early 1960s when executions were practiced, and the general attitudes of inmates immediately following the executions were resentful and reserved. There were no disturbances. The inmate population was simply "up tight" and "on edge" for several days after the execution.

CONCLUSIONS

The maximum security prison promotes a subculture of violence, the intensity of the violence diminishing as custody is reduced and a community culture evolves; too, persons who present fewer security risks and exhibit fewer assaultive tendencies are those selected for the reduced custody environment. The maximum security prison employs an authoritarian regime that has been termed a "miniature totalitarian state." There is no privacy. There is deprivation of goods and services, homosexual relationships abound, and all phases of normal life are stifled. Regimentation is necessary to control these violent people in large numbers. The "inmate code" is developed by inmate society for its members' own protection. Yet society in a maximum security institution is punctuated with assaults, homicides, and suicides. These are some of the reasons that the American Correctional Association has recommended that no prison be built to house more than six hundred inmates. This, however, has been attacked by some administrators and legislators as being too costly a standard. An alternative appears to be better selection and training of all personnel and including the correctional officers in the total program.

CHAPTER QUESTIONS

6-1. What is the mortification process in maximum security prisons?

6-2. What are the deprivations in maximum security prisons to which Sykes refers as the "pains of imprisonment"?

6-3. Why is regimentation necessary in a maximum security prison and what does it do to the residents?

6-4. What is the inmate code?

6-5. What are some significant characteristics of inmate-staff relations?

6-6. What are the results of living in almost constant fear of attacks and gang rapes in maximum custody institutions?

[51]Ibid., p. 10.

6-7.   What is the extent of assaults and homicides in American prisons?

6-8.   Are sexual attacks by aggressors against their targets prevalent in maximum security prisons?

6-9.   What is the extent of suicide and self-mutilation in prisons?

6-10.   What effect do executions in prison have on the residents?

7

RIOTS
AND
DISTURBANCES

Riots and disturbances by large and small groups of men have always been part of prison life. Riots are costly in terms of lives and property damage and are frequently reported by the news media; other disturbances such as hunger strikes, self-mutilation, and work stoppages are less costly and less sensational.

The colonial period of American criminal justice was characterized by free use of the stocks, pillory, whipping, and capital punishment. The prison was introduced to provide humane methods of dealing with offenders. The trend toward the prison, then, was considered to be humanitarian movement. The first prison in colonial America was Newgate, in Connecticut at Simsbury, about 50 miles north of New Haven. Administration buildings were constructed near the shaft of an abandoned copper mine and Captain John Viets was appointed keeper; first-offenders were sentenced for ten years, and second-offenders were sentenced for life. Men, women, and children were kept together in the old mine. The first prisoner was John Hinson, admitted December 2, 1773.[1] He escaped on December 20 with the help of a "strong-handed Phyllis," who worked on one of the neighboring farms and hoisted John up the shaft on a

---

[1]Orlando F. Lewis, *The Development of American Prisons and Prison Customs, 1776–1845* (Montclair, N.J.: Patterson Smith, 1967), pp. 64–67. Published originally by the Prison Association of New York in 1922.

bucket that had been used for raising ore. More prisoners were sent there in 1774, the year of the first prison riot, and the violence, inept management, escapes, assaults, orgies, and demoralization continued through to 1827, when the prison was closed.[2] Riots and disturbances have become a pervasive characteristic of prison life. They have been reported in almost every year for more than the past two centuries.

To make a bomb, you must build a strong perimeter and generate extreme pressure inside. In essence, this is a description of a maximum security prison. The perimeter, characterized by walls and firearms, is strong. Inside, tight control is achieved by segregation and controlled movement of inmates, frequent but irregular searches and shakedowns, complete counts every two hours, the omnipresence of uniformed authority, and other manifestations of authoritative control. When a population drawn from the subculture of violence is placed within these confines, disturbances and riots are likely to result.

Historically, institutions designed to hold offenders had no discipline or internal control—just the strong perimeter. The first inside controls, which were built into the workhouses or bridewells constructed in 1557 and later, were designed to develop work habits in the lazy and immoral poor and minor offenders. When Newgate was built in London in 1769, there was no discipline, no control, and no sanitation inside the walls. These general conditions were addressed by the famous prison reformer, John Howard, in his *State of Prisons*, published in 1777. The first real discipline was introduced by the Quakers when they established the penitentiary movement in 1790 at the old Walnut Street Jail in Philadelphia. In fact, the Pennsylvania system of solitary confinement for the entire prison term eliminated the need for discipline of any sort because there was no opportunity for confrontation or conflict between prisoners.

Even in the most secure prisons today, there are assaults and disturbances. At the federal penitentiary at Alcatraz, where 250 residents and 250 staff were housed between 1933 and 1963, there were assaults, attempted escapes, two disappearances thought to have been lost to the sharks in San Francisco Bay, and one riot. The federal penitentiary at Marion, Illinois, which replaced Alcatraz, has reported assaults, fights, and one rather clever escape by manipulating the computerized locking system.

SELECTED RIOTS AND DISTURBANCES

Prison riots and disturbances throughout the nineteenth century were small and the causes more directly understood, because the prisons were small and the number of people involved was limited. The report of the agent of the Prison Association of New York of October 11, 1852, for example, reported the population of Brooklyn Prison as twenty men, thirteen women, thirty-six boys, and nine girls. Many of the early riots and disturbances were never reported. This writer knows of two or three episodes in the late 1940s that have never been reported. A typical early disturbance was at Auburn, reported "after it came to the atten-

[2]Ibid, p. 65.

tion of the newspapers" when, on Saturday, January 17, 1857, Mr. Curtis, the machine shop contractor, ordered an inmate to perform a task, which he refused to do, and had the inmate placed in solitary confinement. On Monday, January 19, sixty inmates in the shop picked up hammers and other tools for the fight, demanding that the inmate be released. He was released and the inmates went back to work. An attempted mass escape at Sing Sing occurred later the same year, on May 10, 1857, when going from the mess hall to the chapel, inmates armed with slingshots, knives, hammers, and other tools broke into a gang fight with the guards in what was called an attempt at mass escape, a popular early explanation of riot and disturbance, but the mass escape was prevented by guards using firearms.

As prisons grew bigger, so did the riots. The first large riot was on June 5, 1917, at Joliet, Illinois, when National Guardsmen were called to control a thousand rioting inmates who had set fire to buildings. On July 22, 1919, there were three thousand men in the military prison at Fort Leavenworth, of whom twenty-three hundred were involved in a strike; the guards employed perimeter security, only, and the men went back to their cells. These were strikes, not riots. There was no fighting. The men at Leavenworth went on strike three times in six months.

The first known riot in an institution for females occurred at the Bedford Reformatory for Girls in New York on July 24, 1920, when 150 white and black women began fighting after a black woman threw an iron at a white woman with whom she was arguing. Police broke up the riot by force.

On Monday, November 24, 1927, between twelve hundred and two thousand inmates battled National Guardsmen at the California state prison at Folsom. The four hundred National Guardsmen surrounded the building that the hard-core inmates were defending, tanks were brought in, National Guard airplanes were in action, one-pound artillery was set up, and a Southern Pacific Railway switch engine trained floodlights on the building. The troops fired round after round. By the time Governor Young arrived and ordered the attacks to cease, nine inmates had been killed, thirty-one had been wounded, three fatally, and two guardsmen had been killed and three had been wounded, one fatally. An aged officer died from the excitement. Governor Young's action prevented what some thought would have been a massacre. Lack of food placed time on the side of the prison officials and the inmates were starved out.

At the Colorado state prison at Canon City on Friday, October 3, 1929, 150 inmates obtained four rifles and barricaded themselves in Cell House 3, holding seven officers hostage. They demanded that they be permitted to escape or they would kill an officer on the hour every hour until their demands were met or until they ran out of officers. The body of Guard J. J. Elles, the hangman, was the first to be thrown out of the cell house. Armed guards had isolated the riot to one building, National Guardsmen were called, bringing in an airplane and several 3-inch artillery pieces. The Catholic chaplain, Father O'Neil, set the charge of dynamite at the end of the cell house and exploded it. The inmates continued to fight. As their ammunition ran out, inmate leader Danny Daniels shot his lieutenants and then shot himself. The toll was seven guards and five inmates killed.

The greatest loss of life reported from a riot or disturbance was at the

Ohio state penitentiary on Monday, April 21, 1930, when a fire was set by inmates apparently with a view toward creating diversion and then escaping. Two thousand prisoners were in the yard threatening violence that did not materialize. Guards would not open the cells and 317 prisoners were reported to have died.

An escape from Michigan's branch prison at Marquette on September 25, 1939 was handled differently. Forty prisoners had captured the three-man parole board and the prison physician and demanded that the gates be swung open so they could leave. The gates were swung open and the prisoners escaped with their hostages. A few miles from the prison, they released the four hostages. All escapees were captured within a few hours. No one was killed, no property was damaged, and no one escaped.

The riot at the state prison of southern Michigan at Jackson, Sunday, April 20, to Thursday, April 24, 1952, had the largest number of participants. The prison had a population at that time of 6,500 men, 5,000 of them inside the walls. There were 179 in the disciplinary cell block, referred to as 15 block, and they had overpowered a guard and captured all four guards assigned to 15 block and held them hostage. Through Sunday night, the problem became one of how to feed the rest of the prison beginning Monday morning.

Warden Julian Frisbie chose the most "liberal" approach, that of unlocking the north side of the prison first to serve breakfast and return the inmates to their cells and then repeating the procedure on the south side. The first part went tensely, but well. When the south side was unlocked, however, the 500 men who had entered the dining hall began to riot. A deputy warden entered into communication with the leaders of 15 block and with the men on the yard, talking (or coaxing) about 150 men off the yard. The Michigan State Police came in, entered the yard about 2:00 P.M. and had it cleared by 5:00 P.M. One inmate had been killed, which was the total death toll for the riot. By this time, additional men had entered 15 block and the interchanges for the next three days were sensitive. Several hostages were released as gestures of good faith during the negotiations. Finally, on Thursday, the remaining hostages were released and the inmates surrendered at 4:00 P.M.[3]

On January 13, 1970, a white guard opened fire on a group of brawling inmates in maximum security at the California correctional training facility at Soledad, killing three black inmates and wounding a white inmate. A subsequent finding of "justifiable homicide" resulted in the death of a white guard who was thrown off the third gallery of a cell block to the concrete floor below. Three black men, subsequently referred to as "the Soledad brothers," the best known being George Jackson, were transferred to San Quentin. On August 7, inmate James D. McLain was on trial for stabbing to death a white guard in San Quentin, when Jonathan Jackson, younger brother of George Jackson, came into the courtroom armed with a carbine and several pistols. Before the incident was

---

[3]This writer was involved in the riot. Literature that resulted includes "How I Broke the Michigan Prison Riot," *Collier's*, July 12, 1952 (lead article); "L'apaisement d'une penal Révolte de Prisonniers," *Revue de science criminelle et de droit pénal comparé*, Paris, July 1953, pp. 471–88; *Violence Behind Bars* (Westport, Conn.: Greenwood Press, 1973); "Emotional Dynamics in Group Violence," *Archives of Criminal Psychodynamics*, October 1957, pp. 255–77.

over, Judge Haley, Jonathan Jackson, and two inmates were dead. Angela Davis was charged with smuggling a gun into the courtroom, but she was acquitted on June 5, 1972, after a fourteen-week trial. On August 21, 1971, three white guards and three white inmates were killed in the disciplinary unit at San Quentin. George Jackson had just received a visit from lawyer Steven Bingham and had produced a pistol from his long Afro hair, yelled, "This is it!," and killed Sergeant Jerre Graham and shot others. Jackson was killed as he ran for the gate to break out of the unit.

The riot at the Attica correctional facility in New York, Thursday, September 9, to Monday, September 23, 1971, erupted after a year or more of tension. The social distance between the officers and the inmates was basic to the situation. Most of the residents, about 76 percent, were black and Hispanic from New York City, while the officers were from the rural area around Attica, situated between Buffalo and Rochester. There were no Spanish-speaking officers. The all-white personnel carried nightsticks and claimed that they never used them, but many referred to them openly as their "nigger sticks."[4] After a touch football game in the yard on Wednesday afternoon, a black inmate and a white inmate started to brawl, but the inmates said one was just demonstrating the moves of a lineman to the other. The situation was too tense to make an arrest in the yard, so the officers waited until the inmates were locked up for the night and removed them to disciplinary status. Through the night, rumors of beatings and name calling permeated the prison. In the morning, the atmosphere during the first breakfast was tense, but the meal service was without incident. Marching to the second breakfast, an inmate released another inmate who had been "keep-locked" in his cell. Confusion among the guards as to how to handle that situation resulted in explosive action and the inmates took over the prison in about ten minutes. Officer Quinn was beaten, thrown from the roof, and died Saturday in a Rochester hospital. The inmates captured thirty-eight hostages and secured D block's yard.

Efforts between the inmates and Commissioner Russell Oswald failed. The inmates tried and executed three of their number, one as the head of the gambling syndicate inside the prison and the other two for trying to slip notes to guards. By Sunday, the position of the administration had hardened. An observer's team wanted Governor Rockefeller to come to the prison, but he declined. The story was told that an attack was necessary because inmates had been seen slashing the throats of the hostages and one had been emasculated and his sex organs shoved into his mouth. On Monday morning, September 13, helicopters dropped containers of CS gas and the state troopers fired into the group of inmates and hostages, killing thirty inmates and nine hostages. Medical Examiner Dr. John F. Edlund reported that all thirty-nine deaths were by gunshot and that no throats had been cut! The state brought in two pathologists to "correct" the findings, but they supported Dr. Edlund. The New York State Special Commission on Attica said that, with the exception of Indian massacres in the late nineteenth century, the state police assault that ended the four-day prison upris-

---

[4]Herman Badillo and Milton Haynes, *A Bill of No Rights: Attica and the Prison System* (New York: Outerbridge and Lazard, Inc., distributed by E. B. Dutton & Co., 1972), p. 26.

ing was the bloodiest one-day encounter between Americans since the Civil War.[5]

The Oklahoma state penitentiary at McAlester sustained a hunger strike on January 22, 1973. On July 27, the inmates seized control of the prison and took twenty-one guards hostage, but the guards were released within ten hours. A full-fledged riot erupted on July 28 and lasted eight days until August 4, when National Guardsmen with bayonets, together with the Oklahoma Highway Patrol, gained control of the prison. During the riot, there were four inmates killed, one escape from the hospital, and considerable property damage from fire bombs and gasoline ignited by matches. The actual property damage is uncertain, since most of the structures destroyed were slated to have been replaced anyway. Oklahoma officials have avoided estimating the "property damage" but have estimated $20 million of "replacement value," and some have indicated that the inmates may have saved the state some money by doing the demolition themselves!

At the Southern correctional facility at Lucasville, Ohio, the "Lucasville 14" demanded to renounce their U.S. citizenship and be permitted to go to Russia. To dramatize their demands five members cut off a finger beginning November 29, 1977 and sent them to governmental officials, including Assistant Secretary of State for Human Rights Patricia Derian and Attorney General Griffin Bell.[6] One of the five, David L. Cattano, cut off one finger on each hand. They were placed in strip cells and were placed "off limits" to the news media, which Cattano interpreted as an effort to silence them before they became an embarrassment to the President or to the Department of State.

The riot at the New Mexico penitentiary at Santa Fe, February 15–16, 1980, was completely inmate dominated. There were four large cell blocks holding a total of slightly over a thousand inmates. One cell block held people under protection, primarily informants and "rats." The other inmates broke open this cell block and killed thirty-three people, some burned by torches beyond identification. One national publication carried a cartoon of an officer in a guard tower on the telephone, the caption reading, "Tell the governor not to sweat it—we'll have all murder, mutilation, brutality, rape, and mayhem back to the normal acceptable levels in no time."[7]

PATTERNS OF RIOTS

Prison riots generally undergo the following stages:

1. Explosion
2. Organization

[5]New York State Special Commission on Attica, Robert B. McKay, chairman, *Attica: The Official Report of the New York State Special Commission on Attica* (New York: Bantam Books, Inc., 1972), p. xi.

[6]"Q & A with the 'Lucasville 14'," *Fortune News*, March 1979, p. 4.

[7]"The Killing Ground—When Will It Happen Again?" *Newsweek*, February 18, 1980, pp. 66–68 (cartoon on page 68).

3. Negotiation
4. Termination
5. Explanation

The forms these stages take can vary widely from riot to riot.

The *explosion phase* is the spontaneous uprising during which inmates gain control of part of the prison. (It should be noted that riots are not planned, but are spontaneous.) While talk of assaults, disturbances, and riots can be heard in every prison almost daily, any serious planning generally results in a sit-down strike, a hunger strike, or some other nonviolent expression of hostility and resentment. The inmates know who has the firepower and the perimeter security. Inmates have never "won" a prison riot. They know that custodial control will always be regained. They know that inmates who commit crimes, such as assaults, homicides, kidnappings in the case of hostages, or other criminal offenses, can be tried in court. Further, any plans for a riot or an escape will be transmitted by inmates to an officer or an official in the hope of future reward and better treatment.

The *organizational phase* is reached when the inmate leadership emerges and staff members take on various leadership roles. The inmates' leader tends to be a person capable of moderating extremes of those who want to kill everybody and those who want to provide information and assistance to the administration. Inmate leadership calls for considered modification—somebody who can hold acting-out persons of diverse views together. Staff leadership, however, generally follows the table of organization, with the warden and/or the director of the state system handling public relations and approving strategy. Generally, the deputy warden in charge of custody is responsible for the control inside the perimeter.

Various personalities, however, may cause this leadership to shift. At Attica, for example, Warden Vincent Mancusi, an old custodial figure, was effectively blocked out as Commissioner Russell Oswald assumed leadership and instituted frequent contact with Governor Nelson Rockefeller in Albany. Sometimes, it takes hours or a day or so if the riot is permitted to go on that long for the effective leadership to be revealed. In the case of inmate leadership, a vociferous spokeperson may or may not be the real leader. In the case of staff, persons occupying certain positions in the table of organization may not have the best attitudes and personalities to handle a stress situation. A deputy warden in charge of custody who is action oriented may feel impotent, for example, when he no longer has unquestioned control of his prison. In general, inmate leadership emerges by personal interaction among the residents, with the person exhibiting greatest stability assuming charge by consensus, while staff leadership generally follows the chain of command.

The *negotiation phase* can range from warning, ultimatum, and firepower to long, drawn-out discussion. Most correctional administrators agree that, if there are no hostages, the warning ultimatum and firepower is the quickest and easier way of ending the riot. If the inmates are disorganized, and the dissidents are short-timers with parole available in three to five years and first-offenders, the probability of their killing hostages is low. On the other hand, older multiof-

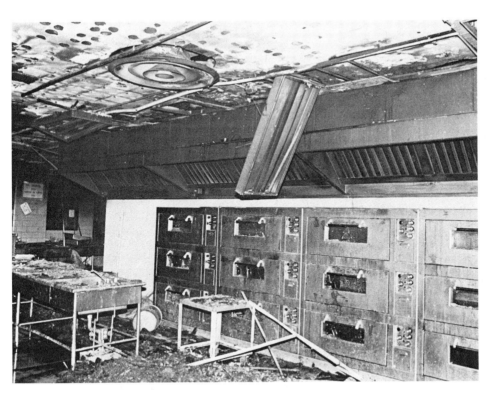

Riot damage.
Courtesy of the Washington State Department of Corrections.

fenders who have records of assaults and homicides and are doing life or other long sentences have little or nothing to lose and may kill hostages.

If hostages are held and the probability of their being in danger is high, then long, drawn-out discussions appear to be the wisest tack. The approach to these types of discussion should not be confused with rational mediation, however, as the tension of a riot and the personalities of the inmates involved provide a highly emotional situation in which logical bargaining is hardly possible. The purpose of "negotiation" in this case is simply to keep the inmates talking and to observe the shifts in group cohesiveness to detect when the leadership begins to lose its support but is still strong enough to play the negotiating role. Frequently prisoner complaints are the brutality of a few custodial officers, poor preparation and lack of adequate food, inadequate medical care, and conservative parole policies. The connection between the demands of prisoners and the actual situation in the prisons appears to be fairly tenuous where a series of demands are presented. It is interesting to note that complaints about food, medical services, and brutality have come from prisons generally conceded to be among the better ones, for example, those under the aegis of the U.S. Bureau of Prisons and those in California, Michigan, New Jersey, and Massachusetts. On the other hand,

Riot damage.
Courtesy of the Washington State Department of Corrections.

some prison systems that do not enjoy good budgets and are considered by correctional administrators and professionals to be most in need of improvement have never reported a riot! It becomes apparent that prisoners' demands are really a sort of rationalization for the riot itself. This is one reason why prisoners' demands have not been linked to the causes of riots.

The *termination stage* of the riot can be accomplished by firepower, by nonlethal force, or by agreement. Many prisons have used nonlethal force by going in with clubs, sometimes with football helmets and chest protectors, to clear out an area. Sometimes, nonlethal gas, such as tear gas or CN, may be used. As indicated previously, most agreements in riots are face-saving devices designed to give the riot leaders an honorable way out, when group cohesion falls apart and leaders begin to be threatened. These agreements should be framed in such a way that there is an honest possibility of honoring them, which is easy to do, because most correctional administrators want a better food budget, better medical care, and other improvements.

The *explanation stage* is the most difficult step in the progression. Every major riot is generally investigated by several committees and consultants. It is necessary for the political leadership to explain what was wrong at the prison and to assure the public that the complaints have been resolved. Frequently, a top administrator is fired so that a "cause" has been eliminated. This "scapegoat" technique, which is used frequently, is generally accompanied by legislative, gubernatorial, and other committees and commissions designed to "investigate" the situation, find causes, and recommend correction. The "appearance" of finding causes and their correction, generally transferring or dismissing somebody, is more important than the substance, because it reinforces public confidence in the remaining power structure.

CAUSES OF RIOTS AND DISTURBANCES

The causes of riots and disturbances are difficult to identify. Official reports and most articles on the subject focus on overcrowding, poor administration, insufficient financial support, political interference, lack of professional leadership, ineffective or nonexistent treatment programs, disparities in sentencing, poor and unjust parole policies, enforced idleness of prisoners, obsolete physical plant, and the influence of small groups of hard-core and intractable prisoners.[8] Psychological viewpoints focus on aggression and acting-out in the prison population. For example, see the late Dr. Ralph Banay's excellent articles on causes of riots.[9] The problems in identifying causes are apparent when all the sociological conditions mentioned in the official reports exist in most prisons, but the majority have not experienced riots. Further, all major prisons hold aggressive, hostile, and acting-out offenders. Consequently, these "causes" do not realistically differentiate between the prisons that experience riots and those that do not.

The total social situation contained within the strong perimeter must be examined to get clues as to the causes of any riot. Riots occur in maximum and medium security institutions, not in minimum security or community-based facilities where strong perimeters do not exist and the general social atmosphere is relaxed. In maximum and medium security institutions during riots, the inmates want to smash the system that keeps them hopeless, anonymous, and desperate, and they will destroy at random.[10] They become so alienated from society that they regard violence as right and proper. The American Correctional Association developed a manual on riots in 1953 and a revision in 1970.[11] The general conclusion was that it was not possible to identify a cause or set of causes, that simple explanations do not exist, and, further, that there is no set of rules outlining how a riot must be handled. While the general pattern is similar, the specific situations and personalities involved differ, so assessment of the situation and discretion in its resolution are essential.

---

[8]Clarence Schrag, "The Sociology of Prison Riots," *Proceedings of the American Correctional Association, 1960* (New York, 1961), pp. 148.

[9]*The New York Times*, July 26, 1959, Sec. 6, p. 8; August 9, 1959, Sec. 6, p. 2; August 6, 1959, Sec. 6, p. 72.

[10]"Violence and Correction," *The Correctional Trainer*, Vol. I, no. 4 (Spring 1970), pp. 56–91.

[11]Committee on Riots and Disturbances, William D. Leeke, chairman, *Causes, Preventive Measures, and Methods of Controlling Riots and Disturbances in Correctional Institutions* (Washington, D.C.: American Correctional Association, October 1970).

Causes must be divided into *predisposing causes* and *precipitating causes*. Just as in civil disobedience, there has to be "readiness" to riot. Then, there has to be a "trigger." The official reports and the literature on riots tends to emphasize the predisposing causes, such as overcrowding, poor administration, insufficient financial support, and other factors that are almost always found in these reports and that exist in almost all prisons.

Riots do not occur in prisons with exceedingly high morale. Neither do they occur in prisons where morale is so low that the residents endure penal oppression in a docile manner so that they break their own legs and cut their own heel tendons, as they have in Georgia and Louisiana in the 1950s, or engage in sit-down or hunger strikes. Riots occur in prisons where inmates have medium to high morale and where some conflict occurs in the staff, probably between controlling behavior or custody, on the one hand, and changing behavior or treatment, on the other. Riots seem to occur in prisons where there is a balance between these two philosophies but where there is not a full commitment to either.

There is also an apparent direct relationship between news coverage by the media and the incidence of demonstrations, riots, and civil disturbances, suggesting an emotional contagion that promotes these disturbances.[12] This is apparently why riots tend to cluster in terms of time.

One contributor to prison insurrection in the 1950s was a decision on the part of many administrations to reverse the drift toward greater inmate control through inmate councils and self-government.[13] That resulted, also, in an increase in inmate litigation against prison administrations in the areas of constitutional and civil rights. This trend continued through the 1950s and 1960s by various means, generally through the politicization of prisoners, litigation by prisoners against the administrations, and the development of grievance procedures.

In summary, the total social situation in the maximum and medium security society must be reviewed to find the elusive clues as to the cause of riots and disturbances. The general predisposing causes so frequently repeated in official reports and articles must be included in the consideration, together with the general social atmosphere within the institutions and the detonating or "triggering" devices.

ADMINISTRATIVE REACTIONS TO RIOTS AND DISTURBANCES

Administrative reactions during the riot or disturbance must be focused on regaining the custodial control of the institutions and neutralizing criticism from the news media. After riots or disturbances, administrative reaction is focused on explaining to political leaders and the public what caused the situation, assuring

[12]David L. Lange, Robert K. Baker, and Sandra J. Ball, *Violence and the Media* (Washington, D.C.: Government Printing Office, November 1969), pp. 614.

[13]Gresham Sykes, *The Society of Captives* (Princeton, N.J.: Princeton University Press, 1958), p. 144.

them that the cause has been corrected or eliminated, and providing assurance that the remaining power structure is in firm control. Of course, preventive measures to reduce the predisposing causes of riots should have been addressed long before the violent incident. Good food, plentiful and well prepared, can counteract many other administrative mistakes. Napoleon's famous remark that an army marches on its stomach could be applied to any group of men. Food becomes a primary source of pleasure to men deprived of many of the comforts of normal life and, conversely, can become a tangible vehicle that carries generalized hostilities and resentments that might, in fact, come from other sources. Consequently, an administrator should spend a little extra time and effort to find a good steward to handle food services and pay special attention to the food budget. It must be noted here that many riots are started in the dining room, even though the "trigger" may have occurred in the yard as it was in Attica, the reinforcing "trigger" being "salt in the coffee" or somebody heaving a tray.

Despite other abuses, riots do not generally occur in prisons that are essentially run by inmates, such as in Southern prisons that never reported riots when inmates carried guns to guard other inmates. Conversely, the social distance between the rural, white custodial force guarding a majority of black and Spanish-speaking inmates from New York City precludes a common ground for communication between the guards and the inmates that could have mediated or prevented the riot at Attica. Good communication between the inmates and the administration, generally through the custodial force, has obviated many complaints and has reduced the predisposing causes of the riots. Inmate leadership is present in all prisons, as leadership is present in all groups of people. Constructive use of inmate leadership and positive communication can reduce tension that contributes to the predisposing causes.

Whether power or negotiation should be primary or secondary depends upon the situation. "Negotiation" with "convicts" is always unpopular with the public and political leaders. On the other hand, firepower in a democratic society, while favored by many conservative citizens and political leaders, violates the general principle of using the minimum amount of force and destruction needed to accomplish the objectives.[14] No administration ever *needs* to "negotiate" with rioting prisoners. The prisoners know this. If hostages are held, then negotiation becomes a real possibility, depending upon other factors. If the rioters are short-term prisoners, primarily property offenders, the chances of hostages being killed is reduced and the risk of force can be considered. In the Michigan riot of 1952, the decision to negotiate was not made until the files of all the inmates holding the hostages in the disciplinary block had been reviewed, about one-third of whom were serving for first-degree murder with records of one to nine previous killings. Negotiation was apparently the only way in which to save the lives of the hostages. This was supported by subsequent report by the inmates and by nationally known clinical psychologists brought in for impartial investigations as part of the "explanation" phase.

The best time to use force is at the initial stage of the riots, before inmate leadership has emerged in the organization stage, whether or not hostages have been taken. During the riot at Attica, Governor Nelson Rockefeller and two

---

[14]See George R. Berkley, *The Democratic Policeman* (Boston: Beacon Press, 1969).

aides considered loading the drinking water at the prison with Librium, a strong tranquilizer. Unfortunately, at Attica, the custodial force was as disorganized and confused as the inmates, and both factions organized their resources simultaneously. The custodial force has no advantage in such a situation. A well-prepared riot plan could possibly have given the custodial force an almost automatic advantage by immediate reaction to disturbances. Then riots could be "nipped in the bud." Unfortunately, most riots are characterized by mutual surprise on the part of the inmates and the custodians.

Legal problems may be increasing with the growth of litigation by prisoners. Every person, including the incarcerated felon, has the right to be free from *fear* for his personal safety and from *actual* bodily attack. Persons who violate either of these rights can be held liable, civilly and criminally, unless such conduct is privileged. It has generally been recognized that prison officials have the privilege to use force against inmates in (1) self-defense, (2) defense of third person being attacked, (3) enforcement of prisoners' rules and regulations, (4) prevention of escape, and (5) prevention of crime.[15] These would support the use of firepower in the case of prison riots and disturbances. Excessive and unnecessary force, however, has been declared unconstitutional.[16] Problems facing the police in the 1960s generally anticipated the problems facing correctional administrators in the 1970s.[17] The law has prohibited shooting a fleeing felon, even if already convicted, but if the shooting occurs, it must be supported as having been necessary and not excessive.[18] If the felon escaping is a property offender and not a murderer, the officers and the prison in which he is employed had better have good reasons for the shooting. There has been a discernible trend away from the use of deadly force in the police system and in the entire criminal justice system.[19]

After the riot is over, the correctional administrators must determine the "cause" of the riot and take steps toward its elimination. Many investigating committees from governmental offices, legislatures, or other political entities seek simplistic answers that seem to construct the interpretations according to their own best interests. Many consultants are invited from outside jurisdictions as impartial advisors. The experts tend to protect the persons or groups who invited them, which is logical. Diplomatic writing is a consultant's art. Other consultants invited from outside generally are not sufficiently acquainted with the underlying intricacies of the power structure to understand the local situation. When all the reports are in—and sometime before—generally, somebody gets blamed and disciplined. The firing of a top official who has been in the news in connection with the riot is a popular solution. A "get-tough" policy is also popular. Whether "scapegoat" or real, the transfer of top administrators or

---

[15]John W. Palmer, *Constitutional Rights of Prisoners*, 2nd ed. (Cincinnati: W. H. Anderson Publishing Company, 1973), p. 15.

[16]*Inmates of Attica Correctional Facility* v. *Rockefeller*, 453 F. 2d 12 (2d Cir., 1971).

[17]*Wolff* v. *McDonnell*, 418 U.S. 539 (1974).

[18]Steven C. Day, "Shooting the Fleeing Felon: State of the Law," *Criminal Law Bulletin*, Vol. 14, no. 4 (July–August 1978), pp. 285–310.

[19]*Johns* v. *Marshall*, 528 F. 2d 123, 139 (2d Cir., 1975).

middle management or their dismissal frequently takes care of the situation for the public and the political leadership.

All major facilities have correctional emergency response teams (CERT) trained and equipped to deal with a wide range of emergencies, including riots, fires, and natural disasters. Special training and equipment are provided. Correctional officers who volunteer for CERT duty undergo rigorous physical examinations and training. Equipment has been bulletproof vests, gas masks, and related protective equipment. Larger facilities have two or three such teams.[20]

DISCUSSION

Many of the problems within the prison are related to similar problems outside. The handling of hostages can be generalized to many national and international terrorist situations. A model has been developed for the handling of hostage situations, referred to as the negotiation model, that stresses human dynamics, rather than military tactics, and can be applied to prison hostage situations.[21]

After the Attica riot in 1971, the McKay commission pointed out that the inmates perceived themselves as being surrounded by walls and gates and tightly regimented by myriad written and unwritten rules; but when they needed protection, they often had to resort to the same skills that had brought many of them to Attica in the first place.[22]

The atmosphere of prisons has been said to have changed in the direction of a new "breed" of radical political prisoner acting as a catalyst in an atmosphere of hopelessness and violence, which has resulted in epidemics of unrest, such as those at Attica, San Quentin, Rahway, and elsewhere.[23] Overcrowding, barbaric living conditions, and the almost total absence of meaningful rehabilitation programs have been brought to public attention through protests organized by the new politicized prisoners.

Gangs have become an important component in the populations of many major prisons. At least 50 percent of the population of the Stateville correctional center are identified with one of the four gangs that are extensions of racial and ethnic gangs in Chicago.[24] The Latin Kings represent the largest Hispanic gang in Chicago and have between 150 and 200 members inside Stateville. The Black P. Stone Nation, frequently called the Blackstone Rangers or the Stones, is a powerful black gang in Chicago and at Stateville. The Devil's Disciples and the Vice Lords are also powerful black gangs in Chicago and at Stateville.

[20]*Equity-Justice: Report of Operations and Development for 1976* (Albany: New York State Department of Correctional Services, 1976), p. 21.

[21]James P. Needham, *Neutralization of Prison Hostage Situations—A Model* (Springfield, Va.: NTIS, 1976), 167 pp.

[22]Robert D. McKay, *New York State Special Commission on Attica* (New York: Praeger Publishers, Inc., 1974), p. 101.

[23]Burton M. Atkins and Henry R. Glick, eds., *Prisons, Protest and Politics* (Englewood Cliffs, N.J.: Prentice-Hall, Inc., 1972), 180 pp.

[24]James B. Jacobs, *Stateville: The Penitentiary in Mass Society* (Chicago: University of Chicago Press, 1977), p. 146.

In the California state prison system, four major gangs function as the (1) Aryan Brotherhood, (2) Black Guerilla Family, (3) Nuestra Familia, and (4) Mexican Mafia.[25] Within the institutions, they engage in narcotics trafficking, pressuring and physical coercion of inmates, and promulgation of revolutionary political doctrines. With the exception of the Aryan Brotherhood, which includes all races and ethnic groups, the gangs are predominantly racial and ethnic in membership. The best organized and most active gangs are the Nuestra Familia and the Mexican Mafia, and they direct criminal activity in the streets in outside communities.

Other prisons also have gangs, such as the Mexican Mafia in Arizona, but the Illinois and California gangs are most significant because of their size and influence in highly populated states. Many of the gangs in other states become in-house groups that operate the gambling and narcotic enterprises within the institution.

The National Council on Crime and Delinquency proposed in 1974 a seven-point program for reducing causes of conflict and riots in correctional institutions.[26] The points were (1) minimum standards for the protection of rights of inmates, (2) formal procedures for handling grievances, (3) legislation authorizing inmates to engage in negotiation, (4) third-party intervention in case of an impasse, (5) prisoner representation, (6) processes of negotiation in case of a prison crisis, and (7) training of officials and inmates in techniques of conflict negotiation.

Assaults on officers have been frequent in the history of prisons. In fact, sexual attacks or rapes of officers by inmates have been "rumored" less frequently than have outright hostile attacks; nevertheless, this writer has been told of several in private conversations at conferences and meetings with friends and colleagues in the prison business. The incidents are withheld from the news media in the interests of the privacy of the officers. Regardless of how it was done, the rape of an officer by inmates would destroy his usefulness in almost any job in criminal justice, much less his self-respect and reputation.

For example, a full-scale riot occurred at the Illinois state penitentiary at Stateville on April 29, 1973, which was really a rumble between two prison gangs, the Stones and the Disciples, after a known gang member killed an inmate and wounded another in retaliation for their interference with a homosexual prostitute "belonging" to the Stones. A lock-down of six months was ordered, the longest lock-down that Stateville had experienced. By September 6, 1973, all but two cell blocks had been released. On the day of the final release, the largest cell block at Stateville was seized and ten officers were held hostage. At the subsequent trial of the ten inmates identified as the leaders, it became obvious that several of the guard hostages had been "raped" by the inmates.[27] At the word "several," all the guards left room to preserve the anonymity of those

---

[25]*Prison Gangs in the Community: A Briefing Document for the Board of Corrections* (Sacramento: California Board of Corrections, 1978), 139 pp.

[26]NCCD Board of Directors, "Peaceful Settlement of Prison Conflict: A Policy Statement," *Crime and Delinquency*, Vol. 20, no. 1 (1974), pp. 1–3.

[27]Jacobs, *Stateville*, p. 166.

involved. The news media subsequently praised Governor Walker and Director Sielaff for having negotiated the end of the riot "peacefully."

CONCLUSIONS

Riots and other violence have been part of the prison scene since the first prison opened in the American colonies as Newgate, in Connecticut, in December 1773. The patterns include (1) explosion; (2) organization of leadership on the part of the inmates and of the administration; (3) confrontation by negotiation, "keeping them talking," or force; (4) termination by force or negotiation; and (5) explanation to the public and the political leadership as to what happened and what corrective measures have been taken. In the last stage, the words of the late President Theodore Roosevelt after the acquisition of the Panama territory for the canal seem to be appropriate:

> they are eager to take advantage of the deeds of the men of action when action is necessary and then eager to discredit him when the action is once over.[28]

This refers to the fact that many "explanations" place blame on the persons who were closest to the riots and leave those who appear to have been least involved in the remaining power structure. After Attica, in particular, regardless of the viewpoint, many began to ponder the social consequences of a poor penal system.[29] Society is the only loser if a prison system fails to rehabilitate its inmates. In the prison, however, there is hardly a way to avoid violence.

CHAPTER QUESTIONS

7-1.   How prevalent are riots and disturbances in maximum security prisons?
7-2.   What are the causes of riots?
7-3.   Through what stages do riots progress?
7-4.   Are prison riots planned?
7-5.   What is the negotiation stage?
7-6.   Why is the explanation stage the most important in terms of public policy?
7-7.   What is the relationship between inmate morale and prison riots?
7-8.   When is the best time to use force in a prison riot?
7-9.   What legal problems have appeared regarding use of force in riots and disturbances?
7-10. What was the seven-point program for reducing causes of conflict and riots in correctional institutions proposed in 1974 by the National Council on Crime and Delinquency?

[28]Edward Wagenknecht, *The Seven Worlds of Theodore Roosevelt* (New York: Longmans, Green and Co., 1960), p. 272.

[29]John R. Dunne, "An Eyewitness Report on Five Terrible Days at Attica," *The American Annual,* 1972, p. 48.

8

EFFECTS
OF
IMPRISONMENT

Long-term imprisonment has a perceptible impact on most people who experience it. The rigidly controlled, regimented, structured environment of the maximum and medium custody institution requires a type of individual adaptation unlike the normal social adjustment in the free community. The younger the person and the longer the period of years he or she is subject to that constant supervision and regimentation, the greater will be the impact. In fact, juvenile institutions that receive youngsters from juvenile courts, generally youngsters between their twelfth and seventeenth birthdays, frequently report an even more severe impact than do institutions for adults. On the other hand, if a person is sent to a correctional institution for the first time after the age of 40, the impact will not be so discernible.

There is a wide diversity among prisons and correctional institutions. And variations exist in competency and attitude of staffs, strengths of the treatment programs, living conditions within the institutions, living space that may be reduced with overcrowding, and many other conditions that affect the style of life.

The personality of the individual experiencing these institutional pressures also makes a difference in the effects that the institutions may have. Some persons are highly vulnerable and susceptible to outside influences; others with greater emotional security and resistance can remain relatively insulated from the impact of the institution. Although there is general tendency for the institutional experience to change social behavior, it is not universal, and the variations in vulnerability and resistance among different personalities may vary widely.

It should be pointed out that minimum custody institutions without a strong perimeter and without pressure inside do not have these adverse effects on the residents. Further, neither riots nor serious disturbances are reported from these institutions. They tend to have an atmosphere more like a summer camp than a secure custodial institution. Community-based facilities are even less restrictive. Community-based facilities are designed for people who can work or study in the community, but need their evenings and weekends controlled. Even so, the control is minimal and the impact of the institutionalization is greatly reduced. In fact, minimum custody institutions and community-based facilities are frequently used in the process of decompression as the individual leaves a maximum or medium custody institution and progresses toward eventual release into the community.

In 1974, 39.5 percent of inmates in state institutions were in maximum custody, 23.9 percent were in medium custody, 21.8 percent were in medium security, and 4.8 percent were in community-based facilities.[1]

PRISONERS' ATTITUDES AND VALUES

Attitude is denoted by the readiness to act in a certain direction in specific social situations. It refers to the personal and social orientation of an individual and is generally conditioned by his or her personal and social experiences. Values are the priorities that the individual places on various components of society in terms of need, attitude, or desire. Values refer to the interacting relationships that exist among needs, attitudes, and desires, on the one hand, and the object component on the other. Attitudes in prisons generally involve conflict with authority and consequent feelings of resentment and face-saving explanations of the inmates.

Other attitudes involve inmate-staff relations. The greater the social distance between inmates and staff, the greater the mutual distrust and hatred. Most staff—fortunately not all—view prison residents as "convicts" and dangerous troublemakers. Many residents, particularly "repeaters," see officers as vindictive and brutal, counselors and treatment personnel as ineffective eunuchs, and administrators as political hacks. Many inmates ask how any self-respecting individual could take a job and receive pay to guard his fellow man. The fact that anybody would work for money in the criminal justice system, be it in police departments, courts, or prisons, degrades them in the view of many inmates. In summary, prisoners tend to deny the offense in various ways and to project blame on the society that has victimized them.

The value system in prison relates to common needs, attitudes, and

[1]Nicolette Parisi, Michael R. Gottfredson, Michael J. Hindeland, and Timothy J. Flanagan, eds., *Sourcebook of Criminal Justice Statistics—1978* (Washington, D.C.: National Criminal Justice Information and Statistics Service, June 1979), p. 631.

desires of the residents. In the broad perspective, the two primary needs are (1) to get out one way or the other and (2) to make life as tolerable and pleasant as possible during this time in prison. Getting out can be accomplished in one of several ways, the most preferable one being acquitted in a new trial or being pardoned by the governor, the next being an early parole, the third being expiration of sentences or, when all else fails, possibly escape. Making life bearable inside the institution presents problems. In most prisons, the best jobs go to long-term trusted inmates who serve in responsible positions, such as clerks for the deputy warden, captains, chaplain, psychologist, and classification personnel. These people may dress in civilian clothes and often have limited contact with the outside.

These long-term trusted inmates have frequently been sent on extended trips alone, for example, returning an older car to the central motor pool and picking up a new one to return to the institution, sometimes at a distance of 500 miles. This is done to save the time and salary of an officer who may spend a day going, a day of layover, and a day returning, when a trusted inmate could do it for expenses.

Long-term trusted inmates frequently identify with the administration and staff more than they do with the general population of the prison. Beginning with the lowest of the status jobs, such as a runner for a cell block officer, up to the warden's driver, they provide a valuable service in the prison. They must still observe the inmate code and not "squeal" on other inmates to maintain their trust and their own personal safety. On the other hand, they can explain to the other inmates in the general population why certain unpopular actions may have been taken by the administration, for example, why a reduced budget is reflected in food services or why the deputy warden had to place certain inmates in administrative segregation. Also, they can relate to the administration and staff some of the concerns of the general population, so that remedial action can be taken. Consequently, the service of this group of inmates goes beyond their immediate jobs and promotes better communication between the administration and staff, on the one hand, and the general population of the prison, on the other.

While some of these long-term trusted inmates in good jobs may misuse their positions, most do not. Those guilty of misuse are frequently clerks in key positions who make changes in assignments of jobs and cells. In some cases, an order for a change of job or cell may get "lost" until the recipient comes up with a carton of cigarettes as payment to the clerk. If the delay happens to be discovered and challenged by an officer, the "lost" order can always be "found"! The majority of these long-termers in good jobs, however, protect their statuses. It has taken a long time for them to achieve their positions and they do not want to jeopardize them. Many have been repeaters, many have been institutionalized in the prison process, and all have seen that escapees seldom stay out for long and are more severely restricted when they are returned.

Back in the general population where good jobs do not exist, however, the values are changed. As a result of the deprivations and restrictions, simple things become important, such as the day's menu, the quality of the cooking, the weekly movie, "store day" or the day the inmates can go to the inmate commissary and buy candy bars and other items not issued by the prison, "yard" or recreational periods outside, and many other commonplace and simple goods and activities.

Sex becomes important, as was indicated in Chapter 7, and aggression and rape, both individual and gang, are constant threats. Gambling, which takes on importance as an opportunity "to get something for nothing," is widespread in prisons. The primary difficulty related to gambling in terms of the safety and security in the institution is that people frequently gamble beyond their means and are not able to pay their debts, which results in violence. As was pointed out in Chapter 7, the first rioter tried and executed by the inmates at Attica during the riot of 1971 was the head of the gambling syndicate inside the institution.

In summary, the attitudes and values in the maximum and medium security prisons are an unusual amalgam of frustration that generates aggression, attempts to maintain a concept of self-worth that results in paranoid thinking, struggles to get out, and attempts to make life as pleasant as possible. The results are manifested in trying to move one's time along, exploiting others for gain or pleasure, and living on a day-to-day basis. Very seldom have long-term "friendships" been made in prisons.

INSTITUTIONALIZED PERSONALITY

The "prisonization" process develops the institutionalized personality. Prisonization was first discussed lucidly by Donald Clemmer in his *The Prison Community* in a pioneering case study of the Illinois state penitentiary at Menard,[2] and the literature is now replete with studies of this process. Prisonization refers to the acquisition of prison culture and prison norms, attitudes, and values. Hayner and Ash began developing a theoretical framework for the prisonization process as an consequence of the acceptance of these cultural norms in prison in the late 1930s,[3] and Sykes's classic work in 1958 in New Jersey supports Clemmer's observations by suggesting that it results from the "pains of imprisonment," which he lists as (1) deprivation of liberty, (2) deprivation of self-concept, (3) deprivation of goods and services, (4) deprivation of heterosexual relationships, and (5) deprivation of security.[4] A prison inmate can never feel safe, nor relate to an unstable world based on aggression and exploitation in a setting he perceives as unjust and which has victimized him or her as a prisoner.

Authoritarian personalities abound in prison, both among the inmates and the staff. They tend to be power oriented and vindictive, and they possess strong opinions and attitudes regarding the power structure, social injustice, and other areas.[5] This creates a "pressure cooker" atmosphere characterized by frustration, hopelessness, and identification with the inmate code that calls for doing one's own time on a day-to-day basis and not bothering anybody else

[2]Donald Clemmer, *The Prison Community* (Boston: Christopher Press, 1940), reissued by Holt, Rinehart and Winston, 1958, p. 298.

[3]Norman Hayner and E. Ash, "The Prison Community as a Social Group," *American Sociological Review,* Vol. 4 (1939), pp. 362–69.

[4]Gresham Sykes, *The Society of Captives* (Princeton, N.J.: Princeton University Press, 1958), pp. 63–83.

[5]T. W. Adorno, Elsie Franken-Brunswick, Daniel J. Levinson, and R. Nevitt Sanford in collaboration with Betty Aron, Marcia Hertz Levinson, and William Morrow, *The Authoritarian Personality* (New York: Harper Brothers, 1950).

unless one is strong enough to do it. The social compression referred to by Martinson exists in this social arrangement where communication, movement, interaction, and the total social structure are severely restricted and controlled.[6] Stress between staff and inmates is characterized by mutual distrust and occasional violence. Stress between inmates tends to fragment groups according to minorities, ethnic groups, rival gangs, or other identifiable characteristics.

Living for a period of years in this stress-ridden environment, always fearing for one's safety and experiencing all the deprivations that imprisonment entails, frequently results in the institutionalized personality. According to Tom Runyon, a lifer at the Iowa state penitentiary at Fort Madison and editor of *The Presidio,* the prison paper, it takes about five years to develop the institutionalized personality in most men, pointing out that life in prison is characterized by frustration, loneliness, boredom, and futility, a "kind of dry, aching misery that lets a lifer know that the yokel who wrote, 'Stone walls do not a prison make, nor iron bars a cage,' never did a day's time in his life."[7] The result of the highly structured and well-regulated life in maximum security is dehumanizing. Prisoners are told when to get up, when to go to bed, when to eat, when to send in their laundry; as a result, they make very few constructive decisions. The individual learns to respond with superficial courtesy to authority figures and develops flat emotional responses to others and the environment because it becomes dangerous and futile to invest in others.

Some prisoners develop a prison psychosis commonly called "stir-bugs," a syndrome characterized by emotional distance and the inability to do anything correctly. Rather than a psychosis, however, most psychologists agree now that Ganser Syndrome is a hysterical type of neurosis, as though the individual were acting out an artificial psychosis. It can be precipitated by anticipated or actual incarceration in some form, and it is the most common psychiatric disorder in prison inmates. Some psychiatrists refer to it as chronophobia or fear of time.[8] Many psychiatrists hold that, sooner or later, all prison inmates develop chronophobia to some degree. It appears suddenly and frequently, at between three and five years. The inmate becomes essentially an indifferent automaton, who serves the rest of his sentence by the clock, living one day at a time, and cannot relate logically to reality. The duration and the immensity of time become terrifying to the individual. It is contended that it occurs in every potential neurotic who goes to prison after the "novelty" of prison life has worn off and the actual length of the sentence is realized.

The patterns of prisonization have been studied at length. According to Wheeler, persons are more susceptible to the prison customs and folkways during the middle part of their sentences. They tend to focus on outside customs and values when they first arrive and when they are about to leave the prison.[9]

[6]Robert Martinson, "Social Interaction Under Close Confinement," *Psychiatry,* Vol. 30, no. 2 (1967), pp. 132–48.

[7]Tom Runyon, *In for Life—A Convict's Story* (New York: W. W. Norton & Company, Inc., 1953), p. 9.

[8]Leland E. Hinsie and Robert Jean Campbell, *Psychiatric Dictionary,* 4th ed. (New York: Oxford University Press, 1970), p. 130.

[9]Stanton Wheeler, "Socialization in the Correctional Community," *American Sociological Review,* Vol. 26 (1961), pp. 679–712.

Thomas has more recently suggested that prisonization theory may derive from social, political, and economical institutions with which the prisoners have weak ties and, therefore, foster alienation and negative reactions.[10]

Scales measuring attitudes toward legal and judicial systems and measure of alienation have accounted for almost one-half of the variance in female prisoners' degree of prisonization and 35 percent of males' prisonization.[11]

Many of the attitudes in the prison population involve rationalizations designed to protect the individual from self-blame. The two techniques used most by prisoners for this protection are denial and projection—denial that the crime occurred or denial of responsibility for it and projection of the blame for any crime onto society or others, in which case the offender becomes the victim.

Sykes and Matza identified five principal techniques of denial in their theory of neutralization.[12] First is denial of responsibilities, which involves lack of intent. Justice Oliver Wendel Holmes observed that even a dog distinguishes between being stumbled over and being kicked. Lack of intent or the absence of *mens rea* has long been a legal defense against criminal prosecution, particularly in insanity. Further, the individual may claim that he was drunk and did not know what he was doing or was "temporarily insane" in the heat of anger. More recently, the blame has been attached to poverty, a slum or ghetto environment, cruel or unloving parents, bad companions, and other social and economic causes.

Second is denial of injury, which refers to the legal distinction between acts that are wrong in themselves or *mala en se,* such as murder, on the one hand, and acts that are illegal but not immoral or *mala prohibita,* such as evading taxes, on the other. Moonshining in the rural South has been considered by the participants and their customers as an occupation providing services. Prison inmates, themselves, frequently go much farther. Bank robbers and burglars frequently say that nobody was hurt, since any losses were covered by insurance. Auto thieves frequently say that they just borrowed the car and that the owner got it back intact.

Third is denial of the victim, which is simply a justification of the defense because the victims "ask for it." Actually, the defense has been successful in courts when the victim had also fired a pistol or rape victims "had asked for it." Sometimes, offenders choose a person who "deserves" to be a victim, for example, a drunk whom they "rolled," someone making unwelcome homosexual advances, a prostitute who stole a "customer's" wallet, and many other victims who are in a weak position to file a complaint.

Fourth is condemning the condemners, that is, verbally attacking the police or the court system as being more guilty of misdeeds than the alleged offender. This happens frequently in many prisons, when inmates see officials stealing state gasoline, taking food from the kitchen's commissary, and having suits made for themselves and/or friends in the institutional tailor shop or when

[10]Charles W. Thomas, "Theoretical Perspectives on Prisonization," *Journal of Criminal Law and Criminology,* Vol. 68 (1977), pp. 135–45.

[11]Geoffrey P. Alpert, "A Comparative Study of the Effects of Ideology on Prisonization: A Research Note," *LAE Journal,* Vol. 41, no. 1 (Winter–Spring 1978), pp. 77–86.

[12]Gresham Sykes and David Matza, "Techniques of Neutralization: A Theory of Delinquency," *American Sociological Review,* Vol. 22 (1957), pp. 664–70.

inmates refer to victims of burglaries and robberies who exaggerate or "pad" their losses to be covered by insurance.

Fifth is appeal to higher loyalties, which means that the individual will not "squeal on" or testify against friends, even though the individual is not involved in any wrongdoing. This occurs not only in prisons and correctional institutions but also in police departments, where officers are "loyal" to fellow officers, in politics, in government, and in private business.

In summary, the regimented and highly controlled institution places pressures on its inmates that have to be met by various adaptations on the part of those inmates. This is why the inmate code is present in most institutions. It explains why confined prisoners change their value systems to protect their own egos or self-respect. It also explains much violence and exploitation among the inmates.

INFORMAL SOCIAL CONTROL

While friendships made in prison seldom last in the outside community, the oppression of the maximum security prison makes prisoners accept a group loyalty that protects everybody. It resembles the behavior exhibited in a riot in which not everybody wants to participate but many feel compelled to support the group. During normal times or in the absence of disruption, informal social control appears to be carried out by small groups that attempt to control extreme aggressors who may precipitate tighter control that would make living conditions in the prison more difficult. These types of groupings were reported by Clemmer in his classic *The Prison Community*, first published in 1940.[13] In this study, 41 percent were "ungrouped" or "loners" who associated very little with others, but were sufficiently civil to avoid altercations. In this grouping of "loners," 50.6 percent of the long-termers were loners versus 32.9 percent of the short-termers. At the other extreme, 17.4 percent of the inmates were in close groups of 2 to 7 members with an average of 4.4 members, 16.9 percent of the long-termers being in this group versus 19.2 percent of the short-termers. In between was the "semiprimary" group whose members were defined as being friendly with a certain small group but did not constitute a close group. Increasing length of residence reduces the number of primary groups and increases the number of loners. It is interesting to note that the primary problems of violence and disruptions occur within the group, either primary or semiprimary, because of interpersonal conflicts that arise in them. On the other hand, these groups also have the power to control disruptions and frequently handle it before it gets to the officials' attention. Many times in a prison, a disruptive inmate has appeared in the cell block or dining hall severely bruised and lacerated, but simply explains that he fell downstairs.

While informal social control by inmates occurs in all prisons to some extent, its effectiveness varies widely according to the strength of the custodial force.[14] In some states, such as New York, which enjoys fairly good budgets and

[13]Clemmer, *The Prison Community*, pp. 113–20.

[14]James B. Jacobs, *Stateville: The Penitentiary in Mass Society* (Chicago: University of Chicago Press, 1977), p. 146.

a staff-inmate ratio above the national average, inmate social control is minimal. At the other extreme, prisons traditionally operated with a low staff ratio, such as those in Arkansas, Mississippi, and Louisiana, inmates' social control has been strong. For example, when Arkansas Governor Winston Rockefeller wanted to reform that state's prison in 1967 and 1968, there were twenty-two hundred prisoners versus twenty-two staff members, six of whom held part-time contracts, such as the physician and the chaplain. An interesting story about that situation was told by Carl Freund, reporter for the *Dallas Morning News*, when he telephoned the Arkansas state penitentiary's Cummins Unit to inquire about a story. The person who answered the telephone explained fully and completely what had happened. Mr. Freund then asked whether he was the warden. The response was, "No, I am doing ninety-nine years for armed robbery, but I handle the P.R. around here."

It is apparent that the social groupings have been constant in most prison, for a long time, but this has been modified by some larger groupings in a few places like San Quentin and Stateville. Even there, the non–gang members hold the same groupings as those found by Clemmer.

INMATE LEADERSHIP
AND SUBMISSION PATTERNS

Inmate leaders in prisons are generally those who have committed murder or other crimes of violence (64.3 percent) or property offenses (22.4 percent).[15] Sex offenders and child molesters are seldom seen as leaders, except sometimes by other sex offenders and child molesters. Leadership in prison is exercised by criminally mature inmates serving long sentences for violent crimes. Prison culture seems to be organized around values of its most persistent and least improvable members, stimulating the aggressive, antisocial behavior and minimizing the status of first-offenders. On occasion, a notorious first-offender convicted of murder and accompanied by wide publicity at the trial may be accepted in some form of leadership. On at least one occasion, the district attorney in a large urban area was sentenced for obstruction of justice and was sought out by many inmates whom he had prosecuted, who thought he might be able to find "loopholes" in their cases. Physical propensities become an important determinant of influence and leadership in prison. The influence of close prison encounters, especially with cell partners, seem to be most effective.

RESULTS
OF INSTITUTIONALIZATION

The results of institutionalization have been debated intensely. Certainly long-termed institutionalization develops the institutionalized personalities through the prisonization process in which an individual becomes dependent on outside structure for his decision making and life-style. Many inmates claim to have

---

[15]Clarence Schragg, "Leadership Among Prison Inmates," *American Sociological Review*, Vol. 19 (February 1954), pp. 37–42.

entered prison as trusting and gentle youths but have left the prison as irritable, ungovernable men.[16] They cannot even order food from a complicated menu, find it difficult to get their laundry in on time, are unable to get to bed in the evening and get up in the morning in time for work, and exhibit many other types of dependency on the institutionalized system.

Many have pointed out that the prison experience makes big resentments out of little ones so that individuals are worse off when they come out than when they go in. Studies have shown that prisons cannot change basic personality patterns. Overt behavioral change can be obtained, however, indicating that they may "learn" to get along or develop an institutionalized personality that makes them respond to structured situations.[17]

Many writers, such as Kropotkin in 1886, Joseph Wilson in 1950, and Karl Menninger in 1968, have suggested that prison be eliminated. Others, for example, Ernest van den Haag (1975), James Q. Wilson (1978), and Andrew von Hirsch (1978), have suggested that offenders should be locked up and the key be thrown away. More moderate writers, for example, Norval Morris (1971, 1974) and Gordon Hawkins (1974), have indicated that prisons have been overused and that they are not needed to the extent that we have them.

The only agreement appears to be that arrest rates are higher at age 16 and tend to go down slowly until age 35 throughout the general population. Maturation apparently is of assistance. This means that many prisons are simply "warehousing," "deep-freezing," and detaining people as a holding operation without putting into the program sufficient treatment personnel to counteract the ill effects of the prisons.

An exhaustive study of 1,345 young adult males who entered the federal correctional institution at Tallahassee, Florida, during a two-year period from November 3, 1970 to November 2, 1972, which included extensive testing at intake and exit for comparison, interviews to learn the residents' evaluation of their experiences in the institution, and measures of recidivism based on total arrests, concluded that the popular impression that *all* inmates emerge from *all* prisons more disturbed, bitter, and inclined toward more criminal behavior is false.[18] Approximately 1,214 men participated in the testing and interviewing phase before data collection ended in June 1974. In the longitudinal follow-up, 1,008 men who had been released for an average of three and a half years revealed that an average of 45 percent had no subsequent arrests, 71 percent had no subsequent convictions, and 72 percent had not been returned to prison for any reason. Some men leave prison improved, some are unchanged, and still others are worse off than when they arrived.

---

[16]Hans Toch, *Living in Prison: The Ecology of Survival* (New York: The Free Press, 1977), p. 178.

[17]Sheldon B. Peizer, "What Do Prisons Do, Anyway?" in Clyde B. Vedder and Barbara A. Kay, eds., *Penology* (Springfield, Ill.: Charles C. Thomas, Publishers, 1964), pp. 292–99.

[18]Edwin I. Megree and Barbara Cadow, "The Ex-Offender and the 'Monster' Myth," *Federal Probation*, Vol. 46, no. 1 (March 1980), pp. 24–37.

CONCLUSIONS

A process of mortification occurs in all total institutions, according to Goffman.[19] Separation from society results in role displacements that can be found in monasteries, convents, mental hospitals, military academies, and like establishments. Total institutions deny all actions that in civilian society would identify a person as having some control over his or her world by stripping a person of his or her name, by imposing restrictions, and by employing other approaches to self-mortification. In religious institutions, this self-mortification derives from identification with the precepts of the religion and rejection of self. In concentration camps and, to a lesser extent, in prisons, punishment to the point of mistreatment is used if the inmate does not facilitate his or her own destruction. Over an extended period of time, the total institution alters markedly a person's previously "normal" personality and ability to take responsibility in a free society.

The penal system was intended to be a means of reform and correction, as well as punishment, but prison becomes a way of life.[20] It is predicated on an artificial environment that negates normal social interaction. Imprisonment removes responsibility from people. Prison, itself, is a means of establishing and reinforcing ties between the individual and criminal society. Imprisonment over a long period of time produces habitual prisoners who are not intentionally antisocial in many instances but have lost whatever potential they may have had to live in freedom.[21]

CHAPTER QUESTIONS

8-1. What is the approximate distribution of the prison population at different levels of custody or security?

8-2. What impact does long-term imprisonment have on people experiencing it?

8-3. What generally are the prisoners' attitudes and values in a maximum security prison?

8-4. How can long-term social relationships be characterized in the maximum security prison?

8-5. What is the prisonization process?

8-6. Why are authoritarian personalities present so frequently in prison staffs?

8-7. What are the five techniques in the theory of neutralization proposed by Sykes and Matza?

8-8. What is the pattern of loners and groupings in the maximum security prison?

8-9. What are the characteristics of inmate leadership in prisons?

8-10. What are the results of institutionalization?

[19]Erving Goffman, "On the Characteristics of Total Institutions: The Inmate World," in Donal E. J. MacNamara and Edward Sagarin, eds., *Perspectives on Corrections* (New York: Thomas Y. Crowell Company) pp. 31–61. Also the opening section of Erving Goffman, *Asylums: Essays on the Social Situation of Mental Patients and Other Inmates* (Garden City, N.Y.: Doubleday & Co., Inc., 1961).

[20]Bruno M. Cormier, *The Watcher and the Watched* (Montreal: Tundra Books, 1975), p. 21.

[21]Ibid., p. 21.

9

CONTACTS WITH THE OUTSIDE

Contact with the outside mediates the prisonization process that results from the strict regimentation and control employed in the maximum security prison. Probably the most restricted prison in modern time was the federal penitentiary at Alcatraz, which opened in 1933 and closed in 1963. The prisoners were cut off from the outside almost completely, with no radio, television, or newspapers. At the other extreme, minimum security institutions and community-based facilities have only a few simple rules designed to promote smooth operation on a regular schedule, much like the "rules" or customs in a normal family. The residents in these facilities are not in fear of attack as they are in maximum and medium custody institutions. The population of these minimum security and community-based facilities is selected with care. Although disciplinary problems exist, they are generally handled by reprimand. Serious disciplinary problems are transferred back to maximum security institutions. In minimum custody and community-based facilities, the prisonization process does not occur. The environment is "normal" in comparison with maximum and medium security institutions.

In maximum and medium security institutions, the greater the contact with the outside, the less the impact of the prisonization process. Newspapers, radio, and television, in that order, have come into the institutions. Visits and correspondence from family and friends maintain the home ties. The rapid development in the 1960s of furlough programs, work release, study release, and community-based programs has reduced the isolation of prisons from society. During the 1960s, also, the courts became interested in the rights of prisoners, and lawyers began visiting prisons more frequently. Inmate litigation averaged about five hundred cases a year in the 1950s, but rose to about twenty-three thousand cases per year by 1980. This interest and activity by the courts has tended to "open" the maximum and medium security prisons and correctional institutions.

NEWSPAPER, RADIO, AND TELEVISION

Newspapers and some magazines and journals have traditionally been permitted inside most prisons and correctional institutions. The residents can order newspapers of their choice. Traditionally, newspapers are delivered by the publisher or distributor in bulk, not to the resident who ordered them, and they are delivered by inmate runners to the appropriate cell block where, in turn, the cell block runner may deliver them to the appropriate cells or the resident may pick them up from the table near the officer's desk.

Single subscriptions of newspapers and journals come directly from the publishers by mail. Traditionally, these have been heavily censored. As recently as the early 1960s, many prison systems, including those run by the U.S. Bureau of Prisons, cut out articles about prisons, advertisements of ladies' lingerie they considered provocative, and other "undesirable" items. By the 1970s, however, this type of censorship had ceased in most institutions. Some prison systems prevented some newspapers like *The Freeworld Times* and *Penal Digest International,* both of which became defunct in 1974 for lack of funding, from coming into the prison because they were considered to be critical of the prison system and hence "inflammatory." Other prison systems have accepted anything that could come through the mails.

The Committee on Institutional Libraries of the American Correctional Association has developed and maintained a list of periodicals recommended for approval. It is constantly changing the list to keep it up to date. "Girlie" magazines are generally considered to be provocative and are not permitted, although some prisons welcome these magazines on the grounds that, as long as men are responding to the female body, homosexual inclinations will be reduced.

Censorship problems appear in the penal press, namely, the newspapers published by the inmates within the prison, such as *The Spectator* at the state prison of southern Michigan at Jackson, *The Presidio* at the Iowa state penitentiary at Fort Madison, *The Kentucky Inter-Prison Press,* and many others. All have been censored or "reviewed" by the administration in some way to suppress unwelcome criticism and controversial views. The Supreme Court has held that such censorship is subject to a standard of review before denying prisoners the exercise of their First Amendment liberties and must be done in a manner no greater than is necessary for the protection of the institution and the state.[1]

---

[1]*Procunier* v. *Martinez,* 416 U.S. 396 (1974); *Pell* v. *Procunier,* 417 U.S. 817 (1974); *Antonelli* v. *Hammond,* 308 F. Supp. 1329 (Mass., 1970); *Bailey* v. *Loggins,* 156 California Reporter 654 (Calif. App., 1979).

Radio came to prisons in the 1930s, generally via a central radio with lines run to each cell where the inmate could plug a head set into two or three channels. In smaller institutions, an inmate may have a radio in the cell; in larger institutions, a radio in every cell playing different programs would create intolerable levels of noise. Radio serves a broader segment of the prison population than do newspapers given the small percentage of prison inmates who subscribe to or read newspapers or periodicals.

Television, which came into the prisons gradually in the 1950s and 1960s, has been the greatest technological advance in helping inmates in maximum and medium security prisons to maintain contact with the outside. This writer knew a lifer who had been sentenced in 1928 and was transferred by bus twenty-five years later from a branch prison to the central prison 500 miles away. Looking at the cars on the road, he noted that "everybody is going fishing." A fellow prisoner being transferred who had been in prison less than ten years told the lifer that those were not fishing poles on the automobiles but antennas for their radios, to which the long-term prisoner responded, "In their cars?" Maximum security inmates are no longer confined to perceiving the world as it was when they entered prison.

The introduction of television into prisons was resisted by many people as a luxury. Even some old-time guards had to be assured that the state did not pay for the television sets; rather, they were being bought with inmates' welfare or commissary funds. Television is now so important to the inmates, however, that fights frequently develop over what channel should be shown. Consequently, most institutions have an officer change the channel in accordance with some type of voting by the residents.

VISITS, CORRESPONDENCE, AND TELEPHONES

Contact with family and friends is generally maintained through visits, correspondence, and telephone calls. The origin of the family visiting persons in prisons is obscure, but there is record of visiting prisoners in the "Old Stone Prisons" in Philadelphia that opened in 1718. Undoubtedly, visits by the family were originally a privilege, as indicated by the minutes of the board of the Old Walnut Street Jail in 1808, which noted that visiting was permitted for prisoners who conducted themselves properly and worked diligently. Visiting procedures have ranged from severely restricted to very loose, for example, permitting the family to have Sunday picnics on the institutional grounds in many minimum custody institutions.

In severely restricted visiting, residents and visitors are placed in two different rooms separated by a window of plate glass, sometimes bulletproof, so they can see each other, and a telephone device is used for communication. In most maximum and medium security institutions, however, there is a visiting room equipped with a long table or two where the resident sits on one side and the visitor sits on the other. The resident is thoroughly searched and, perhaps, has a change of clothes before entering the visiting room, a process that is repeated when the prisoner leaves the visiting room. In most institutions, the resident and his wife may embrace each other under supervision of an officer at the beginning and at the end of the visit. The officer watches the embrace very carefully because narcotics and other contraband may have been exchanged from mouth to mouth during kissing and from hand to pocket or hand to hand during the embrace. Visiting in maximum security institutions is closely supervised by an officer or officers in the visiting room.

There was a trend in the 1960s to relax the supervision of visiting. Many medium custody institutions eliminated the long tables and introduced smaller tables around which the resident and the family could sit and visit in a more informal manner. In minimum custody institutions, as mentioned previously, the family can bring a picnic lunch and eat on the lawn or at picnic tables provided for the purpose.

Dangers in security emanate from the introduction of contraband, the most serious being gun smuggling. For example, George Heureaux obtained a gun from his wife and killed Deputy Superintendent Godwin at the Florida state prison in 1956, and George Jackson at San Quentin obtained a gun from his attorney and brought it into the disciplinary unit. In the minimum security setting, the introduction of contraband is a lesser problem because the residents have been selected on the basis of their trustworthiness. A frequent difficulty that occurs on picnic visits, however, is the inmate engaging in illicit sexual activity with the visitor. Punishment for this misbehavior is generally suspension of visiting privileges.

In matters of visitation, the courts have generally granted prison administrations a wide range of discretion, still recognizing the need for an inmate to maintain family and community ties. The courts will also intervene when policy is based totally on the unlimited discretion of the administrator.[2] Persons eligible for visits are those who have a "constructive influence" on the inmate. Inmates need to maintain contact with family and community. Attorneys, of course, can visit at any time in the line of duty. Supervision of the visiting room should not include monitoring or eavesdropping on any inmate-visitor conversation, yet it should be sufficient to prevent the introduction of contraband.

Lay visiting has existed for two centuries in England, being promoted by Elizabeth Gurney Fry (1780–1845), after whom the Elizabeth Fry Society was named. Visitors from the society attempted to provide persons in prisons who were not being visted by the family with some outside contact. This type of visiting is generally done by individuals, although the professional visitors, from the Salvation Army, Volunteers of America, and other religious groups, are permitted as well. In recent years, there has been more frequent and purposeful visiting by lawyers representing the American Civil Liberties Union and its subsidiaries, the Prison Project of the American Bar Association, and other smaller organizations.

Correspondence in prisons is limited to an approved mailing list. This mailing list is usually made up soon after the resident arrives in the prison and is checked against the inmate's social history. Relatives, particularly the immediate family, generally have no difficulty being approved. Friends are frequently checked out by a probation or parole officer or other means before being ap-

---

[2]*Houston Chronicle Publishing Co.* v. *Kleindienst*, 364 F. Supp. 719 (S.D. Tex., 1973).

Italian-American Day at the Elmira Correctional Facility.
Courtesy of the New York State Department of Correctional Services.

proved. Members of the clergy and other religious officers are generally approved. Mail was censored heavily through the 1950s, but censoring is now generally done on a spotcheck basis when the prison administration or staff considers it valid. Censoring permits the staff to deal with disturbing letters and threats and to assess the resident's relationships with his or her family. On the other hand, censorship is time-consuming and, therefore, costly and adds to the degradation of the prisoner. The approved list appears to be an appropriate alternative. In one case, a prison system decided to permit Christmas cards to be mailed to anybody, whether on the approved list or not. The result was a large volume of mail to the prison administration from angry husbands! The system went back to the approved list. The mailing of contraband, escape plans, and other items—reasons frequently offered by security-oriented personnel desiring censorship of mail—do not constitute a serious problem.

Two types of correspondence, over and beyond personal correspondence, exist in prison: "special-purpose" letters and letters to the state officials, members of the judiciary, and attorneys. A special-purpose letter is one generally involving business or an inquiry to an individual not on the approved mailing list. These letters are reviewed by staff, frequently by counselors, and are approved or disapproved. Letters to the state commissioner or director of corrections and to the director of the U.S. Bureau of Prisons, U.S. attorney general, governors, judges, lawyers, and reputable legal organizations are permitted without censorship.

Payment of postage is generally a responsibility of the prison. Experience has indicated that the accounting procedures and personnel needed to record postage and to collect it from inmates' accounts is far more costly than is using a postage machine and charging the postage to the prison budget. Both practices can be observed in correctional institutions around the country, however.

The telephone has come into common usage in the prison and correctional institution in the late 1960s and 1970s; prior to that time, use of the telephone was highly restricted. In minimum custody institutions and community-based facilities, a pay telephone is available in the day room or other places convenient to the residents. Most prisons do not permit the residents to have money on their persons, but inmates can obtain change for the telephone from the office or the front desk and it can be charged to their accounts. Residents in community-based facilities are generally permitted to have money. In maximum and medium security institutions, the telephone calls are arranged individually.

By 1979, all states but Ohio allowed inmates to make telephone calls.[3] The vast majority of states permitted long-distance collect calls. Approximately half the states permitted inmates to receive telephone calls. The differences in inmate phone access usually relates to custody status, with maximum custody prisoners permitted fewer calls.

In summary, visiting, correspondence, and telephone calls help to maintain family and community ties for the resident of prisons and correctional institutions. As late as the early 1960s, all contact was severely restricted. Visits were degraded by excessive searches and supervision. Correspondence was routinely censored by mail room staff or by officers on the night shifts. There were very few telephone calls and those permitted were only in the case of extreme emergency. By the 1970s, restrictions on visiting had been relaxed in most prisons, censorship of mail had ceased as a general practice, and contact with the family by telephone had become common practice. These contacts with the outside have retarded the prisonization process and have reinforced family and community ties for the residents of prisons and correctional institutions.

CONJUGAL VISITS

Conjugal visits are visits during which wives are permitted to be with their husbands in private. Mississippi was the first state to introduce the conjugal visit in 1900, when the Mississippi state penitentiary at Parchman was opened. Parchman was a planter who donated the land for the prison to the state and became its first superintendent. He used inmates as guards and in other capacities to help operate the prison. The system of conjugal visit was apparently initiated by the inmates and was permitted by the administration to improve morale. As time passed, a wooden building was constructed behind each of the seventeen camps located in an arc or semicircle that made up the penitentiary. Each house was placed in charge of an inmate who collected rent. In 1952, however, several legislatures objected to having an inmate placed in this situation and a sergeant was then placed in charge. The rules in Mississippi were that whites had to be married and blacks had to be "consistent." This system was generally acknowledged, but it was not made public until 1958 at the Southern Conference on

---

[3]"Your Number, Please," *Corrections Compendium*, Vol. 3, no. 9 (April 1979), pp. 1–3.

Corrections at the Florida State University, after which it became the subject of an article in the national news magazine, *Parade,* by Ernest Mitler, an attorney from New York City, who had attended the conference. The reason that it had not been made public officially was that it appeared to be inconsistent with our puritanical Anglo-Saxon culture. Another issue yet to be resolved regards the fate of children born out of these relationships. Columbus Hopper has examined the Mississippi conjugal visiting program at length.[4]

California and some other states have also experimented with conjugal visits. Residencies some distance from the prison can be occupied by a man and his family for a weekend, an experiment first started at Tehachapi and then expanded to other institutions in California in the early 1970s. By observation, administrators considered it to be a success.

Several problems have plagued the conjugal visit. First, most prisoners are not married and do not qualify for the program. Then, some of the inmates, specifically, those in Mississippi, consider it to be degrading to their wives. Also, many wives do not want conjugal visits for a variety of reasons, including the pain of subsequent separation.[5] In addition, many wives tend to resent, despite the undesirable conditions, the fact that their husbands are provided the basic necessities of food, clothing, and housing by the prison and are, at least temporarily, spared the struggles of making a living. In the California plan, where residences are provided for "family visits," those spaces are empty during the week, even in the face of overcrowded prisons.

Conjugal visits or family visitation has been slow to develop in the United States and Canada, but it exists in many other countries, for example, Bolivia, Brazil, Ecuador, El Salvador, Guatemala, Honduras, Mexico, the Soviet Union, Denmark, and Sweden. Problems with family visiting, according to a 1980 survey, were contraband, enforcing proper behavior, poor morale on the part of inmates who do not have these visits, and having too many people appear for the visit.[6] The Mississippi and California systems have reported no problems, but other sources report resentment from inmates who do not have these visits and, where the visit is obviously conjugal, some resistance on the part of inmates who do not want to embarrass their wives. There are no reports of conjugal visits in prisons for women, a situation that has also generated resentment among women in Latin America.

Conjugal visits have joined other goods and services as contraband in some institutions and are now being distributed illegally for profit.[7] Usually in prisons that permit conjugal visits, the demand exceeds the supply because of limited space and, where it is done surreptitiously, the demand may carry with it some type of reward. While assignments of these visits are supposed to be supervised by an official, the actual assignments are sometimes done by an inmate clerk because the official does not have time to do it. When an assigned and

---

[4]Columbus B. Hopper, *Sex in Prison: The Mississippi Experiment with Conjugal Visiting* (Baton Rouge: Louisiana State University Press, 1969).

[5]A. Crosthwaite, "Punishment for Whom, the Prisoner or His Wife?" *International Journal of Offender Therapy and Comparative Criminology,* Vol. 19, no. 3 (1975), pp. 275–84.

[6]"Family Visitation," *Corrections Compendium,* Vol. 4, no. 7 (January 1980), pp. 2–5.

[7]John Irwin, *Prisons in Turmoil* (Boston: Little, Brown and Company, 1980), p. 210.

Family visiting at the United States Penitentiary at Lompoc, California.
Courtesy of the Federal Prison System.

approved visitor does not show up, then her place can be taken by another "waiting in line." Where prisoners actually administer these lists, there is the possibility of "selling" these visits.

In summary, proponents of conjugal visits claim that they reduce homosexuality, whereas opponents hold that it degrades the female participant and introduces pregnancies and venereal disease.[8] The inmates who participate in these programs are enthusiastic, but there are many who cannot because they are not married, space is not available, and they lack the good conduct record to be eligible. There is some evidence that the provocation of seeing others participate actually drives the ineligible residents to homosexuality.

FURLOUGHS

A furlough is a short-term leave from the prison or correctional institution. Furloughs for emergencies, such as a serious illness or a death in the family, have been traditional. In these instances, however, the inmate or his family must pay expenses, including the salary of the accompanying officer. The more recent version of the furlough as a short-term social visit began in many states in the 1960s. The length of time is generally one or two days, frequently over a weekend. For several years, Mississippi has offered two-week Christmas furloughs.

By 1979, furloughs were available in thirty-nine states.[9] Generally, the

[8]Sue Titus Reid, *Crime and Criminology,* 2nd ed. (New York: Holt, Rinehart and Winston, 1979), pp. 721–22.
[9]"I'll Be Home for Christmas," *Corrections Compendium,* Vol. 4, no. 6 (December 1979), pp. 1–7.

family or other approved person checks the resident out of the institution and agrees to return him or her at a specified time. Some states have permitted girlfriends and boyfriends to check out a resident for eight hours; other states are more conservative. Many correctional administrators view the furloughs as more desirable than the conjugal visiting programs in maintaining family ties. The furlough is focused not so much on sex as the conjugal visit is, but more widely on social interaction. Some furloughs are granted to residents about to be released on parole for the purpose of finding employment.

WORK RELEASE

Work release is a program in which sentenced offenders may leave the institution or community-based facility and take a regular job in the community. Many of the jobs are in construction, gas stations, and restaurants, although a variety of jobs has been held by work releasees.

Work release began for misdemeanants in Wisconsin under the Huber Law in 1913 when the state senator whose name the law carries objected to persons in jail sitting in idleness while being supported by law-abiding taxpayers. The law was used rarely at first because some sheriffs indicated that they did not have the personnel to operate it and some citizens object to the freedom it provided to some "convicts who ought to be in jail." Several states experimented with it on the misdemeanor level. North Carolina expanded work release to felons in 1959 for economic reasons. In 1965, Congress passed the Prisoners' Rehabilitation Act that provided for work release and other community-based programs within the U.S. Bureau of Prisons. The terminology and conditions of work release vary, but the basic principles are similar. California copied Wisconsin's Huber Law and refers to its program as "work furlough." Michigan refers to it as "day parole."

The procedure in all programs is essentially similar in the classification process. Residents selected do not present an obvious escape risk and generally have less than a year left until they are eligible for parole. A job counselor finds employment for the resident at the going rate of pay to avoid exploitation and consequent resentment on the part of the resident, which would be counterproductive. The money earned is used to defray expenses of the program, to help support the family still at home, and to provide a savings account in preparation for release. There is a daily maintenance charge, frequently around $5.00 per day, for board and room and a transportation charge, frequently around $1.50 to $2.50, for taking the resident to and from work. Most work releases are in community-based facilities, but some are in maximum or medium custody institutions and residents are permitted to go out through the front gate in the morning and return at night.

Keeping work releasees in community-based facilities together with other community custody residents is a more economical and satisfactory approach. When residents are permitted to leave maximum and medium security institutions in the morning and return at night, they tend to be subjected by other inmates to accusations that they are "pets" of the administration and, even worse, are subjected to requests to bring in contraband for other inmates with "enforcement" by doing fellow residents a favor or by threats of physical violence. In the community-based facility, however, all residents have the same status and such pressures can be avoided.

The most frequent problems in work release generally include alcohol and drugs. Many have returned to the facility under the influence of alcohol or drugs, whereas others, fearing disciplinary action, have failed to return at all. Those who return to the facility under the influence of alcohol or drugs are generally kept at the facility and are provided counseling, frequently by other residents in group sessions; those who fail to return to the facility are considered to be escapees and may be returned to a more secure institution. Another problem occurs when the employer is not satisfied with the performance of the resident. In such cases, the job counselor discusses the problems with the resident and may find another job for him or her. In most systems where work release is used liberally, the resident is placed in a community-based facility and is provided with a job in his or her home community. When released, the individual keeps the job and simply moves home. It should be noted here that the timing of assignment to work release programs is important. The best timing is generally six months to one year prior to parole eligibility release date. Persons on work release for more than a year tend to develop morale problems, since they have made friendships on the job but cannot participate in social activities fully on evenings and weekends.

STUDY RELEASE

Study release is similar to work release, except that the residents attend school. They may attend any kind of school ranging from vocational-technical and high school to the university. Most jurisdictions permit the family to pay tuition and other costs, or the resident may pay his or her own way through scholarships, veterans' benefits, or other means. Some jurisdictions have paid the cost of education for residents considered worthy of it on the basis that it costs less to send a person to college than it does to keep him or her in a maximum security institution and, further, that society has its chance to gain from the contributions the individual might make in the future and from termination of a criminal career.

Education of this type began in Oregon in 1967 under the leadership of Thomas Gaddis, author of *Birdman of Alcatraz,* when he established the NewGate program funded by the Office of Economic Opportunity. Professors would go to the prison and instruct residents to be released in the near future. As they were released, they would go to a university, live in a halfway house or other facility near the university, and attend classes. That program soon spread to six states. Some states, such as New Mexico, permit offenders to live in the dormitories at the university. As study release grew, it developed in other states with their own resources and not identified with the NewGate program or funded by OEO. South Carolina, for example, has an independent program that, according to Commissioner William D. Leeke, will send residents to "any college that will accept them" and where they may use college or university housing.

Political and legal problems sometimes frame the pattern of these community-based programs. For example, the Ohio Constitution prohibits state prisoners from working for private persons or firms, which eliminates work release. Therefore, Ohio has concentrated on study release.[10] In 1975, the Florida legislature eliminated study release in an angry reaction to a judge's son being "bumped" from admission to law school by a "convict" who had scored higher on the admissions examination. By 1978, all but six states had work release or study release.

CONDITIONAL MANDATORY RELEASE

Conditional mandatory release or supervised mandatory release refers to the release of residents of prisons and correctional institutions a short time before the expiration of the maximum sentence without going through the parole board. Brief supervision is provided by parole agents in the community. There is some variation among jurisdictions as to the time of supervision. Some compute the good time earned and permit supervision between the expiration of sentence. Some jurisdictions have a flat 120-day release period, providing four months of supervision, which helps an individual to get going on a job and establish a residence. Approximately 6.1 percent of all releases in 1975 were by conditional mandatory release.

PARDONS, COMMUTATIONS, AND EXPUNGEMENTS

Pardons, commutations, and expungements refer to legal modifications of a sentence. Pardon refers to executive clemency. In most jurisdictions, a pardon can be issued by the governor. A pardon board that includes the governor exists in some jurisdictions, and still other jurisdictions rely on a recommendation to the governor by the parole board. Controls were established after some abuses of pardon power before World War II. The pardon was originally and still remains the primary technique of correcting what is interpreted as a miscarriage of justice. In recent times, the pardon has been used to accomplish desirable objectives. For example, under the immigration and nationalization laws, undesirable aliens must be deported. When an immigrant has not taken American citizenship and his offense was not serious, sometimes a technical pardon has been used to avoid deportation. The pardon is still an integral part of the justice system, well exemplified by President Gerald Ford's pardon of former President Richard Nixon on grounds that he has been "punished enough." Having grown out of the principle of benefit of clergy in a religious society, the pardon has assumed broader ethical connotations available to all to correct miscarriages of justice or to avoid further damage to an individual considered to be unwarranted.

[10]George J. Denton and N. Gatz, "Ohio's Work Furlough: College for Felons," *American Journal of Corrections*, Vol. 35, no. 3 (1973), pp. 44–45.

Commutation has been used in much the same way as pardon. Commutations refer to the governor's or the president's power to reduce sentence. Commutations are used when it has been determined that an offender has received an unusually long sentence in proportion to the seriousness of the offense and after years of good behavior in the prison and correctional institution. It has sometimes been used for political purposes. In the early 1950s, for example, a governor in one state had been elected by a narrow margin with the help of labor unions. When an official of the labor union was convicted of a relatively minor offense involving union activities, his sentence was commuted as he entered the lobby of the prison. Fortunately, this kind of activity is at a minimum, and most commutations are the result of recommendation by the paroling authorities to the governor to reduce the sentence from life, for example, to time served. In the majority of cases, commutations have been used constructively and judiciously.

Expungement is the clearing of a record of conviction for an offense. Expungement status generally refers to first-offenders not considered to be dangerous to society and after a period of time, sometimes three years, of successful adjustment in the community. A petition for expungement can be filed with the convicting court in these jurisdictions. The court may then expunge the record. The role of expungement is an enabling statute to help the ex-offender to reintegrate into society without continuing the legal stigma that prevents him or her from participating in several types of employment.[11] All states have enacted some barriers preventing ex-felons from entering some occupations, including barbering, cosmetology, insect extermination, and others considered to be sensitive. Some jurisdictions have listed more than two hundred occupations from which ex-felons are barred. Expungement eliminates this handicap. By 1978, fourteen states had expungement laws. Yet the expungement alternative is not well known. Ohio and Washington have probably used it more than others. Some problems have arisen with acceptance because of police records. Newspaper stories cannot be expunged and sealed as can court action. Nevertheless, the American Bar Association and other legally oriented groups are optimistic about its future use.

PAROLE

Parole consists of release of residents from prisons and correctional institutions by action of a parole board and subsequent supervision by a parole agent. The length of this supervision has frequently been three or four years, although some jurisdictions have imposed life supervision for capital crimes after release from prison. Experience has shown that most parole violations are in the first weeks or months of release under supervision. By the time that two years under supervision have been completed successfully, the risk of violation is reduced. In the late 1950s and 1960s, between 55 and 63 percent of all releases in the United

[11]Leslie D. Stickler, "Expungement: An Enabling Statute—A New Alternative to the Effect of Legal Stigma," *Proceedings of the 23rd Annual Southern Conference on Corrections*, March 5–7, 1978, Tallahassee, Florida, pp. 235–50.

States were by parole. While nine states, beginning with Maine in 1976, have eliminated or drastically reduced the use of parole and have gone to determinate or flat sentencing, the use of parole throughout the country has risen in recent years. By 1976, releases by parole had risen to 69 percent[12] and continued to rise in 1977 to 77.2 percent,[13] but showed a slight decline in 1978.[14]

A primary problem with parole relates to the residue of dissatisfied residents who have been rejected by the parole board. This creates a morale problem and is one reason that "causes" of riots and disturbances identified by dissident inmate groups invariably include "parole policies." Residents rejected for parole often say that the parole board is "after them" and is being unfair.

Regarding the use of parole, some states, including New Hampshire, Michigan, and Washington, parole almost all their first releases; other states, including South Carolina and Oklahoma, parole considerably fewer inmates than the national average. Another concern is the observation that parole boards generally release the best risks and place them under supervision, yet they hold the worst risks until expiration of maximum sentences and then release them into society with no supervision. Conditional mandatory release, of course, has mitigated this problem in some jurisdictions.

CONCLUSIONS

Most prison inmates lack social ties.[15] Inmates are twice as likely as the general population to have never been married. They are three times as likely to have been divorced, separated, or widowed. Of the married persons, they are half as likely to have been living with their spouses. In terms of age, about 10 percent of the prison population in Illinois, for example, is 18 and 19 years of age, as compared with 5 percent in the general population, whereas only 6 percent of the prison population are 45- to 54-year-olds as compared with 24 percent of the general population.[16]

Families of prison inmates suffer considerably in modern society. Probably half consider divorce and some complete this transaction. Children are frequently protected from the information that their father is in prison, but, sometimes, they are told that their father was no good, anyway. Friends Outside is the only nationwide organization specifically concerned with the problems derived from being in an inmate's family.[17] Many women whose husbands are in prison

[12]James L. Galvin, Cheryl H. Ruby, Cynthia Mahabir, Paul Litsky, and Ellen L. McNeil, *Characteristics of the Parole Population, 1977,* (San Francisco: NCCD Research Center West, April 1979), pp. 13–17.

[13]"Use of Parole Increases Sharply," *Criminal Justice Newsletter,* Vol. 9, no. 17 (August 28, 1978), pp. 5–6.

[14]James L. Galvin, Cheryl H. Ruby, John J. Galvin, Paul Litsky, and William Elms, *Parole in the United States—1978* (San Francisco: NCCD Research Center West, July 1979), p. 1.

[15]Ellen Handler and Lori Schuett, "Are Prison Inmates Really 'Naked Nomads?'" *American Journal of Correction,* Vol. 39, no. 6 (December 1977), p. 16.

[16]Ibid., p. 17.

[17]Laura J. Bakker, Barbara A. Morris, and Laura M. Janus, "Hidden Victims of Crime," *Social Work,* Vol. 23, no. 2 (March 1978), p. 144.

tell friends and neighbors that they are separated or divorced or that it is none of their business.[18]

Residents of prison and correctional institutions can maintain contact with the free community in several ways. Newspapers and radios have long been available. Television has been probably the most effective way of keeping in contact with the free community, particularly in maximum security institutions. Through this medium, residents of the institution can keep abreast of clothing styles, automobile model changes, and many other social and cultural changes that came as a shock to long-term offenders released prior to World War II through the early 1950s. No longer will these long-term offenders be frightened by the heavy traffic and not be able to comprehend traffic lights that flash red, amber, and green. No longer will long-term inmates see antennas protruding from automobiles and interpret them as fishing poles, only to be told that they are car radios. Modern technology has eliminated this problem.

In addition, newer programs have brought families closer together by permitting furloughs, more liberal visiting, correspondence, and community-based programs. While the physical security of walls, fences, and guard towers will remain in many prisons, the communication between the inside and the outside will reduce the shock of reintegrating into society.

CHAPTER QUESTIONS

9-1.   Why are contacts with the outside important to prisoners?
9-2.   Why is television a positive influence on long-term inmates in prison?
9-3.   How are contacts with the family and friends outside maintained in the prisons?
9-4.   What are the advantages of furloughs from prisons?
9-5.   What is the advantage of work release?
9-6.   What is the advantage of study release?
9-7.   What is conditional mandatory release?
9-8.   What are pardons, commutations, and expungements?
9-9.   What are the advantages and disadvantages of conjugal visits?
9-10. Is parole affected by the variations in intensity and frequency of outside contact by inmates to be paroled?

[18]Pauline Morris, *Prisoners and Their Families* (New York: Hart Publishing Co., 1965).

10
STAFF SOCIETY

Special influences of the prison are felt by the staff as well as by the inmates or residents. Living in the "social pressure cooker" known as the prison, there are pressures and stresses much different from those found in businesses, educational institutions, and other facilities in the community. Many lawyers, insurance underwriters, corporation executives, and political leaders make many contacts on a friendly basis in the community and at social events. Prison society is characterized by adversaries, with one group of people guarding another group of people with the intention of keeping the latter alive. Even the adversary posture of the criminal court is less hostile than prison society because the primary effort there is to provide a fair and impartial trial with an adequate defense for the defendants. It is generally known that police and law enforcement agencies spend about 10 percent of their effort in criminal cases, whereas all the effort in prison is directed to criminal cases.

There is considerable literature on pressures on police, but they are in contact with the public, while personnel in maximum security prisons are isolated even from the public and remain invisible, behind the walls.

GEOGRAPHIC AND SOCIAL ISOLATION

Finding the site for the construction of a new prison correctional facility is difficult and is frequently preceded by a series of public hearings, as noted in Chapter 2. Many residents of urban centers do not want a prison or correctional institution built in their neighborhoods because they fear that the value of their property will decline. On the other hand, rural areas that are relatively poor and sparsely populated see the introduction of a correctional facility as providing a substantial payroll and other economic advantages.

Even where prisons are located not far from large urban areas, wardens and superintendents frequently recruit correctional officers from other, more rural places. For example, under Warden Joseph Ragen of the Illinois state penitentiary at Stateville (now called the Stateville Correctional Center), almost a suburb southwest of Chicago, lieutenants and officers were sent in teams to southern Illinois, Missouri, and Kentucky to hire correctional officers.[1] The majority of prisoners were from urban Chicago, but the prisons were staffed from rural southern Illinois. To secure the isolation, a trailer park was developed near the prison to keep the personnel away as much as possible from nearby communities such as Joliet. Still in 1977, eight of the nine guards at the captain's level and above were not from northern Illinois and the trailer court adjacent to the prison had yet to be integrated by a nonwhite family.[2]

The staff was in a relatively closed community, socializing with other staff, and maintaining social distance from the prisoners, many of whom were urban blacks or Hispanics, with little common ground for communication with the correctional officers from rural southern Illinois. A similar situation occurred at the Attica correctional facility in New York, which broke into a riot September 9–13, 1971. About 76 percent of the prisoners were blacks and Spanish-speaking persons from New York City, while the correctional officers were from the rural areas around Attica between Rochester and Buffalo. The social distance between these two groups resulted in considerable tension, which contributed to the riot. The California state prison at San Quentin is 12 miles north of San Francisco, but has its own housing adjacent to the prison for its personnel. The residential areas near the federal institutions are generally called "The Village."

Regardless of how it happens, whether by original construction in a remote rural area or by policy of the administration in hiring, many American prisons have isolated their personnel from the rest of the community. To provide housing for the staff, most prisons and correctional institutions have constructed their own "villages." Consequently, many practitioners and administrators in prison today were born and raised on prison property in a prison social setting. The most famous was Warden Clinton Duffy of San Quentin, whose father was a guard at the prison and who went into the prison ranks, following his father, when he reached maturity and subsequently rose to the wardenship.

---

[1] James B. Jacobs, *Stateville: The Penitentiary in Mass Society* (Chicago: University of Chicago Press, 1977), p. 40.
[2] Ibid., p. 252.

A televised interview on September 18, 1977 reinforced this trend.[3] James W. McLendon, author of *Deathwork*,[4] noted, "I was nine years old before I knew I was living in a penitentiary." His father, R. P. McLendon, had been an officer and administrator in the Florida state prison at Raiford for thirty-nine years before his retirement and had participated in 114 executions. *Deathwork* is a novel that summarizes R. P. McLendon's career. Many of the details concerning execution procedures and experiences were drawn from stories he had heard from his father as a child and as a young man.

An interesting account of being raised in prison is contained in the following letter from James B. Godwin, superintendent of the Florida Reception and Medical Center at Lake Butler.[5] His father had been assistant superintendent of the Florida state prison at Raiford, lived on prison property where James was born and raised, and was killed in 1956 by an inmate, George Heureaux, whose wife had smuggled in a pistol on visiting day. Subsequently, a metal detector was installed at the front gate.

Dear Vernon:

Having been born at Florida State Prison with its rural location in 1930, the real early years seemed as normal as any other child. But from the beginning, I associated with inmates in our home, cooks and maids, and had almost free run of the institution. There were quite a number of children that resided on the institutional grounds. All of the families were of moderate income groups, so entertainment was simple and life mostly like that of any rural family.

I remember my association with many of the old timers inside the fence. They took care of making toys and trinkets for most of the kids. I really felt sorry for most of the inmates because during that stage most all convinced me that they were "victims of circumstances." Many of my inmate friends were used as guards or foremen over other inmates, but I went all over the institution without ever being involved in an incident with an inmate.

During this stage of Florida's Prison System, most of the hardened criminals were transferred to the Road Prisons. Every inmate at that time was required to work during the daylight hours Monday through Saturday and during the summer months the days were quite long. I remember this particular type inmate as caring more for his fellow inmate and showing more respect for them. I think because of this, the children were permitted to attend movies inside the compound and I don't recall any incidents arising from this.

I remember an incident that happened during the early years of World War II that certainly had to be a first in Florida. One of the inmates being

---

[3]"McLendon to Be on TV," *The Gainesville Sun* (Florida), September 18, 1977, p. 1.

[4]James McLendon, *Deathwork* (Philadelphia and New York: J. B. Lippincott Company, 1977, Bantam edition, 1978).

[5]Personal letter from James B. Godwin, superintendent of the Florida Reception and Medical Center, dated October 24, 1977.

used as a tower guard, lowered a rope to another inmate inside and pulled him up in the tower with him. They then took the guns and escaped. I was allowed to ride in the dog wagon during the search which was successful.

As a youngster, I played on the prison baseball team. Their semi-pro ball club was one of the top teams in North Florida. Later on, I was employed to organize and coach the first football team at Florida State Prison. I remember even with outstanding athletes, few had attended school long enough to participate in football. They were a tough bunch and during the season, we tied Stetson and beat Jacksonville Naval Air Station. Funny thing, I still have my tight-end with me thirty years later.

I don't think I ever had any intentions of working at a prison as during those years it was mostly a system of punishment and that did not appeal to me. I was encouraged by my parents to complete my education and not be associated with prison work.

I married while attending the University of Florida and decided to go to work. I began work as a Correctional Officer at Glades Correctional Institution. Belle Glade was a Farm Camp and the total program was farming. We worked long hours but generally the administration was fair, however, there was little to learn for inmates or personnel.

I transferred back to Florida State Prison as Manager of the Cattle Industry. Working there eight years before being promoted to Chief Correctional Officer. I was promoted to Assistant Superintendent six years later. In 1970, I was promoted to Superintendent of Desoto Correctional Institution. In 1973, transferred to the Reception and Medical Center as Superintendent.

I think the most interesting part of Corrections is the fact that it continually changes. Methods that worked last year have to be altered or completely changed to be effective. Problems we solve today are obsolete next month.

We have devoted many hours to training personnel, building institutions to cope with our population of 19,600. I certainly could not have imagined this on my first visit to a prison.

Sincerely,

J. B. GODWIN
Superintendent

Another example of socialization in the prison environment emerged when the wedding picture of a son of a prison official in a northern state appeared in *The Detroit Free Press* during a turbulent "investigation" in the 1940s. The attendants at the wedding were identified as a murderer, a rapist, an armed robber, another murderer, and other convicted offenders. No one at the wedding was from the free community. This writer began to be concerned in the early 1950s at the same institution when his 4-year-old daughter traded a peanut butter sandwich with a lifer completing twenty-five years assigned to the prison housing property for a paint job on her tricycle!

These cases demonstrate the compelling influence of prison society that renders people born and raised there somewhat uncomfortable in other societies. Much has been written about the stress of police work and what it does to the personalities of police officers and members of their families.[6] The factors affecting law enforcement officers are exaggerated in prison society, where the prison staff, unlike the police officer who lives and works in the community, is almost completely closed off from the free society.

EXPOSURE TO PARANOID THINKING PATTERNS

The danger of exposure to paranoid thinking is that one becomes involved in it. Few people in a democratic society are exposed to paranoid thinking more than correctional officers.[7] Even psychiatrists and mental health workers in the paranoid-schizophrenic wards are less exposed because the mental patients are not in touch with reality, whereas angry and violence-prone inmates of maximum custody prisons are able to "interpret" reality. Correctional officers are constantly exposed to persecution and must resist the ever-present temptation to become persecutors. In the deprivation of liberty, staff and inmates alike are condemned to be watchers and watched, and this situation in prison not only changes prisoners, but it changes their keepers, probably more deeply.[8] Many officers and prison personnel have "done more time" than most of the inmates.

Salaries of correctional officers are low, and most new officer recruits take these jobs until they can get something better, which leaves the prisons with "pedestrian" personnel.[9] When these people are exposed to the inevitable degrading and brutalizing aspects of day-to-day work in the prison, together with the regimentation of numbering, counting, checking, and locking-up, the regimentation of the officers is not too different from that of the prisoners.[10] Consequently, some officers become more institutionalized than the prisoners.

Corruption of staff by residents is a frequent problem in most prisons. Sometimes, inmates can "con" a staff member to bring in contraband or carry out underground mail. In one extreme case, an officer was persuaded to bring $2,500 into a prison for a hired killing. In another, a chaplain was blackmailed into bringing liquor into the prison. In that case, an old-time inmate clerk played on the sympathy of the chaplain and prevailed on the chaplain to mail a letter to an "old aunt." When a response came to a chaplain's house, the chaplain reprimanded the inmate clerk, but he was persuaded a couple of months later to take

---

[6]For example, see Jerome H. Skelnick, "The Policemen's Working Personality," in his *Justice Without Trial* (New York: John Wiley & Sons, Inc., 1966), pp. 42–62.

[7]Bruno Cormier, *The Watcher and the Watched* (Montreal: Tundra Books, 1975), p. 12. Also, see Lucien X. Lombardo, *Guards Imprisoned: Correctional Officers at Work* (New York: Elsevier-North Holland, 1981).

[8]Ibid., p. 308.

[9]Harry Elmer Barnes and Negley K. Teeters, *New Horizons in Criminology*, 3rd ed. (Englewood Cliffs, N.J.: Prentice-Hall, Inc., 1959), p. 359.

[10]Ibid., pp. 359–60.

out another letter. One day, the inmate clerk told the chaplain that he was in debt in the yard for gambling and needed money. The chaplain refused such a request as being ridiculous. The inmate clerk asked him how long he had to go to retirement, to which the chaplain replied that he had two more years to go to get the needed twenty-five years. The inmate clerk said, "Chaplain, do you think you will make it?" and reminded him that he had taken out underground mail, which was against the rules of the institution. The chaplain was coerced to bring in the liquor so the inmate could pay his gambling debts in the yard. After the gambling debts were paid, the inmate could continue to have a source of income. Later, the chaplain was discovered and was dismissed and put on probation, after explaining that he thought he had a chance of beating the administration, but he had no chance of beating the inmate!

It is obvious to most correctional practitioners and administrators that it is very dangerous to accept gifts or favors from the residents or their families. Those who do risk dismissal. In one case, an officer permitted a representative of organized crime to pay off his home mortgage in return for several favors, while others have permitted their automobile loans to be paid. Fortunately, these cases of corruption are comparatively rare and are always subject to dismissal and, perhaps, charges in criminal court. The chaplain who brought in contraband liquor was convicted of bringing contraband into a prison and was placed on one year's probation.

In summary, exposure to paranoid thinking patterns affects almost everybody connected with the prison in some way. Only a small percentage engage in illegal activities, but enough do that many correctional administrators have said that, if they could straighten out staff problems, they would have little problem with the inmates.

THE BURNOUT SYNDROME

There has been a growing interest in burnout in recent years,[11] though it has been recognized by correctional administrators and practitioners since World War II, when real attempts at counseling began in the prisons. This writer has referred to burnout cases as persons who are "case-hardened," a process of heating, carburizing, and quenching ferrous alloys in cold water to make the surface layers harder than the interior. In the prison, it meant exterior hardening or callousing by increasing cynicism at successive failure in their cases. In mental health, it is referred to as insensitivity. Some have referred to Sisyphus, the legendary king who was condemned throughout eternity to pushing a heavy stone up a steep hill, only to have the stone roll back to the bottom.[12] The labors of Sisyphus are characterized by continual but often ineffective effort.

The physical signs of burnout have been identified as (1) feelings of exhaustion and fatigue and being physically run down, (2) frequent headaches

[11]Jerry Edelwich with Archie Brodsky, *Burn-out: Stages of Disillusionment in the Helping Professions* (New York: Human Sciences Press, 1980).

[12]Clemens Bartollas, "Sisyphus in a Juvenile Institution," *Social Work*, Vol. 2, (September 1975), p. 366.

and gastrointestinal disturbances, (3) weight loss, (4) sleeplessness, (5) depression, and (6) shortness of breath.[13] Behavioral symptoms include (1) lability of mood, (2) blunting of affect or emotional flatness, (3) quickness to anger, (4) diminished frustration tolerance, (5) suspiciousness, sometimes approaching paranoia, (6) feelings of helplessness, and (7) increased levels of risk taking.[14] Of course, not all these conditions have to be present in every case of burnout.

Burnout is a syndrome of emotional exhaustion and cynicism that frequently occurs among individuals who do "people work" and spend considerable time in close encounters with others under chronic tension and stress.[15] High burnout is often associated with family stress. Heavy use of tranquilizers, alcohol, and drugs is correlated with burnout.[16]

Burnout relating to staff members' treatment orientation includes such factors as cohesiveness in philosophy and approach, confrontation with each other, and personal relations with residents; burnout relating to administration includes such factors as involvement in decision making, autonomy in work, maintaining open communication between staff and administration, and knowledge of the results of their work.[17] Staff members tend to range widely from those with good job satisfaction and little burnout to those most dissatisfied and a high level of burnout.

A study of the correctional workers' and volunteers' development of careers in working with offenders has revealed that disappointment and frustration lead to their being worn down or "burned out" in about two years.[18] Because rehabilitative aspects of corrections are based on superficial conceptualizations of the offenders' inherited maladies, workers fail to achieve the goals and hence feel cheated. Then, they acquiesce to the organization's primary responsibility of protection of the public by incarceration.

It is not a syndrome limited to correctional officers in the United States. It is international. Correctional officers tend to have the highest rate of illness among all government workers in Japan.[19] They experience more strenuous mental and physical labor than do other government employees due to irregular working hours and constant contact with clients who are criminal and emotionally disturbed. Correctional officers are generally in excellent mental and physical health at the point of entry into correctional service. Effective programs

---

[13]Richard C. W. Hall, Earl R. Gardner, Mark Perl, Sondra K. Stickney, and Betty Pefferbaum, "The Professional Burn-out Syndrome," *Psychiatric Opinion*, Vol. 5, (April 1979), p. 12.

[14]Ibid., p. 12.

[15]Christina Maslach and S. Jackson, "Burned-out Cops and Their Familes," *Psychology Today*, May 1979, p. 59.

[16]Ibid., p. 62.

[17]Knowlton W. Johnson, William T. Rusinko, Charles M. Girard, and Marvin G. Tossey, "Job Satisfaction and Burn-out: A Double-Edged Threat to Human Service Workers," in John A. Conley, ed., *Theory and Research in Criminal Justice: Current Perspectives* (Cincinnati: W. H. Anderson Publishing Company, 1979), pp. 127–50.

[18]M. H. Moynihan; *Getting Burned—A Study in the Socialization of Correctional Workers* (Ann Arbor, Mich.: University Microfilms, 1976), 203 pp.

[19]Toru Yoshinage, "Health Control for Correctional Officers—Including Mental Health," *Japanese Journal of Correction*, Vol. 86, no. 2 (1975), pp. 29–38.

of relief and other types of health control need to be implemented to maintain the health of correctional officers.

In this regard, William Nagel has pointed out that

> Warm people enter the system wanting desperately to change it, but the problems they find are so enormous and the tasks so insurmountable that these warm people turn cold. In time, they can no longer allow themselves to feel, to love, to care. To survive, they must become callous.[20]

He continues to reiterate that the prison is corrosive for those who guard and those who are guarded.

While penal institutions determine the expectations of their own guards' social roles, adequate performances of the role depends upon self-perceptions of the guards and the extent to which their own expectations are associated with those of the institution.[21] Correctional officers' attitudes contain a high level of cynicism, which is really an adaptation to conflict situations.[22]

While much of the literature is focused on correctional officers or guards because they are in closer daily contact with the residents, it is also true of the counselors, social workers, psychiatrists, psychologists, educators, and other professional and administrative personnel. Staffs must justify to themselves and to others what they are doing in the prison or correctional institution and how they contribute to the correctional process. Custodial staff and administrative officers can rely on the idea that they are carrying out the mandate of the courts to keep convicted offenders institutionalized, at least for the duration of the minimum sentence. It is really more difficult in many cases with professional staff because their objective is to reintegrate the offenders into the community as self-respecting, wage-earning, taxpaying citizens, a task unmeasurable at the present. When offenders return months or years in the future, the inability to explain failure becomes a source of stress that contributes to burnout.

It must be pointed out that not everybody experiences burnout. There are many correctional officers and other personnel in prisons and correctional institutions who have hope for everybody, and who indicate that if they can help only a few "make it," then the effort will have been worth it. Many correctional officers have been promoted to "counselors" because of their empathic skills, their ability to relate to and work with the residents. Further, many of these good people have been promoted up the ranks to wardens of institutions and to directors of prison systems. Burnout has telling effects on some, resulting in turnover of staff or a retreat from hope of rehabilitation to a hardline custodial orientation. On the other hand, many personnel in prisons, both correctional

---

[20]William G. Nagel, *The New Red Barn: A Critical Look at the Modern American Prison* (New York: Walker and Company, published for The American Foundation, Inc., Institute of Corrections, Philadelphia, 1973).

[21]P. Peretti and M. Hooker, "Social Role Self-perceptions of State Prison Guards," *Criminal Justice Behavior*, Vol. 3, no. 3 (1976), pp. 187–96.

[22]R. E. Farmer, "Cynicism: A Factor in Corrections Work," *Journal of Criminal Justice*, Vol. 5 (1977), pp. 237–46.

officers and others, experience burnout only momentarily without holding unreasonably high expectations, but with some hope for all.

LOYALTIES AND BUILT-IN CONFLICTS

The staff tends to develop loyalty to "prison people" to insulate them against any intrusion or criticism from the outside community, news media, political investigations, and other attacks on them and their colleagues. The U.S. Bureau of Prisons goes so far as to refer to its group as "the Federal Family" and no outsider, even from other prison systems, participates in its official and self-contained parties, retirement dinners, and other social events. Many systems have been that rigid in insulating their "brotherhood" from "outside contamination." The adversary position that many correctional personnel take with the residents is also taken with "outsiders." Although more has been written about the loyalty of police to their colleagues, this behavior also occurs among companies, corporations, and civic and fraternal social groups such as lodges and clubs. Even the Bell Telephone Company is referred to by its employees as "Ma Bell." Nevertheless, this loyalty appears to be stronger and have more meaning in the criminal justice system than in most other groups.

Within their own group, however, the conflicts and factionalization among correction personnel is strong and sometimes vicious. One broadly-based built-in conflict in correctional institutions is that among the administration, custody, and treatment personnel. The administration views lack of escapes and maintaining peace and order inside the institution as essential to public relations, that is, relations with the political leadership, the news media, and the community. Custody has the responsibility of keeping the inmates locked up securely in accordance with the mandate of the court and maintaining peace and order within the institution. The treatment people see their objective as rehabilitation through education, counseling, religious instruction, and other approaches that have as their final goal the release of the offender to the community as a free and law-abiding citizen. The inmates want to get out any way possible. Therefore, a built-in conflict is between custody and treatment, with the administration generally behind custody, since the administration and custody want to hold the inmates securely, inmates want out, and the treatment people also want the inmates out, which places the treatment people "on the side of the inmate"!

Staff members in the average prison tend to group themselves along a continuum ranging from strong support for the administration to disregard for the objectives of the institution in favor of their own welfare and desires. This type of grouping, or course, can be found in any organization. For purposes of study, these groupings can be classified, in their order of decreasing identification with the institution, as (1) *claques*, who strongly support the institution and its leadership; (2) *loyalists*, who become the institution's solid citizens; (3) *cabals*, whose members needlessly withdraw from support or opposition but maintain concerned interest in the institution; (4) *cliques*, whose members are generally withdrawn from the institution in spirit but frequently cause irritation because of conflict with other cliques; and (5) *factions*, whose members become primary friendship groups frequently based on ethnic, racial, sexual, political, religious, or other common factors, not really concerned with the welfare of the institution.[23] The staff members of the institution, then, become divided according to their identification with the institution and their perceptions of their own self-interests.

The claques support the warden or superintendent and attempt to neutralize opposition to the administration. Members of claque groups are frequently promoted more rapidly. The loyalists maintain a balance and sense of humor in the institution and their roles in it. They have "made peace with the system" and give it an honest day's work. The cabals are politically sensitive and maneuver within the institution to win people over to their views; they flourish when key members of the institution are replaced and when those more loyal to the administration are not considered for the key positions during the change of direction. The cabals tend to fill middle management roles, such as captains, lieutenants, and department heads. The cliques do not have much impact on the institution as a whole, but tend to be disruptive because of their continuous fighting among themselves. The factions retreat from the institutional objectives and passively play their roles; they frequently fight among themselves, as do the cliques, causing irritability and conflict within the institution. Their real concern is not the institution; rather, they "put in their time" and look forward to evening and weekend socialization, anticipate vacations and time off, call in sick frequently, and plan an adequate retirement as early as possible, or, in many cases, another job.

The table of organization of an institution can be drawn clearly, but interpersonal relationships, intergroup competitiveness, jealousy and envy of others, and incompetent personnel can sometimes "snag" its smooth operation. The table of organization is a theoretical blueprint of the organization, but it is the personnel and these intrainstitutional cooperational efforts or struggles that determine how this blueprint *really* works. A good administrator and his top management will be sensitive to these potential impediments and attempt to smooth them in the day-to-day operation of the institution. If left without a competent and strong administration, these problems will render the institution and its objectives helpless and hopeless.

Conflicts arising between custodial and treatment personnel within the correctional setting are not the result, really, of mutually exclusive goals, but have been seen as managements' failure to deal adequately with role conflict and interest group formation.[24] Some of the conflict between custody and treatment personnel results from educational differences. In many prisons in the United States, custodial personnel do not need a high school diploma. In fact, there are officers on duty in some states who cannot read or write. On the other hand, the vast majority of treatment personnel have college degrees. This causes some significant problems. For decades at Stateville in Illinois, for example, educators

[23]Howard W. Polsky, "From Claques to Factions: Sub-Groups in Organizations," *Social Work,* Vol. 23, no. 2 (March 1978), pp. 94–99.

[24]Paul Maxim, "Treatment-Custody Staff Conflicts in Correctional Institutions: *A Re-Analysis,*" Canadian Journal of Criminology and Corrections, Vol. 18, no. 4 (1977), pp. 379–85.

like Ferris Laune, Saul Alinsky, Daniel Glaser, Han Mattick, and Donald Clemmer, among others, were harassed and sometimes prevented from entering the prison, but when they did function, their contact was only with inmates and they had no impact whatsoever on the day-to-day operations of the prison.[25] The 1937 Illinois Prison Inquiry Commission said that university people interested in social questions could contribute much to prison operation, but the officials of the prison continued to look upon them as nuisances.

Criminal justice, be it police, courts, or corrections, involves constant adversary confrontation. The social and emotional support from peers in the same work in criminal justice may help to build a positive *esprit de corps* and morale that reduces stress and burnout. Too frequently, however, even peers in the same organization break into clique groups that generate internal resentment and feuding, which increase and reinforce stress and burnout.

Cynicism questionnaires administered to fifty-six randomly selected correctional officers in a northeastern state employed in three county correctional institutions revealed a moderately high level of cynicism.[26] There were almost twice as many cynics in the group of officers from the "treatment" institution as there were from the other two more traditional "custodial" institutions. The cynical responses by the officers were interpreted as adaptations to a conflict situation in which "treatment" was intended, but custody tended to prevail.

The level of conflict in a prison or correctional institution is a function of several factors: (1) the extent to which organizational goals permit the staff group and individuals to pursue compatible policies, (2) the degree of ambiguity in the relation of administrative means to organizational ends, (3) the extent to which organizational behavior cannot be scrutinized but, instead, requires continuous choice in new directions, and (4) the degree of independence of staff groups.[27] The power balance model of conflict can predict dissension within the institution. A custodial-oriented prison tends to follow the rules exactly, and any deviation is generally at the expense of treatment staff. Further, treatment staff in this type of institution seldom have any input into institutional policies. They are considered to be "low man on the totem pole" in prison politics. On the other hand, a minimum security, treatment-oriented institution generally has counselors, psychologists, social workers, teachers, and other "treatment" staff establishing policies. Inmates who need stricter custodial control are generally transferred out of the minimum custody institution into a more secure facility.

STAFF SOCIAL PERSPECTIVES

An officer in Connecticut has said that his entire family are masons in the construction business. They can show him a completed building with a feeling of accomplishment. Then he was asked, "But you come out of a prison . . . and

---

[25]Jacobs, *Stateville*, p. 19.

[26]Richard E. Farmer, "Cynicism: A Factor in Corrections Work," *Journal of Criminal Justice*, Vol. 5, no. 3 (1977), pp. 237–46.

[27]Mayer N. Zald, "Power Balance and Staff Conflicts in Correctional Institutions," in Lawrence E. Hazelrigg, ed., *Prison Within Society: A Reader in Penology* (Garden City, N.Y.: Doubleday & Company, Inc., 1968), p. 398.

what can you show somebody?"[28] Another officer said that the guards are all doing time, except that guards are on eight-hour shifts.[29] Guards often see themselves as being exploited by "the system" without having any input and, positioned between "the system" on the one hand and the inmates on the other, must develop their own protective society.[30] Some scholars have observed that, if police work is a tainted occupation, then prison guard work is tainted utterly.[31]

Many professional people, while interested in offenders, do not want to be identified with the prison. This is why many psychiatrists from nearby medical schools are assigned to the prison on a part-time basis. They may work at the prison one to four days a week, but they want the university to be their professional address and identification. Many institutional doctors are there because they have not passed the state examination and cannot enter private practice. Many accept institutional jobs until they can pass the examination and then leave for a more lucrative private practice. Further, as previously mentioned, prisons located long distances from universities and cultural centers have difficulty in recruiting and retaining social workers, psychologists, counselors, and other professional personnel.

Another source of stress in corrections is the implied threat or reality of adverse investigations and comments by politicians, investigative reporters, consultants hired by the governor's office, and editorials. Investigative reporters have won Pulitzer prizes for exposing corruption in state correctional systems. Crusading legislators have made names for themselves by attacking the prison system. Outside consultants with various viewpoints, right or wrong, can criticize the system, such as the consultant in New Mexico in 1979, who indicated that state officials were "playing Russian roulette with the lives of inmates, staff and the public," and he was right in this instance. There are many more instances, however, where the consultants' reports have simply been efforts to attack the prisons in a way desired by the person or group who hired them. Political investigations by the governor's office or by legislative committees are by far the most demoralizing to correctional personnel and administrations.

Prison administration is a confining business, also, because administrators must be available at all times to the news media, to political leaders who want to ask questions, and to the families and attorneys of residents and in case of emergency. If an administrator is unavailable when an emergency breaks out, he has a lot of explaining to do! During this writer's career in prison administration, his wife reluctantly accepted the view that most effective prison administrators must or should be at the prison on New Year's Day, Easter, the Fourth of July, Labor Day, and Thanksgiving, but she could never accept his not being home with his family on Christmas Day. These holidays frequently have special programs that need monitoring; there is always a pervading attitude that the normal

---

[28]Edgar May, "Prison Guards in America: The Inside Story," *Corrections Magazine*, Vol. 2, no. 6 (December 1976), p. 48.

[29]Ibid., p. 3.

[30]G. L. Webb and David G. Morris, *Prison Guards: The Culture and Perspective of an Occupational Group* (Dallas: Coker Books, 1977).

[31]James B. Jacobs and Harold G. Retsky, "Prison Guard," *Urban Life*, Vol. 4 (April 1974), p. 10.

rigid regimen of the prison has been relaxed, which is conducive to untoward incidents and fights; and relatives and friends visit in some prisons and correctional institutions and many want to talk with the administrators responsible for the welfare of their loved ones in prison.

The families of many of those working with the criminal justice system, particularly police and correctional officers, are subjected constantly to shift rotation, interrupted plans, and haphazard holidays, all of which combine to make family life difficult.[32] This adds to the high rate of alcoholism and divorce, although these trends tend to be mitigated in isolated prison settings because of less contact with the general public that reduces social availability. Nevertheless, these problems are high in criminal justice occupations.

A study by Kroes and his colleagues revealed that seventy-nine of eighty-one married police officers reported that their home lives were affected by their jobs.[33] The same problem, for the same reasons, affects personnel in prisons and correctional institutions. The problems found to be associated with the job were (1) retardation of nonpolice (and nonprison) friendships, (2) inability to plan social events, (3) tendency to take job pressures home, (4) tendency for wives and children to be affected by a negative public image, (5) wives' dislike of being left at home alone when their husbands are on the night shift, and (6) hardening of emotions resulting in lessened sensitivity for their families. The problem of "other women" did not appear because it tends to be generalized to many fields of work and is not peculiar to police work. Many correctional and police administrators have referred to these problems as "the four D's": drugs, drink, debts, and dames!

The Attica correctional facility remained a "powder keg" into 1979. Stabbings, fights, sexual assaults, cell burnings, and "pipings" (clubbings) among inmates were commonplace. One guard who participated in the New York guards' strike of April 18 to May 4, 1979, indicated that

> You come into this place and it's a whole new ballgame. Maybe this prisoner didn't get a letter from his wife. You're the first person he sees and he takes it out on you. He spits in your face. I didn't know how many times I've been spit on, punched, had s- - - thrown on me. You name it.[34]

Evaluation of a training program of 1,012 correctional officers in Virginia between 1974 and 1976 indicated greatest learning in the areas of searches, security and control, inmate supervision, and related areas.[35] The least learning was in the philosophy of corrections, court decisions, probation and parole,

---

[32]Pat James with Martha Nelson, "The Police Family—A Wife's View," *FBI Law Enforcement Bulletin*, Vol. 44, no. 11 (November 1975), pp. 12–15.

[33]W. H. Kroes, J. Hurrell, and B. Margolis, "Job Stress in Police Administrators," *Journal of Police Science and Administration*, Vol. 2, no. 4 (1974), pp. 381–87.

[34]Joel Freedman, "Attica State Prison: Still A Sociological Powder Keg," *NASW News*, Vol. 24, no. 6 (June 1979), p. 7.

[35]Ronald J. Scott and Raymond P. Cienek, *Correctional Officer Training in Virginia: A Final Report* (Richmond: Virginia Commonwealth University, Department of Administration of Justice and Public Safety, Correctional Training Evaluation Project, August 1977), p. 36.

development of corrections, the criminal justice system, and similar topics more removed from the immediate everyday functioning of the correctional officer. About two-thirds of the officers (68 percent) were raised in rural areas or communities smaller than ten thousand population. About 42 percent had completed high school, 23 percent had some college, and 4 percent had bachelor's degrees, while 22 percent had had some high school, 5 percent had completed grammar school, and 4 percent had had some grammar school education.[36]

The social perspectives of correctional workers, of course, is quite wide. Most see themselves as being in a type of work that, while ostensibly "helping" some people and "protecting society," is underprivileged at budget time and in the social hierarchy of the community. They tend to remain in their own society, alienated from the free community, and in confrontation with many of the residents they are trying to "help." There are exceptions in both directions. A few identify with the free community, live "downtown," and see the prison as a place in which to earn a living, but not as a socializing center; others become loners, retreating from everything but their own lives and families. In general, the social perspectives of prison personnel are within a self-contained society that satisfies all social interaction as well as common occupational identification.

THE SOCIAL PROBLEMS

As mentioned in the previous section on social perspectives, family problems frequently arise in all criminal justice occupations. Stress, uncertainty, and negative self-concepts appear to be primary in correctional institutions.

There is a high incidence of suicide and emotional problems among police and correctional workers. Stress is more important in coronary heart disease than is smoking, diet, and exercise combined.[37] At its onset, diabetes is related to periods of high job stress and emotional upset.[38] In 1959, police had the highest death rate of any profession due to arteriosclerotic heart disease, diabetes, and suicide.[39]

Alcoholism as a response to stress has appeared in law enforcement and correctional personnel rather frequently. This is an old method of reducing anxiety. One of the oldest temperance tracts on record was written in Egypt about three thousand years ago under the title, *Wisdom of Ani:*

> Take not upon thyselves to drink a jug of beer. Thou speakest and an unintelligible utterance issueth from thy mouth. If thou fallest down and thy limbs break, there is none to hold out a hand to thee. Thy companions in drink stand up and say, 'Away with this sot' and thou art like a little child.

[36]Ibid., p. 23.

[37]W. McQuade, "What Stress Can Do for You," *Fortune*, Vol. 85, no. 1 (1972), pp. 102–07.

[38]W. H. Kroes, *Society's Victim—The Policeman* (Springfield, Ill.: Charles C. Thomas, Publishers, 1976).

[39]I. L. Guralnick, *Mortality by Occupation and Cause of Death*, Vital Statistics Special Reports, Vol. 53, no. 3 (Washington, D.C.: U.S. Public Health Service, 1963).

Employees who are dependent on alcohol are characterized by late arrivals to work and early departures, absenteeism, poor judgment, erratic and decreased productivity, failure to meet schedules, lowered morale, resentment from other employees, a waste of supervisory time and effort, and other drains.[40] Approximately 10 percent of the people in the total work force face this problem. In the criminal justice system, the problem is exacerbated by the contempt from the inmates when the officer is supposed to be responsible as "his brother's keeper" and cannot "keep" himself or herself.

Because of union contracts controlling termination of employment and the time and effort it takes to defend such termination, either by union activity or by direct litigation brought by the individual, many law enforcement agencies have established formal treatment programs, and many correctional agencies and institutions have instituted treatment procedures more informally. The Los Angeles Sheriff's Department, for example, has established a formal program of alcohol recovery followed by counseling, having found that it is almost impossible to help the alcoholic employee—to resolve resulting family, financial, emotional, and job-related problems effectively—if it fails to direct the officer into an alcohol recovery program first.[41] Several correctional programs offer similar assistance to employees on an informal basis, sometimes transferring the employee to a position in which he or she does not come into contact with inmates—a position more difficult to locate in a correctional facility than in a police department—and follow-up assistance is provided. In some cases, private organizations are brought into the situation to assist without terminating employment.[42]

CONCLUSIONS

Staff societies in prison and correctional institutions live and work in situations unnatural to the rest of society. They serve as their "brother's keepers," not in a loving sense but as adversaries. Consequently, they are often viewed with some contempt by the residents, who refer to them as "screws" or "hacks" as well as by many citizens in the free community, who see them as lazy and stupid individuals who cannot get a job anyplace else.

A similar situation occurs with professional staff members—the psychiatrists, physicians, psychologists, and other treatment-oriented individuals. Many within the prison and some in the free community believe that no competent professional staff member would work in a remote rural area far removed from cultural and educational centers. Unfortunately, some of this is true; many prison physicians and psychiatrists do not have licenses to practice in the state in

---

[40]Quoted in S. George Clark, ed., *A Guide to Community Alcoholism Programs* (Tallahassee: Florida Bureau of Alcoholic Rehabilitation, n.d., issued in 1979), p. 1.

[41]Ibid., p. 53.

[42]John G. Stratton and Brian Wroe, "Alcoholism and the Policeman: Identifying and Dealing with the Problem," *FBI Law Enforcement Bulletin,* Vol. 48, no. 3 (March 1979), pp. 20–23.

which they are employed, but they can be hired by an institution not engaged in private practice.

This leaves the society of correctional personnel accepted neither in the free community nor by "insiders." They perceive themselves to be in a "no-win" situation that is not conducive to feelings of self-worth. In a self-contained society, however, prison people do not have to compete for social status with the business tycoons and the "pillars of the community" outside.

Correctional personnel are a society of captives, themselves, locked into a tradition of roles, responses, expectations, fears, and attitudes that may no longer be valid or functional.[43] The underlying problem appears to be in part a reliance on a perception of individual responsibility that places emphasis on division of labor, roles, and educational preparation for professionals in corrections. Correctional personnel need a broader perspective, including attention to social responsibility in a way that permits them to take their legitimate place in the free community.

There is a move nationally to eliminate prison housing, although it will be slow, which will tend to reduce the impact of the self-contained prison staff community.[44] Prison systems that did not provide housing in 1980 are those in the District of Columbia, Alaska, Colorado, Delaware, Maine, New Hampshire, Oklahoma, Utah, Guam, and most Canadian provinces. Several states, such as Michigan, have reduced that housing in the past several years, while some others have increased it, particularly where the prison is in a rural area. Nevada is currently phasing out such housing. The U.S. Bureau of Prisons has adopted a policy of not constructing any more officer housing. The reduction and elimination of prison housing for staff will tend to reduce the isolation of prison staffs in the future.

CHAPTER QUESTIONS

10-1. Why is prison staff society different from that of many other social groupings engaged in specialized occupations?

10-2. How does growing up in a prison community affect people in the closed prison society?

10-3. What factors have an impact upon the person living and working in a maximum security prison?

10-4. What are the problems that come from long-term exposure to paranoid thinking patterns?

10-5. What are the physical signs of burnout?

10-6. What are the behavioral symptoms of burnout?

10-7. How long does it take for the burnout syndrome to develop?

10-8. How does building conflict affect staff members in prisons?

10-9. What are the general perspectives of the staff members toward themselves and society?

10-10. What social problems are experienced by correctional workers?

[43]Charles S. Prigmore and John C. Watkins, Jr., "Correctional Manpower: Are We 'The Society of Captives'?" *Federal Probation*, Vol. 36, no. 4 (1972), pp. 12–19.

[44]"A House Is Not a Home," *Corrections Compendium*, Vol. 5, no. 2, (September 1980), pp. 1–5.

11

JAIL AND LOCAL DETENTION

The jail was the first institution in the criminal justice system to be constructed specifically for the detention of accused offenders. It was authorized by King Henry II at the Assize of Clarendon in 1166 A.D., along with reformulating the old jury system and the delineating of the duties of the sheriff. The jail has become the most numerous of institutions in the criminal justice system and the most frequently used, although for short periods of time. As pointed out in the first chapter, detention had been used for centuries before, particularly for holding accused persons awaiting trial, and the Roman Catholic Church had begun condoning the use of imprisonment for punishment, but these facilities had all been constructed for different purposes. The jail and local detention, despite its being the oldest institution in the criminal justice system, is the most neglected in funding and staffing.

FUNCTIONS OF THE JAIL

The jail has four primary and many miscellaneous functions. The four primary functions of the jail are (1) to hold accused persons awaiting trial, (2) to hold persons convicted of minor offenses and misdemeanors and those serving short-term sentences, (3) to hold convicted persons awaiting sentencing or execution of sentence, and (4) to hold material witnesses who might disappear prior to trial in major cases.

In addition, miscellaneous uses of the jail generally involve makeshift dispositions on a temporary basis because more appropriate facilities are not available. Some of these miscellaneous functions include holding children when no local detention home exists, holding mentally ill or insane persons in the absence of more appropriate facilities, providing overnight care for transients who have not been arrested, and other catch-all local holding and domiciliary functions in emergencies and in the absence of more appropriate facilities.

JAIL, STOCKADES, AND LOCK-UPS

Prior to the *1970 National Jail Census* performed by the LEAA (Law Enforcement Assistance Administration) in cooperation with the U.S. Bureau of the Census, the actual number of jails in the United States was not known. The reasons involved the definition of a jail as compared with other local detention facilities. The 1970 national jail census indicated that there were 4,027 locally operated jails with the authority to detain prisoners for forty-eight hours or longer.[1] Probably the best estimate before that was in an outstanding criminology text-book published in 1959, which stated, "There are over three thousand county jails in this country in addition to some ten thousand city and town lock-ups. There are fewer work houses, or 'houses of corrections'."[2] In addition, there are about fifteen state-operated jails in Connecticut, Rhode Island, and Delaware. In addition are a number of stockades, which may be local confinement facilities for untried prisoners, local confinement for short-term offenders, who are not security risks, or places of confinement on military posts. There are about 41,000 police jurisdictions in the United States that have some sort of detention facility, if only a room or an arrangement with neighboring jurisdiction that has a jail or lock-up. One precinct in New York has handcuffed people it wanted to detain around a pipe running from the floor to the ceiling. By 1972, the number of state-operated jails had been reduced to 3,921.[3] This was the result of jails being condemned and not rebuilt, primarily for lack of funds. The population of the 3,921 locally operated jails as of July 1, 1972 was 141,588. This was a reduction from the 160,863 inmates held on March 15, 1970.

By February 1978, there were 3,493 jails and 158,394 people being held in them.[4] Of these, 1,611 were juveniles. There were 9,277 adult women or

[1]Law Enforcement Assistance Administration, *1970 National Jail Census* (Washington, D.C.: LEAA, 1971), p. 19.

[2]Harry Elmer Barnes and Negley K. Teeters, *New Horizons in Criminology*, 3rd ed. (Englewood Cliffs, N.J.: Prentice-Hall, Inc., 1959), p. 387.

[3]Law Enforcement Assistance Administration, *The Nation's Jails: A Report on the Census of Jails from the 1972 Survey of Inmates of Local Jails* (Washington, D.C.: National Criminal Justice Information and Statistics Service, LEAA, May 1975), p. 22.

[4]Law Enforcement Assistance Administration, *Census of Jails and Survey of Jail Inmates— 1978, Preliminary Report* (Washington, D.C.: U.S. Department of Justice, LEAA, 1979), p. 3.

about 6 percent of the total adult population. Of the juveniles, 278 were girls or about 17 percent. Nearly half the people held in jail were not convicted but were awaiting trial. The median age of inmates was 25.3 years, 57 percent were white and 41 percent were black, the median educational level was 10.2 grades, and the median income prior to arrest was $3,255 annually.[5]

JAIL DESIGN
AND CONSTRUCTION

Probably one of the best guides regarding design of jails is the *Handbook of Correctional Institution Design and Construction,* published by the U.S. Bureau of Prisons in 1949 with a supplement in 1960.[6] It provides plans for one 25-inmate capacity jail, two 50-inmate capacity jails, and a 250-inmate capacity jail. There is no plan in this publication for the one-cell or two-cell jails frequently found in rural areas, the cage or "tank" sometimes found in smaller cities, or facilities for the large city jails such as those found in Chicago, New York City, and Los Angeles that frequently house between 4,000 and 9,000 inmates. Accreditation standards in 1977 called for cell size of at least 60 square feet if the individual spends ten hours or less per day in the cell, but they should be 70 square feet if more time is spent in the cell.[7] There should also be at least 35 square feet per inmate in day space.

JAIL PERSONNEL

Personnel in jails must be selected and then provided with in-service training. Unfortunately, the salaries are generally so low that the sheriff or jail administrator has a difficult time attracting people who can adequately perform the demanding tasks required for successful operation of a jail. An even temperament and patience are basic requirements in jail personnel, since they deal with people in trouble and in emotional crisis and people who are angry and frustrated, many of whom think they have been mistreated. Those who perform jail work must be able to withstand provocative behavior.

Jail personnel who deal directly with the misdemeanants and clients in the jail need to be physically healthy and strong enough to avoid being overpowered or otherwise lose control. At the same time, empathic skills or the ability to relate to others is basic to working with people. Knowledge of behavior, alcohol and drugs, and physical illness sufficient to make intelligent referrals to medical staff and the ability to give respect to the citizen-offender or accused citizen are all basic to the task of the jailer. Such well-rounded persons are very difficult to locate.

[5]Ibid., p. 2.

[6]U.S. Bureau of Prisons, *Handbook of Correctional Institution Design and Construction* (Washington, D.C.: Federal Prison Industries, 1949), pp. 168–87.

[7]Commission on Accreditation for Corrections, *Manual of Standards for Adult Local Detention Facilities* (Rockville, Md.: CAC, December 1977), p. 21.

Aerial view of the Los Angeles County Central Jail. Jail is in the foreground.
Courtesy of the Los Angeles County Sheriff's Department.

After recruitment and selection, in-service training is essential for the appropriate functioning of personnel. One good source is the *Correspondence Course for Jailers* published by the U.S. Bureau of Prisons. The National Sheriff's Association also has excellent material for jail instruction.

RECEIVING AND RELEASING PRISONERS

Receiving prisoners must be planned thoroughly and implemented meticulously to avoid errors and incidents that might have to be corrected. After receiving many prisoners under arrest and in various emotional states, many jailers tend to become careless, rude, and antagonistic and, further, tend to prejudge the arrested citizen. It is sometimes difficult to remember that persons entering jail are still legally innocent. In any case, any person coming into the jail will respond with greater respect and confidence if he or she is treated in a decent and orderly manner. Jailers work better with inmates and, simultaneously, do not

173

upset themselves when they can work with prisoners without displays of emotion or unnecessary solicitousness or aggressiveness, but respect them as human beings and as citizens with constitutional and civil rights.

New prisoners must be searched. A complete strip search of the prisoner is the only way of preventing contraband from coming into the jail. Guns, hacksaw blades, files, narcotics, and explosives are only a few of the items found on incoming prisoners. Failure to search each incoming prisoner thoroughly may endanger jail personnel and invite escape attempts.

The prisoner's property and money should be removed from him or her and placed in plain view on the table, where all items are listed. The jailer and the prisoner should check the listing together and each must sign the form acknowledging the correctness of the listing. One copy of the form should be given to the prisoner and the original should be filed in the property records of the jail. All prisoners should be fingerprinted and photographed as a routine part of the receiving procedure. For purposes of hygiene, all newly admitted prisoners should be instructed to shower after having been given soap and towels before entering the main part of the jail. Appropriate notations should be made of significant medical observations for reference, and any unusual or immediate medical problems should be called to the physician's attention. Uniform jail clothing should be given to all prisoners as they come out of the shower, and the prisoner's personal clothing should be stored. In the case of sloppy and nauseated drunks, the use of jail coveralls is recommended until the prisoner has sobered up and can be issued regular clothing. A set of simple and understandable regulations in the jail should be given to each prisoner at the time of admission.

Release procedures must be followed as carefully as admission procedures. Many jails have released the wrong prisoner and have had to follow through with escape procedures. In small jails, where the jailers can recognize individual persons, this risk is considerably reduced. In larger jails, however, identification of the individual to be released should be identified by photograph and by fingerprints. In any case, the check-out procedure must assure that the right person is being released. Persons should be released in their own clothing, laundered and repaired, if necessary. On occasion, destitute persons or others needing assistance may be referred to community agencies for help in returning to the community.

SECURITY OF THE JAIL

While the physical plant, including bars, should be designed for visibility as an important part of security, the real security is in constructive and intelligent supervision of prisoners by the staff. Attempts to construct "escapeproof" jails have been disappointing. Even remote-control, computerized locking systems have been manipulated by ingenious inmates for purposes of escape. Whether by saw, computer, or other means, the physical plant is essentially designed to slow down the escape long enough to permit the staff to get into action.

Firearms do not belong in the jail in any form. Any jailer, police officer, or anybody else who walks into a jail with a revolver or pistol is inviting trouble. Firearms should be stored in a secure armory or other safe place outside the section where the inmates are jailed, probably in a secure place in the jailer's office. Firearms have legitimate uses in jail operation, but they should be used primarily for perimeter control and for manhunts following escapes.

Gas is rarely used or necessary in a jail. It should never be used on individuals or small groups of prisoners. It should be reserved for purposes of gaining control over a large group of prisoners who present a danger to jail security and to each other. Indiscriminate use of gas can generate disruption and confusion. It can generate hostility and anger that has in the past contributed to riot. Gas should be used only as a last resort in gaining control.

Shakedowns or searches of prisoners and physical facilities is merely a procedure whereby a jailer is assured that prisoners are not in possession of contraband. The most dangerous items are guns, knives, hacksaw blades, files, and other items that would injure others or be tools for escape. In addition, alcohol, narcotics, money, and other contraband tend to disturb the security and order of the jail. Money can be used for purchasing all sorts of favors, for buying bus tickets in case of escape, and for inviting strong-arm robbery and attacks by other inmates to get the money. A correct shakedown is thorough to the extent that many inexperienced officers and other persons might regard it as "over-kill," but it is much better to avoid trouble than to try and stop it after it has started.

Key control is essential in jail security. Carelessness in the handling and security of keys has resulted in many escapes, some of which have involved assaults and killings of jail personnel. A jail key is simultaneously a key to security and a key to escape. Also, tools need to be controlled. Generally easiest to obtain in jails are kitchen tools, such as knives and cleavers. Other tools, such as hammers and wrenches, are also frequently available.

FOOD SERVICES

Food is important in any institution, for both morale and nutrition. A wholesome and balanced diet is a basic human right that cannot be denied to prisoners. Simultaneously, because of the low budgets in most jails, it must be economical.

Historically, jails have not fed prisoners well, generally offering a good breakfast and a sandwich evening meal. In many cases, inmates would send out to hamburger stands or other commercial establishments to obtain food to supplement the jail diet. This situation was even worse when the old fee system provided many of the expenses of the jail. The fee was a stipend for each prisoner held. The money came from fines, but it was sometimes supplemented by a budget from the county commission with a certain amount allowed for food. The sheriff's revenues would go up if the jailer could reduce the food expenditure below the allowed amount.

The wide variation in sizes of jails and inmate populations, of course, make a standard procedure in food services impossible. Many jails use inmate

Los Angeles County Central Jail dining room.
Courtesy of the Los Angeles County Sheriff's Department.

cooks. The larger jails have a staff with a steward who uses inmate assistants. In any case, an efficient, controlled food service program results in better meals at less cost and better morale in the jail.

HEALTH SERVICES

Health services in jails are essential to meet the responsibilities of serving the citizens who are confined there. The most acute problems have historically related to the admission of inmates who are ill and are under the influence of alcohol. While the majority of people who are arrested and are staggering, unsteady, and incontinent are intoxicated, a significant few are diabetics, a condition that not treated may lead to coma; victims of heart attacks; and people sustaining severe head and other injuries. In fact, many of the deaths in jails soon after admission can be attributed to misinterpretations of medical conditions. In the receiving or booking process, someone with basic instructions from a physician or other medical expert should be available to make a judgment as to whether a physician should be called.

Medical services in jails are also required in cases of assault or attempted suicide. Many of these assaults are simply fights between two or more inmates, some, unfortunately, homosexual rapes of younger prisoners by one or more older and more mature inmates. The problem of gang rape appears in most jails, among both males and females.

Suicides are more frequent in jails than in some other institutions. Individuals there are stressed, frustrated, desperate, and without hope. Most of the suicides in jail are by persons there for the first time.

A small jail, one with fewer than 300 prisoners, cannot afford a full-time physician. This means that the vast majority of the nation's jails do not have a full-time physician on the staff. Of the 3,921 locally operated jails reported on in 1972, only 113 had 250 or more inmates. Medical and dental services in jails, then, are generally contracted services to be used as needed or, sometimes, as available.

While many organizations recommend that every prisoner coming into the jail have a physical examination at the time of admission to detect communicable diseases and to discover any condition requiring prompt medical attention, many jails do not have the resources for this service. Special medical or psychiatric cases, as well as homosexuals and other unusual cases, are frequently simply thrown in with the rest of the inmates. This causes considerable difficulty in future jail operation, which, in turn, makes it important to have a person with some instruction from physicians and other experts available during the booking process.

Every jail, regardless of size, should have an area set aside for medical services and holding people with communicable diseases. This jail infirmary has frequently forestalled many potential difficulties.

Sick call is a regular daily procedure in which prisoners who are ill or require medical attention can report to the jail's physician for examination and treatment. In most jails where the physician is under contract, the physician may set a sick call at his convenience so that it does not interfere with his private practice. While sick call is advisable on a daily basis, in many jails with contracted physicians, sick call may be weekly or not at all. Sometimes, sick call has been dispensed with and the jailer calls the physician as needed. Diseases that can be readily detected by the inmate or the jailer can receive immediate attention. Complaints of inmates with diseases having internal symptoms sometimes result in suspicion and disbelief by the jailers, but they should be checked out, since the jailer is not a physician and is not capable of diagnosis. Sometimes, mental and emotional disturbances take longer to identify and receive attention.

In any case, good medical services become "good business" for the jail because it protects the public by preventing the spread of disease and promotes higher inmate morale, and the sheriff or jailer who provides good medical service can avoid criticism in some cases, including inmate litigation.

The American Medical Association initiated the Program to Improve Medical Care and Health Services in Jails in the mid-1970s after its 1972 survey, *Medical Care in the U.S.* By 1978, there were thirty-eight pilot jail projects, twenty-two of which had achieved accreditation from the American Medical Association.[8] This project has been continued and has improved significantly the medical services in jails into the 1980s.

---

[8]"Overview of AMA Jail Project," *The Correctional Stethoscope*, Vol. 1, no. 8 (February 1978), p. 1 (publication of the American Medical Association).

Working in a jail or a prison is most difficult for new physicians who have not learned to work with the inmate population.[9] Many people in the correctional system have learned to manipulate authority, and many desire drugs of almost any description. Since heroin and other hard narcotics are not available in these institutions, the residents will settle for Valium, Thorazine, or anything else they can get. When new doctors start working in jails and prisons, the number of drug prescriptions rises perceptibly, but the level declines within two or three months when the physician begins to learn the behavior of his offender-patients. The inmates view relationships with staff as adversary, rather than collaborative, and try to outwit and manipulate staff.

It has been observed that many inmates who go on sick call are not sick but are trying to get out of their cells for a half-hour or longer to break the monotony.[10] They make unrealistic demands on doctors, which contributes to the callousness of many doctors in jails and prisons. It is not surprising, since the physicians' own psychic survival is at stake, but it does make it difficult for inmates who are really sick to get adequate treatment. It takes an alert and sensitive physician to separate the malingerers from those who are really in need of medical treatment. When in doubt, it is better for the physician to provide services rather than to risk an erroneous and tragic judgment of suspected malingering. Unfortunately, too many of these unfortunate judgments are made by officers and jail staff without medical training and who have become cynical after having been "burned" several times in the past.

HOUSEKEEPING AND MAINTENANCE

Good sanitation and a well-kept physical plant make jail operation simpler and less dangerous. Dirt and filth always increase the dangers of vermin, and hazards to health escalate sufficiently that medical services and other problems can become overwhelming. Maintenance of a sanitary jail must be based on planned procedures, training of staff and inmates in cleanliness and sanitary procedures, persistent application of cleaning and other sanitary procedures, and frequent regular inspections. Constant supervision produces the best results, including regular inspections. Prisoners must arise each morning in time to clean cells, make beds, and wash themselves before breakfast. Toilets, wash basins, sinks, and other plumbing equipment need special attention. Dogs, cats, and other pets should not be in the jail. Some smaller jails have used cats to control rats and mice, but regular application of ordinary sanitary procedures should eliminate this approach to pest control. There are several rat poisons that are safe for use in jails. Good light and frequent changes of air are helpful in housekeeping and sanitation. Good water supply and adequate waste removal are necessary. One of

[9]*Orienting Health Providers to the Jail Culture,* LEAA Grant 77-ED-99-0011, (Chicago: AMA Pilot Program to Improve Medical Care and Health Services in Correctional Institutions, 1977), p. 7.

[10]Donald Robinson, "The Scandalous Medical Care in Our Jails," *Parade,* June 19, 1977, pp. 9–11; from the AMA's survey of medical care in 1,083 jails.

Metropolitan Community Center, which serves as a jail, in San Diego.
Courtesy of the Federal Prison System.

the most important services in jails is the laundry, which should be in continual operation in a jail of any size.

The cost of jail construction is greater than is that for other local institutions, such as schools and hospitals, because of the extra steel needed for security. Security windows, doors, cells, locking devices, walls, entrances, and internal grills and gates are only a few of the considerations that increase the cost of constructing jails. Maintenance of the jail plant and replacement of equipment is essential to good jail administration. While vandalism in schools may be at an all-time high, attacks on bars, locks, and other hardware in jails as well as obscene and hostile graffiti on the cell walls and elsewhere in the local jails have exceeded all other vandalism for populations of similar size. Constant maintenance, cleaning, and painting is an everyday procedure in jails, not just "spring cleaning" once a year. Many middle-sized and larger jails have a maintenance shop that helps to keep the jail in good repair without having to call outside locksmiths, metalworkers, or other related artisans. The maintenance shop should also maintain a key-making machine and reserve one key for each lock simply for the purpose of making duplicate keys. Of course, when a key is lost, the locks have to be changed. Jail doors always show considerable wear because of their weight and constant use, so they must be greased or graphited regularly. They present a special problem in jail maintenance, because they are generally the first point of attack by prisoners attempting to escape. The jail should be constructed so that there is little access to outside windows. The water system, sewage system, steam or heating system, and the electrical system all require constant attention for purposes of maintenance. The communications equipment, including radios, televisions, intercoms, two-way radios or CBs, telephones, listening devices, and alarm systems, are all essential to jail operations and have to be maintained.

Skillful maintenance of the jail and its equipment is sometimes overlooked by jail administrators because the short-term view in which the jail functions tend to eclipse the long-term requirements. As with a home, a school, an industrial plant, or any other building, constant maintenance, while sometimes immediately demanding, becomes cheaper and more cost effective than having to do a major overhaul of the facility when it begins to break down.

USE OF INMATES IN JAIL OPERATIONS

Most jails need to use inmates to perform certain jail operations because the budget will not support sufficient civilian staff to maintain the jail. In many jails, the inmates operate the kitchen completely. Also, all jails use inmates for maintenance of various sorts. Trusted inmates are used for landscaping, mowing the grass, and maintaining the outside of the facility. Inmates are used for sanitation and cleaning chores. Under close supervision, some trusted inmates may even be used to assist in physical maintenance.

There are many abuses that can enter into the use of inmates to maintain the jail. Consequently, careful selection of inmates and constant supervision is necessary. Supervision of personnel is important, too, since inmates have been known to be used for the personal gain or assistance of jailers.

CONVICTED PRISONERS

Convicted and committed prisoners can be held in jail under the normal conditions affecting their status. They can be assigned to jobs and be subjected to other requirements appropriate to their convictions or commitments. A convicted person is one legally guilty of a crime. In the case of a misdemeanor, he or she may be serving a short term in the jail. In the case of a felony, he or she may be awaiting sentence or transfer to the main prison after sentence. A committed person has been adjudicated into a legal status by a court in civil procedure, as in the case of juvenile delinquency, insanity, feeblemindedness, or epilepsy, that provides public care and treatment through the civil court process according to the laws of the respective jurisdictions.

UNCONVICTED PRISONERS

Unconvicted prisoners in the jail are citizens who are legally innocent. Regardless of the jailer's informal opinion, any presumption of guilt violates the basic principle in American jurisprudence that a person is innocent until proven guilty. Often, even the prosecutor does not know whether he is going to press a case and may not take a position until he examines the evidence after the indictment, at which time he may call for arraignment, where the charges are read to the defendant in open court; even then, he may decide for a variety of reasons not to proceed with prosecution.

A report by the LEAA indicated that 53 percent of the cases made by law enforcement agencies in Los Angeles County in 1972 were not prosecuted because of problems of evidence, problems of due process, and other issues that made prosecution questionable. There is a difference between *actual* guilt and *legal* guilt. It is *legal* guilt that counts in the criminal justice system. In working with unconvicted citizens, all constitutional and civil rights, as well as the personal treatment, respect, and deference due a citizen, should be afforded the convicted prisoner. Jail staffs cannot by law assign unconvicted persons to jobs of any sort. Unconvicted persons cannot be worked.

Jail conditions for pretrail detainees must be better than those for convicted inmates.[11] Conditions for detention must not only be equal, but superior to those permitted for prisoners serving sentences for crimes. On the other hand, the U.S. Supreme Court has indicated that doublebunking of pretrial detainees in the Metropolitan Community Center in New York City does not violate the "cruel and unusual punishment" prohibition in the Constitution's Eighth Amendment.[12] In any case, the unconvicted prisoner is a legally innocent citizen and has to be treated as such by jail personnel.

JAIL ADMINISTRATION

Jail administration refers to the policymaking, planning, budgeting, managing, public relations, and other activities required in responsible jail operations. Usually it is the sheriff who carries out these duties, sometimes with a jailer who works under his direction. In some large jurisdictions like that in Cook County (Chicago), Illinois, a separate department of corrections operates the jail.

While it has been estimated that there are about 41,000 law enforcement and police jurisdictions in the United States, the largest number are small-town and rural, with the urban jurisdictions employing many more personnel. The U.S. Bureau of the Census surveyed in January 1970, with follow-up, the criminal justice agencies that were operative in communities of one thousand persons and more in 1960.[13] Of the 19,310 agencies found, there were 54 sheriffs with

[11]*Ahrens* v. *Thomas*, 434 F. Supp. 873 (W.D. Mo., 1977).

[12]*Bell* v. *Wolfish*, No. 77-1829 (May 14, 1979).

[13]Timothy J. Flanagan, Michael J. Hindelang, and Michael R. Gottfredson, "Criminal Justice Directory Survey—Methodology and Definition of Terms," in *Sourcebook of Criminal Justice Statistics—1979* (Washington, D.C.: Criminal Justice Research Center, U.S. Department of Justice, LEAA, 1979), p. 723.

multiple jails (0.3 percent), 2,579 sheriffs with single jails (13.4 percent), and 438 sheriffs without jails (2.3 percent).[14] There were 6 county police agencies with jails (less than 0.1 percent) and 68 county police without jails (0.4 percent).[15] There were 713 municipal police departments with jails (3.7 percent) and 12,562 municipal police departments without jails (65.1 percent).[16] The remaining agencies were special police, state police, and medical examiners' offices without jails. Of the 3,852 jail jurisdictions covered in this Bureau of the Census survey, then, 2,633 or 68.4 percent were operated by sheriffs, 54 of them with multiple jails.

Because no complete survey of jails has been made, the American Correctional Association developed a survey form and mailed it to over 3,300 jails in 1978. Only 1,203 responded, and these were compiled into the most complete jail survey to date on the national level.[17] It included information on salaries, budgets, physical plant, program elements, and other pertinent concerns. As mentioned earlier in this chapter, there were apparently 3,493 jails in the United States in 1978.

Some of the policy decisions made by the sheriff involve the extent to which he or she will cooperate with the city police and other law enforcement agencies. Whether the intention is to promote a program or to save money, or to hire a professional staff or "good ole local boys," are other decisions relating to policy. The budget is the single most important phase in the implementation of policy and control by the administrator over the jail operation. Generally, the administrator must work out the budget, usually on a line-item basis indicating where all monies are to be expended. Then, the total budget must be presented to the county commission and be defended. The county commission must evaluate how much revenue the county will be obtaining the following year, whether additional taxes will be needed and how much, the attitude of the people paying these taxes with a view toward the next election of the county commission, and the size of other requests in the county budget; then the committee reaches some decision by majority vote as to how much of the budget requested by the sheriff can be appropriated. Generally, the final budget is less than that requested, and the sheriff has to go back and decide where cuts can be made.

Public relations refer to the jail's image in the opinion and view of the voting public. This involves many areas, including the news media, relations with other units of government and local colleges and universities, as well as relation with outside organizations, such as the state and national sheriff's associations, the National Jail Association, and other professional organizations and persons. A sheriff who becomes a president or other officer in one of these organizations also helps the jail's public relations. It should be noted that it is dangerous to build an "image" that does not reflect reality. On the other hand, a jail or any other organization has to *look* good as well as *be* good. Unfortunately, these aims are not always congruent. It is easier to make a good jail look good.

[14]Ibid., p. 4.

[15]Ibid., p. 4.

[16]Ibid., p. 4.

[17]American Correctional Association, *National Jail and Adult Detention Directory* (College Park, Md.: ACA, December 1978).

Table 11-1 Budgetary Information for the Leon County Sheriff's Department

1. Law enforcement expenditure, total	$2,267,753.29
2. Court services expenditure, total	501,025.29
3. Corrections expenditure, total	793,770.42
4. Categorical breakdown of correctional expenditures	
Salaries	$366,673.00
Travel (prisoner transport)	9,053.00
Uniforms	3,960.00
Food	109,905.00
Medical expenses[1]	75,649.00
Supplies for the jail	12,483.00
Plumbing and exterminating	2,560.00
5. Other miscellaneous expenditures	
Attorney fees	1,092.00
Insurance	24,031.40
Dues and subscriptions	2,180.00
Training fees	777.00
Other contracted services	422.00
Equipment	8,705.00
Matching funds for personnel	98,315.95

[1]Including doctors fees and medication plus clothing and bed supplies for the jail.

Provided by Ken Katsaris, sheriff of Leon County, Tallahassee, Florida, November 10, 1977. Reprinted by permission.

The jail administrator has to be knowledgeable in the law of legal liability to avoid suits in civil liability. A successful lawsuit can be based on the following: (1) the jail administrator "knew or should have known" that rights have been violated, (2) the administrator did nothing about it, and (3) this negligence was the proximate cause of the violation. There are also various liability suits against administrators and supervisors, such as (1) negligent hiring without checking background, (2) failure to direct appropriately, (3) failure to train adequately, (4) negligent supervision, (5) negligent assignment to inappropriate duty or duty above the individual's capability, (6) negligent retention when a person should have been dismissed, and (7) negligent entrustment. Many other sources of liability exist and the jail administrator must be aware of them and be able to take appropriate action. Monthly publications focus on these problems.[18]

An example of a budget and a table of organizations for a sheriff's office in a county of between 125,000 and 150,000 population are presented in Table II-1 and Figure 11-1.

According to a survey done by LEAA in April 1977, more than 350 local jails were under court scrutiny.[19] Seven jails were ordered closed, 28 were under federal court order, 144 were under administrative review, 95 were prevented from accepting more prisoners, and 87 were cited for failing to meet state

[18]For example, see the *Jail & Prison Law Bulletin* published by the Americans for Effective Law Enforcement, Inc., San Francisco, California.

[19]"NIC and Its Jail Center Provide Training, Technical Assistance, Vital Information and Money," *Jail Administration Digest,* Vol. 1, no. 1 (January 1978), p. 2.

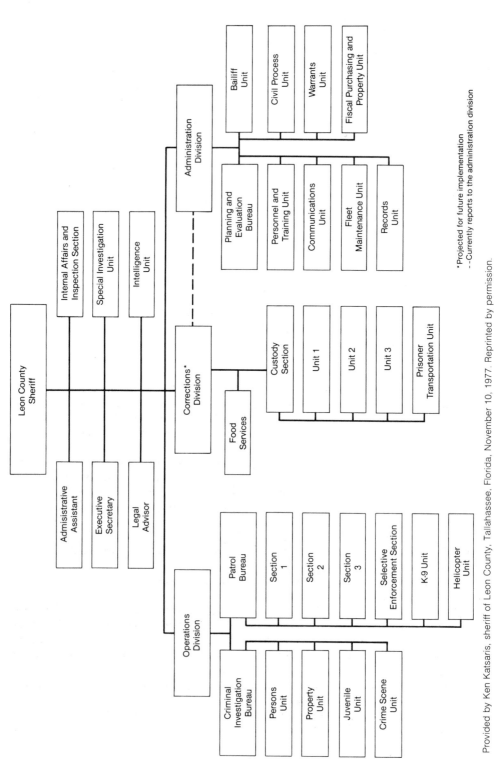

*Projected for future implementation
--Currently reports to the administration division

Provided by Ken Katsaris, sheriff of Leon County, Tallahassee, Florida, November 10, 1977. Reprinted by permission.

Figure 11-1 Table of organization for a sheriff's office in a county of 120,000 to 150,000 population.

standards. The critical problems of jails are widely known and well documented in several jail surveys.

The National Institute of Corrections established a National Jail Center in cooperation with the Boulder County Justice Center in Boulder, Colorado, in 1977, the purpose being to advance correctional progress in American jails. Overall objectives were to upgrade jail staff; to provide information services for jail administrators, elected officials, and concerned citizens; and to provide technical assistance to state and local jails. It was located in Boulder because the Boulder County Jail is a new facility that reflects contemporary thinking on physical design and philosophical approaches to correctional institutions.

CONCLUSIONS

The jail is the oldest institution in the criminal justice system, but the most neglected. Locally operated jails generally have poor budgets, resulting in understaffing and underfunding, together with all the difficulties that accompany such a situation.

Chapel services at the Los Angeles County Central Jail.
Courtesy of the Los Angeles County Sheriff's Department.

On the other hand, the jail is in the most strategic position to provide constructive service to the criminal justice system. Besides adding staff to the jail, community resources can be brought into the jail to assist in providing these services. More information can be collected and recorded on people entering the criminal justice system in the jail than in any other place of entry. Unfortunately, it is in the other stages of the criminal justice system—in probation and prison—that much of this information on presentence investigation and classification or admission derives. Short-term instruction, counseling, and other services would be most useful in jails.

A professional and well-motivated sheriff and jailer can bring in programs of alcohol and narcotic rehabilitation, educational programs, and other services that could help the jail realize its potential. Better public understanding of the function of the jail and its problems could mobilize the support of the community. The potential of the jail may be realized in mutual interaction, understanding, and service between the jail and the community that it serves.

CHAPTER QUESTIONS

11-1.   What are the functions of jails?

11-2.   How many jails are there in the United States and how many people are being held in them?

11-3.   What do the accreditation standards call for in terms of cell space in jails?

11-4.   How should jail personnel be recruited and trained, and what characteristics are desirable?

11-5.   What are the desired procedures for receiving and releasing prisoners?

11-6.   What procedures are generally required for security of the jail?

11-7.   Why is food service important in jails?

11-8.   How should health services be provided in a jail and what are some of the problems involved?

11-9.   What are the problems relating to handling unconvicted prisoners in the jail who are citizens and are legally innocent?

11-10. Why are public relations important in jail administration?

12

INSTITUTIONS FOR JUVENILES

Institutions for juveniles are generally smaller than are those for adults, they tend to have better programs in education and counseling, they are fewer in number, and they hold smaller populations than do institutions for adults. Residential facilities for juveniles in the local communities are more numerous, though smaller, than are institutions for adults. This reflects the philosophy that society is more willing to take risks with troubled children than with adult criminals. If the juvenile presents a danger to society, however, long-term training schools away from the community may be used.

The first public training school for boys was established in Westboro, Massachusetts, in 1846, and the first public training school for girls was instituted at Lancaster, Massachusetts, in 1854.[1] Since then, the training school has become the last resort for dealing with delinquent youths. In 1876, a private industrial school for girls was opened in Illinois to prevent "depraved," "unprincipled," and "impure"girls from growing up to "reproduce their kind three- to five-fold."[2] In 1877, the Illinois State Reform School contracted children as

[1] Lloyd E. Ohlin, Robert B. Coats, and Alden D. Miller, "Radical Correctional Reform: A Case Study of the Massachusetts Youth Correctional System," *Harvard Educational Review*, Vol. 44, no. 1 (February 1974), pp. 74–111.

[2] Anthony Platt, *The Child Savers: The Invention of Delinquency* (Chicago: University of Chicago Press, 1969), p. 110.

cheap labor to industry, a process that was called the institution's primary educational program. Incorrigible boys were transferred to adult prisons.

By the mid-1970s, children between the ages of 10 and 17 accounted for 16 percent of the general population, but they accounted for 45 percent of all arrests for serious crimes, making the need for institutions for juvenile offenders and other programs to re-educate or rehabilitate juveniles central to the justice system.[3] It should be noted that, when this age group is enlarged to include those 21 and under, juveniles account for 61 percent of all arrests for serious crimes. Expanding the age group to those 25 and under, 75 percent of arrests for serious crimes are included. This dramatizes the need for youthful offender programs for those between 18 and 25 years of age, which are being developed in many states. The present concern, however, is the institutional treatment of juvenile offenders 18 years of age and under.

TRAINING SCHOOLS

Training schools are long-term institutions for juveniles who have been committed by the juvenile court. This group includes juvenile adjudicated delinquents and children or persons in need of supervision, generally known as "status offenders," who have not committed what would have been a crime had they been of age but have been truant from school, have acted in an incorrigible manner, have violated curfew laws, and have exhibited other noncriminal behavior.

As of June 30, 1975, there were 874 public facilities for juveniles and 1,277 private facilities.[4] In the public sector, there were a total of 37,926 boys and 4,878 girls in custody.[5] In the private sector, there were a total of 27,290 juveniles, of whom 19,152 were boys and 8,138 were girls.[6] Public facilities care for 64.8 percent of the juvenile case load, while private facilities are responsible for 35.8 percent of the juveniles needing attention in juvenile institutions. There were 189 public training schools, 347 detention centers, 195 halfway houses or group homes, 103 open institutions that included forestry camps and farms, 23 shelters, and 17 reception or diagnostic centers.[7] In the private sector, there were 65 training schools, 3 detention centers, 851 halfway houses or group homes, 295 open institutions that included forestry camps and farms, 58 shelters, and 5 reception or diagnostic centers.[8] The average stay in public training

[3]Birch Bayh, "A New Deal for Children in Trouble," *Skeptic,* Vol. 4 (November–December 1974), p. 52.

[4]*Children in Custody: Final Report on the Juvenile Detention and Correctional Facility Census of 1975* (Washington, D.C.: U.S. Department of Justice, LEAA, 1979), reported in Timothy J. Flanagan, Michael J. Hindelang, and Michael R. Gottfredson, *Sourcebook of Criminal Justice Statistics—1979* (Washington, D.C.: U.S. Department of Justice, LEAA, National Criminal Justice Information and Statistics Service, 1980), p. 163.

[5]Ibid., p. 624.

[6]Ibid., pp. 262, 622.

[7]Ibid., p. 164.

[8]Ibid., p. 165.

schools was 228 days or about seven-and-a-half months, while the average stay in private training schools was 324 days or just under eleven months.[9] The total cost of public detention and correctional facilities for juveniles was about $594,146,000 or $12,126.91 per capita; the cost of private facilities was about $273,644,000 or $10,027.26 per capita.[10] It should be noted that there is wider variation in costs among private facilities than among public institutions.

There were 29,229 adjudicated delinquent boys and 4,878 adjudicated delinquent girls in public facilities as of June 30, 1975.[11] Persons or children in need of supervision (PINS or CINS) included 2,539 boys and 1,955 girls. There were 236 dependent and neglected boys, as compared with 215 girls in that category. Approximately 14.3 percent of the delinquents were girls, 43.5 percent of the children in need of supervision were girls, and 47.7 of the dependent and neglected children were girls. While 21 percent of all juveniles arrested are females, they constitute 30 percent of the total population in local detention facilities and 22.2 percent of the training school populations.[12]

The short-term institutions in the juvenile system are detention centers, shelters, and reception or diagnostic centers. Detention centers are local facilities designed for security. Shelters are local centers not designed for security that frequently house dependent and neglected children in need of supervision. Reception and diagnostic centers have clinical staffs for the purpose of evaluating children with emotional problems. There are public and private institutions in each of these classifications.

The long-term institutions are training schools; ranches, forestry camps, or farms; and halfway houses or group homes. Training schools are designed to hold adjudicated delinquents for extended periods in relatively secure settings. The ranch, forestry camp, and farm are designed to house juveniles in minimum security for extended periods of time. Halfway houses and group homes are local facilities designed to hold small groups, probably 10 to 25, in residential situations from which the residents can go to local public or private schools and participate in community programs. Again, there are public and private facilities in each of these classifications.

There are sharp differences among the approximately 450 training schools, 300 of which are for boys, 125 for girls, and 25 coeducational, only a few of which have been able to mount treatment programs by 1974.[13] Rather than contending that training schools be abolished, as many writers and commissions have suggested, it would be more beneficial to society to narrow the differences between them by improving the treatment programs in the vast majority of them that do not have realistic treatment programs but continue as warehousing custodial operations.

Private training schools are generally better than public training schools

[9]Ibid., p. 627.

[10]Ibid., pp. 168, 172.

[11]Ibid., p. 624.

[12]*Little Sisters and the Law* (Washington, D.C.: Office of Juvenile Justice and Delinquency Prevention, 1977), p. 33.

[13]Raymond L. Manella, "The Case for Residential Treatment of Delinquent Children," *Juvenile Justice*, Vol. 25, no. 1 (May 1974), pp. 2–12.

and cost less. Ira Schwartz, administrator of the Office of Juvenile Justice and Delinquency Prevention, has advised people to send delinquent youths to a private institution where "a kid gets better help, cheaper, in a private facility. It's a sad situation."[14] The cost of holding a child in a state institution averages about $20,000 per year. In New York, it can run to $40,000 or $45,000 per year.

Financing the private school is generally by donations and some fees from the courts. A private school can develop many sources of donations. Many individuals would prefer to give money to a charity than to pay it in income taxes to the federal government. Consequently, some private schools have amassed considerable financial reserves and can pay high salaries to their staffs. On the other hand, some of the new, small, private institutions developed simply to "make money" and "bid" for juveniles from the courts are not well financed and do not have good programs.

Small counties have a difficult time in providing for their children with problems. Muskingum County, Ohio, with a population of less than 100,000, built a detention home with fourteen spaces in 1963.[15] Because it was larger than the county needed, neighboring counties used it, also, making it a regional operation. In addition, a program involving foster homes, group homes, intensive probation, and volunteers was developed, all for the purpose of reducing commitments to training schools. In that, it has been successful. The primary shortcoming is the absence of facilities for girls. While many authorities have held that the only way in which to increase community-based programs is to close the state training schools, it may be that the only way to close state training schools is to reduce commitments to them by increasing community-based programs.

LOCAL DETENTION HOMES

There are 347 local detention homes in the United States, generally in the areas of higher population. Smaller counties do not have the resources to construct detention homes and tend to use other available facilities, be it the jail or other alternatives. Detention homes generally hold between twenty and fifty juveniles, a small section being reserved for girls, and are operated by the juvenile court. A detention home administrator supervises the operation of the detention home.

The majority of detention homes are operated by the county and are directly under the supervision of the juvenile court, although some are separate juvenile detention homes operated away from the jurisdiction of the juvenile court and directed by a separate administrator hired by the county; in other cases, a contract for a juvenile detention home is entered into by the county with a couple who has a large home that can be used as a detention facility and the couple is paid to permit the county to lodge juveniles there. Transportation problems tend to militate against the regional facilities.

Many jurisdictions without detention homes and some with detention

[14]Bill Ryan, "Should Delinquents Be Locked Up?" *Parade*, October 12, 1980, p. 21.
[15]Holland M. Gary, "A Small County's Answer to Community-Based Programs," *Juvenile Justice*, Vol. 26, no. 2 (May 1975), pp. 21–26.

homes make use of the standby foster home in which a certain amount of money is provided to a family on a standby basis, such as $10 or $15 per day, to be receptive to placement of juveniles as needed. When a juvenile is placed in the home, an amount of money is added for the support of a child, generally $20 to $25 over and above the standby fee. This has been considered to be cheaper and more effective than other detention alternatives. It saves construction costs and general maintenance and personnel salaries. Only a few detention homes have a full program that includes education and counseling. Unfortunately, the majority of detention homes are simply a holding action. This is why many professional organizations concerned with children recommend against building a detention home and favor finding more suitable alternatives.[16]

Juvenile court counselors serve as liaison between the detention home and the juvenile court. While the counselors in the detention home, if available, serve in the detention home, the juvenile court counselor provides the transportation and other counseling for juveniles in the detention home and in the juvenile court.

Detention can be a rehabilitative experience if sufficient resources are provided. The Children's Court Center at Pittsburg, Kansas, draws on professional assistance and community agencies to attend to the needs of the young people detained there, to make their contacts with the establishment useful experiences, and to provide alternative means of dealing with the power structure.[17] Young people of today are the leaders of tomorrow, which makes the future dependent upon developing the people in detention as functioning and productive members of society.

ORGANIZATION OF PUBLIC TRAINING SCHOOLS

Juvenile training schools exist in all states except Massachusetts, where they were closed in 1972 by then Commissioner Jerome Miller. Dr. Miller, then Commissioner for Youth Services, thought the institutions were doing more harm than good. The public training schools receive their funds through tax money appropriated by the legislatures. Traditionally, the juvenile institutions have been supervised by the state department of welfare or its counterpart. Some states have an agency specifically designed for youth, such as the Ohio Youth Commission. Still other states, such as Florida, have the Youth Services Program within a larger department, for example, the department of health and rehabilitative services. Figure 12-1 is a chart of the organization of a typical juvenile training school.

Most juvenile training schools have three primary departments or efforts. First, juvenile institutions are concerned with education. Much of the education is through the eighth grade followed by vocational training of some sort.

[16]Sherwood Norman, *Think Twice Before You Build or Enlarge a Detention Center* (New York: National Council on Crime and Delinquency, 1968).

[17]Karen Wilson, "New Concepts in Detention," *Juvenile Justice*, Vol. 28, no. 1 (February 1977), pp. 19–23.

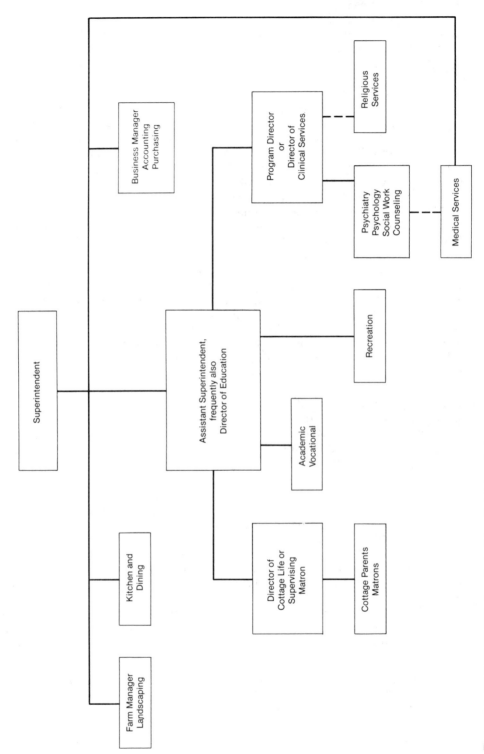

Figure 12-1 Table of organization for a "typical" juvenile training school.

Second, most juvenile institutions have a series of "cottages" in which the youths live, the size of the cottage generally housing twenty to fifty juveniles each. Each cottage is supervised by a matron or cottage parents. The selection of the type of supervision has never been resolved satisfactorily. When a couple serves as cottage parents, in-house duties are primarily performed by the wife, with the husband assisting, which does not give the juveniles a good image of the cultural definition of masculinity. More successful, apparently, is the matron or cottage mother, although they are difficult to find and recruit. A difficulty in some states is that the legislated forty-hour workweek requires three or four shifts in cottage supervision and hence does not promote continuity. The supervising matron or director of cottage life frequently has in-service training sessions to assist persons responsible for supervision within the cottage to understand deviant behavior of the delinquent.

Third, programs for treatment and counseling are generally under a program director or director of clinical services. Sometimes, they are in a social services division. Most frequently, they include social work and counseling services. On occasion, a psychologist may be on the staff. Psychiatrists are sometimes available on a consultation basis, but they are generally not on staff. In a few institutions, a permanent psychiatrist is the program director. The primary focus of this department of social or clinical services has been largely on behavioral problems. Problems of discipline are handled in this department in some of the better schools, although in less progressive schools, the disciplinary problems are handled sometimes in a punitive way within the educational program.

Release procedures in various institutions are generally in two broad categories. The first depends on a specified length of time or number of points earned each month as a result of evaluation by the staff. The second depends on clinical judgment as to whether the juvenile is ready for release. Some institutions use the old Irish system in which they are incarcerated by stages. The more clinically oriented programs use observation and clinical judgment to determine whether the juvenile is ready for release.

GROUP HOMES

Halfway houses and other community treatment programs have increased rapidly since the mid-1960s into the 1980s. Halfway houses are residential community-based programs for sixteen to thirty youths who attend local schools and participate in other programs in the community. Group centers are residential programs for fifteen to twenty-five youths. They are similar to halfway houses, except that educational and vocational programs are within the center and the residents are not involved in community activities. Small group homes provide four to eight youths with a homelike atmosphere, usually under the supervision of a husband-and-wife team. Large group homes have nine to fifteen youths and the programs are similar to the small group homes, frequently a husband-and-wife team providing a homelike atmosphere and participation in local schools and programs. Day care programs are nonresidential centers that provide work or school activities and recreation as well as more intensive treatment services in the form of counseling and group sessions. The youths live at home and report to the program daily.

Standby foster homes have been a viable alternative to the detention home. As mentioned, a standby foster home is an approved family who will admit juveniles into its home as part of the family on a contract with the juvenile court; the standby parents may receive $10 to $15 a day when the home is empty and an additional $20 to $25 a day when the home is used for the placement of a juvenile. The costs are much less than the construction and maintenance of a detention home program and less damaging because the juveniles are permitted to remain in the community and attend the schools they attended when they were at home. These facilities are used for juveniles who need to be removed from their homes but do not have to be sent to a larger institution with higher security. The basic ingredient leading to the success of a standby foster home is the personality and empathic skills of the foster home parents. Runaways are not an important problem in the standby foster home, since most juveniles who run away go home. Most are not gone from home for an extended period of time.

A good directory is available to identify programs in the United States and Canada.[18] It provides information on construction costs, annual costs per child, numbers of boys and girls to service, average length of stay, types of commitment, treatment services available, and other information on each program.

PROGRAM APPROACHES

The training school in historical perspective was a military organization. It was generally supervised by a retired military officer rather than by an expert in behavior. Some were supervised by former police administrators. As a consequence, the many training schools into the 1930s featured close-order drill and a generally military atmosphere.

The inspirational-repressive approach is generally present in a religiously oriented institution or in an institution where the superintendent or staff is concerned with motivation through inspiration and eliminating undesirable behavior through social disapproval.

The traditional training school is geared to education, hard work, and discipline. The primary focus is on education and discipline. When out of school, hard work is assigned, all the way from farming to landscape gardening.

The behavior modification or operant conditioning approach involves punishment and reward. A good monthly evaluation of performance results in additional merits or points. These points can be traded later in a canteen or store for candy or other items appropriate for juveniles. This giving and withholding is a conditioning procedure that operates in many institutions.

The orthopsychiatric approach is the clinical approach. Frequently supervised by psychiatrists or clinical psychologists, it focuses on the emotional stability of the juvenile.

---

[18]*Directory of Halfway Houses and Group Homes for Troubled Children* (Tallahassee: Florida Division of Youth Services, 1974), prepared by Richard L. Rachin. Subsequent directories are planned.

Institute students participating in the sinking of a derelict aircraft which will become part of an artificial reef. This project provides the opportunity for the students to actively use the skills they learn in the Marine Institute program. The community also benefits because the artificial reef increases the commercial and recreational fishery habitat.

Courtesy of the Marine Institute.

Evaluations of the various approaches indicate that the orthopsychiatric is the most effective, although the most expensive. The education, hard work, and discipline approach appears to be next best in terms of effectiveness. The difficulty with the inspirational-repressive approach is that it is dependent upon the personalities that are present at the time. The difficulty with the behavior modification or operant conditioning approach is that juveniles can learn to "play the game" of rewards and punishment in an institutional setting. But, when released, these same reward and punishment pressures do not exist in community life. Rather, the old pressures of the community become paramount again.

Many other approaches to delinquency not associated with the juvenile training school exist. Outward Bound in Denver, Colorado, for example, is a wilderness survival program. And other similar programs involve long hiking and canoeing trips that take six weeks or longer, during which time the youths learn to get along with each other through the process of interdependence for survival and success of the venture.

The Oceanographic Education Program of the Associated Marine Institutes was begun in Florida in 1969 as a rehabilitative project for juvenile

[19]Frank A. Orlando and Robert A. Rosof, "An Alternative to Institutions: Victory at Sea," *Juvenile Justice*, Vol. 27, no. 3 (August 1976), pp. 25–29.

[20]For more information, contact Robert A. Rosof, executive vice president, Associated Marine Institutes, 1500 Southeast 3rd Court, Deerfield Beach, Florida 33441.

offenders, engaging them in small-boat operation, diving, and specimen collection on the coastal shelf.[19] By 1976, the program was in five metropolitan areas: Panama City, Tampa, Jacksonville, St. Petersburg, and Miami.[20] Basic subjects in the program are Red Cross first aid and life saving, skin and scuba diving, seamanship, and oceanography. Elective subjects include marine maintenance (motor and boat repair), advanced training in preparation for the Coast Guard captain's license, underwater photography, and advanced NAUI certification in diving. From September 1969 to April 1975, 576 boys had been enrolled and 78 percent had completed the program. Based on experience, the program could be broadened and extended, and, further, it could be used effectively in other areas, such as forestry and geology.

Approaches to delinquency programs can take a variety of approaches, depending upon the personalities of the workers and of the delinquent youths. The problem is to fit the program to the needs of the youths involved.

PROBLEMS IN INSTITUTIONS

The major serious problems in institutions are (1) theft, (2) homosexuality, (3) bullying, and (4) runaways. Fights occur frequently as a result of interpersonal disputes, but bullying, in which the strong boys victimize the weak, is more persistent. They work out the "pecking order" or the pattern of dominance and submission among the residents, just as happens at recess and after school in the free community, but it is more intense in institutions. In many institutions, aggression and bullying have racial overtones. Blacks tend to be stronger than whites and dominate most physical events. Many white runaways explain that it was fear of the blacks that caused them to run. Conversely, many blacks who run away explain that they have been mistreated by the white staff.

Theft is frequent in institutions for juveniles. Generally, it is not a matter of need but of acquisition. Psychiatrists contend that insecure people practice petty theft to gain security, which is apparently supported by the fact that many youths in institutions steal items they do not need or cannot use. One boy, for example, stole belt buckles until he had accumulated a bushel basket of them. Minor theft, then, is an emotional problem, and punitive overreaction on the part of institutional personnel could well be counterproductive and compound the problem of insecurity.

Homosexuality occurs in juvenile institutions to a lesser extent than it does in jails and other institutions, but it does occur and it is damaging. In juvenile institutionalization, youths are sent to a unisexual or "homosexual" institution right in the middle of their psychosexual developmental process. It is surprising to many in the field of child development that people are so oblivious to this developmental problem. Emotionally troubled youths exposed to this deprivation frequently become arrested developmentally and never have satisfactory heterosexual relationships as adults. It is for this reason that some states, such as Florida, are experimenting with coeducational juvenile training schools.

Runaways from juvenile institutions are a persistent problem. Experience has indicated that the number of runaways per year might be about half the population size of an institution, but involve only about 20 percent of the residents, since some leave several times. The rate of runaways varies according to the location of the institution, among other factors, so that an institution isolated in a distant rural area with probably only one main road nearby will have fewer runaways than will an institution in or near an urban center with a variety of roads and means of transportation. Studies of runaways have indicated that whites run away significantly more often than do blacks.[21] Further, the factors that generate the runaway behavior in an individual are loneliness, fear, and resentment. In running, youths draw the line separating a surrogate community, which is tolerable, from imprisonment, which is not.

Overcrowded facilities has been a problem for all criminal justice systems. Judge Tom Dillon of Fulton County, Atlanta, Georgia, issued an order in December 1972 to the effect that the seventy-two available spaces in the Atlanta detention home would be filled on the basis of pressing priorities but that the facility would never exceed its seventy-two space capacity.[22] The priorities were identified and listed from 1 to 8, ranging from those charged or adjudicated with an offense as severe as a capital felony to a child just being held without any specific charge.

EFFECTS OF JUVENILE INSTITUTIONALIZATION

The effects of juvenile institutionalization involve emotional development. Normal emotional development takes a long time to achieve and requires the inculcation of cultural values and the development of an identity and self-concept that are constructive and positive, both of which come from the family between birth and puberty. Full and secure interpersonal relationships at and after puberty require an interaction between the family and the "outside world," with the family being the primary group that provides a haven from the outside, emotional security, self-concept, and identity. When these services are deficient, emotional development may be arrested, regression may occur, and traumatic events may precipitate deviant behavior. The institution removes the developing personality from the family and normal interaction in society.

Emotional deprivation and feelings of insecurity and failure become obvious in an institutional setting for juveniles. No longer is mother or father there to provide emotional support. Rather, the cottage parents or matron becomes an authority figure to twenty-five to fifty youths. The youth begins to develop flat emotional responses to others, begins to relate without meaning in an impersonal way as a manner of "getting along," and develops some automatonlike behavior. The youth loses what identity and self-concept he or she has. It

[21]Robert Johnson, James Lewis, and Patricia Gail Young, "The Training School Absconder: A Preliminary Assessment of Antecedent Problems and Motives," *Juvenile & Family Court Journal*, Vol. 29, no. 3 (August 1979), pp. 3–8.

[22]George B. Collins III, "One Solution to Overcrowded Detention Homes," *Juvenile Justice*, Vol. 25, no. 3 (November 1974), pp. 45–49.

is another step in the development of a self-concept that is self-fulfilling in failure, "born to lose."

Group living with twenty-five to fifty other youths in the cottage and about two hundred in the institution—although some are much larger—generates the type of social adaptation one would anticipate when existence is based simply on living space and where friendships and emotional attachments are lacking. The society of strangers known as institutions results in a survival-of-the-fittest approach without emotional investment in or commitment to others. The frustration-aggression hypothesis permeates the institutional population, where the frustration of conflict and confrontation leads quite naturally to aggression, assaults, and fighting. When adolescents in their formative years grow up in this environment, this mode of social adaptation may remain with them for the rest of their lives.

The rejection by society after release from the institution, who identifies the youth as a "reform school graduate," is pervasive. Very seldom do boys or girls released from juvenile institutions return to the public school and re-enter their grades and classes, even though they may have been gone only a few months. Consequently, juvenile institutionalization changes the potential careers for all that it graduates. Only a few can "fight back" and earn their academic credentials to go to college and enter the middle-class work force in business or in the professions. The label "reform school graduate" remains with the youths for the rest of their lives in many cases. This is the reason, at least in part, for the high rate of failure of juvenile institutions. Generally, two out of five commitments to juvenile institutions return to the institution, another two grow older and go to a prison for adults or other correctional institution, and only one of the original five commitments does not come into contact with the law again. As a result, there is a strong move in the juvenile justice system today toward de-institutionalization and is the reason why Massachusetts closed all its juvenile institutions in 1972.

Experience in the juvenile justice system has convinced many that, where possible, boys should not be placed in institutions. Where more control is needed than that provided in the home, the group home might be an acceptable compromise. Data on group homes, however, indicate that not all types of offenders can benefit from this community-based facility.[23] People who have been institutionalized before, those who are significantly older or younger than the majority of residents of the facility, and people too emotionally disturbed to live in group situations do not respond to group homes. Even so, group homes appear to be the best long-term alternative available because they keep the youths in the community and in the schools and programs that they know. They are successful because of the integrated approaches they use in programming within a relatively natural setting. Most important in any program, however, is systematic follow-up after release to assist in the transfer of the essentials in the program to outside society.

[23]Delos H. Kelly and Joseph F. Weider, "The Effectiveness of Rural Group Home for Boys: A Descriptive Analysis," *Juvenile Justice*, Vol. 28, no. 1 (February 1977), pp. 47–59.

THE MOVE TOWARD
DEINSTITUTIONALIZATION

The move toward the deinstitutionalization of juveniles has been strong since the 1970s and into the 1980s. The National Council on Crime and Delinquency has called for deinstitutionalization since the mid-1960s. The Office of Juvenile Justice and Delinquency Prevention adheres to a policy made in the late 1970s that no state that institutionalizes status offenders along with adjudicated delinquents will receive grants of funds for any projects from that program. It should be noted that deinstitutionalization of persons dependent upon tax funds for their care is a continuing concern. For example, since the 1930s and the development of the social security system and sophisticated welfare programs, the old county poorhouses have disappeared and welfare recipients receive their checks through the mails. After World War II, the government established the National Institute of Mental Health and supported the move to the deinstitutionalization of the mentally ill as much as possible and has created local mental health clinics to assist in this process. In fact, the deinstitutionalization of the mentally ill, the retarded, and the juvenile and adult offender has been seen as a trend in the future.[24]

The juvenile justice system is under criticism for ineffectiveness, and, simultaneously, many writers are calling for deinstitutionalization. Some have indicated that the approaches that could be used to cope with serious juvenile delinquency might be to (1) lower the age at which a youthful offender could be tried as an adult, (2) sentence the youth to a secure facility for a determinate amount of time, (3) divest the power of handling youths from such agencies as divisions of youth services to the courts, (4) regulate youth services through administrative reorganization within youth agencies and/or merging youth and adult correctional agencies, and (5) move the incremental return from a system built primarily on small, open, community-based facilities to a network of larger, restrictive, institutionlike facilities to centralize service delivery for better cost-effectiveness in working with delinquents.[25]

The Youth Opportunities Upheld, Inc., program (YOU) is supported by the Massachusetts Committee on Law Enforcement Assistance Administration to find and develop new and innovative ways in which to deal with behavioral problems among youths.[26] It attempts to find ways in which to handle the delinquency problem in the absence of state training schools, which were closed in Massachusetts in 1972. Many previously institutionalized youth, about twelve hundred annually, can be helped more effectively by a wide range of communi-

---

[24]Bernard J. Coughlin, 'Deinstitutionalization: A Matter of Social Order and Deviance," *Child Welfare*, Vol. 56, no. 5 (1977), pp. 393–99.

[25]Richard E. Isralowitz, "Deinstitutionalization and the Serious Juvenile Offender," *Juvenile & Family Court Journal*, Vol. 30, no. 3 (August 1979), pp. 21–29.

[26]Maurice J. Boisvert, Helen J. Kenney, and William C. Kvaraceus, "Massachusetts Deinstitutionalization: Data on One Community-Based Answer," *Juvenile Justice*, Vol. 27, no. 2 (May 1976), pp. 35–40.

ty-based programs. Experience by YOU indicates that the extreme positions sometimes expressed by citizens and political leaders that all offenders should be kept on the streets, on the one hand, or that all offenders should be locked up, on the other, are both unrealistic. A broad range of programs is needed to meet the needs of youths.

The population in juvenile institutions is declining. In 1965, there were approximately 40,000 juveniles in public institutions, but by 1970, the number had declined to 37,000 and still further to 26,000 in 1978.[27] The population of juvenile institutions is less than one-tenth the population of adult institutions. Reasons for the drop in population of juvenile institutions are (1) the increased use of community-based facilities such as group homes and intensive probation supervision, (2) the removal of status offenders or those who are not delinquent but need supervision from the juvenile institutional population in many states, and (3) the lowering of the average age of prisoners received in adult facilities, indicating that more younger offenders are going to prison.

CONCLUSIONS

The juvenile institution as a separate entity is only about 150 years old, although there were earlier institutions, somewhat isolated in time, such as the Hospice di San Michele built in Rome by Pope Clement XI in 1704 and the famous "asylums" from the sixteenth century to the Industrial Revolution. Throughout the history of family life from ancient times when the father had power of life or death, through the history of brutality and beating of children, to the formation of the Society for the Prevention of Cruelty to Children in 1874 and the child labor laws of 1912, and on to more humane treatment of children, the place of the welfare of children has always been at issue. When Napoleon issued his famous decree in 1811 that the state was responsible for the welfare of its children and the declaration by the House of Lords in England in 1828 of the doctrine of *parens patriae* (the state is responsible for the welfare of its children), governments had accepted responsibility for the children for the first time. It is interesting to note that the Society for the Prevention of Cruelty to Animals was created in 1824, exactly half a century before the same protections were afforded children!

Institutions will still be needed for some juveniles with serious problems, but community-based programs, especially those utilizing group homes, can reduce the cost and reduce the damage of institutionalization for the majority of juvenile offenders.[28] A specially designed group home with resource room teachers can focus on youth competence rather than on incompetence, can coordinate community agencies and school programs, can contribute to develop-

[27]Rob Wilson, "The Long-Term Trend Is Down," *Corrections Magazine,* Vol. 4, no. 3 (September 1978), pp. 3–11. This issue featured "Where Have All the Juvenile Offenders Gone?"

[28]Ronald F. Kingsley and Joseph N. Murray, "Institutions and Community-Based Programs," *Journal of Juvenile & Family Courts,* Vol. 29, no. 1 (February 1978), pp. 31–37.

mental needs while employing peer modeling, can encourage participation in short-term programs, can intervene in the mildly or moderately involved behavioral problems, can maintain liaison with all residential centers, and can reduce the cost of treatment.

The Massachusetts Task Force on Secure Facilities made a thorough study of the ways in which its Department of Youth Services (DYS) was handling the problem of delinquency after the institutions were closed in 1972.[29] The task force began its study in April 1976 and submitted its report in November 1977. The conclusions were that the vast majority of juvenile offenders could be handled in community-based programs but that secure facilities were needed for a few. With some provision for secure facilities, however, other programs of the DYS must be integrated with them. The task force reported that a major need would be for DYS to "put its own house in order" and that all recommendations would be futile if DYS did not respond.

The National Institute for Juvenile Justice and Delinquency Prevention established in 1976 an Assessment Center Program in accordance with the mandate of the Juvenile Justice and Delinquency Prevention Act of 1974, to collect and synthesize knowledge and information on all aspects of juvenile delinquency that could be applied practically to the field. Among the recommendations of this group were that continued support be provided for the broad-based studies and plans of intervention of the type carried on by the Harvard Research Group, which studied alternative plans after Massachusetts closed its juvenile institutions in 1972; further experimentation with and use of paraprofessionals and community workers, together with volunteers, to strengthen community-based programs; and the maintenance of intensive intervention, casework, and treatment of hard-core, violent offenders in a small, closed residential center or in several such centers with a variety of treatment models.[30]

CHAPTER QUESTIONS

12-1. How many public and private facilities are there in the United States for juveniles and how many persons do they hold?

12-2. What types of public and private juvenile facilities exist in the United States?

12-3. Why are group homes considered to be better than local detention homes?

12-4. How are the majority of juvenile training schools organized?

12-5. What are the various philosophies used in juvenile training schools?

12-6. What are the primary problems encountered in juvenile institutions?

[29]Richard E. Isralowitz and L. Scott Harshbarger, "The Massachusetts Task Force on Secure Facilities: An Examination of the Issue of Security in a Community-Based System of Juvenile Corrections," *Juvenile & Family Court Journal*, Vol. 30, no. 2 (May 1979), pp. 29–36.

[30]Charles P. Smith and Paul S. Alexander, *Reports of the National Juvenile Justice Assessment Centers—A National Assessment of Serious Juvenile Crime and the Juvenile Justice System: The Need for a Rational Response* (Washington, D.C.: National Institute for Juvenile Justice and Delinquency Prevention, LEAA, April 1980), pp. xxi–xxii.

12-7.   What is the effect of juvenile institutionalization on the boys and girls held in training schools?

12-8.   What does juvenile institutionalization do to the heterosexual development of institutionalized persons?

12-9.   Why is the failure rate in juvenile institutions so high?

12-10.   Why is there a move toward deinstitutionalization of juveniles?

13
INSTITUTIONS
FOR
FEMALES

Correctional institutions for females serve a far smaller population than do institutions for men. Between 5 and 6 percent of the prison population is female. Consequently, institutions for females tend to be small and few in number. There were thirty-eight separate prisons for women in the United States in 1978 and twenty coeducational or co-correctional institutions housing men as well as women. In New Hampshire, the only state without a women's prison, there is a women's unit in the main prison. In New Hampshire in 1979, six females were sentenced by the courts, four of whom were housed in the Women's Correctional Facility in Niantic, Connecticut, under the New England Interstate Corrections Compact and two of whom were housed in a county house of correction in New Hampshire. It is noteworthy that some coeducational facilities are instituted without much publicity, probably because of fear of criticism. Among juvenile institutions listed in the directory compiled by the American Correctional Association, twelve listed themselves as being simply for girls, while thirty-six listed themselves as coeducational, and the rest identified their resident population as "adjudicated juveniles," which generally means that it is primarily a boy's institution with a girl's unit under the same administration.[1]

[1]American Correctional Association, *Juvenile and Adult Correctional Departments, Institutions, Agencies, and Paroling Authorities—United States and Canada—1978* (College Park, Md.: ACA, 1979).

Data from the U.S. Bureau of Prisons and from fifteen sample states chosen on the basis of size and geographic location indicated that women's prisons are, in fact, considerably smaller and more remote than are men's prisons.[2] Women's prisons are small because of the small female prison populations, which means that there is less stringent classification in women's prisons, where all offenses and ranges of seriousness of crimes are together and where there are wide variations of lengths of sentences and other problems as well as a lesser variation of available programs. Women's prisons have less concern for custody than do men's prisons. These are only a few factors that have given rise to recent concerns about the "equal protection" clause of the Fourteenth Amendment and of equal rights legislation.

THE FEMALE OFFENDER

An overview of the female offender provides some reference points as to the needs that correctional institutions for women must meet. In a survey by the Women's Prison Association, approximately 42 percent of female prisoners in the United States are white, 24 percent are currently married, and 67 percent have children.[3] Further, there is a national trend toward more serious offenses being committed by women. Because women traditionally constitute only about 5 percent of the total number of prisoners, prisons for women are woefully inadequate and without a diversity of programs found in prisons for men.

Most female offenders come from racial or ethnic minorities, are younger than the general population, have less education, and have had troubled and/or abused childhoods.[4] Alternatives to incarceration and probation could meet the needs of most female offenders. For those incarcerated, an effective link between the institution back to the community is imperative to provide a meaningful reintegration into society.

At the close of fiscal year 1976, the female population of the U.S. Bureau of Prisons was 1,406.[5] The ages ranged from 17 years to over 60, and the racial mix was 34 percent white, 54 percent black, 6 percent Hispanic, and the remaining 6 percent other ethnic and racial groups. Available statistics indicate that 38 percent were single and 26 percent were married, but the marital status of the rest was not identified.

Approximately 25 percent of the general population in the District of Columbia Department of Corrections had been involved in drugs.[6] The drug

---

[2]R. F. Arditi and F. Goldberg, "Sexual Segregation in American Prisons," *Mental Health Digest*, Vol. 5, no. 9 (September 1973), pp. 18–26.

[3]Omar Hendrix, *A Study of Neglect: A Report on Women Prisoners* (New York: The Women's Prison Association, financed by the Ford Foundation, mimeographed, n.d., but released in early 1973), p. 38.

[4]*Female Offenders—Who Are They and What Are the Problems Confronting Them* (Washington, D.C.: U.S. Bureau of Prisons, 1977), 35 pp.

[5]E. Foster, *Female Offenders in the Federal Prison System* (Washington, D.C.: U.S. Bureau of Prisons, 1977), 35 pp.

[6]Stuart Adams, *District of Columbia—Narcotic-Involved Inmates in the Department of Corrections* (Washington, D.C.: District of Columbia Department of Corrections, 1969), 28 pp.

problem is more acute among women inmates than it is among men. More programs need to be developed to combat addiction. A study of population movement of women brought to a District of Columbia detention center and in the Department of Corrections admissions indicates that the criminal justice system penalizes the black female offender unfairly.[7] In addition, women are detained excessively in terms of the kinds of offenses for which they are arrested and in terms of the final dispositions of their cases.

In recent years, levels of female incarceration for property crime have risen at a faster pace than have male levels, but only for larceny-theft and fraud-embezzlement.[8] Absolute differences between male and female offenses have indicated that female property crime still lags far behind that of males in the criminal justice system. Dividing the data between the periods of 1960 and 1967 and 1965 and 1968 suggests that no influence has been due to the women's movement.[9] Women are still typically nonviolent property offenders, and the "new female criminal" is more of a social invention than an empirical reality.

Women in the U.S. Bureau of Prisons facilities constitute 6 percent of the inmate population. They tend to be 31 years old, black and single, have responsibility for two children, and do not have a high school diploma.[10] Nearly 70 percent have been arrested four or more times, blacks having an average of eight and whites an average of five arrests. Most of the women come from five states and the District of Columbia, including California, Florida, Michigan, New York, and Texas. Approximately 41 percent of the women are serving for property-related crimes, 24.4 percent for drug-related crimes, 17.9 percent for homicide and other violent crimes, and 11 percent for forgery. The problems associated with geographic placement of women's facilities are the small number of female inmates that makes cost-effectiveness of providing several appropriately programmed institutions for women questionable.

JUVENILE GIRLS

Juvenile girls present a different problem in institutions than do juvenile boys in several ways. They tend to arrive at juvenile institutions about a year-and-a-half younger than boys, approximately 14.6 years of age as compared with 16.1 years of age for boys, due to their more rapid early developmental growth rates. They tend to be committed more than boys for "status offenses," such as running away, inappropriate sexual behavior, truancy, incorrigibility, and similar "offenses" that would not be offenses had they passed their age of majority beyond school attendance and other laws relating only to juveniles.

[7]C. Barros and A. Slavin, *Movement and Characteristics of Women's Detention Center Admissions, 1969* (Washington, D.C.: District of Columbia Department of Corrections, 1971), 37 pp.

[8]D. J. Steffensmeir, "Crime and the Contemporary Woman—An Analysis of Changing Levels of Female Property Crime, 1960–1975," *Social Forces,* Vol. 57, no. 2, special issue (December 1978), pp. 566–84.

[9]Ibid.

[10]Ilene R. Bergsmann, "The Federal Female Profile," *Prison Law Monitor,* Vol. 2, no. 4 (September 1979), pp. 92–94.

One institutional program designed to treat "unmanageable" delinquent girls took the following sequential order: (1) behavior modification based on a sophisticated token economy program, (2) behavior modification based on a token economy on a few specified positive social acts, (3) behavior modification plus peer and reinforcement therapy, and (4) peer therapy alone.[11] Only peer therapy resulted in successful institutional adjustments. It was obvious that direction by staff and behavior modification had little or no effect. In fact, behavior modification may have even been slightly counterproductive.

Another classic study of work with delinquent girls was based on four hundred girls selected from a vocational high school designed for these special problems in New York City.[12] Two hundred girls were selected randomly as an experimental group and the other two hundred were designated as a control group. The two hundred girls in the experimental group were referred to the Youth Consultation Service whose professional staff provided individual casework and group therapy. After following the girls through their school careers, the experiment showed that potentially delinquent girls could be identified and engaged in programs designed to interrupt their deviant careers. On the other hand, the services had limited success in actually reducing the delinquency in which the girls engaged.

Potentially disruptive and runaway girls apparently can be identified through personality characteristics and be assigned to programs within the institution according to their needs.[13] The runaway girls tend to be more introverted, less emotionally stable, more compulsive, and more spontaneous than the nonrunaways. The girl who is disruptive tends to be more compulsive, individualistic, practical, and sensitive than the girl who is not disruptive. Treatment of girls in juvenile institutions tends to be even less successful than the treatment of boys in institutions.[14] Family love and security are seen as the most profound needs for adolescent girls. Delinquent behavior is seen as symptomatic of a need for such help. Certainly, the administration of juvenile institutions for girls should not be left to amateurs.

In Romig's survey of a series of approaches to effective behavior change among delinquent youth,[15] casework (ten studies) turned out to be conclusively negative, that is, not effective; behavior modification (fourteen studies) was not useful because delinquent behavior is complex and is a response to complex

[11]Robert P. Ross and H. Bryan McKay, "Study of Institutional Treatment Programs," *International Journal of Offender Therapy and Comparative Criminology,* Vol. 20, no. 2 (1975), pp. 165–73.

[12]H. Meyer and Edward Borgatta, *Girls at Vocational High: An Experiment in Social Work Intervention* (New York: Russell Sage Foundation, 1965), 225 pp.

[13]A. M. Bergmann, *Identification of Differentiating Characteristics Among Delinquent Girls in a Correctional Institution* (Ann Arbor, Mich.: University Microfilms, 1967), 58 pp.

[14]H. P. Lampman, *Wire Womb—Life in a Girls' Penal Institution* (Chicago: Nelson-Hall, 1973), 189 pp.

[15]Dennis A. Romig, *Justice for Our Children* (Lexington, Mass.: Lexington Books/D. C. Heath Company, 1978). Reported in Malcolm W. Klein, "Deinstitutionalization and Diversion of Juvenile Offenders: A Litany of Impediments," in Norval Morris and Michael Tonry, eds., *Crime and Justice: An Annual Review of Research,* Vol. 1 (Chicago: University of Chicago Press, 1979), pp. 171–72.

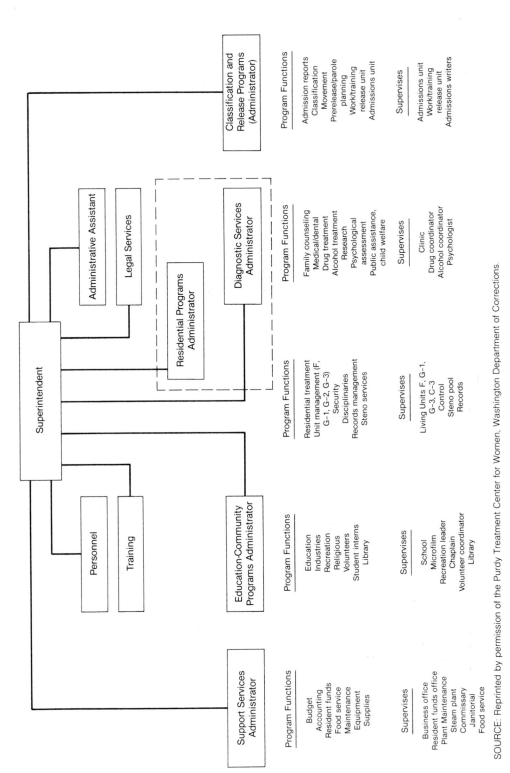

SOURCE: Reprinted by permission of the Purdy Treatment Center for Women, Washington Department of Corrections.

Figure 13-1 Purdy Treatment Center for Women: Organizational units (State of Washington).

community and social factors, while behavior modification is a simplistic approach in a controlled institutional environment and does not transfer to the community; group counseling (twenty-eight studies) tended to improve adjustment inside the institution in some cases but did not transfer outside to the community; individual counseling and psychotherapy (ten studies) resulted in nine negative results and one positive; and family counseling (twelve studies) showed the most promise, especially when parenting skills, such as communication, problem solving, and disciplining, were stressed.

ORGANIZATION

The organization of an institution for females is not as broad as that of a major prison for men. The average women's prison has about three hundred inmates or residents. The command staff generally includes a superintendent and an assistant superintendent or a captain to supervise the custodial staff. An educational program and a system of classification is the other primary function. Of course, the housekeeping and business functions have to be carried on by specialists in those areas. Figure 13-1 shows the organizational structure of one women's prison.

STAFFING

The staff of most women's prisons and institutions is primarily female. While many institutions for females have male superintendents, this role has been challenged by women who think that women should serve as superintendents of institutions for females.

There are a few male officers in most institutions for females, but they are selected carefully and are generally more mature than the rest of the prison population so that they will be "safe" when dealing with the female residents. Further, they are not assigned to dormitories but, rather, to peripheral security.

In 1974, an affirmative active program for female employees was initiated in the California corrections system to expand the number of officers to a ratio similar to the employment of women in the community.[16] It was thought that female employees could perform in correctional work situations equally as well as males. About one hundred female officers were assigned to such jobs as safety coordinator, chief of inmate appeals, parole agents, and counselors. All California institutions now employ female officers and some have opened all posts to females, including those that require direct contact with inmates. It has been observed that the female officers do perform equally as well as their male counterparts and that many have been accepted by the male inmates and seem to have improved the behavior of some of them.

When male guards had been assigned to the Bedford Hills Correctional Facility for Women in New York because of the absence of sex discrimination in

[16]A. M. Becker, "Resolution of Correctional Problems and Issues" *Issues in Criminology,* Vol. 1, no. 4 (Summer 1975), pp. 19–21.

1977, the females objected. The male guards had been assigned to Bedford only after the prison administration and the guard's union determined that Title VII of the 1964 Civil Rights Act required the assignment.[17] An informal settlement has since been made, leaving the assignment of officers inside the institution to the union. In turn, the union assigns men to those posts that are not inside the women's housing quarters.

There was strong objection made in 1977 by women in the Kentucky Correctional Institution for Women at Pewee Valley because male correctional officers had access to female dormitories at any time without the presence of a female officer, which was seen as a gross invasion of the women's privacy.[18] On one occasion, the male assistant superintendent came to inspect the bathroom facilities and ordered a woman taking a shower to come out so he could count her, since he had to see a "body." Other examples were cited, with a request that concerned citizens write to Commissioner Bland to express their opinions.

A survey of eleven state and U.S. Bureau of Prisons women's institutions has revealed that nine institutions used male correctional officers.[19] Only two institutions in this survey did not use male officers. The small population of women that required all personal services made the use of male staff counterproductive. Posts held by male officers in female institutions were confined to positions outside the offenders' housing units.

SELECTIVE POPULATION IN GIRLS' SCHOOLS AND WOMEN'S PRISONS

There were 4.7 men arrested for every woman in 1977, which represents a significant increase in arrests of women over previous years when the ratio was around 6.5 to 1.[20] On December 31, 1975, there were 25.3 men in state and federal prisons for every woman.[21] This was down slightly from the previous 27 to 30 men in prison for every woman, again representing an increase of women in the criminal justice system. It is apparent that the rate of female crime and sentencing is rising, but the difference is still significantly wide. Among juveniles, there were 4.5 boys adjudicated delinquent for every girl in 1974.[22] At the same time, there were 3.4 boys in juvenile institutions for every girl.[23] Compared with previous figures, this also reflects a significant increase in the number of

---

[17]Title 18 U.S.C., Sec. 242.

[18]Judy Wood, "From Kentucky Women," *Fortune News*, February 1977, p. 1.

[19]"Man on the Floor!" *Corrections Compendium*, Vol. 3, no. 15 (October 1979), p. 1.

[20]Federal Bureau of Investigations, *Crime in the United States—1977* (Washington, D.C.: FBI Uniform Crime Reports for release October 18, 1978), p. 177.

[21]Law Enforcement Assistance Administration, *Prisoners in State and Federal Institutions on December 31, 1975* (Washington, D.C.: U.S. Department of Justice, LEAA, 1977), pp. 3–7.

[22]Law Enforcement Assistance Administration, *Children in Custody: Advance Report on the Juvenile Detention and Correctional Facility Census of 1974* (Washington, D.C.: U.S. Department of Justice, LEAA, 1977), pp. 48–59.

[23]Ibid., pp. 42–45.

girls adjudicated and committed. As noted in Chapter 12, girls tend to be committed at an average age of about 14.6 as compared with boys at 16.1, the girls tending to mature earlier. Further, girls tend to be committed for status offenses more than boys, such as running away from home, truancy from school, and sex offenses, whereas boys tend to be adjudicated for burglary, vandalism, and other similar types of delinquency. It is interesting to note that girls tend to be adjudicated delinquent for sex offenses while their male partners tend to be treated less severely by the courts.

EDUCATIONAL PROGRAMS

Educational programs in institutions for females are academic, for preparation for a career. The academic school in a juvenile institution, of course, is a primary effort. Usually, however, the academic school does not go beyond the eighth grade. This, of course, is true of the adult women's institutions as well, although the effort is not concentrated on academics in those prisons. Many of the vocational or career training programs involve domestic work, which is rejected by some and accepted by others.

Two career areas popular in women's institutions are key punch operating and beauty culture. Unfortunately, many states do not license persons with felony records for beauty culture. Even so, it is a handy skill to know. Sewing, cooking, and other domestic skills exist in most women's institutions, sometimes only to maintain the kitchen and dining room or to maintain clothing. Realistically, there are very few viable vocational training programs in women's prisons.

The lack of substantial inmate population in women's prisons makes implementation of a full vocational training program costly.[24] The training programs open to women in institutions tend to reflect the traditional attitudes toward their roles in society and in the work force. It is hoped by many organizations and correctional administrators that this limitation in job opportunities for women will be ameliorated through a coalition of unions, criminal justice committees, women's organizations, and others, such as the American Bar Association. Viable programs must be implemented so that female offenders have a better chance of returning to their communities as highly motivated, taxpaying wage earners, not as additions to the welfare rolls.

PHYSICAL AND MENTAL HEALTH CARE

Experience has indicated that women need considerably more medical attention than do men in their respective institutions. Some of the need for health care results from pregnancies when they arrive in the institution. In addition, superintendents have indicated that women tend to be more emotional and sensitive to these needs. Whatever the reason, the cost of health care in women's prisons is

[24]D. S. North, "Women Offenders—Breaking the Training Mold," *Manpower*, Vol. 7, no. 2 (February 1977), pp. 13–19.

significantly higher than the per capita costs in men's prisons. The number of women who enter prison while pregnant and require prenatal care serves to raise medical demands still further.

Persistent problems in women's prisons include the lack of feminine hygiene articles and other personal items, lack of adequate soap and deodorant, having to fight for their womanhood in the absence of adequate protection in the dormitories and elsewhere, and fighting gnats and cats in the dining and kitchen areas.[25] Many of the programs in women's institutions can be good, but these little, but important, deficits persist.

Sociopathy ratings based on evaluations by staff psychologists and four scales of the MMPI were compared with ethical risk taking on thirty-eight female inmates.[26] A correlation between sociopathy ratings and total risk taking was significant at the .05 level, although the evidence is meager that high and low sociopathic groups were differentially affected by the determinants of risk taking. It appears that the major consideration affecting judgments of unethical behavior in this female population was the maximization of gain, not the avoidance of censure.

A study of ninety-five prisoners from the Framingham Institution for Women in Massachusetts were studied to determine psychiatric differences among women who were homosexual prior to prison, those who became homosexual in prison, and those who remained nonhomosexual female offenders.[27] There were twenty-six self-reported homosexuals, forty-two were considered to be homosexuals by the prison staff, and twenty-seven were nonhomosexuals. Characteristic of the homosexual group were suicidal thoughts and attempts, psychiatric problems during menstruation, and a history of violent crimes against persons. Characteristic of the nonhomosexual group were a history of crimes against self and property and a history of alcoholism. Aggressive impulses may be expressed either internally or externally, the problem being one of impairment in control mechanisms. Violent behavior in incarcerated homosexual females is multidetermined. The factors that could influence its appearance and expression might be a history of family violence, poor impulse control as children, neurological abnormality, sexual identification problems, biochemical abnormalities as manifested in menstrual irregularities, and impulse control problems.

Tests by the Edwards Personal Reference Schedule to determine the personality needs of 110 adult female inmates of Maine's women's correctional institution indicated that feelings of guilt range wider, both high and low, than they do in the general population.[28] Two types of psychopaths apparently exist: (1) primary psychopaths who exhibit no anxiety and have character disorders

[25]Vivian Mobly and Patricia Paul (letter to the editor from Florida), "Report from 17 Year Olds in Women's Prison," *Fortune News*, February 1977, p.5.

[26]J. P. Stefanowicz and T. E. Hannum, "Ethical Risk-Taking and Sociopathy in Incarcerated Females," *Correctional Psychologist*, Vol. 4, no. 4 (January 1971), pp. 138–52.

[27]C. E. Clement, A. Rollins, C. J. Batinelli, F. R. Ervin, and R. Plutchick, "Epidemiological Studies in Female Prisoners," *Journal of Nervous and Mental Diseases*, Vol. 164, no. 1 (1977), pp. 25–29.

[28]M. Hammer and M. B. Ross, "Psychological Needs of Imprisoned Adult Females with High and Low Conscience Development," *Corrective and Social Psychiatry and Journal of Behavior Technology, Methods, and Therapy*, Vol. 23, no. 3 (1977), pp. 73–78.

and (2) secondary psychopaths who exhibit anxiety and neurotic pathological development. These two groups differ significantly in the need for achievement, exhibitionism, dominance, nurturance, change, and aggression, with the secondary psychopaths or more anxious groups showing greater needs in these areas.

A study of seventy-three women admitted to the Iowa Women's Reformatory based on the usual battery of admission tests plus a twenty-four-item self-concept test with a follow-up after six months indicated that there was considerable improvement in self-concept during incarceration.[29] At time of admission, the female prisoner experiences low self-esteem. During incarceration, the educational programs, the visits to the institutional beauty shop, and the reduction of anxiety tend to produce a person who is more skilled, better looking, and more relaxed. In fact, inmates tended to score higher on intelligence and other usual tests of ability. The only scale that declined was the women's tendency to view themselves as more lazy after six months, which is consistent with the nonproductive nature of the incarceration.

An evaluation of group therapy on a sample of female felon inmates at a Minnesota state correctional institution was done through the use of several scales, such as the MMPI, a behavior rating scale, and the Semantic Differential Behavior Rating Scale.[30] There were no significant changes between the group who participated in the group therapy and the control group who did not participate.

For most female offenders, a male therapist is preferable to a female therapist.[31] Negative relationships with men are most central to deviant female behavior. The extension of empathy coupled with efforts to guide the client toward behavioral change in an acceptable setting may assist in neutralizing the negative relationships with men experienced previously by the female client. Female offenders can train and find employment faster than can male offenders. The hard-core drug abusers and prostitutes find normal work to be an extremely difficult adjustment. The most important part of a treatment program is for the therapist to communicate a genuine appreciation for the uniqueness of each individual and her potential for a satisfying life adjustment.

SPECIAL PROBLEMS
IN INSTITUTIONS FOR FEMALES

Because women tend to be screened so rigidly before being sent to prison, it is undoubtedly true that only the hard-core individuals get to the prison. Superintendents of women's institutions also say that women tend to be more emotional and have more minor fights than do men. Men's fights in prisons are much more

---

[29]T. E. Hannum and F. H. Borgen, "Self-concept Changes Associated with Incarceration in Female Prisoners," *Criminal Justice and Behavior,* Vol. 5, no. 3 (September 1978), pp. 271–79.

[30]N. G. Mandel and H. D. Vinnes, *Effectiveness of Short-Term Group Psychotherapy on the Intra-Institutional Behavior of Female Felons* (St. Paul: Minnesota Department of Corrections, 1968), 39 pp.

[31]E. M. Scott, "Therapy with Female Offenders," *International Journal of Offender Therapy and Comparative Criminology,* Vol. 21, no. 3 (1977), pp. 208–20.

Table 13-1 Types of Disciplinary Offense

MALE (*n* = 243)		FEMALE (*n* = 147)	
Offense	% of Total	Offense	% of Total
Verbal disrespect	11.9%	Verbal disrespect	15.0%
Disobeying verbal order	11.9	Presence in unauthorized area	11.6
Fighting	11.9	Disobeying institutional order	9.5
Unarmed assault	7.0	Possession of contraband	9.5
Unauthorized absence	7.0	Fighting	9.5
Obscene/profane act	4.5	Disobeying verbal order	7.5
Drug possession	3.3	Lying to staff	7.5
Presence in unauthorized area	3.3	Possession of unauthorized clothing	7.5
Possession of unauthorized clothing	3.3	Obscene/profane act	4.0
Possession of stolen property	3.3	Disorderly conduct	4.0
Miscellaneous	32.6	Miscellaneous	14.4
Total	100.0%	Total	100.0%

SOURCE: Charles A. Lindquist, "Inmate Participation in Correctional Institution Governance: An Analysis of Inmate Grievance Mechanism," paper presented at the Annual Meeting of the Academy of Criminal Justice Sciences, New Orleans, March 8–10, 1978, p. 23.

serious and may result in homicides, whereas very few homicides are reported from women's institutions.

The disciplinary problems in women's versus men's prisons appear to be similar, as indicated in a comparison of disciplinary reports in Florida's prisons done by Lindquist (see Table 13-1).[32]

The primary difference between disciplinary events in women's prisons and those in men's prisons is the seriousness of the assaults in men's institutions. It must be noted that there was an increase in population in women's correctional institutions in the 1970s and early 1980s. Part of the cause of the increase is due to the fact that women are no longer "tied to the home like they used to be."[33] They are not committing more crimes, in the opinion of women, themselves, but they are being arrested more. The women's prison population is getting to be younger because of the greater mobility of youth. They are leaving the home at an earlier age.

The first real attempt at making a comprehensive examination of programs and services provided for women in correctional institutions was done by the California Youth Authority in 1977.[34] Sixteen state prisons, forty-five county jails, and thirty-six community-based programs were studied in fourteen states: Colorado, Florida, Georgia, Illinois, Indiana, Michigan, Minnesota, Nebraska,

[32]Charles A. Lindquist, "Inmate Participation in Correctional Institution Governance: An Analysis of Inmate Grievance Mechanism," paper presented at the Annual Meeting of the Academy of Criminal Justice Sciences, New Orleans, March 8–10, 1978.

[33]Kathryn Watterson Burkhart, *Women in Prison* (New York: Popular Library, 1973), pp. 75–76.

[34]R. M. Glick, *National Study of Women's Correctional Programs* (Sacramento, Calif.: Department of the Youth Authority, 1977), 388 pp.

New York, Massachusetts, North Carolina, Texas, Washington, and California. The conclusions support the general consensus that services for women are not equal to those of men, primarily because of the smaller populations of women and because the smaller prisons do not permit the development and maintenance of broad programs.

The woman inmate's social role is generally that of homemaker and she needs a homelike setting with stronger personal ties, which is why she frequently turns to homosexuality.[35] Women inmates tend to be less motivated than men, have lower self-esteem, and need more counseling and positive social involvement. Women need to learn to be independent during and after imprisonment.

A study of violence in a women's prison indicates several variables, but none was of greater importance than the others, according to Glick and Neto.[36] Ninety-five women volunteers participated in the investigation. The variables associated most highly with violence were maternal loss before age 10, severe parental punishment, neurological disorders in relatives, the discontrol syndrome (series of disordered acts that interrupt an individual's typical life-style, both out of character for the individual and inappropriate to the situation), and easy access to weapons.

A problem that occurs in schools for adolescent females is self-mutilation. This self-mutilation may be in the form of eye-gouging, rectal-digging, head-banging, wrist-slashing, flagellation, insertion of objects under the skin, hair-pulling, self-biting, genital mutilation, self-burning, injection of harmful objects, and lacerating the skin. In a Canadian study, 117 of the 136 girls in the institution (86 percent) had carved themselves at least once during their stay in the institution.[37] The majority of girls had carved the names or initials of their "lovelight," a term used to refer to a girlfriend in the institution. In fact, 71.6 percent carved themselves in this manner. Some of the carvings were simple scratches (3.2 percent) and others (12.2 percent) entailed complex statement, such as "To Mom, with all my hate." This is a rather common phenomenon in institutions for adolescent girls and consideration of psychopathology does not play a major role in the development of effective programs to control or prevent such behavior.

In England's Holloway Prison, forty-eight acts of self-mutilation were performed by thirty-nine women in 1974.[38] Reviews of these cases and the administration of personality inventories measuring hostility and direction of hostility indicated that most mutilations were done in the cell, generally cutting the arm with a piece of glass. The self-mutilators tended to be younger than the prison norm, had a higher degree of previous institutional and psychiatric expe-

[35]Ruth M. Glick and Virginia V. Neto, *National Study of Women's Correctional Programs* (Washington, D.C.: Government Printing Office, 1977).

[36]C. E. Clement and A. Rollins, "Epidemiological Studies of Women's Prisons—Medical, and Psychiatric Variables Related to Violent Behavior," *American Journal of Psychiatry*, Vol. 130, no. 9 (September 1973), pp. 985–90.

[37]R. R. Ross, H. B. McKay, W. R. T. Palmer, and C. J. Kenney, "Self-mutilation in Adolescent Female Offenders," *Canadian Journal of Criminology*, Vol. 20, no. 4 (October 1978), p. 378.

[38]H. M. Cookson, "Survey of Self-injury in a Closed Prison for Women," *British Journal of Criminology*, Vol. 17, no. 4 (October 1977), 332–47.

rience, and had committed more violent offenses than a control group had. They also had higher hostility scores, particularly in the self-punitive direction, supporting the idea that self-injury is an act of aggression against self to appease guilt. In some cases, the self-injury was suggested to be a conscious manipulation of the environment and an attention-getting device.

Homosexuality is a widely used adaptive technique in women's prisons.[39] The thief subculture or property is not as important as in men's prisons, even though females are convicted for shoplifting and similar offenses more frequently. Homosexual behavior among females serves to create pseudofamily relationships, whereas homosexual behavior in men's institutions is simply related to physical relief.

A study of 160 inmates of the women's prison in Alabama attempted to determine dominance and submission patterns of women displaying masculine and feminine behaviors.[40] Four characteristically female patterns were delineated: (1) submissive-dependent behavior, (2) nurturance, (3) coquettish-passive behavior, and (4) orientations to others. Behaviors defined as masculine included (1) arguing aggressively, (2) vocal threatening, (3) hitting, (4) taking objects away from others, (5) cursing, (6) indicating a mechanical interest, (7) talking in a low voice, and (8) "rough-housing." The percentage of masculine or feminine varied widely among the women from 100 percent feminine to others characteristically, but not completely, masculine. Persons convicted of violent crimes tended to have a more masculine orientation. Inmates with high masculinity scores tended to engage in homosexual activity, tended to initiate most interaction in the classroom, and provided significant leadership in complaining groups.

The latent cultural identities of female inmates tend to manifest themselves in the form of kinship roles, creating pseudofamilies in the prison.[41] The preinstitutional socialization pattern that the female offender brings with her into prison is traditionally defined as "mother" or "companion." Role playing within a pseudofamily is a nonpathological response to institutionalization of women. By substituting for the women's actual families, the pseudofamilies supply gratification not provided by the institution. The participation rate of female offenders in such pseudofamilies may reach 71 percent. Such factors as staff-inmate relationships and staff disapproval may make some of these dyads hard to find. Most artificial families tend to be matricentric, being headed by an older inmate in a mother's role. The desire for affection and security impels women inmates to form these pseudofamilies.

A study of 105 inmates at the Wisconsin Home for Women at Taycheedah indicated that female inmates who perceived themselves as criminal

[39]David A. Ward and Gene G. Kassebaum, *Women's Prison: Sex and Social Structure* (Chicago: Aldine Publishing Company, 1965). Also see Charles Tittle, "Sex Differentiation and the Influence of Criminal Subcultures," *American Sociological Review*, Vol. 29 (1969), pp. 492–505.

[40]Katherine S. Van Wormer, *Sex Role Behavior in a Woman's Prison and Ethnological Analysis* (Palo Alto, Calif.: R. and E. Research Associates, Inc., 1978), 120 pp.

[41]T. W. Foster, "Make-Believe Families—A Response of Women and Girls to the Deprivation of Imprisonment," *International Journal of Criminology and Penology*, Vol. 3, no. 1 (February 1975), pp. 71–78.

tended to have reference groups that also viewed them as criminal.[42] On the other hand, females who did not consider themselves to be criminal perceived their reference category as noncriminal. Inmates who lacked a criminal self-perception, but who had committed a serious crime, tended not to have negative reference groups. The reference groups among women in the institution tended to coincide with the self-perception of each inmate, individually.

Women in prison have a wide variety of aspirations and objectives in life, ranging from wanting to be a housewife and having children and a husband on whom to depend to exhibiting aggressive independence.[43] Women view other women in prison as inconsiderate, rude, and low class, so that there is no solidarity as there is in men's prisons.[44] Women are not used to "hanging out" in gangs and teams as are men. There is a tendency for administration and staff to ignore women prisoners with the result that most constructive programs are in men's prisons. The wide diversity of the population in a small institution makes adequate programming in any area difficult. Then, women wonder about their children, whether they are healthy and doing well in school, whether they will still love their mother when she comes home, and whether she can make up for the time she was away from them.

In a prison for women, the social structure of the staff, inmates, and their interrelations provide institutional goal conflict, with the staff responding to the society outside the institution and the inmates being confined to the society within the institution.[45] Homosexual alliances are established for the duration of the incarceration and sometimes the partners divorce their respective spouses and continue their relationship outside.

One survey of three thousand women using questionnaires and interviews and undertaken with the cooperation of the National Organization for Women (NOW) discovered that many women preferred other women to men.[46] The reasons were that girls tend to be more tender and loving than men, that going with a female gives the woman an opportunity to be the aggressor, and that no fear of pregnancy existed.[47] They thought that men viewed them either as angels of love or whores. One interviewee said that the best experience a woman had was sexual, not genital.[48] Women want love; men tend to prefer more direct genital activity.

The treatment approach to female offender must differ from that of the male offender because of cultural variations.[49] Women are traditionally raised in

[42]M. R. Earnest, *Criminal Self-conceptions in the Penal Community of Female Offenders—An Empirical Study* (Palo Alto, Calif.: R. and E. Research Associates, Inc., 1978), 114 pp.

[43]Joan Potter, "Women in Prison," *Prison Law Monitor*, Vol. 2, no. 4 (September 1979), pp. 1, 96–97.

[44]Ibid., p. 1.

[45]Rose Giallombardo, *Society of Women—A Study of Women's Prisons* (New York: John Wiley & Sons, Inc., 1966).

[46]Shere Hite, *The Hite Report: A Nationwide Survey of Female Sexuality* (New York: Macmillan Publishing Co., Inc., 1976).

[47]Ibid., pp. 267–69.

[48]Ibid., p. 397.

[49]Joy S. Eyman, *Prisons for Women—A Practical Guide to Administration Problems* (Springfield, Ill.: Charles C. Thomas, Publishers, 1971), p. 185.

a more protective environment than are men within the family. They learn to love before they learn about sex. On the other hand, the male becomes interested in sex before he learns about love in the heterosexual situation. There are many ramifications to this basic difference that must be considered in the treatment programming of institutions for females. An example of differences in social organization is that women tend to form substitute families for intimate dyads or small groups in the unisexual institutions, whereas men tend to be more independent.

An underlying statement by women prisoners has been that women are treated like children and are subjected to petty housekeeping regulations that bear no relationship to the task of learning how to deal with a society that was not familiar to them because of their background.[50] Any dependency that women might acquire along the way is in fulfilling their socially imposed "role" that is reinforced in prison. Not only is it reinforced in prison, but the paternalism and sexism that women encounter in prison do not enhance their self-esteem and self-respect.

RELATIONSHIPS WITH WELFARE AND CHILD-CARING AGENCIES

It has been estimated that, in varying jurisdictions, 65 to 80 percent of adult women going to prison are the sole support of minor children. In addition, when babies are born in the prison, a relative, a welfare agency, or a child-caring agency must be involved. These children need placement, foster care, or adoption.

An estimated twenty-one thousand children are separated from incarcerated mothers on any given day.[51] The risk of damage from disruption of the mother-child relationship is essentially neglected by criminal justice, correctional, and welfare systems. Police do not ask about the children, and welfare agencies place about four out of five children with relatives, friends, or neighbors, while about one in eight is placed in a foster home.

Of the female prisoners in the custody of the U.S. Bureau of Prisons, only 27 percent do not have dependent children and 61 percent of the total female population retain legal custody of these children.[52] Approximately 58 percent were not welfare recipients (food stamps, housing assistance, regular welfare check), 26 percent were welfare recipients, while the remaining 16 percent were unknown.

The nursery is an important part of a prison for adult women. Many are pregnant when they arrive at the institution. Policies vary as to how long a

[50]James L. Potts, "Aspects of Life in a Women's Prison," in Prisoners' Forum, *Prison Law Monitor,* Vol. 2, no. 4 (September 1979), p. 99.

[51]Brenda McGowan and Karen Blumenthal, *Why Punish the Children? A Study of Children of Women Prisoners* (Hackensack, N.J.: National Council on Crime and Delinquency, 1978), 133 pp. Also reported in *Criminal Justice Newsletter,* Vol. 9, no. 10 (May 8, 1978), p. 3.

[52]J. G. Ross, E. Heffernan, J. R. Sevick, and F. T. Johnson, *Assessment of Coeducational Corrections,* National Evaluation Program, Phase 1 Report (Washington, D.C.: National Institute of Law Enforcement and Criminal Justice, LEAA, June 1978), pp. 15–17, 77–78.

mother can keep her child. Some prisons want a child-caring agency or relatives to take the child within the first several months, while others have permitted the mother to keep the child up to three years. The nursery is taken care of by other inmates and the mother is permitted visiting privileges.

CO-CORRECTIONS
OR COEDUCATIONAL INSTITUTIONS

In June 1978, there were twenty coeducational or co-correctional institutions in the United States.[53] They were in Pennsylvania (1971), Massachusetts (1972), Illinois (1974), New Jersey (1974), Delaware (1974), Minnesota (1975), Wisconsin (1975), Connecticut (1975), Missouri (1975), Vermont (1976), Maine (1976), Idaho (1976), Tennessee (1977), and Indiana (1977). Co-correctional institutions of the U.S. Bureau of Prisons held 997 females and 2,077 males. In state facilities, there were 1,232 females and 1,277 males. The total in the United States in these coeducational institutions included 2,254 males and 2,229 females. Co-corrections has been implemented amidst fears of pregnancy, sexual assault, and emotional involvement, which have resulted in better surveillance.[54] Even so, it has resulted in better behavior on the part of both men and women, has reduced institutional violence, and has improved atmosphere, and it seems to have reduced recidivism, but the last benefit is yet untested. It has often been suggested regarding co-corrections that "it develops a normal atmosphere, but then extracts the normal consequences of that atmosphere."

While sex is not "permitted," prison officials do provide birth control and abortion services and try to reduce and control sexual intercourse.[55] Many inmates say that they "know better" than to have sexual relations and risk being discovered. Other inmates say that about 75 percent have managed it undetected, using one of probably a dozen whispered "safe places."

There is general consensus that men behave better and exhibit less violence in the presence of women. Homosexual activity occurs despite attempted custodial control in men's and women's institutions. Similarly, sexual activity occurs despite attempted controls in coeducational institutions or co-correctional institutions, as the U.S. Bureau of Prisons calls them. As of January 28, 1977, after two-and-a-half years of operation, there had been sixteen pregnancies inside the federal correctional institution at Pleasanton, California.[56] Four of the women were married. Ten ended in therapeutic abortions, four women carried the babies to delivery, and two were yet undecided at the time of the survey. One woman had two therapeutic abortions, both unknown to her husband outside. Pleasanton and Terminal Island were closed as coeducational prisons in late 1977, leaving the institutions at Fort Worth and Lexington.

[53]Beth Nissen, "Fort Worth Prison That Quietly Went Co-Ed Is a Success," *The Wall Street Journal*, November 21, 1978, p. 10.

[54]John Ortiz Smykla, *Cocorrections: A Case Study of a Coed Federal Prison* (Washington, D.C.: University Press of America, 1978), p. 111.

[55]Ibid., p. 111.

[56]Ibid., p. 111.

Co-correctional education at the Federal Correctional Institution at Terminal Island, California.
Courtesy of the Federal Prison System.

The female inmate is the client of a male-dominated and male-oriented criminal justice system in which she is a powerless minority.[57] Predominantly male personnel within the system have difficulty in recognizing the needs of the female offender, much less in responding to them. During the 1970s, there has been an increasing awareness of the female offender and her needs and rights, undoubtedly because of the increase of female offenders in the criminal justice system. The female offender tends to be more optimistic and positive about the changing status of women. The female offender tends to be work oriented, with 71 percent of the inmate sample preferring to work rather than to stay home, while 91 percent felt it would be good for a women to have a job even if she had someone to support her. Many women already have skills that tend to be offered by correctional institutions for women, but they have more aspirations for which there is no suitable program available. Coeducational institutions may supply and cheaply meet these needs by bringing the female inmate into already existing programs and resources available to male inmates.

The introduction of opposite-sex inmates to previously single-sex institutions and the opening of new coeducational facilities have produced changes

[57]B. K. Sacks, "Case for Coeducational Institutions," *Offender Rehabilitation*, Vol. 2, no. 3 (Spring 1978), pp. 255–59.

in the realities of institutional life.[58] The availability of traditional women's programs and opportunities for women to hold jobs in prison have been only slightly decreased in coeducational institutions. The shift toward heterosexual relations appears to depend on the actual level of integration. There is little evidence that the "return to street behavior" syndrome is widespread in coeducational institutions. A pattern of "relating to the opposite sex by day and the same sex by night" has been observed, and the women continue their homosexual relationships for emotional support and engage in heterosexual relations when possible for financial purposes. Other effects of coeducational institutions involve power struggles in the presence of the opposite sex, substitute family patterns, and assumed role structure.

Some prison officials do not approve of coeducational prisons because the inmates tend to develop relationships that eventually result in divorce of current spouses outside and new close relationships leading to marriage with the partner inside. Most institutional officials who have worked with it approve of the coeducational arrangement. It is particularly helpful in the juvenile institutions because adolescent boys and girls are in the midst of developing their capacity for intersexual relationships when they are sent to institutions. If they are sent to a unisexual institution, more problems can be expected than if sent to a coeducational institution.

EFFECTS
OF INSTITUTIONALIZATION

The prisonization process for women appears to be similar to that for men.[59] The traditional situational variables in the institution have had apparently the same impact on female prisoners as they have on men. There is a wider variation, however, in the acceptance or rejection of the inmate code among women. Women need a family apparently more than do men. Separation of mothers from their children is damaging to both. In many instances, however, children visiting their mothers in prison have scrawled on the bathroom of the California Institution for Women, for example, "I love my Mom."[60]

Because the proportion of women offenders is so small, they do not have the same status in re-entering society as men, who comprise about 95 percent of the people leaving prison.[61] A female ex-offender has problems of relating to men, trying to be accepted by their own children after lengthy separation, and even dealing with the traffic, subways, and shopping in a supermarket. The children see the mother returning as an intruder, a stranger, and a disruption. It takes a long time to re-establish the mother-child relationships, and it includes

---

[58]J. G. Ross and E. Heffernan, "Women in a Coed Joint," *Quarterly Journal of Corrections,* Vol. 1, no. 4 (Fall 1977), pp. 24–28.

[59]G. F. Jensen, "Perspectives on Inmate Culture—A Study of Women in Prison," *Social Forces,* Vol. 54, no. 3 (March 1976), pp. 590–603.

[60] Kathryn Watterson Burkhart, *Women in Prison* (Garden City, N.Y.: Doubleday & Company, Inc., 1973), p. 436.

[61]"Women Talk About Being Ex-Cons," *Fortune News,* February 1977, p. 4.

many hurts. It takes a long time to re-establish all the relationships of "normal" living and assuming again the expected social roles—and some do not have the emotional security to make it.

A woman offender has broken the law and, in addition, has broken the moral code in a male-dominated society, which complicates the re-entry into society of the female ex-offender.[62] Many have developed a negative self-image and want no part of the "squares" that make up middle-class America. This limits further the jobs and other activities into which she would like to enter and be comfortable. If the male is victimized in a sexist society for being an ex-offender, the damage done to women ex-offenders is real and alarming when caught in the revolving door of criminal justice.

Some women leaving the institution at release time feel the emotions of fear and urgency, aloneness, and exposure. One woman likened it to a child whose mother had kicked him out of the house for the first time—although this "mother" happened to be New York City's Women's House of Detention on Riker's Island.[63] Separated from her children for two years when they were being raised by relatives in another city, her role as an intruder bent on upsetting the status quo in the family became real. Former associates and friends—and even relatives—viewed her as a decadent and undesirable. It is difficult to accept being unloved and unwanted by one's own family. In this situation, a person takes drugs or drinks, and gives up or acquires a new determination to make it, herself. The history of women ex-offenders being released back into society shows many incidents of both types of responses.

CONCLUSIONS

The problems of female offenders have generated little interest in a male-oriented system in the past, but various factors are forcing this to change.[64] While official statistics have supported the assumption that women have been seven to twenty times less involved in criminal behavior than have men, many have thought this was due more to a reluctance to report crimes by women, and some crimes committed by women are not reported because of embarrassment of the victim. A married man away from home will generally not report the loss of his wallet in some situations. Certainly, there has been special handling of the female offender in the criminal justice system. But more female personnel are needed, particularly in corrections, so that they can have an administrative impact on the program development and management of the female offender. The rising female crime rate demands that criminal justice systems plan for improvement of treatment and rehabilitation of female offenders to expand on the paucity of information on them that exists today.[65]

[62]David Rothenberg, "Out on a Limb," *Fortune News*, February 1977, p. 3.

[63]Judy Glass, "Coming Out of Jail . . . A Women's Trauma," *Fortune News*, February 1977, p. 6.

[64]R. R. Price, "Forgotten Female Offenders," *Crime and Delinquency*, Vol. 23, no. 2 (April 1977), pp. 101–08.

[65]Annette M. Brodsky, ed., *The Female Offender*, (Beverly Hills, Calif.: Sage Publications, 1977), pp. 108.

A professional social worker conducted group therapy with female ex-offenders at the Fortune Society in New York in an attempt to assist them in reintegrating into society.[66] The effort was directed toward enhancing self-esteem, developing a more positive identity, becoming goal directed, and learning more effective communication skills. Although she was a "square" without a prison record, the women accepted her, probably because *she* had come to *them* at the headquarters of an ex-offenders' group. It soon became obvious, however, that "labeling," be it male or female, convict or square, black or white, is what produces the prejudices, stereotypes, and self-concepts that prevent people from getting together.

Historically, the Detroit House of Corrections held all the female felons in Michigan. In 1975, the State of Michigan assumed control and administration of the institution. Two years before, the Michigan Department of Corrections report had referred to the women inmates as the "forgotten offenders." The institution was in disrepair, and Michigan did nothing to reconstruct it, but the Department of Corrections promised that it would meet the need of women in a new facility, the Huron Valley Women's Facility. A lawsuit was filed against the state by the women with the assistance of students in *Glover* v. *Johnson* in May 1977.[67] Forty-five women were then transferred to the Kalamazoo county jail. The thrust of the lawsuit was that women inmates in Michigan were being discriminated against in programs offered and the physical conditions of their confinement. Many more complaints have since been added to the lawsuit, but *Glover* v. *Johnson* has indicated that the women inmates *can* change the system.

A journal concerning women in the criminal justice system was begun in 1979 under the title *Women & Criminal Justice*.[68] It reviews all areas of women in corrections under two broad categories: (1) female offenders and (2) programs and training for women employees in the criminal justice system.

The Female Offender Resource Center was established by the American Bar Association in 1975. Since that time, it has accumulated information about other local and regional centers focusing on assisting female offenders. It is apparent that the primary concerns of female offenders are their children, adequate health care, and educational or job opportunities.[69] Assistance to female ex-offenders leaving the institution includes finding adequate and satisfactory employment.

The Association for Women Offenders was established in 1979 at the Y.W.C.A. in Paterson, New Jersey,[70] its purpose being to assist female offenders and ex-offenders to make a smooth transition from the institution to the outside world. It emphasizes providing women with the "life skills" and educational and

---

[66]Roninsine J. Williamson, "A Square Woman's View," *Fortune News*, February 1977, p. 6.

[67]Judith Magid, "*Glover* v. *Johnson*: Totality Litigation Against Women's Institutions" *Prison Law Monitor*, Vol. 1, no. 4 (September 1979), pp. 89–92.

[68]*Women & Criminal Justice*, published by Haworth Press, 149 Fifth Avenue, New York, New York 10010.

[69]American Bar Association, *Female Offenders: Problems and Programs* (Washington, D.C.: Female Offender Resource Center, April 1976), p. 9.

[70]*Corrections Compendium*, Vol. 3, no. 14, (September 1979), p. 7.

vocational training that they will need to get a job and support themselves and their families.

Female offenders have existed in all societies and have been reflected in literature ever since Eve ate the forbidden fruit in the Garden of Eden. Female offenders today can be divided into three groups: (1) the neatly dressed white woman who shoplifts or works as a high-priced call girl; (2) the "fallen angel," for example, Lizzie Borden and Patty Hearst; and (3) the petty criminals.[71] They differ from male offenders in several ways. Men become involved in homosexuality as physical release, whereas women do so to satisfy a need to belong to someone or to relate to a person upon whom they can depend.[72] Female offenders have been seen as "forgotten women," except when they are made the albatross of the women's movement. In treatment, those forgotten and unforgiven women need to view themselves as strong, independent individuals able to make their own decisions and choose their own destinies.

In summary, many factors have increased and reinforced interest in the female offender and her treatment. Court cases and Title VII of the Civil Rights Act of 1964 have been used to push the movement. The literature has been replete recently with articles and research on the female offender. A journal focused specifically on women in the criminal justice system was started in 1979. Many organizations have developed projects in this area. There are many centers in various cities that have become resources for female offenders. No longer is the female offender "forgotten."

CHAPTER QUESTIONS

13-1. Of all the offenders in prisons and correctional institutions in America, what percentage do women represent?

13-2. What are some significant demographic characteristics of the female prisoner?

13-3. How are the problems of juvenile girls in institutions different from those of juvenile boys?

13-4. How do different approaches to delinquent youth vary according to effectiveness?

13-5. What problems have arisen as a result of introducing male personnel into institutions for women after Title VII of the 1964 Civil Rights Act required these assignments?

13-6. What are the trends in arrest and commitments of females as compared with males in the United States?

13-7. Are there any differences between men and women in their respective institutions in terms of physical and mental health care?

13-8. What are the differences between problems in women's institutions and those in men's institutions?

13-9. What are the relationships in women's institutions with welfare and child-caring agencies?

13-10. What is the status of co-correctional or coeducational institutions?

---

[71]Charlotte Ginsburg, "Who Are the Women in Prison?" *Corrections Today*, Vol. 42, no. 5 (September–October 1980), pp. 56–59.
[72]Ibid., p. 58.

14

INSTITUTIONS FOR MENTALLY DISORDERED OFFENDERS

Insanity has been an accepted defense against criminal prosecution since the rule of Edward I (1239–1307) in England, becoming the first and most traditional of the psychiatric diversions from the criminal justice procedures. The child molester laws and the criminal sexual psychopath laws became other diversions between approximately 1910 and 1930, respectively. Other patterns of deviance left in the criminal justice system, but of particular concern to psychiatry and psychology, are the dangerous offender, the sexual offender, and the mentally retarded offender.

The definition of insanity has been subject to debate beginning with the writings on its legal consequences by Henry de Bracton in the thirteenth century. In ancient Rome and into the nineteenth century, it was known as "moon madness" or "lunacy."[1] It inspired the werewolf legends that associate aggressive behavior with the lunar cycles.[2] Treatment between the Roman times and the nineteenth century involved confinement, chains, and torture for purposes of exorcism or chasing out the devils. In 1797, Philippe Pinel removed the chains from the lunatics at the Bicêtre in Paris, some of whom had been confined that

[1]Arnold L. Lieber, *The Lunar Effect* (Garden City, N.Y.: Anchor Press, 1978), p. 129.
[2]Ibid., pp. 8, 11.

way for thirty or forty years, opening a new approach to treatment of insanity. The Quakers who operated the Phildelphia asylum, the first to treat the mentally ill in America in 1723, had used humane methods from their beginning. Dorothea Dix in the mid-1800s campaigned for reforms that brought the treatment of the mentally ill to more modern standards. Auburn prison in New York had a wing for mentally ill offenders in the mid-1800s. The first separate hospital for the criminally insane was opened in Ionia, Michigan, in 1867 and is still operative today. The majority of "criminally insane" offenders today, however, are in forensic units in state hospitals.

While the term "insane" has always been part of the medical nomenclature, today it also refers to a legal category that has no real reference to medical terminology. The modern meaning comes from the McNaghten rules formulated in 1843 by a commission appointed from the House of Lords in England in response to the public furor following the acquittal of Charles McNaghten "by reason of insanity" after he had attempted to assassinate Sir Robert Peel, the prime minister, and had killed Peel's secretary by mistake. The ruling indicated that the offender did not know right from wrong (10 CL and F. 200, 1843), and fourteen states in America have added the "irresistible impulse" clause that indicated that, even though the individual might know the difference between right and wrong, an irresistible impulse prevented him or her from acting on this knowledge.

Many psychiatrists have difficulty with this definition of insanity, since it has no relationship to medical reality. Guttmacher, a Baltimore psychiatrist, has indicated that the psychiatric principles have largely been abandoned in practice, that they are difficult for conscientious people who "juggle them" in testimony to accomplish a purpose, and that the testimony is largely a "sham."[3] These rules have been considered to be necessary in the English legal tradition, however, since the adjudication of insanity is made by a jury of peers rather than by expert witnesses who only testify. The other approach is used in Roman law, the "product test," which is used in the United States only by New Hampshire as a result of the work of Isaac Ray[4] and in one case in the District of Columbia in 1954,[5] in which the criminal act was seen as a product of a mental disease or mental defect.

Recent legal and psychiatric concerns involve the legal and constitutional factors of mentally ill prisoners, civilly committed dangerous offenders, defective delinquents (mentally retarded), sexual psychopaths, and other mentally disordered offenders.[6] The right to treatment, informed consent for some types of treatment, and other varieties of special offenders need adequate psychiatric and legal attention.

[3]Manfred S. Guttmacher, "Introduction," in Richard W. Nice, *Crime and Responsibility* (Tallahassee, Fla.: Dixie Publishers, 1962), p. 10.

[4]"Ray's Enduring Legal Treatise," *Hospital & Community Psychiatry*, Vol. 7 (1976), p. 480.

[5]*Durham* v. *United States*, 214 F. 2d 862-876 (District of Columbia, 1954).

[6]David B. Wesler, *Criminal Commitments and Dangerous Mental Patients: Legal Issues of Confinement, Treatment, and Release* (Rockville, Md.: National Institute of Mental Health, 1976), 94 pp. Available from the Government Printing Office, Washington, D.C. 20402.

MENTALLY DISORDERED
OFFENDERS

"Criminally insane" was once used to identify the severely mentally ill offender, but that designation has lost favor with the psychiatric community, which now prefers "mentally ill offenders" or "mentally disordered offenders."[7] In 1974, this writer attempted to determine the number of persons incarcerated who were "criminally insane" by contacting each state's mental health authorities responsible for the criminally insane. Dr. Harry Kozol, then director of the Massachusetts Center for Identification and Treatment of Dangerous Offenders at Bridgeport, replied, "Those of us who work in the vineyards are not accustomed to this strange terminology." This simply points up the differences between the legal designations of "criminally insane" and the medical designations of "mentally disordered" and the testimony a forensic psychiatrist has to present in court to accomplish the objective of civil commitment to hospitalization. An accurate count of these mentally disordered offenders is still not available because of the confusion in definitions. It must be remembered that "insanity" and "insane" are legal categories, not medical classifications.

The most frightening are the "psychopaths," "sociopaths," or "antisocial personality disorders," terms used to describe the same individual until 1952, between 1952 and 1969, and after 1969, respectively, and trace the changes in nomenclature used by the American Psychiatric Association. In addition to the mentally ill in jail or in prison, there are thousands more in state mental hospitals who have been declared incompetent to stand trial. One New York psychiatrist, Dr. Frank Rundle, has indicated that the largest single health care problem within prisons, as well as in the rest of society, is that of the mentally ill.[8] He estimates that 35 percent or more of prison inmates have serious mental problems. Dr. Dennis Jurczak, medical director for the Michigan Department of Corrections, has indicated that 20 percent of all inmates have some serious mental disorder.[9] Many inmates have mental problems unrelated to their crime, but prison tensions exacerbate already existing problems that society will pay for later.[10] Dr. John Vermeulen, commissioner of Forensic Psychiatry in Ohio, has said that reluctance on the part of mental health services has much to do with failure to work with convicted offenders.[11] Talking about "correctional psychiatry" is a contradiction in terms, almost like talking about "capitalist communism."[12]

The percentage of criminally insane in relation to the prison populations seems to be about 6 percent. In other words, approximately 1 out of 16.7 institutionalized offenders were committed as "criminally insane." In addition, an estimated 2 to 3 percent of prison populations were frankly psychotic when they

[7]Rob Wilson, "Who Will Care for the 'Mad and Bad'," *Corrections Magazine*, Vol. 6, no. 1 (February 1980), p. 6.
[8]Ibid., p. 6.
[9]Ibid., p. 6.
[10]Ibid., p. 6.
[11]Ibid., p. 6.
[12]Ibid., p. 8.

California Medical Facility at Vacaville.
Courtesy of the California Department of Corrections.

were received, but were deemed legally sane because the jurisdiction did not have sufficiently sophisticated resources to determine sanity or insanity. In other cases, such as that of David Berkowitz, the Son of Sam killer, in New York City, in 1978, who thought that his instructions to kill came from a dog whose ancestor, Sam, died six thousand years ago, was never asked that question because he may have been declared legally insane. Wanting to avoid that, the question was never asked in court and the offender was sentenced to life in prison without bringing up the question of insanity.

One survey of federal prisoners showed that 15 percent of five hundred consecutive commitments had recognizable mental disorders.[13] Persons newly committed to the federal prisons are studied thoroughly by caseworkers and undergo extensive medical examinations. If the examinations reveal that the prisoner is of unsound mind, it is mandatory that a board of psychiatric examiners inquires into the probable state of his or her competency at the time of trial. The prisoner may be sent to the Medical Center for Federal Prisoners at Springfield, Missouri, or efforts may be made toward other types of psychiatric treatment.

Of 380 pretrial admissions during fiscal year 1973 to the Perkins Hospi-

[13]C. E. Smith, "Psychiatric Approaches to the Mentally Ill Federal Offender," *Federal Probation*, Vol. 30, no. 2 (June 1966), pp. 23–29.

tal Center in Maryland, 73 were found to lack responsibility for their actions at the time of the alleged offense.[14] The vast majority of these were found competent to stand trial. The insanity defense is popular in Maryland, but this apparently reflects the liberal views of psychiatrists, judges, and attorneys and the willingness of juries to find persons not criminally responsible.

Reports of mentally disordered offenders coming from official sources are very low. Experienced correctional practitioners are frequently surprised at the conservative figures reported. For example, the Florida Department of Corrections, with a prison population of about 20,000, estimates that 4,625 inmates suffer from some sort of emotional stress or mental illness that requires continuous health care.[15] Dr. Benjamin Groomes, director of Health and Education for the department, provided that estimate while preparing a request for an LEAA grant to improve this situation.

In New England's maximum security institutions, nearly 60 percent of the 365 criminal offenders identified as disruptive and diagnosed as having some type of psychiatric disturbance were admitted at once to state mental hospitals. The extent of previous hospitalization suggests that it is imperative that correctional and mental health authorities work more closely together to plan jointly for the care, custody, and treatment of this population.[16]

A summary of some studies of psychiatric evaluations of offenders coming into prisons is as follows in Table 14-1.

The jail is turning into a second-rate mental hospital, according to Joseph Rowan of the American Medical Association.[17] The Los Angeles jail has a backlog of mental health cases waiting transfer to state health facilities in California and in other states. The King County Jail in Seattle has been called a "hellhole," a "snakepit," a "zoo," and other epithets because of the mental patients it holds. A basic principle agreed to by all concerned in the field is that, the earlier a patient is identified and provided treatment, the better for the individual and all of society. When people are caught up in the criminal justice system, it simply means that their treatment has been delayed, which can result in increased seriousness and harm to society.

Antipsychotic drugs are the bedrock of psychiatry, and they are used in virtually all of prison psychiatry.[18] The variety of mind-altering drugs used for psychotic patients includes Thorazine, Prolixin, Loxitane, Mobal, Navane, Stelazine, and Mellaril. Tranquilizers and antidepressants used are Valium, Elavil, Norepramin, Pertiphrane, and Avantil. Dr. John Petrich, head of the

---

[14]Robert H. Sauer, "The Insanity Defense in Maryland," *Maryland State Medical Journal*, Vol. 24, no. 3 (1975), pp. 51–52.

[15]"Florida Moves to Improve Treatment of Inmates Suffering from Mental Illness," *Corrections Digest*, Vol. 10, no. 3 (February 2, 1979), p. 6.

[16]Richard H. Uhlrig, "Hospitalized Experience of Mentally Disturbed and Disruptive Incarcerated Offenders," *Journal of Psychiatry and Law*, Vol. 4, no. 1 (1976), pp. 49–59.

Lawrence A. Bennett, Thomas Rosenbaum, and Wayne R. McCullough, *Counseling in Correctional Environments* (New York: Human Sciences Press, 1978), p. 76.

[17]Rob Wilson, "The Jail: 'A Revolving-Door Psychiatric Ward'," *Corrections Magazine*, Vol. 6, no. 1 (February 1980), p. 14.

[18]Ibid., p. 10.

Table 14-1 Studies of Psychiatric Evaluations of Offenders

SOURCE	POPULATION	DIAGNOSIS	% OF TOTAL
Glueck (1918)	608 Sing Sing prisoners	Psychotic or mentally deteriorated	12.0%
		Normal	41.0
		Mentally retarded	28.1
Overholser (1935)	5,000 felons under Briggs law in Massachusetts	Abnormal	15.0
		Normal	85.0
Bromberg and Thompson (1937)	9,958 offenders before Court of General Sessions, New York City	Psychotic	1.5
		Psychoneurotic	6.9
		Psychopathic personalities	6.9
		Feebleminded	
		Normal or mild personality defects	82.3
Schilder (1940)	Convicted felons, Court of General Sessions of New York City	Psychotic	1.6
		Neurotic	4.2
		Psychopathic personalities	7.3
		Feebleminded	3.1
		Normal	83.8
Banay (1941)	Sing Sing prisoners	Psychotic	1.0
		Emotionally immature	20.0
		Psychopathic	17.0
		Normal	62.0
Poindexter (1955)	100 problem inmates	Mentally ill	20.0
		Normal	80.0
Schlessinger and Blau (1957)	500 typical prisoners	Character and behavior disorders	85.0
		Normal	15.0
Shands (1958)	1,720 North Carolina felon admissions to central prison	Psychotic	3.5
		Personality disorder	55.8
		Psychoneurotic	3.9
		Sociopathic personality	7.0
		Other	5.3
		No psychiatric disorder	4.7
		Transient personality disorder	19.8
Brodsky (1970)	32,511 military prisoners	Character and behavior disorders	77.1
		No psychiatric disease	21.3
		Miscellaneous disease	1.6

American Medical Association, has said that prison doctors are giving the prisoners "a double shot of Thorazine" rather than the "milk of human kindness."[19]

Because of legal and other developments, some security mental hospitals may lose some of their traditional patient residents to community mental health programs, but there appears to be a need to establish more secure forensic units in many hospitals and to upgrade psychiatric services to mental wards within

[19]Ibid., p. 10.

prisons.[20] The civil commitment of "special" offenders, such as the sexual psychopath, the criminally insane, and the defective delinquent, poses two principal problems: (1) indeterminate length of confinement and (2) vague criteria for commitment that foster a system of arbitrary selection. There has been some movement to address these problems, such as to (1) apply the criminal law maximum sentences to all offenders and provide whatever treatment can be afforded in the time available: (2) abolish some special offender commitments, such as Michigan's recent abolition of the Criminal Sexual Psychopath Law; and (3) overcome the intermediate sentence problems and most selection problems without totally abolishing special treatment programs, which involves the requirement that the criminal law sentencing lid apply to both correctional and therapeutic confinements.

Defendants considered to be incompetent to stand trial (IST) may be confined in secure institutions for an indefinite period. There has been a recent movement among hospital staffs and legal staffs to prohibit the indefinite confinement of IST defendants. The "successful" invocation of the insanity defense has frequently resulted in automatic and indefinite mental hospital confinement in a secure facility, which, in many cases, is counterproductive. Transfers from prison to the mental hospitals has sometimes been arranged, but, more frequently, the prison has been forced to develop a mental ward and mental health treatment staff within its own confines. Transfers from mental hospitals to the prisons, on the other hand, has been done with greater ease when a civil patient commits a serious crime "beyond a reasonable doubt" and has become dangerous to other patients. Such transfers do not include a new commitment because the patient is already "insane" as indicated by the civil commitment.[21]

A directory of institutions for mentally disordered offenders was developed in 1972.[22] A total of 262 resources were canvassed by mail questionnaires and were reviewed for inclusion. Of these, 73 were considered to be suitable for the survey. A further directory of mental health and correctional institutions for adult mentally-disordered offenders in 1972 included: 19 security hospitals, 23 mental health facilities, and 26 correctional institutions having comprehensive treatment programs for mentally disordered offenders.[23]

The mental hospital is part of the community's screen that separates, officially labels, and processes the mentally ill psychopathic offender.[24] After

---

[20]David B. Wexler, *Criminal Commitments and Dangerous Mental Patients: Legal Issues of Confinement, Treatment, and Release* (Rockville, Md.: National Institute of Mental Health, U.S. Department of Health, Education, and Welfare, 1976), p. 69.

[21]David B. Wexler and S. E. Scoville, "The Administration of Psychiatric Justice: Theory and Practice in Arizona," *Arizona Law Review*, Vol. 13, no. 1 (1971), p. 186.

[22]Saleem A. Shah, *Director of Institutions for Mentally Disordered Offenders* (Rockville, Md.: Center for Studies of Crime and Delinquency, National Institute of Mental Health, 1972), p. iv.

[23]William C. Eckerman, *A Nationwide Survey of Mental Health and Correctional Institutions for Adult Mentally Disordered Offenders* (Rockville, Md.: Center for Studies of Crime and Delinquency, National Institute of Mental Health, 1972), pp. 11–15.

[24]Aldo Piperno, "Indefinite Commitment in a Mental Hospital for the Criminally Insane: Two Models of Administration of Mental Health," *Journal of Criminal Law and Criminology*, Vol. 65, no. 4 (1975), pp. 520–27.

Atascadero State Hospital in California, considered to be one of the better forensic units.
Courtesy of Atascadero State Hospital.

examining considerable data, it is obvious that the control model of mental health administration is analogous to the control model of administration of criminal justice, emphasizing organizational efficiency, valuing ascriptive personal characteristics, and working with speed, finality, and routine procedures. The treatment model rejects absolute efficiency as a goal in itself and focuses on the welfare of the patient, which does not seem to occur in hospital forensic units.

Data on five hundred admissions to Bellevue in New York City and other state hospitals indicate that the distribution of psychiatric diagnoses for offenders is quite similar to the distribution of diagnoses of these patients as a whole.[25] While conviction records might provide a firmer base for estimating the relation between psychiatric diagnosis and criminal behavior, the fact that most psychotic patients avoid convictions because they are incompetent to stand trial suggests that arrest records are also an important criterion in the understanding of the mentally ill offender in a hospital forensic unit.

The relationships between the legal and mental health systems are at a point of accelerating change.[26] Three moral-legal imperatives are that (1) the

[25]Arthur Zitrin, Anne S. Hardesty, Eugene I. Burdock, and Ann K. Drossman, "Crime and Violence Among Mental Patients," in 128th Annual Meeting of the American Psychiatric Association, (Anaheim, CA, May 5–9), 1975, pp. 140–41.

[26]Allan A. Stone, *Mental Health and the Law: A System in Transition* (Rockville, Md.: National Institute of Mental Health, 1975), 266 pp.

Constitution should be seen as defining specific negative rights against governmental intrusion, (2) the Constitution should be seen as establishing a moral residuum for all social policy, assuring citizens minimum guarantees of a decent standard of life, and (3) the law should be the watchdog of public policy, ensuring that policy systems are coordinated and that the legislative will is worked out in the real world. Specific concerns include the role of the judiciary, the concept of dangerousness, statistics on in-patient care, civil commitment, the right to treatment and the right to refuse treatment, mental retardation, the juvenile system, aging, quasi-criminal confinement, competency to stand trial, and the insanity defense.

Guilty, but Mentally Ill (GBMI) first was passed in Michigan in 1972. It was soon followed by Illinois, Indiana, and Georgia. Kentucky adopted GBMI in 1982. Idaho eliminated the insanity defense in 1982, but did not adopt GBMI.

In a challenge by an offender in Texas who had been found not guilty of criminal charges by reason of insanity, but who had been found to be insane at the time of his trial and was committed to the state hospital, the commitment was unconstitutional. The court stated that "the State has a reasonable interest in releasing only those whom the State considers not potentially dangerous to society."[27] On the other hand, differences in treatment where civilly committed persons are given the highest and best medical treatment and no such provision apply to criminally committed persons are viewed as unconstitutional.

Many people formerly dealt with by the mental health system now come into the criminal justice system. Changes in mental health laws have made it more difficult, procedurally and substantively, to commit persons believed to be mentally ill; they can now be arrested on minor charges and committed as incompetent to stand trial.[28] The objective is to keep the nondangerous mentally ill in the community.

Any psychiatric evaluation or classification of mentally disturbed offenders should include an analysis of motivational factors and prognostic evaluations.[29] Socially and situationally stimulated offenders, except for the few who may be psychotic, should be treated in correctional settings, while the impulsive, compulsive, and catathymic offenders cannot be deterred through ordinary correctional measures, which should include psychiatric assistance. Herstedvester in Denmark may be used as a model for handling these cases.

A study of the California Medical Facility at Vacaville of the effectiveness of group psychotherapy on 257 inmates suffering personality and character disorders indicated that patients who had treatment did significantly better than did the control group at a one-year follow-up but that the positive effects had disappeared after four years.[30] This suggests the need for crisis intervention

[27]"Treatment and Release Procedures for Civilly and Criminally Committed: *Reynolds* v. *Neill* 381 F. Supp. 1374, Texas, 1974," *Mental Health Court Digest*, Vol. 18, no. 11 (1975), p. 4.

[28]Walter Dickey, "Incompetency and the Nondangerous Mentally Ill Client," *Criminal Law Bulletin*, Vol. 16, no. 1 (January–February 1980), pp. 22–40.

[29]Eugene Revitch, "Psychiatric Evaluation and Classification of Anti-Social Activities," *Diseases of the Nervous System*, Vol. 36, no. 8 (1975), pp. 419–21.

[30]C. C. Jew and T. L. Clanon, "Effectiveness of Group Psychotherapy in a Correctional Institution," *American Journal of Psychiatry*, Vol. 129, no. 5 (November 1972), pp. 602–5.

with parolees who complete their first year on parole and the development of a program in the community to continue professional service from the institution and sustain the gains made into the community.

The Patuxent Institution at Jessups, Maryland, was opened in 1955 as a psychiatric treatment center for "eligible persons" who had been convicted of a crime and had at least three years remaining in their sentence, had an intellectual deficiency or emotional imbalance, were likely to respond favorably to treatment, and could be rehabilitated better through the programs and services of the Patuxent Institution than by other incarceration.[31] After considerable litigation and controversy surrounding the allegations that persons sent there for treatment did not receive it, beginning in 1966, a private survey concluded that program alternatives were needed. The program was modified in 1978 and 1979 and continues as a specialized psychiatrict institution for juveniles.[32]

Legal thinking about mental illness concerns moral responsibility as a necessary condition for punishment and holds that excuses in the criminal law, such as insanity, should be guided by reference to these shared moral notions.[33] Three major contentions are that (1) in criminal trials involving the insanity defense, moral responsibility should be adjudicated; (2) the issue of moral responsibility depends upon the degree of irrationality of the accused at the time of the crime; and (3) psychiatrists do have something to contribute to the resolution of that issue in that their insights as to whether the accused is as rational as he or she might at first appear are of value. Too, many mental health professionals are unaware that the law has its own system of psychology and its own explanations for normal and deviant behavior.

The right to treatment in the areas of mental retardation, juvenile detention, and the criminally insane have been upheld in various courts.[34] Psychiatric institutions must be aware of the costs and benefits of the right to treatment litigation and must obtain skilled legal counsel to advise them of their obligations and rights, since litigation is expensive. Psychiatrists must participate in such litigation and help to shape legal standards.

The formal guidelines for prison psychiatric care, as adopted by the American Medical Association and developed in the late 1970s into the early 1980s, are (1) correctional personnel should be trained by medical staff to recognize signs and symptoms of chemical dependency (alcohol and drugs), emotional disturbances, and mental retardation; (2) every new inmate should be interviewed by a psychologist and referred for psychiatric evaluation within fourteen days of admission; (3) inmates awaiting emergency evaluation should be housed in a specifically designated area with constant supervision by trained staff for a minimum amount of time not exceeding twelve hours; (4) before any diagnosed

---

[31]*Annual Report—Fiscal Year 1979—Patuxent Institution, Jessups, Maryland, 20794* (Jessups: Maryland Department of Public Safety and Correctional Services, 1980), p. 11.

[32]*Evaluation of Patuxent Institution* (Belmont, Md.: Contract Research Corporation, 1977), 264 pp.

[33]Michael S. Moore, "Mental Illness and Responsibility," *Bulletin of Menniger Clinic,* Vol. 39, no. 4 (1975), pp. 308–28.

[34] Allan A. Stone, "Overview: The Right to Treatment—Comments on the Law and Its Impact," *American Journal of Psychiatry,* 1975, Vol. 132, no. 11, pp. 1125–34.

psychiatric patient is assigned to programs, prison administrators should consult with the psychiatric staff; (5) patients with acute psychiatric and other illnesses who require health care beyond the resources available in the facility shall be transferred to a facility where such care is available; (6) inmates are to be informed, orally and in writing, of the procedures for access to medical treatment; and (7) a special medical program for inmates requiring close medical supervision should be devised.[35]

DANGEROUS OFFENDERS

Dangerousness and mental illness have long been associated.[36] The forerunners of this thinking were in the forms of demonic possession and witchcraft. From the midfifteenth through the seventeenth centuries, over a hundred thousand people were killed as witches possessed by the devil after having sold their souls to him for special powers. Today, therapeutic and social control objectives have become confused and confounded so the treatment of the "insane" and the dangerous in the mental health and the criminal justice systems require more communication and coordination among lawyers, therapists, and correctional personnel than every before to bring social policies and practices to the mentally ill and dangerous offenders more accountable and less hypocritical.[37]

The relationship between socially dangerous actions (SDAs) and schizophrenia was investigated in 201 patients whose actions had not been subject to criminal proceeding.[38] The most common types of SDAs were suicide attempts (19.4 percent) and attempts to kill friends or relatives (60.4 percent). Among the schizophrenics, 56.2 percent had committed SDAs prior to being admitted to the psychiatric observation. Schizophrenics with paranoid tendencies were found to be the most socially dangerous. Of the patients under psychiatric observation, those who had been subjected to prolonged confinement in a mental institution without benefit of occupational or other therapy were most susceptible to SDAs. Improved psychiatric care in forensic units is essential in treating socially dangerous schizophrenics.

Females can be dangerous, also. Female admissions to the Carstairs State Hospital for the Criminally Insane in Scotland between the time of the first female admission in 1959 and December 31, 1973 constituted 8.1 percent of the total admissions over this period or sixty-six females.[39] The females fell into two

[35]Rob Wilson, "The New AMA Guidelines for Prison Psychiatric Care," *Corrections Magazine*, Vol. 6, no. 1 (February 1980), p. 17.

[36]Henry J. Steadman, "Employing Psychiatric Predictions of Dangerous Behavior: Policy vs. Fact," in Calvin J. Frederick, ed., *Dangerous Behavior: A Problem in Law and Mental Health* (Rockville, Md.: Alcohol, Drug Abuse, and Mental Health Administration, National Institute of Mental Health, 1978), p. 129.

[37]Saleem A. Shah, "Dangerousness and Mental Illness: Some Conceptual, Prediction, and Policy Dilemmas," in ibid., p. 185.

[38]V. V. M. Musayev, *The Nature of Socially Dangerous Actions of Schizophrenics not Subject to Judicial-Psychiatric Examination* (title translated from the Russian), *Medistsinskiy Zhurnal Uzbekistana* (Tashkent, U.S.S.R.), no. 5, (1975), p. 1821, as appeared in Steadman.

[39]Patrick W. Brooks and Geoffrey Mitchell, "A 15-Year Review of Female Admissions to Carstairs State Hospital," *British Journal of Psychiatry*, Vol. 127 (1975), pp. 448–55.

separate subgroups: (1) persistently violent patients transferred from other hospitals and suffering from submentality or personality disorder and (2) patients sent from courts or prisons because of their serious acts of violence often directed at family members and who suffered from a personality disorder or schizophrenia. When the two groups were compared, it was found that the prognosis for the first group was considerably worse than was that for the second.

Resocialization of some recovering mentally ill male criminal offenders through the halfway house program is possible.[40] The care of this high-risk population requires ongoing evaluation and prediction regarding possible dangerousness. These predictions apparently can be made with greater confidence when the halfway resident is part of the treatment plan in the community. Some of the social stigma associated with mental illness may result from psychiatrists' activities and not entirely from public ignorance and prejudice.[41] Psychiatric theories and practices that may contribute to stigma include (1) psychological and educational theory of the etiology of mental illness, (2) overly broad definitions of mental illness, (3) overinvolvement of psychiatry in the criminal justice system, (4) delegation of responsibility for the treatment of the mentally ill to nonmedical personnel, and (5) physical separation of psychiatry from the other medical care delivery systems.

By 1977, eight states had enacted mental health statutes that limited involuntary civil commitments to persons who are dangerous to others or to themselves.[42] The courts have been divided as to whether this overt dangerous behavior standard is mandated by the Constitution, but it may be one way in which to meet some constitutional objections to present civil commitment standards.

Sixty prison wardens responded to a questionnaire regarding administrative segregation of protective custody. The majority was generally unhappy with the existing system and favored separate institutions for the really dangerous prisoners.[43] There was consensus that mentally disturbed offenders should not be in prison, whether dangerous or not. One of the more significant findings was a large increase in the number of prisoners in protective custody, a circumstance attributed to the fact that many rival criminal gangs now travel almost intact from the street to the penitentiary.

The Center for the Diagnosis and Treatment for Dangerous Persons in Bridgewater, Massachusetts, was established in 1959 to delegate primary authority for the diagnosis and treatment of dangerous persons to psychiatry rather than to penology. A study dealing with 592 convicted male offenders sent to the

[40]John Goldmeier, Robert H. Sauer, and E. Virginia White, "A Half-Way House for Mentally Ill Offenders," *American Journal of Psychiatry*, Vol. 134, no. 1 (1977), pp. 45–49.

[41]Richard A. Schwartz and Ilze K. Schwartz, 'Reducing the Stigma of Mental Illness," *Diseases of the Nervous System*, Vol. 32, no. 2 (1977), pp. 101–03.

[42]Reed Groethe, "Overt Dangerous Behavior as a Constitutional Requirement for Involuntary Civil Commitment of the Mentally Ill," *University of Chicago Law Review*, Vol. 44, no. 3 (1977), pp. 562–93.

[43]Robert A. Freeman, Simon Dinitz, and John F. Conrad, "A Look at the Dangerous Offender and Society's Effort to Control Him," *American Journal of Correction*, Vol. 39, no. 1 (1977), pp. 25, 30–31.

center found that 304 of these persons were not dangerous, and they were released into the community after completing their sentences. Thirty-six subsequently committed serious crimes. The courts committed 226 cases to centers for special treatment, after which 82 patients were discharged upon recommendation of the clinical staff, of which 5 subsequently committed serious crimes. Of 49 originally committed and released by court order against the advice of the staff, 17 committed serious crimes, including 2 murders. In summary, it was concluded that treatment was successful in modifying the dangerous potential of a high percentage of patients but that there is need for further improvement in diagnostic and therapeutic competence.[44] Although the Massachusetts Center for the Identification and Treatment of Dangerous Persons has compiled a good record for identifying and treating dangerous offenders, including sex offenders, it has been challenged because of the subjectivity of the clinical judgment of psychiatrists, psychologists, and the clinical teams that make the decisions to hold or to release people.[45]

In the absence of valid definitions for dangerousness, many people are locked up on guesswork.[46] Few former mental patients are arrested for serious crimes. The role of the psychiatrist in court and medical politics is considered to be primarily for the need of the judiciary to determine competence to stand trial and legislative bodies to consider reform.

Despite updated clinical rhetoric, many judges and psychiatrists under various laws involving mental health and dangerousness send people to institutions whose primary purpose is to control and manage rather than to provide therapy.[47] Mentally disordered violent offenders (MDVOs) were central in the consideration of S.B. 42 in California, a bill enacted to abolish parole and introduce determinate sentencing.[48] Fixed sentencing permits release of inmates regardless of their dangerousness to society. Release is based on the time served, rather than on the safety of the offender's release.[49]

It is important for the correctional worker to be able to identify the various clinical groupings that appear in the prison and their potential dangerousness.[50] Personality tests have been used to predict dangerousness. Megar-

[44]Harry L. Kozol and R. J. Boucher, "Diagnosis and Treatment of Dangerousness," *Crime and Delinquency,"* Vol. 18, no. 4 (October 1972), pp. 371–92.

[45]D. P. Ross and J. M. Hochberg, "Constitutional Challenges to Commitment and Release Procedures Under Massachusetts General Laws, Chap. 123A. The 'Sexually Dangerous Persons' Act," *New England Journal of Prison Law,* Vol. 4, no. 2 (1978), pp. 253–308.

[46]Henry J. Steadman and Joseph A. Cozza, "We Can't Predict Who's Dangerous," *Psychology Today,* 1975, pp. 32–33, 35, 84.

[47]D. Oran, "Judges and Psychiatrists Lock Up Too Many People," *Psychology Today,* February 1973, pp. 20–22.

[48]Sheldon L. Messinger and Phillip E. Johnson, "California's Determinate Sentencing Statute: History and Issues," in *Special Conference—Determinate Sentencing—Reform or Regression? Summary Report* (Washington, D.C.: National Institute of Law Enforcement and Criminal Justice, March 1978), conference held at the University of California at Berkeley, June 2–3, 1977.

[49]Frederick Howard Wines, *Punishment and Reformation: A Study of the Penitentiary System* (New York: Thomas Y. Crowell Company, 1919), p. 86.

[50]H. L. Hartman, *Basic Psychiatry for Corrections Workers* (Springfield, Ill.: Charles C. Thomas, Publishers, 1978), 486 pp.

gee and his associates undertook a long-range study that classifies offenders according to aggressiveness and other factors, using the Minnesota Multiphasic Personality Inventory at the federal correctional institution at Tallahassee.[51] For several years, this writer used the individual Rorschach test to identify potential dangerousness in questionable cases for the Michigan parole board, using "infantile," "adolescent," and "adult" responses to color, showing a progression from violence to nonviolence, together with other modulating responses, but this process is too time-consuming for regular usage. Kozol used the case study, history of assaults, and clinical observation at the Massachusetts Center for the Diagnosis and Treatment of Dangerous Persons. Dangerousness with some type of reasonably dependable prediction has been demanded by courts in Alabama and Illinois in 1979 to classify all prisoners in their systems and to segregate the dangerous offenders.

SEXUAL OFFENDERS

The first so-called "sexual psychopath" law was enacted in Michigan in 1935, but it was subsequently declared unconstitutional. These laws tended to replace the "child molester" laws that were enacted in several states after the first White House Conference on Children in 1910 and the child labor laws in Congress in 1912. The Illinois act passed in 1938 was the first upheld in the courts.[52] In 1949, six states passed sexual psychopath laws. By the close of the 1950s, thirty-seven states had adopted criminal sexual psychopath (CSP) laws. They generally identified the CSP as a person not insane, not feebleminded, not epileptic, which eliminated legal categories, but having a "mental derangement" coupled with a propensity toward sex offenses, which was interpreted as referring to those who had committed two or more sex offenses within twelve months. This eliminated forcible rape, which would require longer sentences; rather, it focused on minor sex offenses, such as exhibitionism, child molesting, and other noncapital offenses. Section 7 of that law generally provides that no CSP can be released until he has "fully and completely recovered" from such psychopathy, which does not ever happen in psychiatric treatment. The law worked well in Minnesota, for example, where psychiatrists would testify according to the needs of the court, but not in Illinois, where the political turbulence militated against such "shams" in psychiatric testimony.

California's Sexual Psychopath Law was passed in 1937.[53] In 1963, the state enacted four major changes: (1) the term "mentally disordered sex offender" replaced "sexual psychopath," (2) eligibility for probation was provided, (3) reports were required to include a psychiatric opinion, and (4) credit was to

[51]Edwin I. Megargee and Barbara Cadow, "The Ex-Offender and the 'Monster' Myth," *Federal Probation*, Vol. 44, no. 1 (March 1980), pp. 24–37, at this writing is the most recent of several reports on this project.

[52]*People* v. *Sims*, 382 Illinois, 472 N.E. 2d 703 (1943).

[53]Louise Viets Frisbie, "Treated Sex Offenders Who Revert to Sexual Deviant Behavior," *Federal Probation*, Vol. 29, no. 2 (June 1965), pp. 25–27.

be allowed for time in mental institutions to a person if a prison sentence were subsequently given.

As mentioned previously, Massachusetts sent sexually dangerous persons to the Center for the Diagnosis and Treatment of Sexually Dangerous Persons at Bridgewater, which also received "criminally insane" and "alcoholic" offenders.[54] The initial period was sixty days' observation followed by treatment or transfer to another institution.

Wisconsin has had a Sex Crime Law since 1951.[55] It provides for indeterminate sentencing of selective sex offenders and psychiatric treatment. Release is by a special review board, consisting of a psychiatrist, a social worker, and a lawyer. Criminal sexual psychopaths have a recidivism rate that is significantly lower than offenders who plead "not guilty by reason of insanity."[56]

An accurate determination of sexual psychopathy is most difficult.[57] Potential violence is detectable by the use of projective techniques and psychiatric history and interview. Recently, the primary focus has been on the "dangerous sex offender" rather than on the "criminal sexual psychopath," particularly in Europe and Canada.

Centers for sex offenders in prisons and correctional institutions are providing special treatment in several places. Centers are generally headed by a clinical staff, including a psychiatrist, psychologist, and social worker. Information on twenty programs for treatment of sex offenders in twelve states have indicated that serious offenders incarcerated for long terms tend to fit the Krafft-Ebing pattern of sex offenses.[58] These programs are still quite primitive and need considerable development.[59]

Institutionalization has an undesirable effect on many sexual offenders and often increases the likelihood that they will offend again after discharge.[60] An outpatient program that combines group interaction with behavioral engineering may be a more effective alternative for many nondangerous sex offenders.

It is interesting to note that sometimes the criminal sexual psychopath has been transferred from the hospital to the prison because of incorrigibility or

---

[54]Robert A. Serafian, "Treatment of the Criminally Dangerous Sex Offender," *Federal Probation*, Vol. 37, no. 1 (March 1963), pp. 52–59.

[55]*Wisconsin Statutes*, Sec. 595.15, 1951. Also see Leigh M. Roberts and Asher R. Pacht, "Termination of In-Patient Treatment for Sex Deviants: Psychiatric, Social, and Legal Factors," *The American Journal of Psychiatry*, Vol. 121, no. 9 (1965), pp. 873–80.

[56]William R. Morrow and Donald B. Peterson, "Follow-up of Discharged Psychiatric Offenders—'Not Guilty by Reason of Insanity' and 'Criminal Sexual Psychopaths'," *The Journal of Criminal Law, Criminology and Police Science*, Vol. 57, no. 1 (1966), pp. 31–38.

[57]Thomas J. Meyers, "Psychiatric Examination of a Sexual Psychopath," *The Journal of Criminal Law, Criminology, and Police Science*, Vol. 56, no. 1 (March 1965), pp. 27–31.

[58]Richard von Krafft-Ebing, *Psychopathia Sexualis*, trans. by Frank S. Klaf (New York: Stein & Day Publishers, 1965), 434 pp.

[59]Edward M. Bercher, *Treatment Programs for Sex Offenders* (Washington, D.C.: National Institute of Law Enforcement and Criminal Justice, LEAA, January 1978), p. 72.

[60]Steven N. Silver, "Outpatient Treatment for Sexual Offenders," *Social Work*, Vol. 21, (March 1976), pp. 134–40.

negative prognosis and has been nearly twice as likely to be paroled within any given number of years than are his counterparts who remained in the hospital.[61]

The U.S. Supreme Court has held that the death penalty is a grossly disproportionate and excessive punishment for the rape of an adult woman and therefore violates the Eighth Amendment's prohibition of cruel and unusual punishment.[62]

Illinois had a "sexually dangerous persons act" by 1968, replacing the Criminal Sexual Psychopath Act.[63] By 1973, a "dangerous sex offender" law was proposed for Massachusetts to replace the Criminal Sexual Psychopath law.[64] In the new law, strict definitional criteria were required in terms of predictability, proof of dangerousness, and time-limited commitment.

By 1977, there was considerable variation among states as to the approach to sexual deviancy, with some still retaining the criminal sexual psychopath laws and others going to more generalized "mentally disordered" approach. A national survey resulting in only twenty-seven states responding[65] indicated that fourteen states had abandoned them and thirteen states had other mechanisms for diverting the criminal sexual psychopath or deviant from the correctional system into the mental health system.

The balance between psychiatric considerations and criminal aspects of deviant behavior have been debated for a long time. Abramson suggests that criminalization of mentally disordered behavior would be a possible side effect of some mental health laws.[66] On the other hand, some writers hold that mentally abnormal offenders should be processed through the criminal justice system.[67]

California's version of the criminal sexual psychopath law, the Mentally Disordered Sex Offender (MDSO) Act, appears to be more satisfactory than the old criminal sexual psychopath laws.[68] Florida's MDSO law passed in 1979 accomplishes the latter objective in that offenders are "criminal" first and then may be diagnosed subsequently within the system as "mentally disordered" and provided specialized treatment.[69]

[61]Grant Morris, "Mental Illness and Criminal Commitment in Michigan," *University of Michigan Journal of Law Reform*, Vol. 5, no. 1 (1971), p. 66.

[62]*Coker* v. *Georgia* (1977). Also, see C. R. Lesage, "The Death Penalty for Rape—Cruel and Unusual Punishment?" *Louisiana Law Review*, Vol. 38, no. 3 (1978), pp. 868–74; G. Parnass, "The Disinterment of an Ancient Law: An Eye for an Eye, No Death for Rape," *Brooklyn Law Review*, Vol. 4, no. 3 (1978), pp. 622–36.

[63]L. T. Burick, "An Analysis of the Illinois Sexually Dangerous Persons Act," *Journal of Criminal Law, Criminology and Police Science*, Vol. 59, no. 2 (1968), pp. 254–66.

[64]N. T. Sidley and E. J. Stolarz, "A Proposed 'Dangerous Sex Offender' Law," *American Journal of Psychiatry*, Vol. 130, no. 7 (1973), pp. 765–68.

[65]National Association of State Mental Health Program Directors, *The Status of Criminal Sexual Deviances Law*, rev. (Washington, D.C.: NASMHPD, July 1977), 7 pp.

[66]M. F. Abramson, "The Psychiatrization of Criminal Behavior," *Hospital and Community Psychiatry*, Vol. 23 (1972), pp. 101–05.

[67]J. Monahan, "'The Psychiatrization of Criminal Behavior': A Reply," *Hospital and Community Psychiatry*, Vol. 24, no. 2 (1973), pp. 105–07.

[68]M. L. Frost, *Civil Commitment and Social Control*, Lexington, Mass.: Lexington Books D. C. Heath Company, 1978.

[69]*Florida Statutes*, Chap. 917, "Mentally Disordered Sex Offenders."

MENTALLY RETARDED
OFFENDERS

Mentally retarded offenders or defective delinquents are generally regarded, but not always by the courts, as those with IQs of 70 or below. A large and comprehensive study of the mentally retarded offender in the correctional system was made by the Texas Department of Mental Health and Mental Retardation in the early 1970s financed by a grant from the U.S. Department of Health, Education, and Welfare, now the Department of Health and Human Services since the Department of Education became independent in 1980.[70] Texas and Pennsylvania were the only states at that time with institutions specifically designated as having special programs for "defective delinquents." Other states had them in special programs in other institutions or without separation. The vast majority of mentally retarded offenders in correctional institutions are in the borderline and mildly retarded ranges, and there is no necessary relationship between retardation and criminal behavior or culpability from a legal standpoint.[71] To explain mental retardation, the Texas study called upon religious, physical, and genetic and environmental theories of retardation, including the theories of Lombroso (neurological investigations stemming from Gall's phrenological theories) and a table of anthropological, sociobiological, etiological, and other sociological theories of the genesis of crime.[72] Procedural problems complicated the circumstances under which a mentally retarded defendant might be adjudicated as incompetent to stand trial.[73] Some of the high incidence of mental retardation is associated with administrative defects in the criminal justice system.[74] Of the youthful offenders committed to the state training schools administered by the Texas Youth Council, 12.0 percent of the males and 16.6 percent of the females admitted between September 1, 1969 and August 31, 1970 were designated mentally retarded.[75] The high incidence of mentally retarded youngsters in the Youth Council system is related to the absence of diversionary options available to the juvenile court, and the Youth Council is probably in violation of the Youth Council Act that specifically requires that a "feebleminded" youth be returned to the court.[76] The delinquent retardates found in correctional institutions tend to be more moderately retarded and have more extensive criminal histories than those in state facilities for the retarded. Probation officers in the community have reported that there are no facilities in the community available for working with the mentally retarded group. The retarded delinquent tends to be a member of a minority group living in a family

---

[70]*Project CAMIO* (correctional administration and the mentally incompetent offender), 8 vols. *Florida Statutes*, Ch. 19, "Mentally Disordered Sex Offenders," (Austin, Tex.: Department of Mental Health and Mental Retardation, 1973).

[71]Ibid., Vol. 1.

[72]Ibid., Vol. 2.

[73]Ibid., Vol. 3.

[74]Ibid., Vol. 4.

[75]Ibid., Vol. 5.

[76]Ibid., Vol. 6.

headed only by the mother and receiving public assistance.[77] The mentally retarded offender is now recognized as a significant element in the prison population and must be identified and given treatment commensurate with his or her mental capacity and individual needs, a position supported by the courts and by the state statutes.[78]

The Illinois Youth Commission in the late 1960s proposed that retarded delinquents be committed to schools for the mentally retarded rather than schools for delinquents.[79] In many cases, juvenile court judges have not adjudicated a young person as a defective delinquent. The institution for defective delinquents most frequently considered for such a purpose was the State Correctional Institution and Correctional Diagnostic Center at Huntingdon, Pennsylvania, in 1889 and was converted to an institution for defective delinquents in 1945 and retained this status and function until 1960. There is a move away from naming institutions as being for mentally retarded or defective delinquents. Most programs are parts of a larger institutional entity. The Illinois Youth Commission in the late 1960s recommended that retarded delinquents be committed to institutions for the mentally retarded rather than to institutions for delinquents.[80] In many cases, juvenile court judges, themselves, have not adjudicated a young mentally retarded person as a delinquent.

A national survey of prisons revealed that almost 10 percent of all incarcerated inmates are mentally retarded and require special programs.[81] They tend to be disproportionately from minority groups. They commit more crimes of burglary or breaking and entering than does the rest of the prison population. Prison administrators have indicated that they have more difficulty in adjusting to prison life than do others and do not understand what is expected of them. Also, they tend to be victimized by practical jokes. The treatment of retarded persons as compared with those who are mentally ill has sometimes been confused.[82] Retarded persons have a greater capability to become independent, and that has generally been recognized. Moreover while great heterogeneity and differences in individual need exist, prolonged assistance and guidance can help retarded persons. Retardation has been defined as scores of 70 and below in standardized IQ tests. This lag in normal growth processes results in prolonged dependency of the retarded individual upon others and delayed development of physical, social, and cognitive skills as well as vocational and residential skills that need to be mastered.

[77]Ibid., Vol. 7.

[78]Ibid., Vol. 8.

[79]Russell H. Levy, *Mental Retardation in Illinois*, Vol. 2, no. 2 (Springfield: Illinois Youth Commission, 1968), p. 22.

[80]Ibid., p. 22.

[81]Bertram S. Brown and Thomas F. Courtless, *The Mentally Retarded Offender* (Washington, D.C.: National Institute of Mental Health, Center for Studies of Crime and Delinquency, 1971). Also, see Miles Santamour and Bernadette West, *The Mentally Retarded Offender and Corrections* (Washington, D.C.: National Institute of Law Enforcement and Criminal Justice, LEAA, August 1977), p. 55.

[82]Santamour and West, *The Mentally Retarded Offender and Corrections*, p. 48.

CONCLUSIONS

There are approximately fifteen thousand "criminally insane," "mentally disordered offenders," or other legal designations of mentally ill offenders in maximum security mental hospitals in the United States committed by the courts. The most massive follow-up of a cross section of this population occurred after a 1971 court decision released 586 "mentally ill offenders" from Fairview State Hospital in Pennsylvania, not as "cured" but because the commitment procedures were unconstitutional.[83] Thornberry and Jacoby found that these 586 patients showed no more maladjustment either in the institution or in the community after release than did other noncriminal patients and concluded that holding these mentally ill offenders in maximum security facilities was not necessary.[84] They further questioned "the myth of the sexually deranged violent offender."[85]

The number of retarded adult offenders has been estimated at between twenty-five thousand and fifty thousand.[86] While many states identify juveniles as "feebleminded" or retarded if their IQs are below 70, the identification of a mentally retarded adult offender is much more difficult to accomplish in court. Many psychiatrists do not use IQ, which they consider to be a psychological concept that does not really apply to psychiatry. Consequently, when a psychiatrist testifies that a person exhibits schizophrenia, a recognized mental illness, the courts rule that the individual is not a "defective delinquent" or mentally retarded within the meaning of the law. If the patient becomes cured of the psychosis during hospitalization, then he can become a defective delinquent if he meets the legal tests.[87]

While the courts use psychiatrists in legal testimony to determine whether an accused person is "criminally insane" or otherwise mentally disordered according to the laws of the state, the relationships of psychiatrists in correctional institutions frequently are not congenial. Correctional administrators often complain that psychiatrists simply identify and diagnose, but they do not treat.[88] At the same time, psychiatrists complain that correctional administrators want the doctors to handle their problem cases. The statement has been made that "If the therapist is an employee of the prison system, the prison system is his first client. The prisoner is second."[89]

The best known facility designed for the psychiatric treatment of offenders is the Patuxent Institution in Maryland. Opened in 1955 as an experiment

---

[83]*Dixon* v. *Attorney General of the Commonwealth of Pennsylvania*, 325 F. Supp. 966 (M. D. Penn., 1971).

[84]Terrence P. Thornberry and Joseph E. Jacoby, *The Criminally Insane: A Community Follow-up of Mentally Ill Offenders* (Chicago: University of Chicago Press, 1979), p. 215.

[85]Ibid., p. 214.

[86]Harry S. Dogin, "More Programs Needed for Mentally Retarded Offenders," *Justice Assistance News*, Vol. 1, no. 5 (June–July 1980), pp. 2, 4.

[87]*State* v. *Burton*,. 338 A. 2d 421 (Court of Special Appeals, Maryland, 1975).

[88]Wilson, "Mad and Bad," pp. 13–14.

[89]Ibid., p. 13.

in indeterminate sentencing with an initial confinement for two years, the appropriate court could review each case, and an institutional board of review studied and evaluated individual cases. Treatment consisted of individual in-depth therapy, group therapy, and prescription of drugs, with the use of a progressive tier system that classified inmates with reference to progress toward release. Litigation caused the courts to question the adequacy of treatment and released some patients.[90] Its reputation has since been questioned because it has not contributed to the treatment of mentally abnormal dangerous offenders or to the prediction of dangerousness. Lejins has contended that the disenchantment with Patuxent has resulted from a general disillusionment with psychiatric models and a developing emphasis on the rights of individuals, including those of convicted offenders.[91]

The concepts of insanity and of psychopath are disappearing from the legal nomenclature. "Mentally ill" and "insanity" have no precise meaning.[92] They refer to (1) those who are incompetent to stand trial, (2) those who are acquitted because they were mentally irresponsible at the time of the act, and (3) those who are found to be incompetent, disordered, or defective during their incarceration. The term "psychopath" is also in disrepute. It has always been a dubious term in psychiatry and the change in terminology to "sociopathy" or "antisocial personality disorder" does not clarify it.[93] Further, probably no other social institution does a better job than the prison in promoting sexual perversion.[94] Because of the confusion in concepts and the difficulty of applying correct psychiatric testimony to legal concepts in a court of law, these terms and concepts are fading from the vocabulary.

CHAPTER QUESTIONS

14-1. When did "insanity" become an accepted defense against criminal prosecution and what have been some of the problems in defining it since?

14-2. What have been the recent developments regarding "insanity" and the legal and psychiatric concerns that tend to be in conflict?

14-3. What is the most serious mental health problem in prisons, as well as in the rest of society, and what percentage of prison inmates experience it?

14-4. What changes in the law tend to reflect this debate between "insanity" found in the law and "mentally disordered" or "mentally ill" found in psychiatry?

14-5. What is the relationship between dangerousness and mental illness?

14-6. Is treatment or resocialization a viable approach for the protection of the public and reintegration of the individual into society?

[90]*Sas* v. *State of Maryland*, 334 F. 2d 506 (1964).

[91]Peter P. Lejins, "Patuxent Experiment," *Bulletin of the American Academy of Psychiatry and Law*, Vol. 5, no. 2, *symposium issue* (1977), pp. 116–33.

[92]Sol Rubin, *The Law of Criminal Correction*, 2nd ed. (St. Paul, Minn.: West Publishing Company, 1973), p. 567.

[93]Ibid., p. 478.

[94]Ibid., p. 478.

14-7. What is a criminal sexual psychopath and what was the development of the laws covering that problem?

14-8. What is the status of criminal sexual psychopath laws today?

14-9. What are mentally retarded offenders?

14-10. What is the current status of the treatment of mentally retarded offenders?

15

ADMINISTRATION
OF INSTITUTIONS

Administration refers to the organization and management of the delivery systems that bring goods and services to the consumer. A primary objective of administration is the optimum allocation of available resources. The delivery systems are the programs by which services are channeled to the people who need them. Prison administrators who know management and the objectives of the correctional function and are in tune with the power-oriented political structure are a strong position to effect the delivery of services to the offenders in their prisons.

Public administration styles have changed over the years with the changes in needs. Through the 1800s and before, public and private enterprises were small and most could be handled with a one-person span of control. Large corporations, "big government," and massive prisons and prison systems are twentieth-century phenomenon. Large organizations require various levels of administration and management that do not tax the one-person span of control. Consequently, levels of management and supervisory functions over line operations have resulted in a requisite bureaucracy. Max Weber was the first to discuss the functions of this bureaucracy needed to administer and operate large organizations. The most salient characteristics of this bureaucratic organization were seen as[1]

[1]Max Weber, *The Theory of Social and Economic Organizations*, trans. and ed. by A. Henderson and T. Parsons (New York: The Free Press, 1947), pp. 328–40.

1. A formal structure defined by a hierarchy with centralized authority.
2. A division of labor into functional specialities.
3. Standardized, written operating procedures for the conduct of organizational activity.
4. A formally defined career system with a common entry point for employees, career routes that follow the organizational hierarchy, and promotions based on impersonal evaluation of employees by superiors.
5. Management conducted through a formal, monocratic system of routinized superior-subordinate relationships.
6. A system of employee status that is directly related to positions (jobs) and ranks rather than to birthrights, family status, seniority, or other factors.

In the prison, the administrator is the warden and the deputy warden is management.[2] Lieutenants and department heads are middle management.[3] Sergeants and supervisors in various institutions are supervisory over line operations.[4] The earliest style of administration was "organic"; that is, the organization was initiated or born, grew to maturity, and stagnated and died in old age.[5] Between the world wars, the concept of POSDCORB (planning, organizing, staffing, directing, coordinating, research, and budgeting) emerged.[6] Since World War II, the legal approach—concerned with legal limitations, rules and regulations, collective bargaining agreements with unions, and administrative procedures and codes enacted by legislatures—appeared.[7]

Administrative and management decisions need to be based on information that is accurate and immediately available without having to delay awaiting more information.[8] The "systems" approach has emerged in the last two decades.[9] This requires administration and management to view organizations as a constellation of "systems," which could be departments, inmate bodies, unions, legislatures, and all other systems, internal and external, that impinge on the operation of the organization. Management styles classified as participative management emerged in the 1960s, including the formal plan, leadership model, and management by objectives.[10]

[2]Clemens Bartollas and Stuart J. Miller, *Correctional Administration: Theory and Practice* (New York: McGraw-Hill Book Company, 1978), pp. 111–12.

[3]Ibid., pp. 142–44.

[4]Ibid., p. 144.

[5]Edward W. Bemis, "Local Government in Michigan and the North West," in *Johns Hopkins University Studies in Historical and Political Science,* Study V (Baltimore: Johns Hopkins University Press, 1883).

[6]Leonard B. White, *Introduction to the Study of Public Administration* (New York: Macmillan Publishing Co., Inc., 1926).

[7]"Administrative Procedures Acts and Corrections," *Corrections Compendium,* Vol. 3, no. 2 (September 1978), pp. 1–4.

[8]Steven L. Alter, "How Effective Managers Use Information Systems," *Harvard Business Review,* Vol. 54, no. 6 (November–December 1976), pp. 97–104.

[9]Michael Beer and Edgar Huse, "A Systems Approach to Organizational Development," in Edgar Huse, James Bowditch, and Dalmar Fishar, eds., *Readings on Behavior in Organizations* (Reading, Mass.: Addison-Wesley Publishing Co., Inc., 1975), pp. 409–26.

[10]Bartollas and Miller, *Correctional Administration,* pp. 79–88.

Table 15-1 Phases of MBO Implementation

PHASE 1	PHASE 2	PHASE 3	PHASE 4
1. Establish top management team 2. Develop organization mission statement 3. Establish organizational goals 4. Develop management doctrine 5. Implement organizational management analysis 6. Train top-level administrators in MBO 7. Identify job responsibilities for all top management 8. Establish key results by position 9. Develop short- and long-range objectives for top-level management 10. Institute periodic progress review of objectives	1. Train middle management in MBO 2. Establish management teams at this level 3. Identify job responsibilities by position 4. Establish key results areas for each position 5. Establish objectives and align vertically and horizontally in the organization 6. Institute periodic progress reviews	1. Train lower management 2. Establish management teams 3. Identify job responsibilities by position 4. Establish key results areas 5. Establish objectives and align vertically and horizontally in the organization 6. Institute periodic progress reviews	1. Review system and modify as required 2. Integrate with other components (budget, program, information and evaluations, etc.) 3. Recycle objectives 4. Monitor system and outputs

SOURCE: Frederick E. Schwehr, "Wisconsin Moves out on Management by Objectives: Scraps Crisis Management," *American Journal of Correction*, Vol. 40, no. 4 (July–August 1978), p. 26.

Management by objectives (MBO) has recently been adopted as the style in most progressive correctional systems.[11] MBO, initiated by Odiorne in 1965,[12] focuses on (1) long-range goals, (2) short-range objectives, and (3) the determination of specific job targets for a given time period.[13] The phases of MBO implementation in the Wisconsin Division of Corrections are as noted in Table 15-1.

In addition to federal and state laws and regulations, most jurisdictions operate under administrative procedures acts that require advance public notification and sometimes hearings before changes in departmental or institutional rules and regulations can be implemented. At the federal level, for example, all such information regarding intended changes must be published in the *Federal*

[11]Mark L. McConkie, *Management by Objectives: A Corrections Perspective* (Washington, D.C.: National Institute of Law Enforcement and Criminal Justice, LEAA, July 1975), p. 45.

[12]G. S. Odiorne, *Management by Objectives* (New York: Pitman Publishing Company, 1965).

[13]Harry E. Allen, Eric W. Carlson, Evelyn C. Parks, and Richard P. Seiter, *Half-way Houses* (Washington, D.C.: National Institute of Law Enforcement and Criminal Justice, LEAA, November 1978), p. 80.

Register, available on a daily basis from the superintendent of documents. In addition, each department or institution generally has its own manual of policies and procedures. Grievance procedures have been formalized in most jurisdictions. Consequently, contrary to the almost unfettered power enjoyed by administrators prior to the 1960s, the decisions and activities of the modern administrator are severely restricted, both institutionally and legally.

THE LEGISLATIVE PROCESS

The correctional administrator must be acquainted with the legislative process. The legislative process is the formulation of public policy by elected political leaders; the pertinent bills and acts constitute a major part of the implementation of this policy. Congress or the state legislatures have often established programs and "authorized" funds, but appropriations bills have subsequently eliminated all funding or have drastically reduced the money available for the program.

Because the correctional administrators are interested in new prisons and correctional institutions, new programs like work release and study release, questions concerning flat sentencing and parole, legislation limiting prison industry, and many other programs and policies the corrections administrator would be mandated to execute, they generally have to have friends in the state Senate, the House, or both, to introduce bills into the legislature and campaign for their passage. The correctional administrator, whether the director of the entire system of correctional institutions or the superintendent of an institution, participates in the legislative process by testifying before the appropriate legislative committees that consider the bills before sending them to the floors of the Senate or House. In some jurisdictions, only the director of the entire system participates in legislative activities, although generally, the superintendents testify as well. Wardens in the Federal Prison System, Inc. (formerly the U.S. Bureau of Prisons, name changed in 1981), do not testify before congressional committees, as this activity is, by policy, done only by the director of the system. In New York State, legislative activity is by the commissioner of the Department of Correctional Services rather than by the superintendents of institutions. In most other jurisdictions, participation in legislative activity is engaged in by the administrator of the entire system and by the wardens and superintendents of each institution. The legislative process in most jurisdictions is similar.[14]

The legislative process begins formally with the introduction of a bill on the floor of the Senate or the House by an elected representative. The actual initiative probably came much earlier. For example, a bill can be recommended to a legislator by the governor, a governmental agency, citizens groups or associations, or individuals. If the lawmaker agrees to sponsor the proposal, it must be framed in the proper legal form for a bill by the legislator, by the persons or

---

[14]James W. Hunt and James E. Bowers, *Guide to Legislative Action: A Review of Strategies to Remove Statutory Restrictions on Offender Job Opportunities* (Washington, D.C.: American Bar Association, National Clearinghouse on Offender Employment Restrictions, n.d., ca. 1975), p. 15.

group who recommended it, or by the legislative research drafting service, an office established for the purpose of drafting bills as requested by legislators, sometimes called a legislative reference bureau.

After the bill is drafted, it is introduced in one of the two sides of the legislature or in both, simultaneously, as when companion bills are introduced in both houses. In most states, a statement or memorandum is attached to the bill listing its sponsors, its purpose, and its proposed effective date. The new bill then receives a number or some other identification to indicate its identity, with bills introduced in the Senate prefaced by "S" and bills introduced in the House prefaced by "H," and bills introduced in the Assembly, which in some states corresponds to the House, prefixed by a "A." The bill is then given a "reading" and is referred by the speaker or leader of the chamber to the appropriate committee. The committee conducts hearings to receive testimony from interested persons and groups. In the process, the committee may amend, revise, or rewrite the bill. Also, it might "table" it, in which case it will not get out of committee unless forced out by a majority vote of the Senate or House, depending upon the location of the committee. A bill reported out favorably to the Senate or House is placed on a calendar to await consideration by all members of the chamber. If a majority of members votes for a bill, it goes to the other chamber where the process is repeated. If a majority there also approves the measure or reaches agreement with the other body on changes, it becomes an act of the legislature, and it is sent to the governor for signature or veto. Vetoes can be overriden by two-thirds of the majority of the legislature. On occasion, a bill is considered desirable by both houses of the legislature, but disagreement occurs on certain clauses or language. In these instances, a compromise committee made up of legislators from each branch meets to clear the differences. The bill becomes law when the governor signs it, permits it to become law without his signature, or a veto is overridden.

RELATIONS WITH THE LEGISLATURE AND THE GOVERNOR

Administrators must have close relationships with the legislature and the governor to maintain support for their desired policies and programs and to recognize political opposition and assess it in time to work out acceptable compromises. In all programs, the political concerns must be worked through first. Second, the economic concerns must be worked through in terms of cost, whether the political realities will bear that cost, and in cost-benefit analysis. Third, social concerns must be accounted for with regard to the setting and impact of any correctional program in terms of unemployment; housing; welfare; effects of programs on the family, mental health, neighborhoods, and areas of high delinquency; and other social issues. After these have been worked through, administrators can concern themselves specifically with policies and programs. Political concerns are most important and include the personal relationships between the administrator and the legislature and governor. Institutional wardens and superintendents frequently serve at the pleasure of the governor or the director or commissioner of corrections appointed by the governor. On the other hand, the legislature appropriates the money for programs it approves or does not appropriate funds for programs it disapproves. Consequently, the administrator has to keep close liaison with both the legislature and the governor.

POLICYMAKING

Policy in the prison or correctional institution is a reflection of legal and economic conditions and the personality of the administrator. The warden or superintendent of the institution must have been in tune with the political situation when appointed or the individual would not have been appointed. Some of these relationships have endured over a period of years and even decades. On the other hand, many turn out to be short-term relationships. The stability or instability of policy within the correctional system and the institution is dependent to some extent on the communicative skills of the administrator.

An issue that has been central to policymaking over the years has been the relationship between custody and treatment programs. Many wardens and superintendents, particularly those with law enforcement or legal backgrounds, have placed emphasis on custody to the almost complete elimination of treatment-oriented programs. On the other hand, many administrators have been treatment oriented and have developed counseling and other programs as extensively as possible commensurate with the security of the institution. As has been pointed out, maximum and medium custody institutions tend to emphasize custody because of security needs, but treatment programs vary with the philosophy of the superintendent and available funds. Minimum custody and community-based facilities tend to be more treatment oriented, since their populations are selected for reduced custody. The balance between custody and treatment has always been an issue central to policymaking in prisons and correctional institutions.

Another policy problem relates to whether the program is to be expanded and improved or whether it is more important to save money, a decision generally dictated by the availability of funds in the legislative appropriation process. After the appropriations have been received, some administrators make sure that all available funds are used for the institutional program and operation. This places them in a position to demonstrate the need for increased budget for the next fiscal year. Other administrators, however, pride themselves in turning back to the state unused funds on the grounds that they are conservative and can be trusted to spend only what is needed to operate the institution. Some systems with large farm operations, such as those in Mississippi and Texas, have frequently turned back to the state more than their original appropriations.

One classification of policy has been made by O'Leary and Duffee, who divided policy into the (1) reform model, (2) restraint model, (3) reintegration model, and (4) rehabilitation model.[15] The reform model focuses on the welfare

[15]Vincent O'Leary and David Duffee, "Models of Correctional Policy: A Classification of Goals Designed for Change," *Crime and Delinquency,* Vols. 16–17 (October 1971).

of the community, and persons in custody are expected to conform with the assistance of authoritarian control. The restraint model focuses on neither the individual nor the community and uses punishment only to "keep the lid on," with some administrators explaining that they are simply trying to "keep things normal." The reintegration model focuses on the offender and on the community, but it emphasizes bringing the law-abiding ex-offender back into society, preferably with community-based programs. The rehabilitation model emphasizes the offender with problems and stresses holding him for as long as needed for counseling and treatment with a minimum of legal intervention.

Policymaking can involve many other issues. Some institutions or systems permit the news media free access to the institutions; others limit such access. Some systems and institutions censor the mail and limit the types of periodicals permitted inside; others are far less restrictive.

NATIONAL INSTITUTE
OF CORRECTIONS

The National Institute of Corrections was established within the U.S. Bureau of Prisons as an amendment to the Juvenile Justice and Delinquency Prevention Act of 1974 (Public Law 93-415, Title V, Part B, 18 U.S.C., Sec. 4351). The overall policy and operations of the institute is under supervision of an advisory board of sixteen members. A director of the institute is appointed by the attorney general after consultation with the advisory board. The National Institute of Corrections can receive from or make grants to and enter into contracts with federal, state, and general units of local government, public and private agencies, educational institutions, organizations, and individuals to carry out the purposes of the institute. The institute serves as a clearinghouse and information center for the collection, preparation, and dissemination of information on corrections. It assists and serves in a consulting capacity all these departments and agencies in the development and maintenance of programs and facilities with respect to criminal and juvenile offenders. It assists all agencies in programs to develop and implement improved corrections programs. It conducts training programs, seminars, and workshops in various parts of the country for all persons concerned with corrections, including law enforcement officers, judges, probation and parole personnel, correctional workers, welfare workers, and other persons concerned with the treatment and rehabilitation of criminal and juvenile offenders. Technical assistance, coordinating and conducting research, assisting in formulating correctional policies and goals, and evaluation programs are also included in the mission of the National Institute of Corrections. The purposes of the National Institute of Corrections, then, are broadly focused on assisting in almost every way possible the improvement of programs in juvenile and adult corrections.

A valuable source of information comes from the standards worked out by the American Correctional Association. The *Manual of Correctional Standards* was first published in 1946 and revised in 1959 and in 1966 and has been followed by a series of manuals of standards for all phases of corrections, including juvenile and adult institutions, under the auspices of the Commission on Accreditation for Corrections sponsored by the American Correctional Association in 1977 and 1978. These publications provide recommended standards in all areas of corrections. The coverage of correctional institutions includes standards in many areas for local and central detention and long-term central and special institutions for juveniles and adults.[16] They are used to accredit correctional institutions, depending upon how well they meet the standards.

PLANNING

Planning refers to the adequate preparation for future needs. This type of planning is generally done in the central office rather than at the prison or correctional institution. Nevertheless, each prison or correctional institution must assess its own local needs and transmit the assessment to the central office for inclusion in the total system plan. Planning is based on projected prison population as discussed in Chapter 2, political concerns as depicted in the "War on Crime" and "Get Tough with Criminals" as espoused by some political leadership, fiscal reality or available funds as compared with projected costs, and many other similar concerns.

The first governmental funding appropriated specifically for corrections came as a result of passage of the Juvenile Delinquency Control Act of 1961. Adult corrections was funded specifically by the Omnibus Crime Control and Safe Streets Act passed in 1968 and resulted in the funding by the Law Enforcement Assistance Administration (LEAA), which went out of existence in 1981 when the Congress did not refund it in 1980.

The origin of the grant-in-aid system of governmental funding was based in the Sixteenth Amendment,[17] which allowed the Congress to tax, borrow, and spend money for the general welfare of the country. The first major grants-in-aid were for interstate highways in 1916 and public health in 1918. The Great Depression in the 1930s resulted in grants for welfare, education, and other programs. After World War II, mental health received significant funding. As mentioned previously, it was in the late 1960s that correctional programs were included to any significant amount. By 1977, these grants-in-aid had reached $60.5 billion, about 0.5 percent of the total federal budget.

Other information on planning that would be helpful to correctional administrators includes a directory of computerized data files and other reports from the National Technical Information Service in the U.S. Department of Commerce and abstracts of the literature from the National Criminal Justice Reference Service in the Department of Justice.

---

[16]These manuals are available from the Commission on Accreditation for Corrections, 6110 Executive Boulevard, Suite 750, Rockville, Maryland 20852.

[17]Thomas R. Dye, *Politics in States and Communities,* 3rd ed. (Englewood Cliffs, N.J.: Prentice-Hall, Inc., 1977), p. 43.

SUPERVISING
AND COORDINATING MANAGEMENT
IN INSTITUTIONS

The warden or superintendent of a prison or correctional institution accomplishes the supervision and coordination of management in institutions through top management within the institution, particularly deputy wardens or associate superintendents and those department heads who do not clearly report to these persons. The deputy warden or associate superintendent in charge of custody, recently recalled "operations" in many institutions, is responsible for primary control within the institution itself. The deputy warden or associate superintendent in charge of treatment, called "program" in some institutions, is responsible for education, classification, counseling, the chaplains, recreation, library, and all other phases of the program responsible directly for assisting the residents to prepare themselves for release to free society.

Several other positions in prisons and correctional institutions clearly do not report to anybody, for example, the business manager, personnel officer, record clerk, chief engineer, medical officer, superintendent of farms, director of industries, and some other peripheral positions. When difficulty and conflict arise between people occupying these positions and others in custody or treatment, the warden or superintendent frequently has to determine who more closely meets institutional policy or, at the extreme, who may be dismissed. Some systems, such as the New York State Department of Correctional Services, has introduced a third deputy warden or associate superintendent in charge of administration. These individuals report to the warden.

Frequent staff meetings, including those among top and middle management in the warden's office, appear to be the most satisfactory way of resolving conflicts, working out policy, avoiding some conflicts, and promoting the smooth operation of the institution. Based on these discussions in staff meetings, the development of a manual of policy and procedures in addition to the administrative code of the central department helps to codify problems and resolve issues before difficulties develop.

EMPLOYEES' UNIONS

Guards' unions were formed in some states prior World War II, such as New York, along with the unionization movement in the automobile and other industries. The first correctional officers' union, later the Correctional Officers Association, was part of the AFL-CIO and, later, the Teamsters. The American Federation of State, County, and Municipal Employees (AFSCME), part of the AFL-CIO, began recruiting in New York in 1953 and two-thirds of the security unit membership were correctional officers. By 1972, the Civil Service Employees Association unsuccessfully challenged the AFL-CIO's representation of the security unit, so AFSCME has continued to represent the correctional officers in New York. By 1976, correctional officers were engaged in the collective bargaining through the union, mostly under AFSCME, in thirty-three states, the trend toward expansion of collective bargaining stemming from the congruence of interests among state political leaders, unions, and employees. More than half of all state correctional workers were represented by collective bargaining agreements by 1976.[18]

Even when state laws prevent public workers from going on strike, strikes, "sick-outs," and other work stoppages have been experienced in prisons and correctional institutions in the United States. In most cases, the National Guard and/or state police are called in to control the prison. In a strike in July 1975 in Pennsylvania's Youth Development Centers, 426 of 736 juveniles were furloughed (sent home) for periods of two days to three weeks.[19]

A red alert went out to the Wisconsin National Guard just after midnight on July 2, 1977, when the Wisconsin State Employees Union voted to strike. During the next twelve hours, National Guardsmen replaced the striking employees of Wisconsin's prisons and correctional institutions. During the following sixteen days, several thousand citizen-soldiers carried out the regular duties of the institutions. The League of Women Voters of Wisconsin surveyed the opinions of Guard members, correctional personnel, and residents of five institutions and found rather interesting results.[20] The morale of the residents was higher during the strike than it had been before; inmates helped the Guards in the performance of their duties, and the residents frequently reported, "I was treated like a man."[21] The National Guardsmen were more positive in their attitudes toward the residents than were the correctional officers. On the other hand, supervisory personnel described the correctional officers more favorably than the National Guardsmen.

Correctional officers in New York State went on strike on April 18, 1979 and remained out until May 4.[22] Their functions were taken over by the New York Army Reserve National Guard, by state troopers, and by central office staff members, many of whom worked twelve hours daily. During the April–May 1979 strike of correctional officers in twenty-eight New York prisons, National Guardsmen took over the custodial duties. The prisons ran smoothly, and the inmates stated that the Guardsmen outperformed correctional officers because of the former's positive and fair attitudes.[23] Correctional officers make a living in the prison and must become accustomed to the system. To survive it, the officers become numb to the realities of prison life. A group of fresh townspeople in the National Guard represented a new perspective for the inmates.

Strikes in many other states include those in California, Massachusetts,

[18]M. Robert Montilla, *Prison Employee Unionism: Management Guide for Correctional Administrators* (Washington, D.C.: National Institute of Law Enforcement and Criminal Justice, LEAA, January 1978), p. 337.

[19]Burton Cohen, *Analysis of the Impact of the State Employees' Strike on Juveniles Committed to the YDC's* (Philadelphia: The Wharton School, University of Pennsylvania, 1975), p. 1.

[20]*Changing of the Guard: Citizen Soldiers in Wisconsin Correctional Institutions* (Madison, Wisc.: The League of Women Voters, July 1978), pp. 58.

[21]Ibid., p. 28.

[22]"Central Office Staffers Learn from Emergency Duties in the Field" and accompanying pictures, *Correctional Services News*, Vol. 4, no. 4 (May 1979), pp. 6–7.

[23]David Rothenberg, "Out on a Limb," *Fortune News*, June 1979, p. 3.

and others.[24] In February 1980, there were correctional officers' unions in Alaska, California, Delaware, the District of Columbia, Florida, Hawaii, Illinois, Iowa, Louisiana, Maine, Maryland, Massachusetts, Michigan, Minnesota, Montana, Nebraska, New Hampshire, New Jersey, New York, North Dakota, Ohio, Oregon, Pennsylvania, Rhode Island, Vermont, Washington,[25] Wisconsin, and the Federal Prison System, Inc. (formerly the U.S. Bureau of Prisons).

It is generally conceded that the employees' unions have made administration more complex and difficult because of a new force that has to be considered in each policy decision and in management. It sometimes results in split loyalties in management, as when some officers who have been members of the union are promoted to sergeants, lieutenants, and captains and thus become members of management, no longer eligible to participate in union activities. On the other hand, some observers have held that, while unionization will have profound effects on the administration and organization of prisons, probably requiring a new type of administrative system, it has made the guard force more conscious of its rational self-interest and may lead them to accept and even advocate many prison reforms that they may have rejected in the absence of collective bargaining.[26]

The unionization of prisons has had greater impact on the administration of institutions in the United States and has received more notice outside than almost any other development. Guards' unions have provided massive gains in available jobs, salaries, and work benefits for their members at a time when taxpayers' resistance has resulted in budget costs, layoffs, and hiring freezes for other public agencies.[27] Control of the prison is now hotly contested in some places by a wide assortment of actors, including the correction commissioner, the warden, the custodial force, which has become unionized, newly created official "watchdog" agencies, representatives of the legislature and other governmental units, activists from many special-interest groups, and the prisoners themselves.[28]

PRISONERS' UNIONS

While prisoners' unions have been present in the Scandinavian countries and elsewhere in northern Europe, such as West Germany, since World War II, it was not until 1970 that they were organized in the United States. The first such union in America was the United Prisoners Union developed at the California

[24]J. Potter, "Guards Unions—The Search for Solidarity," *Corrections Magazine,* Vol. 5, no. 9 (September 1979), pp. 25–35.

[25]"Look for the Union Label," *Corrections Compendium,* Vol. 4, no. 8 (February 1978), pp. 1–6.

[26]James V. Jacobs and Norma Meacham Crotty, *Guard Unions and the Future of the Prisons* (Ithaca: Institute of Public Employment, New York School of Industrial and Labor Relations, Cornell University, August 1978), p. 8.

[27]Ibid., p. 8.

[28]Scott Christianson, "Corrections Law Development: How Unions Affect Prison Administration," *Criminal Law Bulletin,* Vol. 15, no. 3 (May–June 1979), p. 238.

state prison at Folsom in 1970. It was a disruptive force at the prison and met considerable resistance from the administration. It was terminated at Folsom, but reorganized again in San Francisco several months later by ex-prisoners, recruited from within the walls of the prisons in California, and soon replaced the earlier union at Folsom with a more conciliatory approach. By 1975, its membership represented twenty thousand prisoners and ex-prisoners in California who were attempting to become the bargaining agent for the prisoners with the State of California. When the state considered seriously the possibility of the California Prisoners Union being recognized as a bargaining agent, the Correctional Officers Union threatened to strike. The result was that no action was taken officially to recognize the prisoners' union as a bargaining agent.

In early 1972, the first labor union of prisoners was at the Green Haven State Prison in Stormville, New York, established with the legal work done by the Prisoners' Rights Project of the Legal Aid Society. This prisoners' labor union notified Commissioner Russell Oswald of New York that it wanted to be recognized as the exclusive bargaining agent for the inmates at the Green Haven Prison. No action was taken. Since 1972, prisoners' unions have been established in Minnesota, North Carolina, Wisconsin, and in New England (the New England Prisoners' Alliance, NEPA). The Washington State Prisoners' Union was terminated in 1975 but reorganized later.

Other inmate groups have organized to represent prisoners without calling themselves "unions." The Incarcerated Veterans Assistance Organization (IVAO) was formed in July 1974 at the District of Columbia Reformatory at Lorton, Virginia, to assure that veterans obtained their minimum GI benefits and that offenders be permitted to serve their time in the military services with time credited toward parole.[29] The National Prison Reform Association was organized and quartered at the Rhode Island Adult Correctional Institution, Maximum Custody Section, in Cranston, Rhode Island. This organization publishes the *NPRA News* to disseminate information regarding lawsuits by inmates and news stories regarding prison events.

Prisoners' unions tend to attract the more militant and politicized inmates.[30] Official recognition of prisoners' unions, however, tends to reduce defiance and broaden the support of the inside politicians and the "square johns." The opportunities that prisoners' unions provide include reduction of the potential for violence by providing a legitimate channel of expression, opening communication with the administration, and fostering greater personal responsibility among prisoners.

Prisoners' unions have been encouraged by some legal groups and have been defended under the provisions of the First Amendment of the Constitution providing the right of peaceful assembly and organization to redress grievances.

The early stance of the courts was cautious regarding the balance between the First Amendment rights of the inmate-citizens and the security of the institution. *Paka* v. *Manson* in 1974 discussed this balancing of the interests of

---

[29]"Inmate Veterans Organize in DC," *Target* (newsletter of innovative projects funded by LEAA), Vol. 4, issue 5 (May 1975), p. 4.

[30]Stephen Woolpert, "Prisoners' Unions, Inmate Militancy, and Correctional Policymaking," *Federal Probation*, Vol. 42, no. 2 (June 1978), pp. 40–45.

inmates with the state's interest in institutional security and decided against the union, suggesting the alternatives of selective interviews of inmates by authorities and a full-time correctional ombudsman.[31] In *North Carolina Prisoners' Union* v. *Jones* in 1976, the lower court decided in favor of the inmates, but the Supreme Court reversed the decision the following year, holding that, if the administration could show that the union constituted a threat to institutional security, the administration could prevent the formation of a union.[32] On the other hand, the decision in a Florida case in 1977 upheld the right of prison authorities to prevent the formation of a prisoners' union.[33]

COLLECTIVE BARGAINING

Collective bargaining agreements had been made with employees' unions by 1976, but no such agreements have been consummated with prisoners' unions. These collective bargaining agreements, which have been extensive in the late 1970s and early 1980s, cover such general issues as lobbying for favorable action in the legislature to rights for participation in management.[34] Specific issues relating to employment benefit provisions include negotiations and agreement on (1) salaries, (2) grievance procedures, (3) overtime and sick leave, (4) job security, (5) seniority provisions for job assignments, (6) seniority provisions for promotions and transfers, (7) employee orientation and in-service training, (8) leaves with pay, (9) holidays, (10) employee time off for union business, (11) leaves without pay, (12) rest periods and meals, (13) uniform allowances and replacements, (14) shift and other pay differentials, (15) length of service pay, (16) labor relations neutrals (third parties in collective bargaining), (17) temporary assignments to higher or other classes, (18) shift overlap, (19) retirement benefits, and (20) other miscellaneous contract provisions and omissions.[35] General issues involving the union role in state correctional administration include (1) emergency plans related to strikes and job actions, (2) security, (3) conditions of work and employee safety, (4) discipline of employees, (5) affirmative action and equal opportunity for employment, (6) fitness for duty standards and medical examinations, (7) noncustody matters (restricting union involvement in noncustody issues such as education, prison industries, health care, recreation, and other programs affecting inmates directly), (8) position classification and pay plans, and (9) responsibilities of correctional management in personnel administration.[36]

[31]*Paka* v. *Manson*, 387 F. Supp. 111 (D. Conn., 1974).

[32]*North Carolina Prisoners' Union* v. *Jones*, 409 F. Supp. 937 (E.D. N.C., 1976). Reversed by U.S. Supreme Court, 21 CRL 3190 (June 23, 1977). Also, see *Goodwin* v. *Oswald*, 462 F. 2d 1237 (2d Cir., 1972).

[33]*Brooks* v. *Wainwright*, 439 F. Supp. 1335 (M.D. Fla., 1977).

[34]M. Robert Montilla, *Prison Employee Unionism: Management Guide for Correctional Administrators* (Washington, D.C.: National Institute of Law Enforcement and Criminal Justice, LEAA, 1978), pp. 20–202.

[35]Ibid., pp. 203–334.

[36]Ibid., pp. 335–419.

Some collective bargaining difficulties have involved the issue of standardization of rules and regulation in state civil service and merit systems being incompatible with collective bargaining. It is frequently recognized that standard qualifications based on examinations, education, and other factors militate against minority groups and need to be negotiated. Since Wisconsin passed the first statute in 1959 formally recognizing employees' unions right to collective bargaining, approximately forty states had enacted similar legislation by 1976.[37] It should be pointed out that, while the first formal legislation granting bargaining rights was in Wisconsin in 1959, previous bargaining occurred in the earlier unions in New York and elsewhere directly with the civil service commission or other personnel agencies, departments of corrections, and other agencies on an administrative basis rather than as a legislative right. In the bargaining process, administrators and management must develop knowledge and skills considerably above those that had been required in precollective bargaining times, which means that education and training are necessary for the administration and management to fill successfully the new roles.

Almost all the collective bargaining contracts in corrections include a no-strike agreement accompanied by a no-lock-out provision.[38] To circumvent this provision, there have been many instances of guards "calling in sick," as happened at the New Jersey state prison at Trenton on August 2, 1968; the Adult Correctional Institution at Cranston, Rhode Island, on August 25, 1969; the Suffolk County Jail, New York, on June 3, 1971; again at the Adult Correctional Institution at Cranston, Rhode Island, on October 19, 1972; the New Jersey state prison at Leesburg on September 26, 1973; all New Jersey prisons on April 4, 1974; all Ohio prisons on July 14, 1974; New York City prisons on July 7, 1975; the New Jersey state prison at Trenton on January 4, 1976; and other instances. Despite this provision, some strikes have been called, such as those at the Ohio state penitentiary at Columbus on February 5, 1969; the jail at Atlanta, Georgia, on March 23, 1970; the Chillicothe correctional institution in Ohio on February 1, 1971; the Erie county jail in Pennsylvania on August 1, 1973; all Ohio prisons on July 14, 1974; all Connecticut prisons on April 4, 1977; and elsewhere. In reaction to the strike, despite the provisions of the collective bargaining agreement, many prison systems have dismissed the striking guards. In very few instances, however, have the dismissals been effective. In most cases, further union activity and negotiation have resulted in the reinstatement of the guards.

An extensive questionnaire was mailed to correctional agencies and institutions in late 1976 to determine the extent to which unions and the return rate reached 99.0 percent. Collective bargaining agreements were reported in eighteen states and the District of Columbia.[39] In case of strikes, five states

[37]J. P. Morgan and Richard J. Korstad, *Impact of Collective Bargaining on Law Enforcement and Corrections* (St. Petersburg, Fla.: Public Safety Research Institute, 1976), 55 pp.

[38]Joann B. Morton and Nicholas Beadles, "Collective Bargaining Activity in State Correctional Agencies," in *Readings in Public Employee-Management Relations for Correctional Administrators* (Athens: Southeastern Correctional Management Training Council, University of Georgia, 1974), pp. 83–154.

[39]Charles A. Kuhl and J. Keith Rodgers, "Collective Bargaining in Correctional Institutions," *American Journal of Correction*, Vol. 39, no. 6 (November–December 1977), pp. 14–15, 37.

reported that they had coverage by the National Guard, seven states indicated coverage by the state police, twelve states had coverage by administration and management, and seven states had a combined coverage of these units. In case of impasses in bargaining, mediation by an outside arbitrator was considered the best method in ten states, binding arbitration was considered the best in eight states, advisory arbitration was recommended by three states, a regulatory method was recommended by two states, and a combination was recommended by nine states.

A Management-Employee Relations in Corrections (MERIC) project surveyed all states to determine the developments in collective bargaining. The findings revealed that prison management had been weakened, that direct and indirect costs of security personnel had increased significantly, and that most correctional unions tended to oppose the reforms suggested by the National Advisory Commission on Criminal Justice Standards and Goals.[40] The increasing influence of employees' unions has led to increased salaries and better working condtions, but not all the changes have increased the efficient operation or effectiveness in corrections.

INMATE SELF-GOVERNMENT AND PARTICIPATORY MANAGEMENT

Informal social control by the residents or inmates of the prison or correctional institution has long been a significant factor in institutional management. Many correctional administrators have said that most prisons are run by the inmates because they provide some clerical and technical skills to prisons whose budgets are too low to hire civilian help. Most prisons rely on inmate clerks, inmate carpenters, inmate plumbers, and other contributions from the general population of the prison. The most extreme cases have been in some Southern prisons, such as those in Arkansas, Mississippi, and Louisiana, where inmate guards were used until the early 1970s. Prior to that, many other systems, including those in Oklahoma and Texas, used inmate guards as well as other help from the general population. The last inmate to remain in an armed guard tower in Florida was removed in January 1956.

There have been several attempts to formalize inmate self-government. In 1885, Warden Hiram of the Michigan state prison at Jackson devised a self-government system called Mutual Aid League.[41] Thomas Mott Osborne established the Mutual Welfare League at Auburn, New York, during World War I, and it worked well for a few years. Failure of adequate protections and controls resulted in its abolition in 1928 when a few powerful inmate leaders began to use it for their own purposes. Adequate administrative controls and supervision are

---

[40]M. R. Montilla, *Prison-Employee Unionism—Management Guide for Correctional Administrators* (Sacramento, Calif.: American Justice Institute, 1977), 506 pp., sponsored by the National Institute of Law Enforcement and Criminal Justice, Washington, D.C.

[41]Harold M. Helfman, "Antecedents of Thomas Mott Osborne's 'Mutual Welfare League in Michigan'," *Journal of Criminal Law and Criminology*, Vol. 40, no. 5 (January–February 1950), pp. 597–600.

necessary, just as they are necessary for student government in a school or university or for civilian government under military occupation. There have been calls recently for further inmate participation in prison management or control. Participatory management has come to refer to the participation of inmates or residents in the control of the prison or institution.

Participatory management that includes the inmates' subcultures could lead to improved institutional functioning.[42] The inmates' subculture is a major impediment to successful intervention within the prison setting. Participatory management would neutralize these effects by giving inmates increased responsibilities for decision making. A coalition of staff and inmates reduces the traditional opposition of staff-inmate relationships and tends to promote proactive group behavior by taking advantage of many inmates' tendency toward conventional norms and restoring dignity and a sense of responsibility to an oppressed group.

The inmate council appears at present to be the most viable method of such participation. In this system, residents of living units or the institution itself, depending upon its size, are elected by the other residents to meet with the warden and management staff to report and discuss grievances by the other inmates, specific problems in the institution, and other needs of the general population of the institution. The results have been favorable in that many adjustments can be made easily when brought to the attention of the administration. Probably the first inmate council was inaugurated by Superintendent Howard B. Gill of the Norfolk Prison Colony in Massachusetts in 1927.[43]

INMATE LITIGATION

Prior to the 1960s, the courts maintained a hands-off policy regarding administrative procedures in the institution. They considered prison administration to be beyond the purview of the courts. Beginning with *Fulwood* v. *Clemmer* in 1962, the courts began to take an interest in the prison. By the late 1960s, the courts were in the prisons, and many prison systems operated under court orders by the mid-1970s. In the 1950s, about 500 cases annually were brought to litigation by inmates. By the late 1960s, about 1,000 such cases a year were brought to litigation. In 1976, 19,809 petitions were filed by prisoners in the federal courts. By 1979, the number of such cases exceeded 20,000 a year by a wide margin.

The increase of prisoners' civil rights litigation has required prison officials to become more aware of the defenses to these actions. An excellent bibliography on correctional law was published in 1977 by the American Correctional Association.[44] It provides guidelines for access to courts and counsel,

---

[42]S. A. Bloomberg, "Participatory Management: Toward a Science of Correctional Management," *Criminology*, Vol. 15, no. 2 (1977), pp. 149–64.

[43]Harry Elmer Barnes and Negley K. Teeters, *New Horizons in Criminology*, 3rd ed. (Englewood Cliffs, N.J.: Prentice-Hall, Inc., 1959), p. 502.

[44]Jeffrey Curtis, Richard Crane, and Michael Weisz, *Correctional Law: A Bibliography of Selected Books and Articles* (College Park, Md.: American Correctional Association, February, 1977), 28 pp.

access to the media, behavior modification, civil disabilities, and many other concerns. Specific defenses are in three groups: (1) protection from liability because of the prison official's status as an officer of the state that includes various doctrines of immunity, including the Eleventh Amendment and the defense of good faith and probable cause; (2) the concurrent nature of civil rights suits being amendable to such defenses as *res judicata*, collateral estoppel or abstention, or the Younger doctrine that permits state courts to try state cases free from interference by federal courts (*Younger* v. *Harris*, 401 U.S. 37 (1971)); and (3) the federal character of the action that requires the plaintiff to have standing to sue and that it be a viable case on controversy.[45] There are many other sources regarding correctional law with which the correctional administrator should be acquainted.[46]

A law library is a constitutional requirement for any prison or correctional institution. The only exception is when a prisoner has his or her own attorney. Recommendations for books and other forms and services have been made by and are available from the American Bar Association. New Hampshire, Texas, and Washington have hired their own full-time attorneys to assist inmates in these litigations.

INMATE GRIEVANCE PROCEDURES

Inmate grievance procedures refer to the ways in which individual inmates can appeal or complain about actions and conditions that they consider to be unjust and wrong. Some institutions have an appeals board for this purpose. If it does not satisfy the inmate, then he or she may appeal to the warden. Eventually, the inmate may appeal to the director of the system at the state level or to the director of the Federal Prison System, if he is in the federal system. The advantage of this grievance procedure is that it eliminates many cases that might otherwise go to court.

Inmates contend that the inmate grievance system generally works well.[47] It serves to lessen tensions inside the institution by giving the inmates an avenue through which to express themselves, it can stop some lawsuits from being brought by inmates against the various departments of corrections, and it is good public relations.

---

[45]Michael Weisz, *Defenses to Civil Rights Actions Among Correctional Employees*, rev. (College Park, Md.: American Correctional Association, August 1977), 35 pp.

[46]John W. Palmer, *Constitutional Rights of Prisoners*, 2nd ed. (Cincinnati: W. H. Anderson Publishing Company, 1973, second printing February 1978), and the annual *Supplements*. See also Michele G. Herman and Marilyn G. Haft, eds., *Prisoners Rights Sourcebook: Theory, Litigation, Practice* (New York: Clark Boardman Company, 1973); Sol Rubin, *Law of Criminal Correction* (St. Paul, Minn.: West Publishing Company, 1973); *Prison Law Monitor*, published monthly (Washington, D.C.: Institution Education Services); *Jail & Prison Law Bulletin*, published monthly (San Francisco: Americans for Effective Law Enforcement).

[47]Larry Kenston, inmate, "Inmate Grievance System: Does It Work?" *The Inter-Prison Press* (Kentucky Bureau of Corrections), Vol. 7, no. 6 (April 1979), p. 3. Also, see Alexander Dixon, "Inmate Grievance," *Correctional Services News* (New York State Department of Correctional Services), Vol. 2, no. 8 (September 1977), p. 8.

RELATIONS
WITH OTHER AGENCIES

Prison administrators have close relations with many other agencies because of common problems and ethics. Contacts include those with conservation departments, highway departments, welfare departments, and other agencies. Mutual cooperation and respect is the only viable approach to developing and maintaining these relationships.

PUBLIC RELATIONS

A primary function of the prison administrator is public relations. Good relations with the news media, the community in which the prison or correctional institution is located, and the community's political leaders and other groups are most important. They have an impact in getting cooperation from the governor and the legislature and many other ways. An "open-door" policy with news reporters can reduce suspicion and hostility with the media. Civic activity and visibility by political leaders without being overly aggressive tends to provide a wholesome situation at budget time and when new programs are desired.

CONCLUSIONS

There are five important areas to which an administrator must attend: (1) staff development through careful recruitment, selection, in-service training, and performance ratings, to develop an effective organization; (2) the limitations imposed by constitutional guarantees and the newly developing standards and accreditation procedures by the American Correctional Association and other organizations, such as the American Bar Association, to avoid litigation; (3) conflict and riots that need safety valves, including inmate grievance procedures, a law library and legal service, and other means, to improve morale and to provide legitimate outlets; (4) reasonable and identifiable administrative objectives, so that the entire organization knows the policies and directions in which the prison or correctional institution is expected to go; (5) greater job satisfaction for the many frustrated and "burned-out" correctional officers and other personnel in the prison. Too frequently, many correctional officers and other personnel create a public relations problem by telling friends and acquaintances in the community outside the prison how terrible work in the prison is and how unfair and capricious the warden and other administrators are, often referring to the prison as "the pits" and counting the years, months, weeks, and days to their retirement eligibility. Some do not wait for retirement. The turnover rate of personnel in many prison systems exceeds 50 percent annually.

At one time, the warden had almost absolute authority in the prison, but he has recently been reduced to a role of a negotiator, attempting to maintain the safety and security of an institution, yet lacking any real power to do it. Recent changes have also shifted the monopoly on force from the correctional officers to the inmates.[48] The warden today must be familiar with the language of the Constitution of the United States and know how the courts are interpreting it, the statutes, the administrative procedures acts or their counterparts in the jurisdiction in which he functions, the legislature and governor, the collective bargaining agreement, and many other constraints. Seldom have administrators in any field faced the complex problems, sweeping changes, divisive issues, and social pressures that confront the administration of prisons and correctional institutions in the United States. Prison administrators have suffered from a long legacy of neglect and lack of public support and understanding.

Authority in modern times has diminished in almost all areas of society. Even the divine right of kings has given way with the infallibility of the pope and the church to power struggles between interest groups. Authority in the civilization of man seems to be passing from individual to group decision making where the struggle for dominance is part of the process.[49] As the captain of the Florida road prison said in the film *Cool Hand Luke*, "What we have here is a problem of communication!"

CHAPTER QUESTIONS

15-1. What is administration?

15-2. What is meant by management by objectives?

15-3. What other factors in society must correctional administrators work with and through before they can concentrate on their institutions and programs?

15-4. What new constraints in administration have been brought into the process in recent years?

15-5. What is the National Institute of Corrections and what are its functions?

15-6. What has been the impact of employees' unions in prisons and correctional institutions?

15-7. What has been the impact of collective bargaining on the administration of prisons and correctional institutions?

15-8. What are the status and the problems of inmate self-government and participatory management?

15-9. What has been the impact of inmate litigation in recent years on the administrative procedures in the institution?

15-10. What are inmate grievance procedures and how have they functioned?

[48]David C. Anderson, "The Price of Safety: 'I Can't Go Back Out There'," *Corrections Magazine*, Vol. 6, no. 4 (August 1980), p. 8.

[49]Robert Nisbet, *Twilight of Authority* (New York: Oxford University Press, Galaxy Books, 1975).

16
FISCAL MANAGEMENT

Money is the lifeblood of any organization. Without funding, the organization dies. The primary source of funding for prisons and correctional institutions is in the form of appropriations from the legislatures. There are other sources also, particularly federal funding agencies and private foundations. In some cases, funding is available through contracts with other state agencies generally concerned with conservation projects or roads upon which the residents of a correctional institution may work.

The president of the United States and the governors of the various states are the most powerful administrative leaders in their respective jurisdictions. It is generally conceded, also, that the director of the agency that handles the money is generally the second most powerful in his or her respective jurisdiction. At the federal level, the director of the Office of Management and Budget (OMB) holds this position. In various states, it is the comptroller, or comparable positions by other names. The director of the Office of Management and Budget at the federal level and the comptrollers in the states control expenditures. These offices review and frequently modify budgets before the president presents them to Congress and before governors introduce them to state legislatures. These offices also have annual audits that may criticize the way in which funds were spent. Some of these audits revealed wrongdoing on the parts of the administrators and managers and have resulted in reprimands, resignations, and dismissals, at the least, and even prison terms in some cases. It is obvious that these offices generally have the expertise, knowledge, and ability to manage the businesses of their various jurisdictions.

Fiscal management, particularly the budget and its implementation, is the most significant and effective tool of administration and management of any organization. It becomes most important in the control of programs in prisons and correctional institutions because of the low priority they have in the total fiscal and budget process in any jurisdiction.

MANAGEMENT FUNCTIONS

Management has the function of implementing the policies of the administration. Planned management in prisons and correctional institutions, as elsewhere, assesses the present situation in the organization, plans for the future to improve the program within budgetary limits, and determines how those objectives can be achieved. Unfortunately, management in some institutions has been oriented toward crisis and has focused on "putting out fires and mending fences." Sometimes, managers have dealt primarily with the exceptions or disturbing deviances. The rationale for these approaches is to keep affairs in the prison as normal as possible rather than to develop clear-cut objectives and programs.

As stated in the previous chapter, management by objectives (MBO) has been a recent significant development in management procedures. A statement of goals and admissions precedes a clear fundamental objective and centralized policy direction. Clear lines of executive authority and responsibility have to be drawn. Maximum decentralization of execution is desirable and, in a large organization, results in several levels or echelons of management between administration and direct contact with the residents. Management by objectives then handles significant deviations without overreacting to crisis. Management teams can reduce conflict and factionalism in the prison staff and promote coordination of effort. For example, the top management personnel are the deputy wardens or assistant superintendents for various functions, such as treatment, custody, or administration. Working together as a team, implementation of policy is enhanced. Middle management people are the captain and lieutenants in custody and the department heads in other areas. Similarly, by comparing notes and working together as a team, achievement of objectives can be facilitated. At the supervisory level are the sergeants, counselors, supervisors, and other supervisory personnel. By using management teams in various echelons, operational objectives can be aligned horizontally and vertically in the organization to assure attainment of goals.

The clear lines of authority in MBO permit a clear division of function in any analysis. Consequently, preparation of the budget under this system has proved to be more satisfactory to more people than have most previous approaches to management.

BUDGETS

The budget process is a long one that takes time and effort. Many states and the federal government work on annual budgets because the Congress and many state legislatures meet annually; other states develop biennial budgets because their legislatures meet every other year. Work on the budgets begins in the institutions, generally in July or earlier, and is transmitted to the central office of the department of corrections, or whatever other title is used to designate the prison system, where the budget requests from each institution are coordinated, sometimes modified, and made into a total agency budget that includes the costs of running the central office. The budget is then generally transmitted to the budget director and his or her agency. The budget package submitted by the correctional administrator should include (1) a letter of transmittal; (2) the proposed basic budget for the coming year or biennium, as the case may be; (3) the proposed supplemental programs; and (4) a program of performance statistics, cost-benefit analysis, or unit costs on the basis of previous experience.[1] In the office of the budget, the budget requests from the various state agencies are all coordinated and frequently modified, and all budgets are synthesized to form a total state budget.

This budget is then transmitted to the governor in time for his presentation of the budget message to the state legislature, which, in most states, open their sessions on or about the first day of March or April. The legislature prepares an appropriations bill and sends it to the ways and means committees or other appropriate committees of the House and Senate for consideration. The legislature then considers other bills and programs, most of which need money. At the end of the session, the legislature takes into consideration the budget requests, the recommendations of the committees, and the creation of new programs during the session, after which the appropriations bill is brought to a vote. In case of disagreement and other difficulties, extra sessions of the legislatures have been called, if necessary, to finish work on the appropriations bills.

At the federal level, the Bureau of the Budget in the Office of Management and Budget sends letters to each agency in the first quarter of the calendar year (January to March) identifying major program issues, and the agencies provide the bureau with analytic studies either underway or planned. Between February 15 and July 15, agencies submit programs and financial plans about a year before the Congress that hears it meets.[2] It goes to the Office of Management and Budget for review and presidential decision in September and then is transmitted to Congress in mid-January; after congressional proceedings, funds are made available in October, when the federal fiscal year begins, about a year and a half after the requested budget was begun. Most fiscal years at the state level begin July 1.

Program evaluation, management appraisal, and independent audits by the General Accounting Office are thereafter periodic. For purposes of cost-effectiveness, correctional resource consumption must be goal oriented rather than process oriented.[3] The costs of dealing with offenders are enormous and are increasing. Further, there are no real indications that present correctional

[1]Charles N. Kaufman, "The Budget Process: Dollarizing Law Enforcement Planning," *FBI Law Enforcement Bulletin*, Vol. 38, no. 8, (September 1969), pp. 12–18.

[2]Lance T. LeLoup, *Budgetary Politics: Dollars, Deficits, Decisions* (Brunswick, Ohio: Kings Court Communications, Inc., 1977), pp. 250–55.

[3]Mark S. Richmond, "Measuring the Cost of Correctional Services," *Crime and Delinquency*, Vol. 18, no. 3 (1972), pp. 243–52.

Table 16-1 Congressional Budget Process: Timetable

ON OR BEFORE	ACTION TO BE COMPLETED
November 10	President submits current services budget.
15th day after Congress meets	President submits his budget.
March 15	Committees and joint committees submit reports to budget committees.
April 1	Congressional Budget Office submits report to budget committees.
April 15	Budget committees report first concurrent resolution on the budget to their Houses.
May 15	Committees report bills and resolutions authorizing new budget authority.
May 15	Congress completes action on first concurrent resolution on the budget.
7th day after Labor Day	Congress completes action on bills and resolutions providing new budget authority and new spending authority.
September 15	Congress completes action on second required concurrent resolution on the budget.
September 25	Congress completes action on reconciliation bill or resolution, or both, implementing second required concurrent resolution.
October 1	Fiscal year begins.

SOURCE: Gerald H. Yamada, "New Law Reforms Budget Process: Next Fiscal Year Begins October 1," *LEAA Newsletter,* Vol. 4, no. 6 (December 1974), p. 3.

methods are effective in intervening in criminal careers. Additional problems arise from the failure to define and coordinate criminal justice and correctional goals. Optimum prison size and cost behavior is difficult to resolve because the larger the prison, the cheaper the cost per inmate, but probably the less effective the rehabilitation.[4] To realize the savings resulting from a large-scale operation, planners could centralize many administrative activities. Inmate units could be designed on a smaller scale to meet requirements of inmate services, and administrative savings could be diverted to treatment programs.

The Budget and Impoundment Control Act of 1974 provided a unified congressional appropriation process to assure effective control over the budget, to determine each year an approximate level of federal revenues and expenditures, to establish national budget priorities, and to require the executive branch to furnish Congress with requisite fiscal information.[5] The Budget Act established a House Budget Committee, a Senate Budget Committee, a Congressional Budget Office, and a budget process timetable and provided impoundment controls. The timetable for the federal budget appears in Table 16-1.

[4]V. L. Williams and M. Fish, "Optimum Prison Size: Cost Behavior v. Rehabilitation Goals," *American Journal of Correction,* Vol. 34, no. 2 (1972), pp. 14–19.

[5]Gerald H. Yamada, "New Law Reforms Budget Process: Next Fiscal Year Begins October 1," *LEAA Newsletter,* Vol. 4, no. 6 (December 1974), p. 3.

The General Accounting Office (GAO) is the research arm of Congress. The GAO is frequently asked to evaluate programs before the legislation regarding them has been enacted. For example, H.R. 9400 (1977) was a House bill that required minimum standards for inmate grievance mechanisms for the U.S. Bureau of Prisons (Federal Prison System, Inc., as of January 1981), including time limits. staff and inmate participation, provisions for emergencies, prohibition against reprisals for filing grievances, and outside reviews. The GAO was requested to provide information about this problem. The GAO examined in depth inmate grievance mechanisms used in California, Minnesota, and New York and requested that all forty-three states that had grievance mechanisms at that time provide information about them. An analysis indicated that many of these procedures were in need of further review, themselves, and it was concluded that a need existed for the development of a model inmate grievance management system that could be adapted by the Bureau of Prisons and the states to assess continually the extent to which they are in compliance with standards that the attorney general might promulgate under H.R. 9400.[6] The GAO provides information on all bills as requested by Congress. Information requested by state legislatures generally comes from the office of research evaluation, or other comparable title, in the central office of the agency concerned.

The forms of state budgets have changed through the years. The earliest type of budget, with some less progressive states continuing it in the 1950s, was the lump-sum budget. In this system, the legislature simply appropriated a lump sum to the warden or superintendent of an institution, who could then set up his own system of expenditures within the institution. This system was generally favored in jurisdictions where there was no central control and a single institution served the state.

The next system was the line-item budget in which every expenditure, including salaries of administrative and management personnel, as well as all other categories, were listed. The legislature could modify each line or eliminate it, as it saw fit. This system has become the most popular approach to the budget process as far as the legislatures were concerned, because it provided the budget officials and the legislators greater control over all state operations.

The program planning and budget system (PPBS) enjoyed some popularity in the 1960s. It included a statement of (1) the mission; (2) the need, goals, and objectives; (3) a search for alternatives; and (4) program structure. It was then divided into cost categories and unit costs. In PPBS, programs were planned for the future, frequently four or five years and sometimes more, with budget requests synchronized with the planning. This system encountered difficulty in the political arena, however, because many political leaders are not in office four or five years. Many terms are for two years or four years, and legislators just did not want to be committed for a period of five years. New administrators coming into state agencies also did not feel committed to a plan of which they had not been a part. Consequently, the line-item budget system remains the most popular.

Integrating systems and accounting within a complex organization has

---

[6]"GAO Reports to Congress—Inmate Grievance Mechanisms Need Effective Procedure for Monitoring an Analysis of Data," *Correctional Digest*, Vol. 8, no. 22 (October 28, 1977), pp. 1, 8–9.

long been an ideal of public administration.[7] The budgeter speaks of executive and congressional budget review; the accountant speaks of journals, ledgers, and specialized reports; and the planners and programmers speak of new initiatives. Management accounts structure (MAS) can provide a common framework for all systems and achieve a continuity of data processing and presentation through each phase of the integrated system.

Beginning in the mid-1970s, zero-base budgeting enjoyed some popularity. In zero-base budgeting, budgets are not based on previous years of experience; rather, each activity must be defended as though it had not existed before. This has presented some difficulty for administrators because it takes away a base of the previous year that had been used as a point of origin for preparing the new budget. In addition, sunset laws have been passed in several jurisdictions, so that, after a specific period of time, generally two to five years, each agency must defend its existence or specific parts of its program.

Governmental agencies tend to regard current operating and expenditure levels as an established base and build on it for their budgets. As a consequence of this incremental budgeting, only a small fraction of the total budget dollars really gets an intensive review. Hence, zero-base budgeting that evaluates the entire program provides better analysis of programs.[8] All programs should be budgeted "starting from scratch," with the administrator preparing a decision package as part of the budget justification. The decision package would include an analysis of purposes, goals, objectives, costs, benefits, alternative courses of action, measures of performance effectiveness, consequences of not performing the functions, costs and benefits of spending at the minimal level, or about 75 percent of the current costs, as well as other expenditure levels. With this analytical tool, the manager and the committee discussing appropriation of funds would have a better view of the total expenditure and its effect.

Zero-base budgeting outlines suggested programs and less costly alternatives.[9] From these guidelines, management and planners can see the most logical places in which to cut expenditures. All activities and operations are grouped in "decision packages" that can be ranked and evaluated in their order of importance. There are four components: (1) the design package listing programs and alternatives, (2) the expense listing at all levels, (3) the priority ranking, and (4) the worksheets that provide additional levels of alternatives. These procedures add time to budget planning, but sometimes the additional expense may be justified.

It becomes obvious that the budget process is a system of control and management and that the prisons and correctional institutions are vitally affected by this process. Budgetary reform in the United States has evolved through three distinct stages before getting to PPBS,[10] and it has since ventured into zero-base budgeting. Budget reform is frequently used to attempt to deal

[7]Francis E. McGilvry, "The Management Accounts Structure," *Public Administration Review,* Vol. 26, no. 4 (December 1966), pp. 277–83.

[8]Peter A. Pyhrr, *Zero-Based Budgeting* (New York: John Wiley & Sons, Inc., 1973), 231 pp.

[9]Joseph L. Herbert (ed.); *Experiences in Zero-Base Budgeting,* Lexington, Massachusetts: Lexington Books, D. C. Heath, 1978, pp. 1–30.

[10]Allen Schick, "The Road to PPBS, the Stages of Budget Reform," *Public Administration Review,* Vol. 26, no. 4 (December 1966), pp. 243–58.

Table 16-2 State Purposes: Regular Summary of Appropriations and Changes, Fiscal 1978–1979

	TOTAL		PERSONAL SERVICES	
Program	Recommended	Increase (decrease)	Recommended	Increase (decrease)
Administration	$ 8,319,900	$ 1,424,001	$ 5,468,300	$ 775,976
Support services	68,583,600	3,573,538	29,623,500	1,100,884
Supervision of inmates	122,875,600	11,010,326	116,355,700	6,802,976
Program services	33,531,300	2,537,942	22,540,100	1,310,337
Correctional industry	3,204,300	152,239	3,204,300	152,239
Contract facilities	8,988,100	7,734,751		
Total	$245,502,800	$26,432,797	$177,191,900	$10,142,412

	NONPERSONAL SERVICE		MAINTENANCE UNDISTRIBUTED	
Program	Recommended	Increase (decrease)	Recommended	Increase (decrease)
Administration	$ 2,722,800	$549,225	$ 128,800	$ 128,800
Support services	36,681,700	194,254	2,278,400	2,278,400
Supervision of inmates	1,876,600	(435,950)	4,643,300	4,643,300
Program services	9,076,900	(437,510)	1,914,300	1,665,115
Correctional industry				
Contract facilities			8,988,100	7,734,751
Total	$50,358,000	($150,981)	$17,952,900	$16,450,366

SOURCE: Ms. Ruby Ryles, Deputy Commissioner for Public Relations, New York Department of Correctional Services, Albany, N.Y. Used with permission.
Correctional Services (Albany: New York State Department of Correctional Services, January 1, 1978), p. 119.

effectively with a bureaucracy that not only tends to resist change but increases in size and extends its power apparently as a function of the bureaucracy itself. At the federal government level, Franklin D. Roosevelt introduced "performance budgeting," which was intended to place governmental programs in an hierarchical system of priorities designed to bring the nation out of an economic depression. Lyndon Johnson introduced PPBS, which involved long-range planning for present and future programs. Jimmy Carter introduced zero-base budgeting. This illustrates the budget reform cycle in which political leaders introduce the reform as a means of overcoming the bureaucracy. The bureaucrats are then instructed in how to use it in planning for the future, and, finally, starting from zero in attempting to evaluate the "real worth" of programs.[11]

The budget is divided into categories in various ways; a typical system is as follows:

[11]See Joseph L. Herbert, ed., *Experiences in Zero-Base Budgeting* (Petrocelli, 1977); Joseph S. Wholey, *Zero-Base Budgeting and Program Evaluation* (Lexington, Mass.: Lexington Books D. C. Heath Company, 1978).

Salaries: Funds committed to the payroll for full-time employees.

OPS: Funds for other personal services, namely, funds paid to part-time employees, outside persons on contract, visiting consultants who provide technical assistance, and persons other than full-time employees.

Expenses: Funds for the purchase of expendable supplies, including office stationery, food and clothing for the residents, and other items not on permanent inventory.

CCO: Capital outlay for construction of new buildings and facilities. Frequently, it refers to paint and other supplies necessary for maintenance, although in some systems, maintenance is a part of expenses.

This breakdown is not universal. In some systems, for example, capital outlay refers only to construction of new buildings and facilities.

Salaries account for approximately 65 to 75 percent of the institutional budget. For example, in one federal correctional institution housing six hundred men, salaries were $3,878,750 and all other operating expenses amounted to $1,385,150; in this instance, salaries amounted to 73.8 percent of the operating expenses and equaled the average annual cost of $8,756.50, or $24.00 daily, per resident. This is in line with national expenditures for small institutions in 1978. Of course, expenditures per resident in larger institutions (two thousand to four thousand or more residents) are lower. In any case, the budget procedure is a primary source of control and management.

The New York State Correctional Services budget for 1978–1979 is given in Table 16-2.

ALLOCATIONS AND ALLOTMENTS

The business manager of a prison or correctional institution controls expenditures. Allocations refer to the categories in which the money has been appropriated. Salaries go for salaries. The OPS segment goes for other personal services, such as contract physicians or other employees, consultants coming in for personal services, and personnel other than full-time employees. Expenses go for only those items that are expendable and are not on the inventory, such as paper and other office supplies, food and clothing, and other nonpermanent items. Capital outlay for equipment goes for typewriters, calculators, and office equipment and may go for other equipment throughout the prison or correctional institution, such as kitchen equipment, all of which would be on permanent inventory. Capital outlay for construction goes only for the construction of new buildings and facilities, although it might go for maintenance purposes in some systems of budget and management.

Allotments refer to the time of release of funds. The business manager releases funds in four quarters, beginning July 1 (the beginning of the fiscal year) and on October 1, January 1, and April 1. Some allotments are essentially similar around the year, such as that for food. Other allotments vary from season to season; farms, for example, have heavy expenditures in the spring and fall, relatively heavy expenditures in the summer, and relatively little expenditure in most jurisdictions in the winter. Frequently, middle managers, such as the director of education or farm manager, may request advances on the next quarter. Most business managers are reluctant to make such advances because, if the department head has overspent in one quarter, the advance reduces the funds available for the next quarter. Consequently, it must be a crisis or an emergency before a business manager will release an advance from the next quarter to the present quarter. Some business managers must reconcile the fact that, while they see paint peeling in various parts of the institution, the allocation or allotment for that purpose is gone and that maintenance must wait for the next quarter or the next fiscal year. In summary, the business manager controls the expenditures within a prison or correctional institution.

APPROPRIATED FUNDS

Appropriated funds are those that come from Congress and the legislatures at the federal and state levels, respectively. All these funds, of course, derive from tax revenues. These appropriated funds are delivered to the agency or to the institution in the categories previously mentioned. Appropriated funds must be spent in the category for which they have been appropriated, which is the allocation for specific purposes, such as salaries, construction, or other category.

Most states have a general fund that includes tax revenues over and above the money appropriated by the legislatures. This generally comes from a surplus of tax revenues over expenditures and from unspent money returned to the state by agencies and institutions. From the prison or correctional institution, funds generated by agricultural and industrial production are also returned to the general fund.

INMATE FUNDS AND ACCOUNTS

The private funds of each resident must be accounted. If he or she comes in with $50, it must be deposited and recorded. All incoming funds due each resident, whether brought by family, sent in from outside, or derived from a part of the prison wage system, must be accounted. All expenditures at the inmate store or commissary, by mail order, or other means of expenditure must be recorded and accounted. The bookkeeping and accounting involving relatively small amounts of funds is voluminous.

Prior to 1970, for example, Texas used clerks to post these transactions by hand and to keep inmate accounts up to date. The volume was so great that there was a lag of about six weeks between the time a family would leave $25 for an inmate until the time it was recorded and the inmate could spend it. This resulted in poor morale. In 1970, a computer system was installed at the Huntsville, Texas, facility and has been used for various purposes, including inmate accounting. The time lag for inmate accounting has been reduced to twenty-four hours, one working day. This has improved inmate morale considerably.

Many prisons place inmate funds in a bank to draw interest. This interest goes to the inmate welfare fund. If a resident wants a bank account in his or her own name in a downtown bank, it is permissible, but generally the family or other friend must do the transaction. The work involving a large number of small accounts is simply too prohibitive to do otherwise.

COMMISSARY OR WELFARE FUNDS

Each prison has an inmate store or commissary where inmates can purchase candy, cigarettes, and other items not supplied by the prison. This money goes into the inmate welfare fund and is supposed to be spent for items that the legislature does not appropriate, such as recreation equipment, library books, and extra "goodies" for Christmas dinner.

Some institutions put the money held in the inmate accounts into savings accounts in a local bank, and the interest accrued is put into the welfare fund. This is viewed as a legitimate activity because individual accounts are so small and the paperwork is so great as to make impractical the assigning of interest to each inmate account. Further, an inmate who wants to deposit funds in his or her own name in a downtown bank can usually do it.

Misuse of the welfare fund has been observed in many prisons. Historically, these accounts were not funded by state monies, so they were not audited in many jurisdictions until the 1950s, when better controls were generally applied. In some cases, equipment was bought for the warden or other administrators' houses or other uses from the inmate welfare fund. Sometimes, funds were transferred directly to these people without an audit. For example, this writer was able to review one account in which $500 was listed for "administration" in one month and $72,000 had been deposited in securities with no record as to where the dividends were going. Better auditing and increased control has eliminated many of these misuses. When a prison or correctional institution is being evaluated for effective administration, a review of this account can be most revealing.

FUNDS FROM GRANTS

Additional funds are available to prisons and correctional institutions in the form of grants from some federal agencies, private foundations and, to a lesser extent, contracts with some private companies. Federal funding existed into 1982, but the Reagan administration is closing this source out.

Funds under the Comprehensive Employment Training Act, which was administered by the Department of Labor to provide vocational training to unskilled persons, was available to everyone, including those in prisons and correctional institutions. It was widely used in correctional institutions for younger offenders. Additional support for educational programs, available from the Department of Education, is designated primarily for juvenile institutions and institutions for younger adult offenders.

Various other grants were available from the Law Enforcement Assistance Administration (LEAA) administered through the Department of Justice. Applications for grants were written for almost any type of project, but projects had to be approved by the state planning agency and reviewed by LEAA. Prisons and correctional institutions have received funds from LEAA for various purposes. The National Institute of Corrections functioning within the U.S. Bureau of Prisons also provides training grants and financial assistance to prisons and correctional institutions. The NIC Jail Center at Boulder, Colorado, begun in 1977, serves jails through training, technical assistance, and information services.

Several private foundations have contributed significantly to the correctional effort at various times. The Ford Foundation contributed to the correctional effort in prisons and correctional institutions until the mid-1970s when its attention was diverted to other areas. The Jessie and Clement Stone Foundation in Chicago contributed heavily to self-help and other correctional efforts until the mid-1970s when its attention was diverted to child abuse. It must be noted that a primary reason for private foundations beginning to fund areas other than corrections is that governmental funding, particularly LEAA, had reached a point that the need for private funding was greater elsewhere. The Institute of Corrections of the American Foundation, headquartered in Philadelphia, has maintained its interest in the correctional field. The Sears, Roebuck Foundation continues to fund projects in the juvenile delinquency area. Other smaller foundations fund projects to a lesser extent in the correctional field.

Contracts with private companies have involved research in which the residents of the institution may volunteer for participation in return for compensation. Drug companies have used this approach frequently.

One of the difficulties with federal grants and, to a lesser extent, private foundation funding relates to the extra accounting required. Even if the prison or correctional institution does not receive grants, but its residents receive social security, Veterans Administration benefits, and other federal funds, the entire institution must meet federal guidelines. While a private company may spend over 5 percent of its revenues in accounting and managerial control procedures, the accounting and evaluation for federal funds generally increases this cost by five or six times. Additional personnel must be placed in bookkeeping, auditing, and in clerical positions to meet governmental regulations.

GENERATED FUNDS

Generated funds are those monies earned by farm produce sold to other units of government in the state-use plan, products made by prison industry and sold to other units of government or elsewhere, and any other funds generated by productivity or contracts with the prison. These funds generally go to the general fund of the state.

PROBLEMS IN FISCAL MANAGEMENT

Problems in fiscal management generally involve delays, as mentioned previously. When a cost analysis report remains on the desk of a manager without being processed, it becomes ineffective because it is not used. This inefficiency in the use of money and effort brings no positive results.

Property control is always a problem in fiscal management. While custody is responsible for attempting to keep property from leaving the prison, the business manager has a function in property control through periodic inventories. The inventory is a list of permanent equipment in the prison. This inventory is checked annually or semiannually in most jurisdictions. When property is missing, an attempt is made to determine its whereabouts. A major problem is that property on inventory is too frequently missing and not traceable.

Because of the special need of prisons in terms of security, finding the best times to purchase is sometimes difficult. For example, burning mattresses are a frequent problem in prisons and correctional institutions. Prisons with mattress factories and textile plants have frequent fires started by inmates. They produce large amounts of heat, smoke, and gases. For example, a fire generated by igniting mattresses in June 1977 at the detention center at Saint John, New Brunswick (Canada) resulted in the loss of twenty-one lives caused by a combination of soot inhalation and carbon monoxide poisoning. The mattresses frequently used in prisons and correctional institutions are flame-retardant polyurethane cores covered by removable flame-retardant vinyl or Neoprene-coated nylon. A study of mattresses most resistant to fire found that fire-retardant all-cotton mattresses were best.[12]

COST-EFFECTIVENESS IN CORRECTIONAL INSTITUTIONS

All public policy and programs have as a central question, "Is it worth it?" This is true in the criminal justice system. There is also always the problem as to how much future crime and delinquency is to be prevented. No system is perfect. In fact, obtaining perfect security in a jail, prison, or correctional institution has not yet been achieved. A hypothetical expenditure of $100,000 may, for example, achieve 76 percent effectiveness. Another $100,000 may raise the effectiveness to 90 percent, a rise of only fourteen percentage points over the initial level of security. Another $100,000 may raise it to 93 percent, a rise of only three percentage points. At some point, additional expenditures are not worth the gains. This is a matter of public policy.

Methods of evaluating correctional programs are increasingly becoming a concern in budget requests, legislative appropriations, and grant proposals as to whether the cost of a program is worth it. Recent approaches have been in (1)

---

[12]Michael J. Williams and Hugh J. Campbell, "Flammability of Mattress Materials," *Canadian Journal of Criminology*, Vol. 21, no. 1 (January 1979), pp. 16–21.

cost analysis, (2) cost comparison, and (3) cost benefits.[13] Cost analysis refers to the tracing of the correctional or criminal action or services involved in dealing with specific offenders. Cost comparison compares two or more cost analyses and provides a basis for an evaluative judgment. Cost-benefit comparison estimates the monetary benefit as well as the cost, such as the benefit of reduced recidivism over a period of years compared with the cost of the program that accomplished it. Cost-benefit analysis is open handed, exploratory, and demanding and is most easily applied in conjunction with experimental or experimental research designs where the costs and benefits are calculated for a specific period of time.

To determine whether general revenue sharing funds have really been used for law enforcement and criminal justice to the extent indicated by official Treasury Department statistics, fifty sample jurisdictions were reviewed for 1973 and 1974.[14] The results indicated that officially reported expenditures of shared revenue on law enforcement and criminal justice programs compiled by the Treasury Department's Office of Revenue Sharing were six times greater than the new spending for this purpose out of revenue sharing identified in the Brookings field research in 1973 and four times greater in 1974. The differences were greatest for larger units, those under greatest fiscal pressure, those located in the Northeast, and municipal governments generally. The principal reason for this pattern of variation was the high substitution uses of shared revenue in the Brookings net effect analysis. Many jurisdictions had substituted the revenue sharing funds for programs previously supported by local funds, so the total effectiveness of revenue sharing was significantly reduced.

Purchasing correctional services has proved to be cost effective in many institutions. For example, some institutions are too small to maintain a full-time physician, psychiatrist, or other professional help. The budget in most institutions includes OPS (other personal services) over and beyond the salaries of full-time personnel. In one experiment in Florida, the commerical laundry services for 150-person institutions used one washer and dryer for each 16-person cottage to handle personal clothing and the linens and towels were sent out several times a week.[15] For institutions of 400 persons this included two fully equipped laundromats for the inmates' clothing and with linens and towels sent out. For both institutions, it was found that the commercial services were less expensive than the in-house method.

An evaluation of the Alaska correctional system found the system itself

[13]Stuart Adams, *Evaluative Research in Corrections: A Practical Guide* (Washington, D.C.: U.S. Department of Justice, LEAA, National Institute of Law Enforcement and Criminal Justice, 1975), pp. 74–96.

[14]R. P. Nathan, D. Crippen, and A. Juneau, *Where Have All the Dollars Gone—Implications of General Revenue Sharing for the Law Enforcement Assistance Administration* (Washington, D.C. and Rockville, Md.: Brookings Institution for the National Institute of Law Enforcement and Criminal Justice, 1976), 83 pp.

[15]*Florida Division of Corrections: Comparison of Alternative Laundry Service Costs* (Tallahassee: Florida Division of Corrections, 1973), 8 pp.

not to be cost effective.[16] There was no percentage increase in the number of inmates and only a 2.3 percent increase in probationers and parolees between 1965 and 1973, yet during the same time period, there was a 1.69 percent increase in staff and a budget increase of 2.14 percent. No appreciable increase in service resulted. The construction of the $5.2 million Eagle River correctional facility and continued use of out-of-state prisons were not cost effective. Even if all outside prisoners were returned to Alaska, there would still be at least a 25 percent excess bed capacity for Alaska prisoners. It was recommended that outside contacts should be ended, that increases in personnel should be eliminated, and that no new facilities should be built.

There has been some concern about pharmaceutical firms using inmates to test the effects of new drugs and compounds. On the other hand, the necessity of experimentation and the economic and social condition of prisoners make such experimentation feasible.[17] Inmates are willing to participate in experiments and incur risks at rates in excess of five times the voluntarism exhibited by free persons and at rates of pay below nonprisoners' demand. The savings derived from prisoner experimentation by medical practitioners, social and psychological experts, and pharmaceutical manufacturers runs into millions of dollars annually, but this accrues completely to the experimenters. Areas for future research in this field suggest including an examination of the opportunity costs associated with different allocations of this subsidy now used entirely to reduce costs or outlays of the experimenters.

THE AUDIT

The audit is the analysis of the effectiveness of fiscal management made by the branch of state or federal government concerned with management and budget. Federal auditors from GAO review funds acquired by federal agencies and evaluate their expenditures. At the state level, auditors from the auditor general's office in most states and its counterparts in other states review the funds acquired by state agencies and evaluate the effectiveness with which it was spent. The audit provides an independent check on management. If management is becoming lax, it can provide early warning of difficulties and can be used to prevent further mismanagement as well as detection. Very few agencies come through the fiscal year without varying degrees of criticism from the auditor general at the state level or the GAO at the federal level. The following listing shows the directions taken by auditors.[18]

---

[16]Thomas O. Murton, *Alaska Correctional System—A Preliminary Evaluation* (Rockville, Md.: National Criminal Justice Reference Service, 1974), 36 pp.

[17]P. B. Meyers, *Medical Experimentation on Prisoners—Some Economic Considerations* (Washington, D.C.: American Bar Association, 1975), 66 pp.

[18]Theodore R. Lyman, Thomas W. Fletcher, and John A. Gardner, *Prevention, Detection, and Correction of Corruption in Local Government* (Washington, D.C.: Law Enforcement Assistance Administration, November 1978), p. 37.

1. See that audits include financial record keeping and accounting, including conformance with the law in keeping separate funds separate and in making expenditures, compliance with good practice in accounting methods, and compliance with budgeted allocations.

2. Verify that any monies received are being accounted for and looked after properly. Spotchecks are usually made at unannounced times to verify that cash on hand matches records of receipt.

3. Verify that personnel are being paid according to proper pay scales. How do pay scales conform with averages for similar jobs in other government organizations and in private industry?

4. Verify that everyone on the payroll is actually working or is otherwise properly accounted for. Are promotions, transfers, and dismissals properly documented?

5. Check actual time worked with payroll records, and verify (spot check) that work time is being used for public services.

6. Determine that benefits are being used and recorded correctly.

7. Check inventory. Are pieces of equipment where the records say they should be? Where supplies are used, does the amount on hand (of gasoline, or bullets, or copier paper) conform to the inventory records? Is all the office equipment where it should be, including any typewriter, tape recorder, or dictation equipment that may be checked out for use at home?

8. Check computer use. If your computer is being used to play Star Wars, to cast horoscopes, or for other non-work-related uses, then it may be vulnerable to misuse of worse types (computer crime is a growing field).

9. Check the efficiency and effectiveness of units, using measures of input (allocation, staff, equipment, time) and measures of actual performance (not only number of transactions, but how well the transactions are carried out. Are the streets clean? Are complaints dealt with promptly?).

10. Check transactions with other governments or other organizations within the government. Determine if mandated reports are being provided on time, legal restrictions on grants management are being met, complaints are being resolved swiftly.

11. Check "perks." Are official cars, or club memberships, or travel funds, or expense accounts, or other position-related privileges being used properly?

Some organizations perform an internal audit several times a year or on a continuing basis during the fiscal year to control management from within and reduce the risk of criticism by the outside auditor.[19] These internal audits or

---

[19]Victor Z. Brink, *Foundations for Unlimited Horizons* (Altamonte Springs, Fla.: The Institute of Internal Auditors, Inc., 1977), pp. 3–6.

inspections ensure and promote effectiveness and economy and involve almost every policy, operation, and type of material or facility within the department or institution where it is used. The scope of work to be accomplished by internal auditors is as follows:[20]

1. Reviewing and appraising the soundness, adequacy, and application of accounting, financial, and other operating controls and promoting effective control at a reasonable cost.

2. Ascertaining the extent of compliance with established policies, plans, and procedures.

3. Ascertaining the extent to which assets are accounted for and safeguarded from losses of all kinds.

4. Ascertaining the reliability of management data developed within the organization.

5. Appraising the quality of performance in carrying out assigned responsibility.

6. Recommending operating improvements.

Other procedures that can complement the audit are the performance and evaluation review technique (PERT), which is really the same technique used in the critical path method (CPM), and the "net work analysis," which is useful in tracing the development of a single project rather than an overall audit. Sophisticated charts employ a cost per time unit formula to specify the time and cost for each portion of the project. PERT was developed in the 1950s for the U.S. Navy by Booz, Allen and Hamilton, a consulting firm, as a method of assuring the scheduled completion of the first nuclear submarines and the Polaris missiles.[21] It can be used to trace the implementation of a new counseling program, Youth Corrections Act and program, or any other project in the prison, correctional institution, or entire department.

The audit is the most important control of management that has developed in recent years. It has served to reduce the considerable corruption in prisons and correctional institutions that prevailed prior to World War II. The audit is an indispensable tool for effective and efficient financial management.

CONCLUSIONS

As mentioned previously, money is the lifeblood of any organization. Without it, the organization will die. Efficient use of it, however, can produce an efficient organization.

Efficient use of funds by administration and management requires close knowledge of the budget process, internal accounting, and the internal and

---

[20]Robert H. Gebhardt, "Internal Auditing: A Management Tool," *FBI Law Enforcement Bulletin*, Vol. 50, no. 3 (March 1981), pp. 17–18.

[21]Nicholas Henry, *Public Administration and Public Affairs* (Englewood Cliffs, N.J.: Prentice-Hall, Inc., 1975), pp. 137–38.

external audits. Close control of the use of funds within the prison or correctional institution by the business manager is an essential key to the smooth and successful operation of the institution. The budget and fiscal management constitute the most effective tools available to administration to accomplish this.

CHAPTER QUESTIONS

16-1.   What are management functions in an institution?

16-2.   How is the budget prepared and submitted?

16-3.   What are allocations and allotments in the fiscal process?

16-4.   What categories of accounts must the business office record and supervise?

16-5.   What are the problems involved in the accounting of appropriated funds?

16-6.   What are the problems involved in the accounting of inmate funds and accounts?

16-7.   What are the problems involved in the accounting of commissary or welfare funds?

16-8.   What are some primary problems in fiscal management?

16-9.   What is the problem of cost-effectiveness in correctional institutions?

16-10.   What is the value of the audit?

17
PERSONNEL MANAGEMENT

Personnel represent the most important component in the delivery of services to consumers in a prison or correctional institution, namely, the residents or inmates confined there for purposes of correction. As mentioned in Chapter 16, personnel salaries generally constitute 65 to 75 percent of all operating costs and are higher in smaller institutions than in larger ones.

CORRECTIONS PERSONNEL

Personality and social orientation are the most important factors for a successful career in criminology and criminal justice. The ability to withstand provocative behavior from angry people is basic. If one has to punish people, then one cannot counsel or treat them; if one condones their behavior, one cannot change them. The correctional officer has neither to love the offender nor to hate him. Education and training can improve the skills of anybody, but personality and social orientation must be tested and diagnosed to determine the level of effectiveness of such education and training. The wrong individual trained is still the wrong individual.

Race relations in the prison today reflect both prison reform and black nationalism.[1] The collective adaptations to the prison structure by both the staff and the inmates have resulted in decreased power of the staff and in an informal social organization among the inmates. The influence of race upon staff-inmate relations resulted in the riot at Attica in 1971. The disparity in racial composition between inmate populations and staff has stimulated a move to increase minority hiring in corrections.[2] Recruitment of minority group members and ex-inmates as correctional employees and increased development of community treatment and community-based corrections will increase inmates' involvement with their families.[3] A survey of the fifty-two correctional agencies in the United States indicated that forty-four had dropped whatever blanket prohibitions they may have had in hiring of ex-offenders.[4] Of these agencies, thirty-eight employ a total of 280 ex-offenders. More than half of these employees serve as counselors, teachers, and correctional officers—roles that involve extensive interaction with the inmate population. The performance of the ex-offenders was routinely rated as equal or superior to that of nonoffender counterparts, with the respondents generally advocating more widespread employment of ex-offenders in the criminal justice system. Legislative support, administrative efforts, and judicial decisions have promoted new hiring policies that have been basic to new funding by LEAA to correct these deficiencies.

The presence of women in jails as teachers or other roles breaks the monotony of all-male population and security staff.[5] However, while there is nothing anywhere in the literature to suggest that males are inherently superior to females in administrative ability,[6] it is generally agreed that for cultural reasons most males would prefer to be supervised poorly by a male than to be supervised in any way by a female.[7]

RECRUITMENT AND SELECTION

Policies in recruitment and selection of personnel vary widely in the United States. Some jurisdictions have good civil service procedures, whereas others hire almost anyone available. One state, for example, with a prison "65 miles from civilization" has indicated that it will hire any "warm body." A few of the

[1]L. Carroll, *Hacks, Blacks, and Cons—Race Relations in a Maximum Security Prison* (Lexington, Mass.: Lexington Books D. C. Heath Company, 1974), pp. 272.

[2]Daniel L. Skoler and R. Loewenstein, "Minorities in Corrections: Nondiscrimination, Equal Opportunity, and Legal Issues," *Crime and Delinquency*, Vol. 20, no. 4 (1974), pp. 339–46.

[3]Michigan Committee on Corrections, *Michigan Committee on Corrections—Report 1972* (Rockville, Md.: Law Enforcement Assistance Administration, 1972), 95 pp.

[4]R. R. Smith and M. A. Milan, "Ex-Offender Employment Policies—A Survey of American Correctional Agencies," *Criminal Justice and Behavior*, Vol. 1, no. 3 (September 1974), pp. 234–46.

[5]A. M. Scacca, Jr., "Some Observations About Women and Their Role in the Field of Corrections," *American Journal of Correction*, Vol. 34, no. 2 (1972), pp. 10–12.

[6]C. Bernard Scotch, "Sex Status in Social Work: Grist for Women's Liberation," *Social Work*, Vol. 16, no. 3 (July 1971), p. 9.

[7]Carlton E. Munson, "Evaluation of Male and Female Supervisors," *Social Work*, Vol. 24, no. 2 (March 1979), p. 109.

poorer states do not even require that a guard (correctional officer in other states) be able to read and write.

Recruitment refers to the acquisition of applications from persons who want to be on the staff of the prison or correctional institution in all departments and at any level. Many of these applications are prompted by notification and advertisements by civil service commissions that an examination will be held for a specific position. In many other cases, interested persons may initiate the contact by voluntarily approaching the personnel officer or other person at the institution. In addition, there are several agencies that serve as brokers between applicants and the institutions. Two are the Correctional Service Registry of the U.S. Employment Service and the centralized placement service at the Institute of Contemporary Corrections and Behavioral Sciences at Sam Houston State University in Texas. In many instances, particularly in civil service, a large number of applications can be accumulated to fill available positions. In this case, "many are called, but few are chosen."[8] Unfortunately, many correctional systems have to take whoever is available because of their low status on the budget priority system.

Selection refers to the screening of applicants to determine whom the prison or correctional institution wants to hire. Civil service registers generally have a rule of three, in which any of the top three candidates on the register can be selected for the position.

Who is hired depends heavily on the philosophy of the personnel officer, warden, or other individual or committee doing the hiring. The American Correctional Association has a progressive philosophy and includes the following as a preamble to its code of ethics:

> The American Correctional Association expects of its members unfailing honesty, respect for the dignity and individuality of human beings and a commitment to professional and compassionate service.

To implement this philosophy, the prospective candidates would have to be interviewed and judgments arrived at as to their social orientation, attitudes toward people, and general ability to relate to others. On the other hand, sometimes the administrators and managers want people who can maintain an orderly prison with whatever means necessary.[9]

The four main screening devices employed in selecting line correctional officers are (1) oral interviews, (2) background information and investigations, (3) regular use of testing, and (4) medical examinations.[10] Variations include psychological screening and police record checks. Only half the jurisdictions using written tests make regular use of personality tests, and few medical examinations include psychiatric and psychological assessments, which are considered to be very important in determining the fitness and qualification of line officers to work with inmates.

---

[8]Matthew 20:16.

[9]E. Stotland, "Self-esteem and Violence by Guards and State Troopers at Attica," *Criminal Justice and Behavior,* Vol. 3, no. 1 (March 1976), p. 36.

[10]D. Goldstein, *Screening for Emotional and Psychological Fitness in Correctional Officer Hiring* (Washington, D.C.: American Bar Association, 1975), 19 pp.

The concept of job enlargement, providing increased challenge and work responsibilities as a remedy for worker apathy and inefficiency, has been presented frequently.[11] A modified version of the Hackman–Lawler Job Design Inventory at two time periods separated by an interval of fourteen months indicated that the staff of a juvenile institution were participants in an innovative institutional training program that appeared to be helpful in assessing institutional change, both for inmates and for staff, by permitting them to see the broad, overall, objectives of their jobs, rather than the immediate task.

IN-SERVICE TRAINING

In-service training is provided to new correctional officers in most of the better correctional systems. The Federal Prison System has training centers in several institutions in various geographic locations around the country. Several states have correctional academies similar to those developed by police departments where new employees are sent for their initial training. In these sessions, new employees learn the law under which they function, rules of the institution, elementary personality development, methods of counseling, and defensive tactics and use of firearms. Some jurisdictions require continuous in-service training, generally involving a specific minimum number of hours of lectures and instruction in each quarter of the year.

Training of correctional personnel falls in two categories: (1) career generalists who manage the system, set policy, and perform most of the client-related tasks and (2) specialist employees who fulfill roles assigned by the generalists, such as education and casework.[12]

Training programs are frequently called upon to be instruments of institutional change, and administrators typically turn to the treatment personnel in the institution or persons allied with treatment personnel outside the institution to make up these training staffs.[13] Problems inherent in this training-staff model relate to the treatment-custody conflict. A mixed staff for training purposes from treatment and custody would appear to be more acceptable. On the other hand, some jurisdictions have no training at all and simply assign young officers to a senior officer for several days of observation.

PERFORMANCE RATINGS

Performance ratings on each employee are made by their immediate supervisors annually or semiannually in most systems. Frequently, a form is used to assign one of five levels of ability: outstanding, above average, satisfactory or average,

---

[11]N. D. Greppucci and J. T. Saunders, "Job Design Variables as Change Measures in a Correctional Facility," *American Journal of Community Psychology*, Vol. 3, no. 4 (December 1975), pp. 315–25.

[12]Richard A. Myren, "Education for Correctional Careers," *Federal Probation*, Vol. 39, no. 2 (June 1975), pp. 51–58.

[13]B. S. Brown and J. W. Sisson, Jr., "The Training Program as a Correctional Change Agent," *Crime and Delinquency*, Vol. 17, no. 3 (1971), pp. 302–09.

below average, and unsatisfactory. The factors to be checked include knowledge of the job, efficiency, cooperativeness, judgment, ability to get along with others, and other lesser factors. Conditions that encourage employee integrity involve five management functions: (1) environment conducive to effective operation, (2) management control, (3) audit, (4) training, and (5) investigation.[14] The management team provides central coordinating functions that can develop and apply these elements in an integrated fashion.

Conflict-of-interest legislation, which exists in approximately forty states, requires policymaking administrators and public officers to reveal their private interests in all areas in which the institution or agencies may have dealings, including contracting with companies for services and goods in which the official may have part ownership or friendship in one of the competing enterprises; real estate; or any other types of goods and services in which the official has an interest. These conflict-of-interest laws tend to reduce corruption. A specified number of unsatisfactory ratings for two successive rating periods may be cause for dismissal.

Unfortunately, several less progressive systems of prisons and correctional institutions exist that do not have performance ratings. In these systems, poor performances can be tolerated over a period of years. On the other hand, an individual can be dismissed at the will of the supervisor or the warden regardless of his or her performance.

There has really been no completely satisfactory approach to rating performance because personalities differ and job requirements differ. Many persons, for example, may be "average" in the majority of categories on a rating performance form but be very effective in working with the residents. Conversely, many persons who might be judged "outstanding" in the ratings may not work well with residents. Some systems have gone to open-end narrative ratings in which a supervisor may write or dictate his opinions of the performance of people, which may be one of the better approaches to performance ratings, but it bears the risk of leading to a type of "standardization" of reporting. Unfortunately, personality conflicts or friendships between the rater and the person being rated may enter into the performance rating. This is one of the problems most complained about in the military where officers are rated by their superiors. In any case, some type of performance rating tends to be better than no performance rating at all.

PROMOTIONS

Promotions are made after examination in states with strong civil service systems and in the Federal Prison System. Persons eligible for the higher job to be filled take the examination, which may be written or "unassembled," and frequently an oral interview. In an "assembled" examination, the candidates are assembled and are asked to write an examination under supervision. In an "unassembled" examination, the candidates may furnish an application of their experience and

[14]Theodore R. Lyman, Thomas W. Fletcher, and John A. Gardiener, *Prevention, Detection, and Correction of Corruption of Local Government* (Washington, D.C.: Law Enforcement Assistance Administration, November 1978), p. 42.

background, high school or college transcripts, and other information. Oral interviews become more important as the responsibility of the job increases. For example, a correctional officer may have no oral interview, whereas promotion to warden may require half the examination to be an oral interview. The purpose of this is to determine how the candidates, particularly those in supervisory, managerial, or administrative positions, deal with others on a face-to-face basis. In states with strong unions, the pressure of the union may influence the promotion procedure. For example, the only persons eligible to be promoted to warden in New York State are those who have come up through the custodial ranks and have correctional officer experience, the result of an agreement between the union and civil service commission in the 1950s. When the register is completed, the administrator may select the person to be promoted from the top three persons on the list.

In other systems, where the civil service procedures are not strong or are absent, promotions and demotions may be made at the behest of the administrator. For example, the Illinois state prison at Stateville was dominated personally by Warden Joseph Regan between 1936 and 1961, when he became director of the entire system, and this domination continued until his retirement in 1965. For that entire thirty years, hirings and promotions had to have his approval.

Promotions are an important part of implementing the policies of administrators. While selecting the "right men" by an administrator can be done to some extent in the rule-of-three civil service procedure, it can be done without restraint when promotions, demotions, and dismissals are done or must be approved by the administrator.

PAYROLLS

The preparation of a payroll is fairly standard in all jurisdictions. In most systems, employees are paid on a biweekly basis, although some are paid on a monthly basis. Today, most payrolls are computerized. The information is sent by the prison or correctional institution to the central office of the department of corrections or other designation of that office in the state capital. In turn, the department's payroll is sent to the comptroller's office, where the computerized information is stored and the checks are completed by the computer on the basis of information furnished by each department.

At the institution, central office, or both, depending upon the system, the procedures are fairly standard. The application form of a person newly hired is sent to the payroll office where information is taken for computer storage. A form, variously called report of payroll action or payroll action form, is filled out denoting the date of actual hiring and is sent to the comptroller's office. On this form is the appropriation number from which the individual will be paid, the job classification title, the dates, biweekly or monthly, of salary, social security number, employee number if it is different from the social security number, and other pertinent permanent information. A deduction form includes information on retirement code and deductions, withholding tax for the Internal Revenue Service, social security deductions or FICA, health insurance deductions, any credit union deductions, any union dues deducted, payroll deductions for U.S. savings bonds, and any of several other types of deductions that might be available in any particular system. In case of any changes in salary, promotions, deductions, sick leaves, retirements, or dismissals, a change order or payroll action form is submitted to the comptroller's office. In the case of retirement, the day of retirement and the pay is generally submitted to the comptroller's office by the state retirement system.

Briefly, the procedure in payroll is as follows, with "A" as procedure and "B" as changes:

A. Payroll
    1. Application comes to payroll
    2. RPA (report of payroll action):hiring
    3. Appropriation number from which paid
    4. Classification title
    5. Salary
    6. Temporary employees (OPS)
    7. Change order to comptroller's office
    8. Computer data: social security, classification code, amount of pay, retirement code, state insurance, etc.
    9. Change order for any changes in salary, promotions, dismissals, etc., sick leave.
    10. Retirement: date and pay
B. Changes
    1. Payroll action report
    2. Deductions report
    3. Other reports

PROBLEMS IN PERSONNEL MANAGEMENT

The problems in personnel management are legion. Many wardens and superintendents of prisons and correctional institutions have indicated that, if they could gain control of their personnel and keep them in order, they would have no difficulty with the inmates. The majority of contraband coming into prisons, for example, is brought in not by inmates or visitors of inmates but by correctional officers and other staff who are compensated for it. There have been many examples of correctional personnel caught in this practice and dismissed. Further, many cases have been prosecuted and those found guilty have served up to a year in the prison system.

Public relations becomes an important factor in personnel management. Dissatisfied employees, for example, can "expose" undesirable activities in the institution much to the embarrassment of the administration of the institution. In almost every system, these people have been dismissed or "blackballed." Often, the individual involved does not even know what has happened, and the administration will not tell him or her for fear of increasing the embarrassment or becoming vulnerable to charges by the union, appeal hearings before the civil service commission, or even litigation.

While union activity reduces the administrator's latitude in operating the institution, many personnel problems can be handled through the union. An administrator who realizes that the union is "here to stay" can use the union by openly discussing personnel problems with the leadership and obtaining suggestions for action or letting the union handle it. A good relationship between the administrator and the union can resolve many personnel problems.

EMPLOYEE ASSISTANCE PROGRAMS

Benefits for correctional staff are few and far between when compared with the need for these benefits generated by the stress of confrontation and other factors in the correctional field. At least thirty-one programs in the United States and Canada are operating employee assistance programs (EAPs). These programs offer counseling and other assistance in resolving drug, alcohol, domestic problems and other services to employees in correctional programs.[15] In Canada, the Province of Ontario was the first to offer such a program in 1967, with New Jersey offering the first program in the United States in 1970. EAPs are offered by state councils, federally funded in part or whole, but most are funded by the individual states. Because of the stress experienced in the criminal justice system, EAPs become important for the retention of experienced correctional personnel.

RETIREMENTS

Retirement systems vary very widely. Most state and federal retirement programs are well organized, though some states lack a retirement system of their own and rely solely on social security payments. The length of service required also varies, generally from ten years to twenty-five years. As in the military, some have an "early retirement" at twenty years and provide additional benefits for those in for thirty years of service.

Retirement systems in the Federal Prison System contain cost-of-living increments through the U.S. Civil Service Commission. Other systems have unusual laws, as in the State of Mississippi, which indicates that, when the retirement fund is below that required for a full payment of retirement, the reductions will be pro-rated for the checks of all persons retired. Many systems with better early retirement benefits experience a relatively high early retirement rate, and many retirees go on to a second career, becoming wardens or directors of corrections in various state systems or doing extensive consultation work.

A secure and beneficial retirement program is an attractive recruiting device. It tends to provide the sysem with a better selection of applicants from which to hire new employees.

[15]"Employee Assistance Programs," *Corrections Compendium*, Vol. 5, no. 11 (May 1981), p. 1.

Institutions or organizations that receive federal funds or service clients who receive federal funds come under provisions of the 1964 Civil Rights Act enforced by the Equal Employment Opportunity Commission (EEOC). This includes most public institutions, since most of these entities have veterans who receive various forms of compensation from federal funds and many also receive grants from the Law Enforcement Assistance Administration (LEAA); Department of Labor programs, such as the Comprehensive Employment Training Act (CETA); and various programs of the Department of Health, Education, and Welfare. The Office of Federal Contract Compliance has paid some special attention to policies that exclude persons with arrest records from employment. This brings in the racial issue, because arrest records are disproportionately more frequent among blacks than among whites.

There are many factors that must be taken into consideration by the courts, administrative agencies, and arbiters to determine whether an employer has acted properly in the employment of persons with arrest and conviction records.[16] The employer is responsible for the wrongdoing of an employee that occurs within the scope of his or her employment, regardless of past record. The employer may also be held responsible for wrongdoing outside the scope of employment if the employer knowingly hires someone with a past record of impropriety, violence, and disorder. Some courts have ruled that an employer must investigate the past record of the employee if his or her employment would give the individual access to houses and apartments of others, and the employer must provide necessary supervision to prevent wrongdoing. The employer cannot automatically reject minority group job applicants just because of the arrest and conviction record. There is variation in the legality of an employer's right to inquire about an applicant's arrest record that did not result in convictions, and the Equal Employment Opportunity Commission has ruled that inquiry about arrests is unlawful when applied to members of minority groups unless the necessity for the inquiry can be proved. Inquiries about convictions are legal if there is a relationship to the job to be done, but the inquiries must be accompanied by a statement that the revealed information will not necessarily bar employment and that age and time of the offense, seriousness and nature of the violation, and rehabilitation will be taken into account. An employer's right to discharge an employee who has falsified his or her application form is dependent upon the pertinence of the falsified information to the performance of the job.

The Women's Bureau of the U.S. Department of Labor was created by Congress in 1920 to formulate policy programs and help women to realize their employment goals. In 1978, an interagency committee was established between the Women's Bureau and the U.S. Bureau of Prisons. A central focus of this committee was to expand opportunities for women offenders in apprenticeships and other nontraditional jobs. By 1980, there were twenty women inmates as apprentices in twelve different trades, mostly nontraditional at the federal cor-

[16]*Employing the Ex-Offender: Some Legal Considerations* (Washington, D.C.: American Bar Association, Clearinghouse on Offender Employment Restrictions, November 1976), pp. 11–12.

rectional institution for women at Alderson, West Virginia. The Targeted Jobs Tax Credit (TJTC) program also gives employers tax breaks when they hire these women.[17] A need has been seen to hire more women in the correctional field. Women officers say that, to win promotions, they must work in the housing units of men's institutions.[18] Male inmates say that it violates their privacy. Corrections administrators in several states have been caught up in a tangle of lawsuits filed by women guards and male prisoners, or both.[19] Body frisks and other intimacies have been allowed by the courts. Title VII of the Civil Rights Act of 1964 forbids sex discrimination and, in addition, focuses on sexual harassment of females on the job. Sexual harassment on the job is considered to be sexual discrimination. The guidelines on sex discrimination are included in the Civil Rights Act of 1964 (Title 29, Labor; Chapter XIV, Part 1604).[20]

An enlarged job has been defined operationally as a set of tasks exhibiting (1) skill variety, (2) autonomy, (3) task identity, and (4) feedback. Research in a division of corrections in a midwestern state with 104 participants in a training program responded to a questionnaire that included these characteristics.[21] The results indicated that the perception of the participants to job enlargement depended upon their own levels of motivation, involvement, and satisfaction. Job enlargement was recommended to bring the institution into conformity with environmental reality and to overcome the therapy-custody dichotomy.

In 1969, women in the correctional work force represented 12 percent of the total, whereas in 1978, they constituted 23 percent, most being employed in juvenile work and probation and parole. Equal Employment Opportunity Commission activity and the affirmative action movement have been the primary reasons for increased use of women in corrections. By 1978, many states had hired females as correctional officers in male facilities. Table 17-1 indicates the states that had more than 10 percent women officers in male correctional institutions.

A real problem in using women as correctional officers is inmate privacy.[22] When male officers were assigned to the Bedford Hills (New York) Correctional facility for women in 1978, the female inmates objected so strenuously that the union took over assignment of officers to that facility, which effectively bypassed the nondiscrimination laws of New York. By 1979, the movement to hire women in corrections had taken on national proportions. The prohibition of women correctional officers from contact positions within the prison and from performing all the duties of their job would be discriminatory

[17]Alexis Herman, "Women's Work for Female Offenders," *Corrections Today*, Vol. 42, no. 5 (September–October 1980), pp. 54–55.

[18]Joan Rotter, "Should Women Guards Work in Prisons for Men?" *Corrections Magazine*, Vol. 6, no. 5 (October 1980), pp. 30–35.

[19]Ibid., p. 35.

[20]Dail Ann Neugarten and Jay M. Shafritz, eds., *Sexuality in Organizations: Romantic and Coercive Behaviors at Work* (Oak Park, Ill.: Moore Publishing Co., 1980).

[21]A. P. Brief, J. Munro, and R. J. Aldag, "Correctional Employees' Reactions to Job Characteristics—A Data-Based Argument for Job Enlargement," *Journal of Criminal Justice*, Vol. 4, no. 3 (Fall 1976), pp. 223–30.

[22]Thomas G. Toombs, "Female Officers in Male Institutions—Inmates' Right to Privacy vs. Women's Right to Work," *Proceedings of the One Hundred and Ninth Annual Congress of Correction* (College Park, Md.: American Correctional Association, 1980), p. 266.

Table 17-1 Distribution of Male Versus Female Officers in State Correctional Facilities, 1979

STATE	TOTAL OFFICERS IN MALE FACILITIES	NUMBER OF WOMEN OFFICERS	PERCENTAGE OF WOMEN OFFICERS
Louisiana	1,185	216	18.23%
Wyoming	81	13	16.05
Kentucky	503	80	15.90
Oklahoma	843	117	13.88
South Carolina	883	115	13.02
Kansas	485	61	12.58
Nevada	326	41	12.58
Michigan	1,576	197	12.50
Virginia	2,682	287	10.70

[1]Where women constitute more than 10% of the work force.

Joann B. Morton, "Women in Correctional Employment: Where Are They Now and Where Are They Headed?" *Proceedings of the One Hundred and Ninth Annual Congress of Correction* (College Park, Md.: American Correctional Association, 1980), p. 260.

because it would deny them the opportunity to advance in their chosen profession. In his dissent in such a case involving the State of Alabama, Justice Thurgood Marshall in *Dothard* v. *Rawlinson* held that, if women guards behave professionally at all times, they will receive reciprocal respect from inmates who should see that their privacy is being invaded no more than as if they were being examined by a woman doctor.

The self-perceived variables among thirty-two prison guards at the Indiana state prison in Michigan City indicated that their roles consisted of integration into the correctional system, personal interest and concern for their relation to the inmates, and social distance as limited communication and interaction, but not intimate association with the inmates.[23] Such expectations might delimit role performance and thus increase or decrease role conflict with the institution.

An exploratory survey of the helping potential of a prison staff found that some prison guards are able to play combined custodial and helping roles but that their effectiveness is limited because they have little professional support.[24] Housing black guards in three New York maximum security prisons during 1975 and 1976, all among the most experienced personnel, showed wide disparity in their perceptions of crisis in their units. For example, one officer reported that all the men in his unit experienced personal crisis over the preceding ten months, whereas another on the same shift reported an incidence of 10 percent. Personnel who tried to help reported a variety of responses ranging from simple inquiry to informal counseling, referral, and follow-up, while other personnel reported no interest in such involvement, usually claiming that it is "not my job." If prisons are to develop therapeutic impact or at least reduce levels of stress, efforts to help correctional personnel become more responsive to inmate needs become important.

[23]P. O. Peretti and M. Hooker, "Social Role Self-perceptions of State Prison Guards," *Criminal Justice and Behavior,* Vol. 3, no. 2 (June 1976), pp. 187–96.

[24]R. Johnson, "Ameliorating Prison Stress—Some Helping Roles for Custodial Personnel," *International Journal of Criminology and Penology,* Vol. 5, no. 3 (August 1977), pp. 263–73.

DISMISSALS

Dismissals can be made for a variety of reasons. Dismissals for ineffective performance frequently result from successive unsatisfactory performance ratings. Many dismissals stem from wrongdoing on the part of the employee. Many correctional officers and other staff members, for example, have brought in liquor, drugs, and other contraband for distribution to the prisoners. Others have misused their positions in the prison in various ways, such as checking an inmate's file of the record office and letting the inmate go through it, sometimes making changes, for which the inmate or his family compensates the employee. Many employees steal or convert state property to their own use, much of which results in dismissal, while others get away with it for years, depending upon the rigidity of control in the system.

Many dismissals are the result of personality conflicts or other related problems. For example, some administrators have purposefully and without real justification rated certain employees unsatisfactory for two successive periods for the purpose of dismissal. In highly political systems, many staffs are replaced by an incoming governor and the new group of people assisting him or her.

In cases of dismissals resulting from homosexuality or other activities that would embarrass the administration, the official reasons for dismissal are frequently not the real ones.[25] Conflicts arising between custodial and treatment personnel are not the result of mutually exclusive goals but, rather, the result of management's failure to deal adequately with the role conflict and interest group formation.[26] Interest group conflict can be overcome by management creating a suitable end goal that will encompass the work of all employees. Officers differ considerably from managers in policy and social climate, which suggests that much correctional officer training is ineffective because it is antagonistic to the policy and values of the administration.[27] Small-group dynamics techniques were suggested for changing officers' subculture values and their perceptions of the way in which they are managed.

Staff members are caught between two subcultures, that of the administration and that of the inmates. Attitudes and perceptions of administrative personnel, staff personnel, and inmates toward "restricted" inmates judged to be harmful to themselves and others, and labeled so, were regarded so by some staff and not by others. The necessity for staff to reconcile these apparently irreconcilable attitudes produced a set of values unique to the staff, containing meanings related to both the inmate and the administrative cultures, yet beyond the valuation or understanding of either.[28]

Organizational and occupational rights for the correctional officer have

[25]Brief et al., "Correctional Employees Reaction to Job Characteristics," pp. 223–30.

[26]P. Maxim, "Treatment-Custody, Staff Conflicts in Correctional Institutions: A Re-analysis," *Canadian Journal of Criminology and Corrections,* Vol. 18, no. 4 (1976), pp. 379–85.

[27]D. Duffee, "The Correction Officer Sub-culture and Organizational Change," *Journal of Research in Crime and Delinquency,* Vol. 11, no. 2 (1974), pp. 155–72.

[28]A. D. Cheatwood, "The Staff in Correctional Settings: An Empirical Investigation of Frying Pans and Fires," *Journal of Research in Crime and Delinquency,* Vol. 11, no. 2 (1974), pp. 173–79.

been proposed and include (1) input into decision making and information gathering, (2) defined roles and loyalties, (3) education and training relevant to job activities and career development, (4) differential assignments related to skills and abilities, (5) informal behavioral science consultation on managing people, and (6) development of professionalism.[29]

Institutionalization can also affect prison officers who become highly dependent upon each other.[30] To counteract this process, it is necessary to introduce new treatment methods and philosophies to stimulate personal qualities of individualism. This can be accomplished by frequent changes of job and locale and meetings with those in other branches of the field.

Officers have the right to be protected from the daily threat of injury, hostage-taking, and possible death. The officer needs the support of the public because the public support helps to increase the officer's effectiveness and diminish the chances of danger inherent in the job.[31] Financial support is needed from the public to provide (1) levels of security suited to the needs of the inmate in terms of the program, security, and individual's capability to adapt to these levels of custody; (2) meaningful programs for the inmate in terms of outside community needs and job opportunities, as well as academic and vocational training; (3) extensive personnel training programs for old and new officers.

The captive world of the professional correctional worker exists side by side with the captive world of the inmates.[32] Correctional personnel are locked into a tradition of roles, attitudes, expectations, and attitudes that are no longer functional. The basic problem appears to be in part the reliance on a perception of individual responsibility that underlies the division of labor, roles, and education for professionals in corrections. The cult of individualism is no longer a sound one if the emphasis is exclusive, because correctional personnel need a broader perspective—one that includes social responsibility. Attention must be drawn to the need to change laws, policies, values, and social institutions if viable programs are to be developed for the control and prevention of crime.

EMPLOYEE MISCONDUCT

Experience has indicated that corruption in prisons and correctional institutions may be just as widespread as it is in cities, industries, the business communities, and even legislatures and the Congress of the United States, where the Ethics Committee seem always to be busy. In local corruption, for example, incidents have been reported in 103 cities in all states but North Dakota, South Dakota, and Hawaii.[33] Corruption can appear almost anywhere, and no area of the

---

[29]Stanley L. Brodsky, "A Bill of Rights for the Correctional Officer," *Federal Probation*, Vol. 38, no. 2 (1973), pp. 38–40.

[30]N. G. Silk, "Institutionalization," *Prison Service Journal*, Vol. 5 (1972), p. 16.

[31]Russell G. Oswald, "Rights of Correctional Personnel," *American Journal of Correction*, Vol. 34, no. 6 (1972), pp. 18–20.

[32]Charles S. Prigmore and John C. Watkins, Jr., "Correctional Manpower: Are We 'The Society of Captives'?" *Federal Probation*, Vol. 36, no. 4 (1972), pp. 12–19.

[33]Lyman et al., *Prevention, Detection, and Correction of Corruption in Local Government*, p. 1.

country, type of government, or institution is immune. Corruption involves converting state property to one's own use, outright theft of state property, introducing contraband into the institution for a fee or other consideration, kickbacks on contracts awarded to private firms, nepotism, bribes to inspectors and auditors who overlook some items, use of state automobiles for personal transportation, sending hams or other commodities from the prison commissaries to friends and relatives for Christmas, accepting gifts from inmates, and any of a series of similar incidents.[34] *The New York Times* has estimated that bribes relating to the construction industry alone reach $25 million a year in New York City.[35]

Corruption has three main components that are controllable and one that is not. The three controllable ones are opportunity, incentive, and risk. The uncontrollable one is personal honesty. Many in public service have had the opportunity, incentive, and little risk of being caught. It is apparent that most have not succumbed to corruption, but many have engaged in corruption and have profited personally at the expense of the institution or agency.

Employee misconduct has been widespread in corrections. In 1979, a major scandal in Delaware led to the arrest of the commissioner of corrections and twenty-two others in the midst of an investigation of corruption there.[36] Correctional employees were assisting in inmate escapes, were smuggling drugs and money, and were homosexually raping inmates. Major episodes of serious staff misconduct have occurred in Arkansas, Hawaii, Illinois, New York, and Tennessee, among others.[37] Three models of corruption appear to be (1) the public-office-centered definition, which explains corruption as essentially a violation by an officeholder for personal gain; (2) the market-centered definition of corruption, in which a corrupt civil servant regards his or her office as a business, the income of which he or she seeks to maximize; and (3) the public-interest-centered definition, which regards corruption as the advantage of special interest over common interest.[38]

The majority of staff involved in corruption are correctional officers.[39] Inmates are involved in slightly over half the complaints. Very few involve civilian employees. The commission of offenses were relatively unorganized. The disposition of these cases is seldom prosecution, but dismissal. Many inmates considered themselves as victims.[40] Malfeasance included trafficking, theft, embezzlement, and sexual assault; misfeasance included internal payoffs, influence peddling, acceptance of gratuities, harassment and extortion, and mismanagement; nonfeasance included cover-ups and failure to enforce regulations.[41]

[34]Ibid., p. 3.

[35]Ibid., p. 3.

[36]Bernard Jerome McCarthy, Jr., "An Exploratory Study of Corruption in Corrections," unpublished doctoral dissertation, School of Criminology, Florida State University, Tallahassee, 1981, p. 1.

[37]Ibid., p. 3.

[38]Ibid., pp. 6–7.

[39]Ibid., p. 241.

[40]Ibid., p. 242.

[41]Ibid., p. 247.

Most jurisdictions have internal affairs units, as do police departments in medium-sized and large cities, to control employee misconduct. The Federal Prison System has an Office of Professional Responsibility to supervise ethics, misconduct, and deviant behavior of personnel.

CONCLUSIONS

Many states have indemnification laws to improve and clarify employees' rights. These laws are helpful when employees are sued in state or federal court for acts or omissions that occurred while acting within the scope of employment. While the attorney general's office provides defenses for state agencies and employees, there are times when a conflict of interest or other problem prevents such defenses. Indemnification laws clear this problem. There have been a few occasions, however, when the suit was brought for activities outside the "scope of employment" and the employee had to use his or her own funds for defense and pay damages when found guilty.

The Public Safety Officers' Benefits Act of 1976, administered by the Law Enforcement Assistance Administration, provides $50,000 payment to families of public safety officers killed in the line of duty.[42] Coverage is for officers authorized to be involved in crime and delinquency control or reduction or the enforcement of criminal laws. While regulations refer specifically to correctional, probation, and parole officers in the field of corrections, coverage could be extended to headquarter's personnel and volunteers, provided that they have the necessary authorization.

Title VII of the Civil Rights Act of 1964 was designed to eliminate discrimination in employment practices based on race, color, religion, sex, or national origin.[43] The Equal Employment Opportunity Commission was created by Congress to interpret and administer the provisions of Title VII. Subsequent decisions by the commission and by the courts have generally placed the burden of proof concerning job relatedness to variations under Title VII on the employer.[44]

Personnel is the most important factor in any operation dealing with people. While finances and budgets are basic to any operation, personnel implement the operation, and their performance determines the effectiveness of any operation, including the prison or correctional institution. Consequently, recruitment and selection, in-service training, performance ratings, and all personnel policies are vital to the effectiveness of the prison or correctional institution as well as to any organization dealing with people. A competent personnel officer and personnel office are vital to the administration and management of prisons and correctional institutions.

[42]Richard Crane, "Public Safety Officers' Benefits Act Is Important to Corrections Personnel," *American Journal of Correction*, Vol. 39, no. 3 (May–June 1977), pp. 8, 34.

[43]42 U.S.C. Sec. 2000e.17, Supp. 1, 1972, amending 42 U.S.C. Secs. 2000e–2000e.17, 1970.

[44]Daniel L. Schofield, "Title VII of the Civil Rights Act of 1964: An Overview of Supreme Court Litigation, Part I," *FBI Law Enforcement Bulletin*, Vol. 48, no. 4 (April 1979), pp. 26–31.

CHAPTER QUESTIONS

17-1. What are the most important factors for a successful career in the field of criminal justice?
17-2. Why are recruitment and selection important in hiring employees for correctional institutions?
17-3. What factors are generally reviewed when making performance ratings on employees?
17-4. What are some of the problems in personnel management that appear in prisons and correctional institutions?
17-5. What are some of the problems in handling equal opportunity employment in correctional institutions?
17-6. Why must dismissals be handled carefully and after thorough investigation?
17-7. Why is job enlargement desirable in a correctional institution?
17-8. What would be a set of organizational and occupational rights for the correctional officer?
17-9. What are the controllable and uncontrollable components in corruption?
17-10. What is the function of an internal affairs unit?

18

THE FUTURE
OF CORRECTIONAL
INSTITUTIONS

The future of institutions has been debated for centuries, is debated today, and will continue to be debated for years to come. The problem is that it is difficult to decide how best to handle the illnesses, the poverty, the mental health problems, the criminal behavioral deviations, and the many other problems that demand the attention of an organized society. The primary issues are how these social problems can be resolved (1) most effectively, (2) at least cost, and (3) with the least damage.

CURRENT DEBATES REGARDING INSTITUTIONS

The first serious debates about correctional institutions occurred between proponents of the Pennsylvania system of solitary confinement and meditation and advocates of the Auburn system of congregate labor, silence, and harsh discipline. Because the Auburn system was cheaper, it prevailed in America. In Europe and Latin America, however, the Pennsylvania system was favored. Over the entrance to the Puerto Rico state penitentiary at Rio Piedras, just outside San Juan, for example, appears the phrase, "Odio al Crimen Pero Compadezco al Delincuente," which means, essentially, "Abhor the Crime, but Have Compassion for the Criminal." While there are wide variations in the effectiveness of the application, these philosophies tend to be followed in these various countries.

The debates about standards for the physical plant and for the program continue today. These debates manifest themselves in the literature and in the numerous court actions brought by inmates under constitutional and civil rights acts specifications. The combination of underfunding, understaffing, overcrowding, and court litigation have contributed to the difficulties in administering prisons and correctional institutions, as administrators and practitioners alike are operating in a Catch-22 environment.[1]

Various solutions have been proposed by persons interested in the field. Kropotkin called for the abolition of prisons as long ago as 1887. Wilson has questioned the need for prisons.[2] Menninger has indicated that a prison is inhumane and ineffective and has called for other methods to approach the problem of crime.[3]

There is a strong movement toward no new prison construction. The National Council on Crime and Delinquency (Hackensack, New Jersey) instituted a moratorium on building prisons in 1972 and has pursued this goal vigorously. Many public debates have occurred between people who want to stop building prisons and those who want to build more prisons to house, without overcrowding, the large numbers of offenders the courts are sending to the system. A directory is available of six hundred organizations that want to reform the prisons, many of which want to abolish them completely.[4]

The prison began as a humane gesture, but as the Quakers, who began the penitentiary movement in 1789 and implemented it in 1790, wrote nearly two centuries later,

> The horror that is the American prison system grew out of an 18th century reform by the Pennsylvania Quakers and others against the cruelty and futility of capital and corporal punishment. This 200-year-old experiment has failed. They now want to correct the "error" they made in 1787–1790.[5]

More balanced views are also available in the literature. Gordon Hawkins contends that small, homogeneous countries such as Sweden and Switzerland

---

[1]Joseph Heller, *Catch-22* (New York: Simon & Schuster, Inc., 1961). This is a comic novel about members of the 256th bomber squadron positioned on a tiny island in the Mediterranean during World War II. Members could be discharged from duty by reason of insanity, but when someone came out of combat and pleaded insanity, it was considered to be the sane thing to do, so nobody was discharged.

[2]Joseph Wilson, *Are Prisons Necessary?* (Philadelphia: Dorrance Press, 1950).

[3]Carl Menninger, *The Crime of Punishment* (New York: The Viking Press, Inc., 1968).

[4]Mary Lee Bundy and Kenneth R. Harmon, eds., *The National Prison Directory: Organizational Profiles of Prison Reform Groups in the United States*, base volume (College Park, Md.: Urban Information Interpreters, April 1975). Also, see Mary Lee Bundy and Rebecca Glenn Whaley, eds., *The National Prison Directory: Organizational Profiles of Prison Reform Groups in the United States*, Supplement 1 (College Park, Md.: Urban Information Interpreters, 1976).

[5]American Friends Service Committee, *Struggle for Justice* (New York: Hill & Wang, 1971), p. v.

could eliminate prisons in favor of community-based alternatives, but large, heterogeneous countries such as the United States, which need prisons for a few dangerous people, are now overusing them.[6] Some persons should be retained in prison, but there are other ways of providing cheaper and more effective protection of society without disrupting family life and causing further suffering on the part of innocent dependents.[7] Morris has subsequently indicated that prisons are needed but that they should hold only the most dangerous offenders for the public safety and not exceed a hundred persons in population.[8]

On the other hand, some would like to lock up everybody who may be dangerous to society. One writer has gone so far as to suggest that, even when these persons have completed their sentences, they should be shipped to a distant island if they are still dangerous.[9] Another writer who wants many people locked up says that the offenders escape the full impact of official punishment in the present system of corrections.[10] Wilson wants to lock up all criminals to make the streets safe.[11]

Writers from the legal viewpoint want flat sentencing without parole so that all offenders can be treated equally before the law. Morris and Jacobs contend that the rehabilitative ideal in prisons, like the early Quaker ideal of solitary confinement and meditation, has proved to be unworkable.[12] The use of indeterminate sentencing, coerced cures, and broad administrative discretion in the treatment of prisoners are examples of unjust procedures brought about by the rehabilitative ideal. Humanitarian reform that includes better facilities, more prison activities, prison furloughs, and community-based corrections are needed in the criminal justice system.

The debate continues. Viewpoints range from the abolition of all prisons to building more prisons and arresting more dangerous persons. The viewpoint taken by the majority of correctional administrators is that prisons are overused and that many people in prison today do not need to be there.

CONCLUSIONS

Since the seventeenth century, there has been a movement to make the treatment of criminal offenders more humane. Blackstone (1723–1780) had cataloged among permissible punishments hanging, being drawn or dragged to the place of execution, emboweling alive, beheading, quartering, public dissection, dismemberment by cutting off the hands or ears, and mutilation by slitting

[6]Gordon Hawkins, *The Prison: Policy and Practice* (Chicago: University of Chicago Press, 1976).

[7]Norval Morris and Gordon Hawkins, *The Honest Politicians' Guide to Crime Control* (Chicago: University of Chicago Press, 1970), p. 144.

[8]Norval Morris, *The Future of Imprisonment* (Chicago: University of Chicago Press, 1974).

[9]Ernest van den Haag, *Punishing Criminals: A Very Old and Painful Question* (New York: Basic Books, Inc., 1975).

[10]Andrew von Hirsch, *Doing Justice* (New York: Hill & Wang, 1976), p. 129.

[11]James Q. Wilson, *Thinking About Crime* (New York: Basic Books, Inc., 1975).

[12]Norval Morris and James B. Jacobs, *Proposals for Prison Reform* (New York: Public Affairs Committee, Inc., 1974), 28 pp.

the nostrils or branding the hand or cheek.[13] Imprisonment became a humane replacement for these "treatments." George Bernard Shaw said in the twentieth century, after a century and a half of prisons, that imprisonment is the most cruel of all punishments and those who inflict it without ever experiencing it cannot believe it to be cruel.[14] Today, there are many people calling for the elimination or reduction of imprisonment.

Political, economic, and social concerns need to be addressed before any public policy is changed. The political concern in criminal justice refers to fear of crime and calls for stiffer sentences. "Law-and-order" slogans have been offered by many politicians; others have used the "soft-on-crime" approach. The economic concerns have been the high cost of imprisonment coupled with overcrowding and understaffing. The social damage involves the removal of a man from his family and job, leaving the dependents on welfare. The social damage of locking up women is even greater, because the majority of women in prison are the sole support of dependent children who have to be cared for in other ways. Some writers have predicted that, when the economic cost and the social damages are perceived and appreciated, the political leadership will respond.[15] Carl Menninger has said that the overcrowding of mental hospitals in 1948 has been relieved by a similar change of policy and predicts that the overcrowded prisons today will be similarly relieved in the future.[16]

It is obvious and well documented that there is considerable dissatisfaction with traditional correctional systems.[17] On the other hand, the frontiers are gone; there is no place to "transport" prisoners. Nils Christie has suggested that, in this age of electronics, it would be possible to exercise effective control over criminal offenders outside prisons by implanting radio transmitters almost anywhere in the person's body and using radio locaters to monitor the individual's activities.[18]

The institutional setting really militates against any rehabilitation programs and cannot counterbalance the ill effects of the institution itself.[19] Prisons and correctional institutions are apparently overused in America. Nevertheless, prisons and correctional institutions are needed and will remain a permanent component of the criminal justice system. Depending upon the public's fear of crime, these institutions may increase in number. Dangerous people need secure

---

[13]W. Blackstone, *Commentaries on the Laws of England, 1510–11*, 4th ed. (London: T. Cooley & J. Andrews, 1899). Reported in Ira P. Robbins, ed., *Prisoners' Rights Sourcebook*, Vol. 2 (New York: Clark Boardman Company, 1980), p. 126.

[14]George Bernard Shaw, *The Crime of Punishment* (New York: Philosophical Library, 1946).

[15]Richard A. McGee, "What's Past Is Prologue," *The Annals: The Future of Corrections*, Vol. 381 (January 1969), pp. 9–10.

[16]Carl Menninger, *Quandary in Corrections—History Repeats Itself* (Hackensack, N.J.: National Council on Crime and Delinquency, 1977), p. 11.

[17]Robert Sommer, *The End of Imprisonment* (New York: Oxford University Press, 1976).

[18]Nils Christie, "Changes in Penal Values," in Nils Christie, ed., *Aspects of Social Control in Welfare States*, Vol. 2 (Oslo: Universitets Forlaget, 1968). Reported in Ezzat A. Fattah, "Making the Punishment Fit the Crime: The Case of Imprisonment," *Canadian Journal of Criminology*, Vol. 24, no. 1 (January 1982), pp. 1–12.

[19]Bruno M. Cormier, *The Watcher and the Watched* (Montreal and Pittsburgh: Tundra Books, 1975).

institutions, of course, but the great majority of nondangerous property offenders could be handled in community-based facilities. Whether they are or not remains a political decision.

CHAPTER QUESTIONS

18-1. What are the primary issues related to the way in which an institution, such as a prison or correctional facility, handles social problems?
18-2. What was the philosophical origin of the prison?
18-3. Why is there a strong movement now toward new prison construction?
18-4. What is the attitude of some conservative scholars who have written in the field of criminal justice?
18-5. What is the debate between flat sentencing and indeterminate sentencing?
18-6. What areas must be considered when making policy for correctional institutions?
18-7. Which does the most social damage, locking up a man or locking up a woman?
18-8. What is the social damage done to men in prison?
18-9. How are standards for accreditation of correctional institutions developed?
18-10. What does the future of prisons appear to be?

BIBLIOGRAPHY

ADORNO, THEODOR W., ELSIE FRANKEN-BRUNSWICK, DANIEL J. LEVINSON, AND R. NEVITT SANFORD, IN COLLABORATION WITH BETTY ARON, MARCIA HERTZ LEVINSON, AND WILLIAM MORROW. *The Authoritarian Personality.* New York: Harper & Row, Publishers, 1950.

ARCHAMBEAULT, WILLIAM G., AND BETTY J. ARCHAMBEAULT. *Correctional Supervisory Management: Principles of Organization, Policy, and Law.* Englewood Cliffs, N.J.: Prentice-Hall, Inc., 1982.

ATKINS, BURTON M., AND HENRY R. GLICK, EDS. *Prisons, Protest, and Politics.* Englewood Cliffs, N.J.: Prentice-Hall, Inc., 1972.

BABINGTON, ANTHONY. *The Power to Silence.* London: Robert Maxwell, 1968.

BADILLO, HERMAN, AND MILTON HAYNES. *A Bill of No Rights: Attica and the American Prison System.* New York: Outerbridge and Lazard, Inc., 1972. Distributed by E. P. Dutton & Co., Inc.

BARKER, MICHAEL B. *Building Underground for People: Eleven Selected Projects in the United States.* Washington, D.C.: American Institute of Architects, 1978.

BARNES, HARRY ELMER. *The Story of Punishment; A Record of Man's Inhumanity to Man,* rev. ed. Montclair, N.J.: Patterson Smith, 1972.

———, AND NEGLEY K. TEETERS. *New Horizons in Criminology,* 3rd ed. Englewood Cliffs, N.J.: Prentice-Hall, Inc., 1959.

BARTOLLAS, CLEMENS, AND STUART J. MILLER. *Correctional Administration: Theory and Practice.* New York: McGraw-Hill Book Company, 1978.

BEMIS, EDWARD W.   "Local Government in Michigan and the North West," in *Johns Hopkins University Studies in Historical and Political Science*, Study V. Baltimore, Md.: Johns Hopkins University Press, 1883.

BENJAMIN, HARRY AND R. E. L. MASTERS.   *Prostitution and Morality*. New York: The Julian Press, 1964.

BENNETT, LAWRENCE A., THOMAS S. ROSENBAUM, AND WAYNE R. McCULLOUGH.   *Counseling in Correctional Environments*. New York: Human Sciences Press, 1978.

BERKLEY, GEORGE R.   *The Democratic Policeman*. Boston: Beacon Press, 1969.

BOWKER, LEE H.   *Prison Victimization*. New York: Elsevier-North Holland, 1980.

BRINK, VICTOR Z.   *Foundations for Unlimited Horizons*. Altamonte Springs, Fla.: The Institute of Internal Auditors, Inc., 1977.

BRODSKY, ANNETTE M., ED.   *The Female Offender*. Beverly Hills, Calif.: Sage Publications, 1977.

BURKHART, KATHRYN WATTERSON.   *Women in Prison*. Garden City, N.Y.: Doubleday & Company, Inc., 1973.

CAMPBELL, CHARLES F.   *Serving Time Together: Men and Women in Prison*. Fort Worth, Tex.: Texas Christian University Press, 1982.

CARROLL, L.   *Hacks, Blacks, and Cons—Race Relations in a Maximum Security Prison*. Lexington, Mass.: Lexington Books D. C. Heath & Company, 1974.

CARTER, ROBERT M., RICHARD A. McGEE, AND E. KIM NELSON.   *Corrections in America*. Philadelphia: J. B. Lippincott Company, 1975. Distributed by Harper & Row, Publishers, since 1980.

CHANG, DAE H., AND WARREN B. ARMSTRONG, EDS.   *The Prison: Voices from the Inside*. Cambridge, Mass.: Schenkman Publishing Company, 1972.

CLARK, S. GEORGE, ED.   *A Guide to Community Alcoholism Programs*. Tallahassee: Florida Bureau of Alcoholic Rehabilitation, n.d., issued in 1979.

CLEMMER, DONALD.   *The Prison Community*. Boston: Christopher Press, 1940. Reissued in New York by Holt, Rinehart and Winston in 1958.

COFFEY, ALAN R.   *Correctional Administration: The Management of Institutions, Probation and Parole*. Englewood Cliffs, N.J.: Prentice-Hall, Inc., 1975.

COHEN, ALBERT K., GEORGE F. COLE, AND ROBERT G. BAILEY, EDS.   *Prison Violence*. Lexington, Mass.: Lexington Books, 1976.

COHEN, BURTON.   *Analysis of the Impact of the State Employees' Strike on Juveniles Committed to the YDC's*. Philadelphia: The Wharton School, University of Pennsylvania, 1975.

CONLEY, JOHN A., ED.   *Theory and Research in Criminal Justice: Current Perspectives*. Cincinnati: W. H. Anderson Publishing Company, 1980.

COOLEY, THOMAS M.   *A Treatise on the Law of Torts*, 2nd ed. Chicago: Callaghan and Company, 1888.

CORMIER, BRUNO M.   *The Watcher and the Watched*. Montreal and Pittsburgh: Tundra Books, 1975.

CRESSEY, DONALD R., ED.   *The Prison: Studies in Institutional Organization and Change*. New York: Holt, Rinehart and Winston, 1961.

DE BEAUMONT, GUSTAVE, AND ALEXIS DE TOCQUEVILLE.   *On the Penitentiary System in the United States and Its Application in France*. Carbondale and Edwardsville: Southern Illinois University Press, Arcturus Books Edition, 1979. Published originally in France in 1883.

DI GENNARO, GIUSEPPE, AND SERGIO LENCI. *Prison Architecture.* London: London University Press, 1975.

DRESSLER, DAVID. *Sociology: The Study of Human Interaction.* New York: Alfred A. Knopf. 1969.

DYE, THOMAS R. *Politics in States and Communities,* 3rd ed. Englewood Cliffs, N.J.: Prentice-Hall Inc., 1977.

EARNEST, M. R. *Criminal Self-conceptions in the Penal Community of Female Offenders—An Empirical Study.* Palo Alto, Calif.: R. and E. Research Associates, Inc., 1978.

ECKERMAN, WILLIAM C. *A Nationwide Survey of Mental Health and Correctional Institutions for Adult Mentally Disordered Offenders.* Rockville, Md.: Center for Studies of Crime and Delinquency, National Institute of Mental Health, 1972.

EDELWICH, JERRY, WITH ARCHIE BRODSKY. *Burn-out: Stages of Disillusionment in the Helping Professions.* New York: Human Sciences Press, 1980.

EYMAN, JOY S. *Prisons for Women—A Practical Guide to Administration Problems.* Springfield, Ill.: Charles C. Thomas, Publishers, 1971.

FARRINGTON, FAYE. *The Massachusetts Furlough Program: A Comprehensive Assessment.* Boston: Massachusetts Department of Corrections, 1976.

FOGEL, DAVID. *"We Are the Living Proof . . .": The Justice Model for Corrections.* Cincinnati: W. H. Anderson Publishing Company, 1975.

FOUCAULT, MICHEL. *Discipline and Punish: The Birth of the Prison.* New York: Pantheon Books, Inc. 1977.

FROST, M. L. *Civil Commitment and Social Control.* Lexington, Mass.: Lexington Books D. C. Heath & Company, 1978.

GALVIN, JAMES L., CHERYL H. RUBY, JOHN J. GALBIN, PAUL LITSKY, AND WILLIAM ELMS. *Parole in the United States, 1978.* San Francisco: NCCD Research Center West, 1978.

_____, CHERYL H. RUBY, CYNTHIA MAHABIR, PAUL LITSKY, AND ELLEN E. MCNEIL. *Characteristics of the Parole Population, 1978.* San Francisco: NCCD Research Center West, April 1979.

GIALLOMBARDO, ROSE. *Society of Women—A Study of a Women's Prison.* New York: John Wiley & Sons, Inc., 1966.

GLASER, DANIEL. *The Effectiveness of a Prison and Parole System.* Indianapolis: The Bobbs-Merrill Co., Inc., 1964.

GLASSER, WILLIAM. *Reality Therapy.* New York: Harper & Row, Publishers, 1965.

GLICK, R. M. *National Study of Women's Correctional Programs.* Sacramento, Calif.: Department of the Youth Authority, 1977.

_____, AND VIRGINIA V. NETO. *National Study of Women's Correctional Programs.* Washington, D.C.: Government Printing Office, 1977.

GOFFMAN, ERVING. *Asylums: Essays on the Social Situations of Mental Patients and Other Inmates.* Chicago: Aldine Publishing Company, 1961.

GROSVENOR, MELVILLE BELL. *The Story of Man—Everyday Life in Bible Times.* Washington, D.C.: National Geographic Book Service, 1967.

_____, ED. *Middle Ages.* Washington, D.C.: National Geographic Book Service, The Story of Man Library, 1977.

HALLECK, SEYMOUR L. *Psychiatry and the Dilemmas of Crime: A Study of Causes, Punishment and Treatment.* New York: Harper & Row, Publishers, 1967.

HARTMAN, H. L. *Basic Psychiatry for Corrections Workers.* Springfield, Ill.: Charles C. Thomas, Publishers, 1978.

HATCHER, HAYES A. *Correctional Casework and Counseling.* Englewood Cliffs, N.J.: Prentice-Hall Inc., 1978.

HAWKINS, GORDON. *The Prison: Policy and Practice.* Chicago: University of Chicago Press, 1941.

HAZELRIGG, LAWRENCE E., ED. *Prison within Society: A Reader in Penology.* Garden City, N.Y.: Doubleday & Company, Inc., 1968.

HELLER, JOSEPH. *Catch-22.* New York: Simon & Schuster, Inc., 1961.

HENRY, NICHOLAS. *Public Administration and Public Affairs.* Englewood Cliffs, N.J.: Prentice-Hall, Inc., 1975.

HERBERT, JOSEPH L., ED. *Experiences in Zero-Base Budgeting.* Lexington, Mass.: Lexington Books, D. C. Heath, 1978.

HERMAN, MICHELE G., AND MARILYN G. HAFT, EDS. *Prisoners' Rights Sourcebook: Theory, Litigation, Practice.* New York: Clark Boardman Company, 1973.

HIBBERT, C. *The Roots of Evil: A Social History of Crime and Punishment.* Boston: Little, Brown and Company, 1963.

HINSIE, LELAND E., AND ROBERT G. CAMPBELL. *Psychiatric Dictionary*, 4th ed. New York: Oxford University Press, 1970.

HITE, SHERE. *The Hite Report: A Nationwide Survey of Female Sexuality.* New York: Macmillan Publishing Co., Inc., 1976.

HOFFMAN, ETHAN (PHOTOGRAPHS) AND JOHN MCCOY (TEXT). *Concrete Mama: Prison Profiles from Walla Walla.* Columbia and London: University of Missouri Press, 1981.

HOPPER, COLUMBUS, B. *Sex in Prison: The Mississippi Experiment with Conjugal Visiting.* Baton Rouge: Lousiana State University Press, 1969.

HUSE, EDGAR, JAMES BOWDITCH, AND DALMAR FISHER, EDS. *Readings on Behavior in Organizations.* Reading, Mass.: Addison-Wesley Publishing Co., Inc., 1975.

IRWIN, JOHN. *The Felon,* Englewood Cliffs, N.J.: Prentice-Hall, Inc. 1970.

_____. *Prisons in Turmoil.* Boston: Little, Brown and Company, 1980.

JACOBS, JAMES B. *Stateville: The Penitentiary in Mass Society.* Chicago: University of Chicago Press, 1977.

_____, AND NORMA MEACHAM CROTTY. *Guard Unions and the Future of the Prisons.* Ithaca, N.Y.: Institute of Public Employment, New York School of Industrial and Labor Relations, Cornell University, August 1978.

JOHNSTON, NORMAN, LEONARD SAVITZ, AND MARVIN E. WOLFGANG, EDS. "Rules for Inmates." In *The Sociology of Punishment and Corrections,* 2nd ed. New York: John Wiley & Sons, Inc., 1970.

_____. *The Human Cage: A Brief History of Prison Architecture.* New York: Walker and Company, published for the American Foundation, Inc., Institute of Corrections, Philadelphia, 1973.

KENSTON, LARRY. *Inmate Grievance System: Does It Work?"* Frankfort, Ken.: The Inter-Prison Press, Kentucky Bureau of Corrections, 1979.

KINZEL, AUGUST F., LEWIS MERKLIN, AND WARREN B. MILLER. "Violence in Prison." In *A Handbook of Correctional Psychiatry,* Vol. 1. Washington, D.C.: U.S. Bureau of Prisons, 1968.

KROES, W. H. *Society's Victim—The Policeman.* Springfield, Ill.: Charles C. Thomas, Publishers, 1976.

LAMPMAN, H. P. *The Wire Womb—Life in a Girls' Penal Institution.* Chicago: Nelson-Hall, 1973.

LELOUP, LANCE T. *Budgetary Politics: Dollars, Deficits, Decisions.* Brunswick, Ohio: Kings Court Communications, Inc., 1977.

LEONARD, EILEEN B. *Women, Crime and Society: A Critique of Criminology Theory.* New York: Longman, Inc., 1981.

LEWIS, ORLANDO F. *The Development of the American Prisons and Customs, 1776–1854.* Montclair, N.J.: Patterson Smith, 1967.

LIEBER, ARNOLD L. *The Lunar Effect.* Garden City, N.Y.: Anchor Press, 1978.

LIPTON, DOUGLAS, ROBERT MARTINSON, AND JUDITH WILKS. *The Effectiveness of Correctional Treatment.* New York: Praeger Publishers, Inc. 1975.

LOCKWOOD, DANIEL. *Prison Sexual Violence.* New York: Elsevier-North Holland, 1980.

LOMBARDO, LUCIEN X. *Guards Imprisoned: Correctional Officers at Work.* New York: Elsevier-North Holland, 1981.

MACCORMICK, AUSTIN H. *The Education of Adult Prisoners.* New York: The Osborne Association, 1931.

MACNAMARA, DONAL E. J., AND EDWARD SAGARIN, EDS. *Perspectives on Corrections.* New York: Thomas Y. Crowell Company, 1980.

MCARTHUR, V. A., AND M. R. MONTILLA. *Role of Prison Industries Now and in the Future—A Planning Study.* Washington, D.C.: Georgetown University Institute of Criminal Law and Procedure, sponsored by the U.S. Department of Labor, 1975.

MCGOWAN, BRENDA, AND KAREN BLUMENTHAL. *Why Punish the Children? A Study of Children of Women Prisoners.* Hackensack, N.J.: National Council on Crime and Delinquency, 1978.

MCKAY, ROBERT B., CHAIRMAN, NEW YORK STATE SPECIAL COMMISSION ON ATTICA. *The Official Report of the New York State Special Commission on Attica.* New York: Bantam Books, Inc., 1972.

MCLENDON, JAMES. *Deathwork.* New York and Philadelphia: J. B. Lippincott Company, 1977.

MANOCCHIO, A. J., AND J. DUNN. *Time Game—Two Views of a Prison.* New York: Dell Publishing Co., 1970.

MAURER, PAUL R., AND JAMES C. PAYNE. *A Statistical Study: An Offender Profile—Escape.* Tallahassee: Florida Division of Planning and Evaluation, 1975.

MEANS, ERNEST E. *Prison Industries and Rehabilitative Programs.* Tallahassee: Florida Division of Corrections and Florida State University Institute of Governmental Research, 1964.

MENNINGER, KARL. *The Crime of Punishment.* New York: The Viking Press, Inc., 1968.

MEYER, H., AND EDWARD BORGATTA. *Girls at Vocational High: An Experiment in Social Work Intervention.* New York: Russell Sage Foundation, 1965.

MORRIS, NORVAL. *The Future of Imprisonment.* Chicago: University of Chicago Press, 1974.

———, AND GORDON HAWKINS. *The Honest Politicians' Guide to Crime Control.* Chicago: University of Chicago Press, 1971.

————, AND MICHAEL TONRY, EDS. *Crime and Justice: An Annual Review of Research,* Vol. 1. Chicago: University of Chicago Press, 1979.

MORRIS, PAULINE. *Prisoners and Their Families.* New York: Hart Publishing Co., 1965.

MOYER, FRED. *Correctional Environments.* Urbana and Champaign, Ill.: National Clearinghouse on Criminal Justice Planning and Architecture, 1973.

NAGEL, WILLIAM G. *The New Red Barn: A Critical Look at the Modern American Prison.* New York: Walker and Company, published for the American Foundation, Inc., Institute of Corrections, Philadelphia, 1973.

NEEDHAM, JAMES P. *Neutralization of Prison Hostage Situations—A Model.* Springfield, Va.: NTIS, 1976.

NEUGARTEN, DAIL ANN, AND JAY M. SHAFRITZ, EDS. *Sexuality in Organizations: Romantic and Coercive Behaviors at Work.* Oak Park, Ill.: Moore Publishing Co., 1980.

NICE, RICHARD W. *Crime and Responsibility.* Tallahassee, Fla.: Dixie Publishers, 1962.

NISBET, ROBERT. *Twilight of Authority.* New York: Oxford University Press, Galaxy Books, 1975.

NORMAN, SHERWOOD. *Think Twice Before You Build or Enlarge a Detention Center.* New York: National Council on Crime and Delinquency, 1968.

ODIORNE, G. S. *Management by Objectives.* New York: Pitman Publishing Company, 1965.

PACE, D. C. *Christian's Guide to Effective Jail and Prison Counseling.* Old Tappan, N.J.: Fleming H. Revell Company, 1976.

PALMER, JOHN W. *Constitutional Rights of Prisoners,* 2nd ed. Cincinnati: W. H. Anderson Publishing Company, 1973.

PLATT, ANTHONY. *The Child Savers: The Invention of Delinquency.* Chicago: University of Chicago Press, 1969.

————, AND PAUL TAKAGI, EDS. *Punishment and Discipline: Essays on the Prison and the Prisoners' Movement.* Berkeley, Calif.: Crime and Social Justice Associates, 1980.

POWELL, J. C. *The American Siberia.* Montclair, N.J.: Patterson Smith, 1970.

PYHRR, PETER A. *Zero-Based Budgeting.* New York: John Wiley & Sons, Inc., 1973.

RAGAN, JOSEPH, AND CHARLES FINSTON. *Inside the World's Toughest Prison.* Springfield, Ill.: Charles C. Thomas, Publishers, 1962.

REID, SUE TITUS. *Crime and Criminology,* 2nd ed. New York: Holt, Rinehart and Winston, 1979.

RIBTON-TURNER, C. J. *A History of Vagrants and Vagrancy and Beggars and Begging.* Montclair, N.J.: Patterson Smith, 1972.

ROBERTS, ALBERT R., ED. *Correctional Treatment of the Offender.* Springfield, Ill.: Charles C. Thomas, Publishers, 1974.

ROBINSON, WILLIAM H. *Prison Population and Costs—Illustrative Projections to 1980.* Washington, D.C.: Congressional Research Service, April 24, 1974.

ROGERS, WILLIAM WARREN. *Ante-Bellum Thomas County—1825–1861,* Tallahassee: Florida State University Press, 1963.

ROMIG, DENNIS A. *Justice for our Children,* Lexington, Mass.: Lexington Books/ D. C. Heath Company, 1978.

ROTHMAN, DAVID J. *The Discovery of the Asylum*. Boston: Little, Brown and Company, 1971.

RUBIN, SOL. *Law of Criminal Correction*, 2nd ed. St. Paul, Minn.: West Publishing Company, 1973.

RUNYON, TOM. *In for Life—A Convict's Story*. New York: W. W. Norton & Company, Inc., 1953.

SCHENCK, W. A. *A History of Psychiatry*. Philadelphia: J. B. Lippincott Company, 1952.

SCOTT, RONALD J., AND RAYMOND P. CIENEK. *Correctional Officer Training in Virginia: A Final Report*. Richmond: Virginia Commonwealth University, Department of Administration of Justice and Public Safety, 1977.

SELLIN, THURSTEN. *Slavery and the Penal System*. Philadelphia: University of Pennsylvania Press, 1977.

SKELNICK, JEROME H. *Justice Without Trial*. New York: John Wiley & Sons, Inc., 1966.

SMYKLA, JOHN ORTIZ. *Cocorrections: A Case Study of a Coed Federal Prison*. Washington, D.C.: University Press of America, 1978.

———. *Coed Prison*. New York: Human Sciences Press, 1980.

SOMMER, ROBERT. *The End of Imprisonment*. New York: Oxford University Press, 1976.

SPRADLEY, JAMES P. *The Ethnographic Interview*. New York: Holt, Rinehart and Winston, 1979.

STONE, ALLAN A. *Mental Health and the Law: A System in Transition*. Rockville, Md.: National Institute of Mental Health, 1975.

SUTHERLAND, EDWIN H., AND DONALD R. CRESSEY. *Criminology*, 9th ed. Philadelphia: J. B. Lippincott Company, 1974.

SYKES, GRESHAM. *The Society of Captives*. Princeton, N.J.: Princeton University Press, 1958.

SYLVESTER, SAMUEL. *Homicides in Prisons*. Washington, D.C.: National Institute of Law Enforcement and Criminal Justice, 1976.

———, JOHN P. REEDE, AND DAVID O. NELSON. *Prison Homicide*. New York: Spectrum Publications, 1977.

THORNBERRY, TERRENCE P., AND JOSEPH E. JACOBY. *The Criminally Insane: A Community Follow-up of Mentally Ill Offenders*. Chicago: University of Chicago Press, 1979.

TOCH, HANS. *Living in Prison: The Ecology of Survival*. New York: The Free Press, 1977.

ULETT, G. A., AND D. W. GOODRICH. *A Synopsis of Contemporary Psychiatry*. St. Louis: The C. V. Mosby Company, 1969.

VAN DEN HAAG, ERNEST. *Punishing Criminals: A Very Old and Painful Question*. New York: Basic Books, Inc., 1975.

VAN WORMER, KATHERINE S. *Sex Role Behavior in a Woman's Prison and Ethnological Analysis*. Palo Alto, Calif.: R. and E. Research Associates, Inc., 1978.

VEDDER, CLYDE B., AND BARBARA A. KAY, EDS. *Penology*. Springfield, Ill.: Charles C. Thomas, Publishers, 1964.

VON HIRSCH, ANDREW. *Doing Justice*. New York: Hill & Wang, 1976.

VON KRAFFT-EBING, RICHARD. *Psychopathia Sexualis*. New York: Stein & Day Publishers, 1965.

WAGENKNECHT, EDWARD. *The Seven Worlds of Theodore Roosevelt.* New York: Longmans, Green and Co., 1960.

WALKER, P. N. *Punishment: An Illustrated History.* Newton Abbot, Devon, England: David and Charles, Publishers, Ltd, 1972.

WARD, DAVID A., AND GENE G. KASSEBAUM. *Women's Prison: Sex and Social Structure.* Chicago: Aldine Publishing Company, 1965.

WARREN, MARGUERITE Q., ed. *Comparing Female and Male Offenders.* Beverly Hills, Calif.: Sage Publications, 1981.

WEBB, G. L., AND DAVID G. MORRIS. *Prison Guards: The Culture and Perspective of an Occupational Group.* Dallas: Coker Books, 1977.

WEBER, MAX. *The Theory of Social and Economic Organizations,* trans. and ed. by A. Henderson and T. Parsons. New York: The Free Press, 1947.

WHITE, LEONARD B. *Introduction to the Study of Public Administration.* New York: Macmillan Publishing Co., Inc., 1926.

WHOLEY, JOSEPH S. *Zero-Base Budgeting and Program Evaluation.* Lexington, Mass.: Lexington Books/D. C. Heath Company, 1978.

WILSON, JAMES Q. *Thinking About Crime.* New York: Basic Books, Inc., 1975.

WILSON, JOSEPH. *Are Prisons Necessary?* Philadelphia: Dorrance Press, 1950.

WINES, FREDERICK HOWARD. *Punishment and Reformation: A Study of the Penitentiary System.* New York: Thomas Y. Crowell Company, 1919.

WRIGHT, FRED, CHARLES BAHN, AND ROBERT W. RIEBER, EDS. *Forensic Psychology and Psychiatry.* New York: New York Academy of Sciences, 1980.

YOCHELSON, SAMUEL, AND STANTON E. SAMENOW. *The Criminal Personality.* New York: Jacob Aronson, 1976.

ZIETZ, DOROTHY. *Women Who Embezzle or Defraud: A Study of Convicted Felons.* New York: Praeger Publishers, Inc., 1981.

INDEX